D1717041

The American Martial Arts Film

The American Martial Arts Film

M. RAY LOTT

McFarland & Company, Inc., Publishers
Jefferson, North Carolina, and London

LIBRARY OF CONGRESS CATALOGUING-IN-PUBLICATION DATA

Lott, M. Ray, 1960–
The American martial arts film / M. Ray Lott.
p.   cm.
Includes bibliographical references and index.

ISBN 0-7864-1836-2 (illustrated case binding : 50# alkaline paper)

1. Martial arts films—United States—History and criticism. I. Title.
PN1995.9.H3L68   2004   791.43'657—dc22   2003028283

British Library cataloguing data are available

On the cover: (large image) Patrick Swayze in *Road House* (1989); bottom
left, Jim Kelly in *Golden Needles* (1974), and center and right, Mark Dacascos,
and Paco Christian Prieto with Dacascos in *Only the Strong* (1993)

Manufactured in the United States of America

McFarland & Company, Inc., Publishers
Box 611, Jefferson, North Carolina 28640
www.mcfarlandpub.com

Table of Contents

Preface

The American Martial Arts Film shall certainly not be the last words written about this type of cinema, but most probably they are the first. The origins of this study came while I was doing graduate work in screenwriting at CSU Northridge. My thesis screenplay, *A Fast Getaway*, was developed and written in the vein of the low-budget, high-impact action films that arose during the late 1980s and which continue to line the shelves at various video stores today—films commonly referred to as Direct-to-Video (DTV) releases. As I studied these DTVs, which actually encompass all genres, from horror to sci-fi, from Westerns to thrillers, I found that they are much akin to the old B movies from the golden age of Hollywood cinema, when the studios churned out lower budgeted films to accompany their major releases as a way of giving viewers more bang for their buck. However, in this instance it was not only the studios, but a myriad of independents as well, providing the video market, and their customers, with added viewing selection.

A significant number, if not a majority, of these action flicks were martial arts films. Yet very little had been written about them, not from a historical standpoint, and certainly not from a critical one. I wrote this book to change all that. *The American Martial Arts Film* examines English language martial arts films in terms of both their historical development and their critical relevance. While most other film genres and styles, even subgenres, have been around in one form or another for 70 or more years, and some almost 100, American-type martial arts films are relatively new on the scene—dating back only 30 years or so, to 1973, when *Enter the Dragon* was released and achieved widespread popularity.

This study takes an in-depth look at that film and others, and demonstrates how the tenor of the times is reflected in their narratives—and in some instances, how a film actually influenced the society in which it was released. I also look at the actors and actresses whose athletic abilities (and in some cases, magnetic personalities) have advanced these films so far so fast in the eyes of certain segments of the viewing public. In addition, I observe how the effects of technology, in the form of the video cassette recorder (VCR), as well as alterations in Hollywood marketing strategies, served to end one form of martial arts film—the low-budget theatrical release—while revolutionizing another—DTVs. And finally, I examine what the future holds for the American martial arts film, which trends threaten it, and which developments support its continued growth.

To accomplish this task, I viewed hundreds of martial arts films, or films containing martial arts sequences, so as to present a definitive and comprehensive overview of the material at issue. Whatever strengths this study possesses are shared with the filmmakers and performers who give it their best in each and every film, despite its budget; alas, any shortcomings are all my own.

I'm sure many readers wonder about the acknowledgments that most writers include in the preface of their books. I certainly did. After all, the reader doesn't know these people, right? But now that I have written a book, I realize that the significance of thanking the people who helped, influenced or motivated me is *not* so the reader know who they are, but that those people know I know who they are— and most importantly, how they contributed in no small way to me getting the job done. With that in mind, I would like to offer my thanks to the following people: God; my family; THE PARTNERS; D Watch Patrol; Robin Acosta; John Bangs, Chief of Ontario Airport Police; Lili Berko, Professor, CSU Long Beach; Dr. Lawrence Blum; Claudia; Stephen Cooper, Professor, CSU Northridge; Dorsey; Keri; Lance Lee, Professor, CSU Northridge; Marilyn; Steve Martinez; Dr. Andrei Novac; Paula; Michael Picou; Sherri; Jon Stahl, Professor, CSU Northridge; Dr. Bruce Van Vranken; Bea Williams; Gil-Adrienne Wishnick, VP, Creative Affairs and Development, Promark Entertainment Group; and my darling wife and inspiration Ivy, who sat with me through countless films and never once complained. Ever...

I

Lights ... Camera ... ACTION!

During the better part of the 1990s, film studios worldwide produced hundreds of action pictures. In the five years between 1995 and 1999, more than 900 action films were produced and distributed around the globe,[1] with the majority of them being low-budget films. Of those, a significant number are of the karate or kung-fu variety. Marilyn D. Mintz, in the introduction to her book *The Martial Arts Films*, writes

> All cultures begin in conflict. They hunted food and protected possessions. Only by skill could they survive. Fighting systems were developed in cause and effect terms, then were linked to philosophies and codes for depth and meaning beyond the purely physical.[2]

Many of these "fighting systems" evolved into what is now commonly referred to as "martial arts," which are methodical disciplines of weaponless defense as well as weapon-filled combat that take on a multitude of forms. Some of the best-known styles of martial arts are as follows:

1. *Ju jutsu* [also known as *jujitsu*]
An amalgam of dissimilar combat systems which include methods of kicking, striking, kneeing, throwing, joint-locking, choking, weaponry, holding and tying. It shares some elements with combat sumo, and was used to complement sword-fighting techniques.

2. *Judo*
A form of *ju jutsu* that relies on a precise mode of throwing, grappling and the touching of vulnerable pressure points to subdue an opponent.

3. *Karate*
An overall means of fighting that originated in sixth century India whereby the entire body is developed as a weapon. It employs hand strikes and kicks to various unprotected areas of an opponent's body. Precise breathing and punctuated shouts during the delivery of blows is thought to increase their power and effectiveness.

4. *Aikido*

Another spin-off of *ju jutsu*, it is primarily considered a defensive martial art which avoids injury to opponents. An alloy of various martial arts forms, both Chinese and Japanese, it is manifested through joint-locking techniques as well as some throwing and grappling.

5. *Kung Fu*

A fluid discipline that adapts a wide variety of movements, hard and soft, often named after animals, like "the crane," "the mantis" and so on. Punches, kicks, even throws are employed as the body is used as natural leverage with substantial and insubstantial energy and weight distribution constantly changing. *Jeet kune do* (literally "way of the intercepting fist") is the style developed by Bruce Lee, one influenced by Zen philosophy, that advocates the mastering and then the forgetting of every technique possible, thereby allowing the martial artist to fight without thinking, spontaneously and fluidly, in the most simple, effective and direct way.

6. *Thai Kickboxing*

A fast, efficient and powerful form of martial combat, using high kicks and fists to overcome an opponent.

7. *Tae kwon do*

A Korean style of karate which relies on punches and kicks, particularly the latter. Internal breathing is considered essential for coordinating external movements and for gathering power to "unify force."

8. *Ninjutsu*

A system employing a wide array of weapons and martial arts techniques designed to protect against danger and to facilitate various methods of spying on an enemy. Ninjas are masters of disguise and camouflage, and are experts with edged instruments, shurikens or throwing stars, as well as with swords, spears and halberds. This martial arts form originated in Japan between AD 593 and 628, when espionage before a battle often brought success.

9. *Kendo*

The art of the sword, developed in Japan, and when combined with jujutsu, a very effective method of fighting. Kendo swordsmen view the sword as an extension of self, and the customs developed around the art further the spiritual development of the practitioner. In the Zen approach to swordsmanship, the person who transcends himself no longer fears death and can reach mastery.

10. *Hapkido*

Also a Korean martial art form, this one relying on the unity of opposites: hard and soft; circular and linear; quick and expansive, to obtain maximum mobility. Techniques include circular kicks, spin kicks, jumps and throws.[3]

History of Martial Arts in the United States

The presence of Japanese and Chinese immigrants in America was an important factor in the ultimate development of martial arts in the United States. Two disciplines of fighting predominated: judo and karate (including kung fu). The first known exposure of Americans to judo came in 1879, when former U.S. President

Ulysses S. Grant was in Japan for a visit and was invited to witness a demonstration of judo by Jigoro Kano, who would eventually become an influential teacher of the fighting art.[4] Almost 25 years later, Yoshiaki Yamashita arrived from Japan to teach judo in America. In 1902, Yamashita traveled between New York and Chicago performing demonstrations, and was eventually invited to the White House to illustrate the strong points of judo. Yamashita was pitted in a contest against a Naval Academy wrestling coach; Yamashita won handily. Roosevelt not only decided to take judo lessons from Yamashita, but he arranged for Yamashita to teach judo at the Naval Academy.

On the West Coast, a number of Japanese judo instructors immigrated to the United States, and the first judo dojo opened in 1903. It closed after a few months, but in 1907, Prof. Takuguru Ito opened a dojo in Seattle, Washington. Later, there were a total of six dojos operating in Oregon. In the 1920s, the Tacoma, Washington, dojo was also operating, and during the 1930s competitions began across the West Coast. The onset of World War II interrupted the exposure and growth of judo as many Japanese were interned in relocation camps throughout the United States. However, judo within the camps flourished and some American trainers actually brought their students to the camps for instruction.

Just before and then after World War II, judo began to be taught in physical education departments in college, while the Amateur Athletic Union (AAU) eventually adopted it as an approved sport. In 1953, the first AAU national judo championships were held in San Jose. By the middle of the decade, dojos began spreading again, and various tournaments were held throughout the country. The YMCA started holding training classes, and even the armed forces got into the act. The Air Force began judo training after Gen. Curtis LeMay ordered physical conditioning units set up at various bases and airmen trained in the art of self defense. Many were sent to Japan for instruction.

As judo spread across the country, there was no central organization to keep things regulated. In 1961, the Judo Black Belt Federation began reorganization of national judo clubs and established a national ranking system to stop false claims of belt ranking. By the end of the 60s, judo was the third largest sport in the AAU and was firmly established in the United States as competitive discipline.

Chinese immigrants brought the discipline of kung fu with them upon first hitting the shores of the U.S. in the mid–nineteenth century.[5] The Chinese did not teach the art to outsiders, so it was not until the mid–1960s that it took root in the west. In 1922, the Chinese physical culture association in Honolulu began teaching kung fu to the Chinese community, but again, westerners were excluded from the training. In 1964, Bruce Lee opened his Oakland school to non–Chinese and attracted students from everywhere. Spurred on by the popularity of Lee and his films, kung fu schools spread throughout the country, and now can be found in almost every large city, and some small ones, too.

Karate got its first start in America when Kentsu Yabu, a famous Okinawan master, performed a public demonstration at the YMCA in Honolulu. As time passed, other Okinawan instructors came to Hawaii to practice and teach their art, founding clubs and dojos across the islands. By 1933, westerners were actively studying karate in Hawaii.

Kenpo karate, based on Shaolin kung fu, began in Hawaii under the sponsorship of Dr. James Mitose, who opened up a self defense club in 1942. Mitose's "Kenpo," meaning "first law karate," spread to the mainland through his students, among whom was Ed Parker, who would someday become one of the foremost supporters of American style karate. The first karate school in the mainland was established in 1946 by Robert Trais, who had studied karate while overseas. In 1957, at Brigham Young University, Parker began teaching a karate course which was quite popular, particularly with the law enforcement officers who crammed his evening class.

Korean tae kwon do instructors began immigrating to the United States in the 1960s, many to teach U.S. servicemen hand-to-hand combat. By the early 1970s, more than 1200 tae kwon do instructors were teaching here, though not all could claim to have worked with the military. Jhoon Rhee introduced tae kwon do to America in 1956 and opened his first school in Washington, D.C., where he began teaching to an exclusive clientele, including Congressmen and Senators. Jack Hwang followed, opening his school in Oklahoma City in 1964. The following year he began the All American Open Karate Championships, which were among the most important events on the tournament circuit. By 1974, tae kwon do was reorganized as a separate sanctioned sport by the AAU. A number of important tournaments followed as the United States Tae Kwon Do Federation was founded.

By the mid- to late 60s, franchise karate institutions began making their way across the country, with Chuck Norris and Ed Parker's schools among the most successful. Like with tae kwon do, tournaments for karate also followed. Among the biggest were the All American Karate Championships and the North American Karate Championships. In 1964, Parker started the International Karate Championships in Long Beach, California. Mike Stone won the championship, but Bruce Lee stole the show by demonstrating his enormous power and skill for the audience. As the number of karate tournaments increased around the country, so too did the confusion, as rules, procedures, and formal structures were lacking.

In 1968, the first World Professional Karate Championship opened in Kansas City and was won by heavyweight Joe Lewis. Other world championships followed. Chuck Norris, who was the noted middleweight champion, turned to professional fighting, which was evolving towards more and more full contact.* By 1974, after a succession of various "professional" championships, the Professional Karate Association (PKA) was formed. It standardized rules and procedures, authorized full contact and began the long partnership with television that still exists today.

Now, some 100 years after their introduction to the United States, martial arts schools can be found throughout the country and are an accepted part of life. With the popularity of martial arts, new styles combining individual disciplines have arisen, and in many ways can be called "American," as fighters combine judo, karate, boxing and wrestling to form unbeatable combinations. The Ultimate Fight Championships (UFC), arising in the mid–90s, became immensely popular, and to this day are a pay-per-view favorite. The UFC stages fights in an octagon ring, where two opponents use whatever skills they have to win. The fights are full contact and quite brutal—so brutal, in fact, that the sport is illegal in many states. As

*Up to this point, all martial arts championship fights were amateur in nature. The fighters didn't start getting paid until the end of the 1960s or the beginning of the 70s.

the popularity of the UFC increases, it would not be surprising to see in the new millennium many schools opening up that eschew the traditional teaching of one martial art, like kung fu, to concentrate on providing training in mixed martial arts.

Martial Arts in Cinema

The appearance of these and other martial arts forms in film is not a new phenomenon; in fact, martial arts films have been around almost as long as cinema has been a force in Asia. Among the most popular films in the Japanese film industry were Jidai-geki, historical tales that often featured heroic, martial arts–trained samurai warriors. *Sanshiro Sugata* (1943), Akira Kurasawa's directorial debut, was a nineteenth century action tale that focused on the clash between a young judo fighter who must learn self-control under the supervision of a disciplined master. The film spawned a sequel, launched Kurasawa's career and became an influence on the Hong Kong martial arts films that would later follow.[7]

At the turn of the century, the Chinese film industry found itself enveloped by western culture, which competed with traditional values.[8] The industry responded with long established, conventional stories. Early martial arts depictions were stage-bound affairs, with little unarmed combat and a reliance on the supernatural. From the outset of their film production, the Chinese developed their *wu xia* stories, action genres known as "martial chivalry."[9] The *wu xia* are one of China's principle central myths, much like the American Western, and combine elements of magic and the fantastic with martial arts–trained warriors and monks fighting for any number of noble causes as they wander the land. These films eventually evolved into the unarmed combat cinema of the 1970s, exemplified by Bruce Lee's "Kung Fu" films. Training, dignity and identity were all themes associated with these films.

The Cantonese *Wong Fei Hung* films, based on a real life nineteenth century character who employed his considerable fighting skills to defend the weak and uphold justice, constitute one of the longest series ever, 99 black-and-white films from 1949 to 1970. These films also rejected the stage aspects of earlier martial arts movies and concentrated on proper martial arts forms and genuine weapon conflict. Today, Hong Kong martial arts cinema has exerted its influence on action-thrillers, and well-known western directors such as Oliver Stone, Francis Ford Coppola and Quentin Tarantino have all indicated a certain keenness for the genre.[10] Taiwanese director Ang Lee's *Crouching Tiger, Hidden Dragon* (2000) is just the latest in a long line of *wu xia* films.

Though this style of film is popular in Asia, and with some audiences in the west, the realm of implausibility so readily accepted by Asian audiences limits mass appeal to American audiences, which were more into "realism." Warriors who could flip up to the top of a fortress 30 feet high, or disappear in thin air, or catch knives with their hands and arrows between their teeth did not catch the fancy of the American viewer.*

From these movies evolved a different type of martial arts film that was more suited to American tastes. The "American" martial arts film featured a ritualized style of violence (such as karate, judo, kung-fu, kendo or other forms of martial arts) to advance along a traditional narrative. The films emerged during the mid–70s, and mostly come from America, but productions from other countries like Australia, Canada, Hong Kong and South Africa are also included, so long as the film is shot in the English language.

This study explores the history of the American martial arts cinema, beginning with the arrival of the popular "kung fu" cinema imports of the late 1960s, and then traces the development and evolution of the American martial arts film from the mid–1970s on. The study concludes in the present, where a convergence of economic and technological factors produced the "DTV," or direct-to-video movie, a low-budget format where the American martial arts film has primarily been found.

A Note About Budget

Films are considered low-budget when they are produced for a sum of money considerably less than that of major studio releases, anywhere from a few thousand dollars upwards to a few million, fall into a recognizable genre or exploitation mode, and are intended to produce a profit rather than overt artistic acclaim. Most if not all American martial arts films fall into this category.

However, that is not to say these films can't be art. Since the early 30s, thousands of low-budget films have been made; most are schlock, trash, kitsch. But there are a significant number of good ones, maybe even great ones, which have risen above their production limitations to make a lasting impression on their audience. *Enter the Dragon* (1973), which will be examined in the next segment, immediately comes to mind.

The Velocity of Gary (1996), a disturbing film set in the early 80s about drugs, a bi-sexual man, his girlfriend and boyfriend, and the arrival of a strange new disease (AIDS), cost only a few million to make; whether it fits into a recognizable genre is debatable, but it is clearly a film designed for the critics and art house crowd. It made little money, received some praise and can be seen occasionally on cable late at night.

Armed Response (1985), on the other hand, was produced for about a million dollars, featured David Carradine as a martial arts trained vet protecting his family against gangsters, and was released nationwide with the intent to rake in as much dough as possible. It, too, made little money, received no praise and can be seen at regular intervals on cable late at night. It is just the type of film we are going to explore.

II

The Trendsetters: Enter the Dragon *and* The Yakuza

Most martial arts films, American or otherwise, are of a low-budget variety. While major studios regularly greenlight huge films like *The Hulk* (2003) or *Titanic* (1997) that cost upwards of $100,000,000 or more, the thought of spending that kind of money on a karate film is unheard of. And perhaps it should be. While these extravagant productions spend most of their money on cutting edge special effects and big stars, the appeal of a martial arts film is its action. A good fight choreographer and a decent story go a long way in this genre. However, two martial arts films stand out as "A" level productions. One popularized the form for American consumption and gave us its first superstar; the other assumed the narrative model that most subsequent martial arts films would follow.

Enter the Dragon

Born in San Francisco in 1940, Bruce Lee was a successful child actor who was featured in a number of Hong Kong productions. Performing was in his blood: his father, Lee Hoi Chuen, was a successful Cantonese comic actor. Lee returned to the United States in 1958, where he struggled to break into show business—with mixed results. He became a martial arts trainer to big name actors like Steve McQueen and James Coburn and scored a number of guest shots on television shows, but didn't hit pay dirt until the late 60s, when he co-starred in *The Green Hornet.* Playing the Green Hornet's sidekick Kato, Lee's forte was using his extensive martial arts skills to fight crime.

A few years later, Lee landed a recurring role as Lee Chan in the series *Longstreet,* where he introduced the title character—a blind insurance investigator played by James Franciscus—to his own personal martial arts defense system, Jeet Kune Do. These appearances made a much more lasting impression on audiences. In 1971, when his television work made it to Hong Kong, Lee became wildly popular and was offered the chance to star in a Cantonese martial arts film.

Bruce Lee in the 1967 television series *The Green Hornet*. Reruns of the show playing in Hong Kong made him a star.

Golden Harvest Productions, a Hong Kong–based studio, was churning out martial arts films left and right for its Asian audience. Popular in the Orient, a few of these films began making their way to the United States, where they became a hit quite quickly, mostly with teenage boys. Suddenly, Bruce Lee, now *the* martial arts phenomenon and Hong Kong's biggest star, had been rediscovered. In films like *The Big Boss* (1971) and *The Chinese Connection* (1972), Lee chopped his way to stardom.

The plots of Lee's films, and for that matter other Chinese martial arts films, were often flimsy: small business people needing a hero to fight off the triads; westerners trying to corrupt traditional Chinese values have to be put in their place; Japanese invaders are routed, and their martial arts styles proven to be inferior against the Chinese styles.... Ironically, or sadly enough, depending on one's point of view, a good number of these movies might be considered somewhat offensive, particularly to Japanese and Caucasians.*

Lee made three films for Golden Harvest before entering into a co-production deal with Warner Bros. through his partner and Golden Harvest owner Raymond Chow.† His fourth and last film became the most famous martial arts film of all time. *Enter the Dragon* (1973), which was Lee's American starring debut, was the first decently budgeted martial arts film, yet even with its renowned cast and expert crew from both Hong Kong and Hollywood, it still took five months on location to craft into an instant classic.[1]

Lee became an overnight sensation—and a legend. The film was very well choreographed, with Lee engaged in a number of battles, each one increasing in intensity until he fights off scores of opponents using only a pair of Nunchuckus. To capture Lee's quick movements, cinematographer Gilbert Hubbs had to work minor miracles by adjusting the camera's settings.[2]

Enter the Dragon was also remarkable for both its story and its casting. Lee plays a martial arts expert who lives in a Shaolin temple, teaching his combat skills to a select group of dedicated students. He is recruited by an Interpol-like agency to infiltrate an island off the coast of China that is governed by Han, an infamous drug lord and murderer. Grainy black-and-white footage of some of Han's victims—women dragged from the ocean—underscores the importance of Lee's mission.

The pretense Lee uses to gain entry to Han's fortress is a semi-annual martial arts tournament, sponsored by Han, where the best fighters in the world gather to prove themselves. As the fighting proceeds, Lee infiltrates Han's below-ground drug laboratory but, after fighting off scores of opponents, is captured. Also at the tournament are Roper, a failed businessman looking to win some big money in the fights, and Williams, a black activist who runs afoul of Han. Roper is recruited to move Han's drugs; he refuses, and is pitted against Lee in a fight to the death. Instead, the two men join forces and, in a heated battle, kill Han and take control of the fortress.

While Lee's magnetism is undeniable, the deceptive simplicity of the story itself accounts for much of the film's popularity with its overwhelmingly male audience. In essence, Han's island functions as a male paradise, a place where all needs are met, all wants are fulfilled. Men spend their days training and competing, with no worries or troubles. Fighting becomes a religion, a spiritual release, and the

---

* *Twenty-five years later this is still the case. A 1996 DTV I reviewed in preparing for this paper, American Chinatown, was an ultra low-budget film that was made by Koreans and which had nothing to do with any city's Chinatown. The hero, a Korean, triumphed in a number of battles against other Asian ethnicities: Japanese, Chinese and Filipinos. The "name" in the cast, Robert Z'Dar, best known as the Maniac Cop in William Lustig's low-budget series of the same name, was a racist, and the hero's goal was to get him and his love away from the corruption of America and back to Korea.*

   † *Warners had some familiarity with Lee: He had proposed the television series* Kung Fu. *The idea was made into a television series, but Lee was replaced by David Carradine.*

island a sanctuary where male camaraderie can be celebrated within a heterosexual construct. As Han indicates in his opening address to the men, "You are warriors who thrive on combat."

Symbolism within the film often revolves around animals or insects. Lee's sister is menaced by Han's thugs, and systematically hunted like human prey. Later, in Han's drug laboratory, the exact scene is repeated, only this time it is Lee being chased. When guards conceal a deadly serpent at a secret entry hatch to kill possible intruders, Lee overpowers it so quickly as to remind one of the mongoose, a small but extremely quick and powerful animal. As Lee makes his way out of Han's laboratory, his agility and balance are so great that Williams, who sees him scrambling straight up a high wall, marvels by calling him a human fly! But perhaps the most telling incident occurs on the boat bringing Lee to Han's island, a scene which portends of the conflict to come. The fighters gather around to wager on a battle between two mantises; Lee bets on the smaller insect, Roper the bigger one. In overturning and killing its larger opponent, the small mantis augurs Lee's inevitable triumph over Han's forces.

Women are marginal beings and fall into readily identifiable cultural niches, as either the asexual "good girl" like Lee's sister, and Mai Lin, the undercover operative

Bruce Lee in action. Note the scars on his abdomen courtesy of Han's iron claw. (*Enter the Dragon*, Warner Bros., 1973)

who passes Lee vital information, or as servants and sexual playthings at the fighters' beck and call. At the time, Women's Lib, making its mark in American society, is nowhere to be seen, though significantly enough, Tania, the one woman who asserts her own sexual will by boldly accepting Roper's advances, is killed during the final bloody fracas.

The story, in providing a reactionary knee jerk to feminism, also presents a level of comfort and identification with its psychological division of the main characters. Roper, the breezy, self-assured vet-turned-failed businessman, functions as an ego figure: capable, confident, attractive to the ladies, he is what most men would want to be. Williams serves as a libidinal force, volatile, unrestrained and undisciplined, ready to explode. Where Roper takes just one woman for the evening's pleasure, Williams takes many, while his inability to follow Han's strict rules leads to his death. Lee acts as the conscience, the moral locus of the story. He maintains a strict code of honor, does not use Han's women for sexual purposes and completes his mission despite his reservations.

The last scene of the film, where the government's forces arrive too late to make a difference, played upon two prevalent attitudes of the time: a growing distrust of authority and a concomitant fear that crime was overwhelming said authority and menacing the public. In a time where both *Walking Tall* (1973) and *Death Wish* (1974) were huge box office hits, featuring vigilante-like heroes such as Buford Pusser and Paul Kersey who operate outside of a crooked, or ineffectual legal system, *Enter the Dragon* clearly appealed to an alternately cynical and fearful public. Lee, skeptical from the beginning about his mission, takes it on not out of patriotism but revenge for his sister's murder by Han. Like the Pusser and Kersey characters, he works outside the system, a renegade of sorts, who can only rely on himself to apply the force needed to undermine the drug lord. After Lee finishes off Han, he surveys the scene of carnage, the dead and dying, and shakes his head in open contempt at the approaching government helicopters, cementing his position as rebel in the eyes of the public.

The change between Lee's character in this movie, and those of his previous films, was pronounced. Lee's prior films had always featured him as an underdog, either as a worker or student, who is goaded to fight. However, Warners, sensing that Lee's past film personas would not play to a broader audience, provided him with a new identity, that of a martial arts master turned secret agent. As Randall Clark notes in his section on martial arts films:

> When Warner Bros. studios made Lee's last starring film, *Enter the Dragon*, in 1973, it began the long and gradual process of "whitening" the martial arts film, making it palatable to mainstream American audiences. The studio began with the film's plot. Lee was no longer playing an average Hong Kong youth; he is instead playing an Asian James Bond.[3]

Though the "whitening" aspect of Clark's statement is certainly debatable, the goal of extending the appeal of martial arts films to a larger audience is not. Lee's previous films exhibited a number of predominant themes: xenophobia, class struggle and a commitment to personal discipline. While the first two areas are of particular interest to native Chinese viewers in light of past imperialism by both the West and Japan, they would not necessarily strike a chord in middle-class America.

Unlike the socio-economic disconnect between the black urban culture that produces gangster rap and today's suburban white teens who dress in a hip hop style and listen to it, for these 70s martial arts films to be financially successful, the stories and characters would have to connect with both the steel worker in Allentown, Pennsylvania, and the accountant in Orange County, California and not just various minority groups in downtown theaters.

It is certainly possible that Warners reckoned just that, and wisely eschewed the Marxist aspects and anti–Japanese bias of the Hong Kong films. Rather than "whitening" the genre as Clark maintains, Warner's "widened" it by relying on "B" genre hero types and narratives that had proven successful in the past. Instead of an issue of race, it was clearly a matter of money. Changes would have to be made to fit the martial arts elements into a framework acceptable to the American mainstream.

By featuring Lee as a teacher rather than a student, the story affirmed his position as an active rather than passive instrument in the challenges confronting him— and, by extension, us. With drugs becoming a major problem in our society at the time, Lee becomes a surrogate American hero, breaking up the drug smuggling ring the same way so many old-fashioned heroes of past films did: with his fists. In fact, Lee's character broke with a stereotype of Asians as humble and unassuming and instead positioned Lee as a reserved but self-assured man who goes about his mission with a cynical, detached cool, the same way Charles Bronson and Clint Eastwood, both top stars at the time, did in their respective films.

However, Warners kept the aura of discipline that surrounded Lee, and which in part contributed to his massive appeal and eventual superstardom. Though a small man, Lee was enormously lean and muscular, his body a testament to hours of exercise and training. In the film's opening scene, Lee is observed fighting under the tutelage of the Shaolin masters; when he trains a student, he admonishes him not to think, but to "feel." Later, after battling literally scores of Han's army to a standstill, he is trapped in a cell, where he promptly sits down cross-legged to meditate, demonstrating the discipline behind "not thinking" by not worrying or wasting energy in a futile attempt to escape. In a comical but deadly scene, Lee exercises strict control when fighting to keep a deadly cobra away while he calmly uses a wireless to send the signal the authorities have been awaiting.

While Clark is also critical of Warners' supporting cast, as we shall see in later chapters, it is merely a continuation of past practice. By featuring known American star John Saxon as Lee's ally, and up-and-coming actor–martial artist Jim Kelly as a black militant caught in the fray, the strategy was a clear throwback to the "B" mantra of the '30s and '40s: Place solid talent around a newcomer to enhance not only the film's quality, but its drawing power at the box office.

The resulting film was a huge hit, made a cult classic by Lee's death a few months later under mysterious circumstances.* Fifteen years after its initial release, world-wide theatrical gross was estimated at $150,000,000 and counting.[4] Following the film's success, Warner Bros. purchased and released *Return of the Dragon*

His son Brandon Lee would follow in the father's footsteps, starring in a number of high-quality martial arts films until his own death, under mysterious circumstances, during the filming of The Crow *in 1995.*

Lee squares off against the evil Han in *Enter the Dragon*'s climax. Observe his perfect balance and the wonderful symmetry of his body.

(1973), a Hong Kong film that Lee had lensed before *Enter the Dragon*. However, while the film's title suggested that it was a sequel, nothing could be further from the truth. *Return* featured Lee in his previous persona, one of the little people, a restaurant worker fighting gangsters. The incongruity between the two films is palpable, yet riding on the success of *Enter the Dragon*, and the various conspiracy theories surrounding Lee's untimely demise, *Return of the Dragon* was a success. Co-billed with Lee was six time martial arts champion Chuck Norris, who would soon be making a name for himself in the world of martial arts cinema.

The Yakuza

In 1975, following the success of *Enter the Dragon*, Warner's released *The Yakuza*, a full-blown "A"* martial arts film featuring the likes of Robert Mitchum, Brian Keith, Christina Kokubo and Japanese superstar Ken Takakura. Mitchum

---

* *"A" is the traditional designation given to high-budget films. Its origins stem from the classic days of cinema, when the studios needed to differentiate their various productions.*

starred as Harry Kilmer, a World War II veteran who returns to Japan after a long absence. As a young man right after the war, Kilmer met and fell in love with Eiko Tanaka; they were to be married, but then Eiko's brother Ken, thought dead, returns from the war. Ken is a martial arts kendo expert, a man tied to tradition and honor who cannot immediately reconcile the country's loss during the war. Ken disowns Eiko for associating with the American Kilmer, but is also indebted to him for saving Eiko and her daughter from poverty and starvation. For her part, Eiko would no longer associate with Kilmer, let alone marry him.

At the end of his enlistment, Kilmer borrows $5000 from his Army buddy Tanner and opens a restaurant-bar for Eiko, which she calls Kilmer House. Twenty-five years later, Tanner's daughter is kidnapped by Japanese mobsters—the Yakuza. Tanner enlists Kilmer's help to get his daughter back, knowing that Ken, who was once a powerful Yakuza, owes Kilmer. Ken assists in rescuing Tanner's daughter, but he is identified by other Yakuza and they prepare to come after him, leaving Harry Kilmer with a big dilemma.

The Yakuza is a powerful film which displays a number of similarities with *Enter the Dragon*. Both Lee's character and the Ken character are martial artists bound

In *The Yakuza*, Harry (Robert Mitchum) and Eiko (Kishi Keiko) embrace after 25 years apart. Eiko's secret leads to an ever spiraling cycle of violence—and ultimately redemption.

to tradition and to what many would perceive as an outdated sense of honor. Both films hinge on a journey and a mission: Kilmer's to Japan to rescue Tanner's daughter; Lee's to the island fortress to gain evidence against Han and to save a female police operative. In both cases the law is ineffectual and individual action is the only way to solve the problem. Flashbacks are used extensively in the two films, while the final confrontations feature an Anglo and an Asian pitted against a large number of criminals.

However, unlike *Enter the Dragon*'s rather straightforward plot, *The Yakuza* turns on a complexity that rivals the Greek playwright Euripides' tragic work *Alcestis*. Both explore the depth of human nature, with a particular emphasis on duty and honor that meshes well with the martial arts genre. In Euripides' work, the King is faced with his own death; Apollo intervenes because of a past kindness that the King had bestowed upon him and convinces Death to allow the King to find a substitute. The King is rebuffed by everyone but his loving wife Alcestis, who agrees to die in his stead. While the King is mourning, Hercules pays a visit. The King extends his hospitality, not wishing to ruin Hercules' time. When Hercules discovers the truth, he is impressed by the King's generosity and feels a responsibility to him. Hercules resolves to go down to Hades to bring Alcestis back to the King.

The same tragic sense of duty and obligation form the locus of *The Yakuza*. When Harry Kilmer agrees to rescue Tanner's kidnapped daughter from the gangsters, he is repaying a friend for a past kindness. In seeking Ken's help, Kilmer is relying on a debt that Ken owes him. When Ken is discovered to have helped Kilmer, other Yakuza prepare to kill him, and Kilmer must decide whether to return to Los Angeles, like Tanner suggests, or remain to help Ken. Choosing to stay and help Ken, Kilmer learns that Eiko and Ken are really married, not brother and sister. As he tells Ken's older brother, "If I don't do this, I have no where else to go."[5]

In effect, Kilmer has not only robbed Ken of his wife but, as he says to his partner Wheat, with the killing of Ken's daughter by gangsters, he has also taken away Ken's past and future. Kilmer accompanies Ken to the gangster's base of operation, where they prevail after a brutal fight. Later, Kilmer, in a traditional act of contrition toward Ken, slices off his pinky finger, thereby enabling Ken to reunite with Eiko.

Like *Enter the Dragon*, *The Yakuza* features a set piece where the martial arts protagonist, in this case Ken, faces off with scores of gangsters, all of whom were wielding kitanas, the traditional Japanese sword. Tradition and honor compel the combatants to fight in this manner, though Kilmer, neither Japanese nor a gangster, was not obligated to fight as such and could use other weapons. As Ken masterfully crossed swords with his rivals, Kilmer plowed through the rice paper walls of the manor house like a rampaging bear, armed with a double barrel shotgun in one hand and a .45 semi-automatic in the other. The result was an orgiastic display of violence bordering on art, with the brute force of Kilmer's booming firearms contrasting with the subdued, almost rhythmic clash of Ken's sword.

Unlike its predecessor, *The Yakuza* did not do well at the box office, and spelled the end of big budget martial arts films. Critical reception was mixed, with Pauline Kael calling it "an attempt to sell a romantic view of gangsterism in an exotic setting."[6] Just as it had re-tooled *Enter the Dragon* to attract a mainstream audience,

Warner Bros. tinkered with *The Yakuza*, hoping to lure in an even greater audience. However, ironically enough, the seeds of its failure lay in the very thing the studio considered its greatest strength: a top-notch cast; a talented, future Academy Award–winning director; and a well-written, intricate and emotionally complex story with an ambiguous ending.

Director Sydney Pollack was considered at the time as a man of serious taste, best known for helming such films as *They Shoot Horses Don't They?* (1969) and *The Way We Were* (1972), while Robert Mitchum's great appeal was to older audiences from the classic days of Hollywood. The predominantly younger male audience, looking for a new "cool" hero, didn't find it in either Mitchum, who had been the cool bad boy of 40s cinema, or Ken Takakura, also an older man, and they stayed away in droves.

Paul Schrader, who wrote the original screenplay, gave some insight as to why in an interview during a Directors Guild of America retrospective of his films. Schrader noted that the initial story was a gangster action tale based on the Japanese genre films which his brother Leonard, who received story credit, had become familiar with during his stay in Japan. Leonard originally planned to write it as a

Harry (Robert Mitchum) and Ken (Takakura Ken) plan their assault on Tono's hideout in *The Yakuza*. Both *Enter the Dragon* and *The Yakuza* feature Asian men teamed with Anglo partners to fight the last battle.

novel, but Schrader intervened and convinced him it would make a marvelous screenplay. He called his agent and told him, "This is *The Godfather* meets Bruce Lee."[7] However, unknown to Schrader at the time, Warner Bros. had hired Academy Award–winning screenwriter Robert Towne to re-work the romantic elements of the plot.

The "new" story was both haunting and elegiac, with a transcendent sadness that overwhelmed the reconciliation of the two heroes. Martial arts fans, expecting straightforward action, were disappointed by the story's artistic and elaborate structure, while older fans, expecting to see Mitchum in a romantic thriller, were turned off by the excessive levels of violence and bloodletting. The film's apparent happy ending was overshadowed by the solitary figure of Kilmer, boarding a plane to return to a life of retirement and loneliness, having reunited husband and wife at the expense of his own happiness.

Aftermath

While no studios would since venture into a full-fledged "A" martial arts production, Warner Bros. and others would continue to produce and release such films on a scaled-down model. The importance of *Enter the Dragon* and *The Yakuza* lay in their status as groundbreakers and trendsetters, the fact that they were the first, despite their ultimate success or failure. Warner Bros. and the other studios learned from their mistakes: Future martial arts films would be more akin to "B" productions and exploitation films. For the most part, ambiguity, narrative complexity and open endings would be out; simple stories with readily identifiable heroes and villains would be in.

However, perhaps the most important contribution of these two films to the martial arts genre was their establishment of two distinct prototypical categories that subsequent martial arts films followed: the "pure" martial arts film along the lines of *Enter the Dragon*, whose story reveled in combat and which is usually manifested in the form of "tournament films"; and "story" films, such as *The Yakuza*, where the narratives of any number of genres are enhanced by and chock full of martial arts sequences which move the plot forward. Both categories are popular in American martial arts cinema, though the lion's share of these films fall under the "story" parameters. And as we shall see, both types of films would rely on hero and narrative structures developed in the films of Hollywood's classic era.

III

The Early Days: Martial Arts in American Film

Martial arts films really didn't hit America until the late 60s, which is not to say that elements of martial arts weren't found earlier in other films. In 1937, 20th Century-Fox launched the Mr. Moto series, which featured Peter Lorre playing a Japanese detective. While Moto would solve the mystery by the story's end, usually by his wits, he was not above employing a little jujutsu to get the job done. The series was abruptly cancelled as relations with Japan soured. War was imminent, and a Japanese detective would not be a good draw.

This is not to say that American films were devoid of action. Far from it. Fists and lead flew in the American cinema. The differences between homegrown action films and their Asian counterparts lay in culture and history: the various forms of martial arts were developed in the east, and gradually spread west.[1] While a few dojos existed in Asian enclaves, most Americans were familiar with boxing and wrestling as their primary modes of personal self-defense. The American equivalent to the Japanese samurai, fighting for the honor of his master, or Chinese monk, wandering the land battling evil and oppression, was the cowboy, one of the main character paradigms from which the American martial arts hero would later emerge. Other genres (action-thriller, horror, sci-fi, and war) would later provide consistent narrative frameworks in which the American martial arts film would operate. Mintz notes,

> To put the martial arts films in perspective with other types of films, they combine some significantly similar elements—certain types holding to the specific code of the Western; chases of the thriller-mystery-adventure films; special effects of the fantasy films; gambling and gangsters of the gangster films.[2]

The Western Hero = The Martial Arts Hero

Westerns provide a certain amount of narrative economy because so many of its representations are clearly understood and accepted without further explanation.

Wide open spaces, hats, guns and horses are all notable iconography of the genre. The same can be said of the martial arts hero: whether he be a soldier, a cop, a fighter or the master of a dojo, by his stance and moves, the minute he swings into action with his fist and feet, the viewer knows who he is. Gi's, swords, nunchukus and the like all mark him or her a martial artist.

Both the Western hero and the martial arts hero are usually self-sufficient—he owns his own horse or car, can travel at his leisure, and as often as not has a past that marks him a special man. Familiar too are certain themes that both martial arts and Western films share: tradition versus evolution; law versus morality; the individual versus the group; self-reliance versus help from the outside. Both the classic Western and martial arts protagonists are often loners, though in some films the hero has a sidekick, sometimes supplying comic relief.

Today's martial arts films are most akin to "B" films of the 30s and 40s, both in budget and genres, and its protagonists would particularly embody most aspects of the Western hero. All cowboy heroes and martial artists are good with their fists, not to mention their feet, at least with the latter. Like the cowboy, the martial arts hero usually fights on the side of law, or right, whether or not he has any official position. He or she can be an average Joe with above-average fighting skills, or even a criminal who does the right thing in a pinch. They are not above revenge, though in most instances it parallels justice.

Narrative Patterns

American martial arts films take their narrative patterns from the various "B" genres that appeared in the 30s. Besides Westerns, for instance, there were action-thrillers like *Doorway to Hell* (1930), *Public Enemy* (1931) and *Scarface* (1932) which literally exploded onto the scene, becoming all the rage, with their callous (for the time) violence and not-so-subtle fascination with the mob underworld. Though all three pictures told the same basic story—that of the rise and fall of a gangster—it was the fall that captured the imagination of the audience and his death that made him a hero. Unlike, say, an outlaw in a Western, who is killed by the sheriff and thus squared with the community he preyed upon, the gangster's death usually stemmed from a quirk or weakness in his nature—a thematic aspect of tragedy—which underscored the way he lived, in isolation from society.[3]

Whether these films were merely a reflection of hard economic times and their violent by-product or whether they served to influence the predatory mobsters and gangs that flourished during this period is open to debate. What is not is the influence these movies had on later action films, like the martial arts flicks that emerged decades later. The gangster films featured strong male protagonists, high levels of stylized violence, fistfights, occasional misogyny and an emphasis on criminal activity, or its prevention. Once developed, this paradigm would function for decades to come, mutating somewhat here and there over the years, but staying essentially intact in both crime and action films

Following their Western counterpart, action-thrillers were hardly ambiguous affairs: The audience knew who the hero was from jump street. Like the cowboy and gangster, action-thriller heroes led with their jaws, fighting and shooting their way through whatever and whoever got in their way. G-men and their pursuit of the mob were standard fare; so were the "good" cons in prison routine. Tough newspapermen could also dish it out, and take it—usually after exposing some type of graft or corruption. Boxers, truckers, pilots and detectives round out the genre, getting the job done, no matter what, with no sparing of the fisticuffs. Like the Western, violence in these films becomes the ultimate solution when the social order is faced with criminality; if might doesn't make right, it certainly makes things okay, so long as the authorities are the ones dishing it out.

War, horror and science fiction genres were less significant to the development of the hero paradigm in American martial arts films than they were in providing a receptive narrative framework in which the martial arts hero could later operate. In other words, if the martial artist found himself in a war story, horror tale or some futuristic landscape called sci-fi, it really didn't matter. The fighting would be the same.

War films often concentrated on bringing diverse people together for the purpose of winning the fight, or battle. During World War II, Germans, Italians, Irish, Polish, Mexican, Jews and Gentiles were all shown working together to fight the fascists. In the martial arts war films that followed, camaraderie was of paramount importance, while in horror films, which featured bizarre, evil happenings, or the proverbial monster, self-reliance was a major trait of the protagonist.

Science fiction films are largely based on futuristic ideas, even when they are set in the present. The fascination lies between what is possible in the realm of reality and what is shown to be possible on the silver screen. Space travel, cataclysmic disasters and alien invasion were common topics. *Deluge*, a 1933 RKO release, was a forerunner among apocalypse films, and told of civilization's destruction by atmospheric disturbances that trigger earthquakes and tidal waves. The survivors wander about, trying to avoid the renegades who lurk all around them. Decades ahead of the "Mad Max" films, *Deluge*'s special effects include the destruction of New York City by tidal wave.

The world of these films is a self-contained universe, where the laws of cause and effect are often suspended. A significant number during the classic Hollywood era were originally shot as serials, 15–30 minute shorts that ended with a cliffhanger designed to bring the audience back the next week. *Flash Gordon, Spy Smasher* and *Batman* were all popular in their time. Mascot Productions' *The Phantom Empire* (1935) featured Gene Autry as a cowboy who divided his time between the ranch and an underground world called Murania, located at the bottom of a mine shaft. Autry fought, rode and sang, though not necessarily in that order. Of greater interest than Autry's exploits, however, was the genre-melding of the narrative, in this case Western with science fiction, a ploy we would see decades later, particularly in the direct-to-video martial arts films of the 90s.

First Appearances

Displays of martial arts could sometimes be found in American cinema of the 30s and 40s. In war films, basic training sequences often showed recruits receiving hand-to-hand combat instruction, while every now and again a "flip" or a "chop" would surface in a movie fight scene. One of the first and most intense displays of martial arts in an American film came in 1945's *Blood on the Sun,* a World War II–era film that related a tough newspaper reporter's fight to expose the Japanese plan for world domination prior to the outbreak of hostilities in 1941.

James Cagney plays Nick Condon, managing editor of *The Tokyo Chronicle.* When Nick's friend and fellow reporter Ollie is murdered after coming into evidence that the Japanese were planning to attack America, Nick works to retrieve the documents that Ollie had obtained. One step behind and always over his shoulder are the not-so-secret Japanese secret police, who want Nick to lead them to the hidden military attack plans. After a number of killings and the requisite treachery by the Japanese, Nick succeeds in getting the plans taken out of Japan, but the entire Japanese police force is looking for him and there is only one way into the American Embassy.

The first minutes of the film set the stage for its martial tone. Drawings of samurai warriors shooting arrows and dueling with swords scroll along with the opening credits. The first shots are of a riot in front of *The Tokyo Chronicle,* which has printed a headline story telling of a pending plan for an attack on America. The Japanese police barge into the newspaper, demanding Nick's head on a platter. The focus of the story then shifts to Nick, who is working out in a judo dojo. He is dressed in a gi, faces his opponent and flips him over and again. We can see right off the bat that Nick is a very formidable man.

Two themes stand out in the film: freedom of the press versus censorship, and the superiority of American ingenuity over Japanese blind obedience. When the Japanese question the owner of the *Chronicle* about Nick's story, they advise him that Nick has violated their censorship laws. When they confront Nick, he stands on his right and that of every person to hear, speak and print the truth. Throughout the film, Nick's main resistance comes from those wanting to oppress any freedom of expression. In fact, in one scene, Nick is prevented from boarding a ship to say farewell to Ollie and his wife. One of the men there identifies himself as the "thought" police. However, by continuing to print and seek out the truth, Nick is able to overcome his opponents by exposing them to the light of public inquiry.

The forces arrayed against Nick are both numerous and powerful. However, the militarists and their henchmen in the police force must follow orders by rote, and are not allowed to think for themselves, something always warned about in Allied propaganda films. Nick, on the other hand, improvises repeatedly, keeping the Japanese continually off balance. In one instance, when the police are banging down his door to search his house, Nick hides Ollie's stolen plans behind a picture of the Emperor, knowing that the Japanese will not look at his picture.

Nick's ingenuity also extends to the realm of judo. He has mastered the most Japanese of martial arts, and then turned it against them. In one instance, Nick takes on three police officers, flipping them all around his living room. In another, while chasing the killer of Ollie's wife, he chops one of the men in the chest, knocking him cold. Later, after getting the military plans safely away, Nick is trapped in the wharf-house by the sadistic Captain Oshima, a judo expert with hands of iron. In a brutal free-for-all, Nick and Oshima toss, flip, kick and chop their way through the place, demolishing it and each other. However, again it is Nick who improvises, lacing in good old-fashioned American boxing with his judo to finally knock out

Oshima. Running along the docks, a weary Nick knocks out more police using that combination, eventually escaping to the American Embassy.

After more than half a century, *Blood on the Sun* holds up well, and while it is clearly anti–Japanese, it is not filled with the offensive tone of some films of the same era. Cagney rarely uses any racial slurs toward the Japanese—a "Jap" here and there, and then at the end of the story he calls the police chief a "monkey," hardly strong language considering a war was on—but what was probably more telling was the hard core gangster persona he brings into the film. While the Japanese are polite but devious, Cagney is blunt and rude, yet honest. However, he is not above smacking a woman, either, which he did in his gangster roles, and which he almost does to the mixed-raced Iris when he thinks she has played him into Japanese hands.

The Lady from Shanghai, a 1948 Columbia release, straddled the nether region between "A" and "B" that many noir films shared, and starred none other than Orson Welles and his then estranged and soon to be ex-wife Rita Hayworth. It is worth noting here, for it marked another early showing of a martial arts style fighting. In the story, the heretofore-regal Welles engaged in a couple of very savage fights. Most brawls in film to this point were rough and tumble affairs, hardly scientific or precise, with both dirt and fists flying. However, this film was different because the Welles character, that of "Black Irish" Mike O'Hara, obviously had a martial arts background that was tied to the fact that he was a merchant seaman who had traveled the world, including the Orient. In the film's opening scene, Hayworth is abducted by some robbers, whom Welles dispatches with relative ease, using a form of judo to flip and toss his opponents. The martial arts connection to Asia is reinforced in later scenes in which O'Hara, having escaped police custody, hides out in a Chinese theater, where a costume drama features martial arts–style swordplay.

In *Bad Day at Black Rock* (1954), a one-armed Spencer Tracy makes mince meat of bully Ernest Borgnine using judo chops, while in *Thunder Road* (1958), Robert Mitchum does the same thing, savagely chopping a fellow bootlegger across the chest. In *The Sea Chase* (1955), John Wayne plays the captain of a German merchant ship trying to make it back home at the outbreak of the war. When a Gestapo agent attempts to take control of his ship, Wayne uses a karate kick to knock the gun out of his hand. While what happened was not significant, who did it was. Wayne, the biggest draw in Hollywood at the time, had been associated with two-fisted action since his early days in the "B's." This implicit recognition of the efficacy of martial arts combat became overt in Wayne's 1958 film, *The Barbarian and the Geisha*.

Directed by John Huston, the film chronicles the story of Townsend Harris, the first American ambassador to Japan. In a pivotal scene, a hulking brute of a man and his diminutive friend accost Wayne. Wayne beats the big man but the little man, a judo expert, easily dispatches Wayne. While the sequence appears to champion the superiority of eastern martial arts over western modes of self defense, Huston's light direction and Wayne's hammy response denude the victory's significance by playing off traditional western ideas of fair play.

When the big man starts the fight, Wayne attempts to avoid the confrontation; cornered, he cuts the big man down to size, much to the delight of his Geisha assistant. The little man, less than half Wayne's size, is not taken seriously by him; the idea of a bigger man fighting such a small one being patently unfair. The little man then easily flips Wayne over his shoulder, dumping him on the seat of his pants. Wayne's response to being flipped is closer to bemused surprise than out-and-out anger. Having beaten the threat (the big man), he is bested by an afterthought (the small man) who poses no danger. By not losing his temper, Wayne reserves the right to get up and take care of business if he chooses to take things seriously. Instead he appears incredulous. As the little man stalks off, angry at the big one whom he pulls along behind him, the scene is co-opted, turning it from a serious moment to a comic one.

Robert Aldrich's 1955 noir classic *Kiss Me Deadly* was based on one of Mickey Spillane's potboilers and featured an almost atavistic Mike Hammer, as played by Ralph Meeker. The film is remarkable on any number of levels, but particularly in its scenes of misogyny. Every major character around Hammer is killed, as were the minor ones, while the leads are terminally exposed to radiation. As Nicholas Christopher notes about Hammer,

> [W]e can forget the chivalrous codes of honor of the 1930s detective, and the rough-and-tumble, furnished room, rumpled-raincoat persona of the 1940s private eye.[4]

This version of Hammer is clearly a brute with no idea of what he is getting into when he helps a woman he found running hysterically through the desert. When her assailants recapture the woman, she is tortured and murdered, and Hammer is almost killed. Intellectually deficient but tough as nails, the detective plods through the mystery until he unravels a plot to smuggle nuclear material out of the country. One of the film's highpoints comes when Hammer is being followed, and savagely beats a thug at his own game using a mix of martial arts and boxing. In a world of political intrigue and fugue, where Hammer is clearly out of his element, the fight was an important narrative element in the sense that it provided the detective a chance to excel in the one area where he is not outclassed, and to realistically stay in the hunt as it were. Aldrich shot the scene under a streetlight, with a chiaroscuro lighting style that both made the fight appear shadowy as well as more brutal, reinforcing the impression that if Hammer can't solve the case one way, he could always do it another.

Two films which featured martial arts in a positive light were "B" veteran Albert Zugsmith's *Girl's Town* (1959) and writer-director Sam Fuller's *The Crimson Kimono* (1959). *Girls Town*, the ultimate teen exploitation flick, was probably the most unlikely place to find an exhibition of martial arts, but it was there all right, along with Mamie Van Doren and her rare charms, some drag racing, gang fighting, singing and dancing, a guest appearance by the Platters and none other than Paul Anka! Of course, Mamie was in her late twenties when she shot the film, and was undoubtedly the best dressed impoverished teenager in town, but reality was not what drew in the boys at the box office. Mamie did.

She plays Silver Morgan, a streetwise teen who spends most of her time wise-cracking—that is, when she's not either attracting guys or having to fight them off. Silver is suspected of pushing her date off a cliff, but the police can't prove it. Already on probation, Silver has a choice: go to reform school or Girl's Town, a boarding school run by Catholic nuns. She heads off to the religious school, figuring that she'll get over on the nuns easy enough. However, what she doesn't count on is the other girls, who take a dim view to her antics. Virtually outcast, Silver hits rock bottom when her baby sister is kidnapped by drag racers. The girls from Girls Town then swing into action to help her.

Silver is not the typical teen, but she's not a bad kid either. Representative of the "lost youth" that many of these 50s films featured, she is merely the product of bad circumstances who just needs to be given some love, guidance and a little bit of regulation. Her mother and father have run off, and a very nasty aunt takes care of Silver and her sister, if you can call it that. Silver is so down on the idea of family that when she moves into Girl's Town, Sister Veronica tells her that she may address her as mother. Silver replies something to the effect of "What's that?" She even derisively calls the chief detective questioning her "Dad," as if to say he is old and square.

If the nuns and girls present Silver with an orderly, caring setting, it is just as clear she is not accustomed to it. At first she rebels, and that's when we meet Veda, one of Silver's roommates. Veda takes Silver's smokes because they are against the rules, and Silver fights back, but it isn't much of a fight. Veda flips Silver onto her back with ease. When Silver gets up and charges again, Veda hip tosses her. Turns out Veda's deadbeat dad was a bar bouncer who knew judo.

Silver's calamities in Girl's Town continue, though Mother Veronica advises the other sisters to remain patient with her. She believes there is something good underneath all that makeup and flip talk. However, Silver sneaks out of the school on a Saturday night and meets up with an older man who takes her to a nightclub. When she returns to school, the other girls confront her for going out, and she is forced into a "trial," where she is judged by her peers (the other girls). Silver's punishment is to scrub the floors before the big dance—alone. When Mother Veronica gets on her knees, habit and all, to help, Silver begins to realize that the program only works if she is mature and truthful enough to follow the rules.

As Silver's character changes for the better, her baby sister's predicament changes for the worse. She is recognized by one of the drag racers as the girl who pushed her date off the cliff, even though it was to defend herself from rape. The same drag racer forces her to accompany him in a drag race and, after someone gets hurt, kidnaps her to keep her from talking to the police. Silver and Veda follow him to his hideout, and in a most odd confrontation, Veda battles a very muscular man who is trying to force himself on Silver's sister. First she gets him in an arm lock, then flips him over. Later she pulls his leg out from under him and sends him to the floor, flat on his back. Unlike the battle in *The Barbarian and the Geisha*, this fight is performed seriously, and presents judo as a constructive force that can help good overcome evil. Nonetheless, the effect is slightly bizarre, not only because of the gender difference but because the size difference between the two is so great.

Girl's Town ends on a happy note. Silver and her sister are cleared of the murder charge and the former can leave the school. As she says goodbye to Mother Veronica, she can finally call her "mother." Silver has learned a valuable lesson about taking responsibility for one's actions and rejecting the petty selfishness which marked her earlier life. As Paul Anka pulls up to take Silver away, we can see that Mother Veronica was right. Sometimes a little patience does go a long way.

Sam Fuller's *The Crimson Kimono* was an unsettling probe of east and west culture clash within the framework of a detective thriller. Charlie (Glenn Corbett), a white man, and Joe (James Shigeta), a Japanese man, are best friends, having met in a foxhole during the Korean War. They are also homicide detectives in the Los Angeles Police Department, investigating the murder of a stripper who may have been having an interracial affair. While running down leads, both men meet and fall in love with Chris, a comely young artist living downtown, which complicates matters for the two buddies.

The film's martial arts sequences become mirrors by which we can view the sometimes raw emotions of the characters. The first, in the opening dance scenes, is phony, merely a show for the lowbrow audience. By working within the display of martial combat, the stripper shows her desire to be seen as an artist by attempting to add class to what remains essentially a bump-and-grind routine.

After the stripper's murder, Joe and Charlie track down one of her "samurai" dancers for questioning. He is an accomplished martial artist who puts up a fight. Joe and Charlie, still best friends, fight as a team, like in Korea, using a combination of Japanese karate and American boxing styles to bring the man down. However, later, when Joe and Charlie compete for Chris' affections, the two men engage in a ritual bout of Kendo, or Japanese swordplay. While Charlie looks at the bout as a friendly competition, Joe, agitated over Chris, becomes completely unhinged and loses all sense of self-restraint. He beats Charlie severely, breaking the rules of the sport and upsetting the Japanese audience by his disgraceful conduct.

The film ends on a slightly ambiguous note. Joe has tracked down and killed the stripper's murderer, realizing in the process that he was wrong about Charlie. However, his friendship with Charlie still remains tenuous, and in the film's final shots, Charlie is not seen with Joe but rather another character, leading one to wonder if the two can ever really patch up the relationship.

Like *The Crimson Kimono*, the decade of the 50s ended with a number of issues unresolved. The anxieties produced by the Cold War would linger as America moved into armed combat in Vietnam. The moguls who ruled their studios during the classic age of Hollywood cinema were replaced, died off, or both, and their studios would founder almost beyond hope. Social issues, such as integration, always simmering beneath the surface calm of the "I like Ike" years, were coming to a boil, and would result in the civil rights movement of the 60s. The envelope of the exploitation film would be pushed beyond the limits of what had been imaginable just a decade earlier, and full-blown martial arts films would arrive.

IV

The 1960s: A Time of Transition

As the 1960s dawned, the major studios were struggling, while the independents continued to churn out inexpensive features designed to make a quick buck. Martial arts began to seep into American films more frequently, while a small Hong Kong production company began turning out kung fu movies on a regular basis, some of which made their way to our home shores.

Martial Arts in Television and Film

It was during this decade that martial arts began routinely appearing in fight scenes in movies and on television. *Batman*, one of the hottest television shows in the country during the middle of the decade, featured comic book characters in a cheesy, avant-garde type setting. The fights, of which there were many, were more comical than serious, though co-star Burt Ward, who played Batman's sidekick Robin, often used martial arts moves, such as judo flips and karate kicks. *The Green Hornet*, also a comic book–style show, was spun off from *Batman*, and in an interesting episode, featured Batman battling the Green Hornet, and Robin fighting Kato, who was played by Bruce Lee.

Gene Rodenberry's *Star Trek*, also guilty of employing rather cheesy sets, became one of the most popular television shows in syndication, and created a virtual cash cow for Paramount, which went on to launch a series of big-budgeted, financially successful *Star Trek* films featuring the original television cast. William Shatner, a veteran of some low-budget Roger Corman films, played Kirk, the ship's captain. Invariably, each week would find Kirk either having to defend the ship from rampaging aliens or himself from more anthropomorphic ruffians; he employed combinations of karate, boxing, and judo to dispatch them.

Martial arts even made it into the Western. *The High Chaparral*, a popular television show starring B stalwarts Leif Erickson and Cameron Mitchell as a cattle baron and his younger, high-spirited brother, devoted an entire episode to Mitchell's attempts to defeat a wiry Frenchmen who uses savate, a style of martial arts that greatly relies on kicking. While mostly played for laughs, the story turns on the lesson Mitchell learns: Until he adapts his old fashioned boxing style and uses his legs to kick, he is destined to fail.

In *Hell to Eternity* (1960), Jeffrey Hunter, best-known for his role as Martin Pawley in John Ford's *The Searchers* (1956), plays a young man raised by a Japanese family. When the war breaks out and his family is sent into internment, the young man is drafted into the Marine Corps, where he eventually distinguishes himself heroically.

The story revolves around a series of dilemmas that must be reconciled. As a young boy, Hunter is initially the outsider in a Japanese family; by the time he is fully accepted by them, war breaks out, and it is his foster family who become outsiders to the society at large; the Marines provide a new home, but again he is on the outside looking in, having no great interest in killing Japanese. He visits his foster family in the camps, where his mother tells him he must do his duty. Reluctantly he fights, but the ferocity of combat eventually hardens his heart. It seems by serving his new family, he is destroying his old one. The quandary is resolved when Hunter puts to use his ability to speak Japanese, persuading hundreds of soldiers to surrender rather than be killed.

Hunter's change of character is in no small way mirrored by the discipline of his martial arts training. As a young man he is exhibits the self-control he has learned at the dojo. However, during boot camp, unsure and given to doubt, his resolve loosens and he gratuitously battles a self-defense instructor to a draw in a superior display of hand-to-hand combat. When Hunter and his fellow Marines hit the beach, his humility completely dissolves into anger. He loses control and becomes an unfeeling killer. Only after serious soul-searching does he regain his martial discipline, and uses it to turn from a remorseless killer to a dedicated savior.

The film was one of the first American productions to not only address, if even indirectly, the bigotry involved in sending Japanese-Americans to the internment camps, but to distinguish martial arts as a form of combat that provides discipline and self-restraint to its practitioners.

On a much lighter note, 1964's *Ride the Wild Surf* featured Barbara Eden as a judo expert who beats up a surfer, only to fall in love with him later. Like Veda in *Girls Town*, Eden portrays a tomboyish yet beautiful young woman who has learned judo from native Hawaiians. In a match against one of the locals, she loses easily to him, but when the surfer she's looking to impress laughs at her, she struts her stuff, flipping him a number of times. It takes a while for him to get over his bruised ego, but after he does, it smooth sailing for the both of them.

Karate—the Hand of Death (1964) is an interesting (if not exploitational) film that was shot on location in Japan, and is clearly a forerunner of the American martial arts movies to come. Though it was poorly budgeted, and in some parts very crudely acted, the film featured a good story and was done as well as could be expected considering its financial restraints. The time is 1964, almost 20 years since the end of World War II, and Matthew Carver has returned to Japan to find the ghost of a woman he once loved. He is followed by a pickpocket who steals his wallet; when the police find it, his money is gone but a mysterious coin is in it. Carver soon learns that the coin is the key to a fortune in platinum that was hidden by Nazis during the war. As he unravels the mystery of the platinum's whereabouts, and who the mysterious woman is that resembles his dead lover, his life and world are changed forever.

Like with *Blood on the Sun*, the opening shots of the film set the tone of the story. The credits unfold on boards, which are then broken by punches, chops and kicks, immediately establishing the martial aspects of what is to follow. They turn into an alley that opens onto a major street, with gray slates of rain pouring from the sky seemingly without end. Abruptly, a man pulling a rickshaw-like apparatus casually turns down the alley toward us, while another man slowly walks down the street, clicking some type of ancient plaything, reminding the viewer that old Japan has still not vanished more than halfway into the twentieth century.

Two western men then exit from a building across the street, looking for a cab, which passes quickly by. Modern Japan is also present, and the fact that the Japanese pass off screen before the westerners arrive suggests a certain disconnect between the old and new. When one of the men moves off to find a cab, a silent and unseen killer attacks the remaining man, karate chopping him to death and stealing a valuable coin. Somewhere between the Japan that was, and the Japan that is, lurks a very dangerous and mysterious place, a terrain that Matthew Carver will soon find himself navigating.

That Carver is a kareteka, or karate practitioner, is established early on in the film when he visits the police station to report his stolen wallet. The police detective immediately recognizes a huge callous on Carver's right knuckles, which marks him as an expert. In fact, Carver's reputation has preceded him, and the police know that he is a fifth degree black belt, one of the highest ranking of all karetekas.

But Carver is a bitter man. Having lived his whole life in Japan, and studying karate since he was a boy, he was shattered by the war. Though his sensei was able to get him out of the country, Carver's parents were interned—and died in the camps. Fighting in the Pacific, Carver then finds himself killing Japanese, the very same people he grew up with and loved. By his own account, having killed over a hundred Japanese soldiers, most of them with the deadly martial art he possesses, Carver has now sworn off fighting.

Yet, there is also a kindness in the man. Walking down the street, Carver stops to talk to children and buys them fruit. When he gets his shoes shined, a young girl gives him a flower. Just then the pickpocket strikes, and rather than quickly following the thief, Carver makes sure the little girl is okay before giving chase. Like with the tug-of-war between old and new Japan, Carver is a decent man whose past haunts his present, and prevents him from having any type of future.

The exploitational aspects of the film lie mainly in its approach to karate, and how it is demonstrated on screen. At the time, besides judo, martial arts were not widely known in the States. In presenting karate as an almost magical killing force, a naive audience was led to believe that nothing could withstand the kareteka and his chops. In fact, in this movie most of the emphasis of the art form's deadly nature is concentrated on the karate chops, not the lethal kicks and punches that audiences are most familiar with today. At the beginning of the film, a quick and deadly chop to a victim's face kills him instantly. When Carver is in the police station, his hands have to be "registered" with the police department as deadly weapons! Later, when Carver has a flashback to the war, he fights and kills three Japanese soldiers using just his bare hands, again mostly through the deadly "chop" but also with some kicks. Carver eventually gives up his vow not to use karate when Rohmer, one of the men searching for the platinum, has him pistol-whipped. In probably the best fight scene in the film, Carver chops his assailant and then easily flips him over his shoulder. After Carver unravels the mystery surrounding the platinum, he is forced to fight an expert as great as he, but fueled by the anger inside of him, he beats the karateka by killing him with a chop to the throat.

Though *Karate—the Hand of Death* was filmed with the assistance of the Japanese Karate Association, fight choreography is almost non-existent on this film, and it shows. Most of Carver's fights look completely rigged, his kicks slow and amateurish, and the scene in the jungle, where he takes on the Japanese unit single-handedly, is hardly believable as the kicks don't land and the chops appear to be pulled. Similarly difficult to swallow is Carver's facial contortions and hissing noises when he takes a position to use his karate. Of course, to audiences who don't know better, the more bizarre the action, the more appealing the story.

To its credit, *Karate—the Hand of Death* is free from many of the stereotypical features that plagued other films, both martial arts and non–martial arts ones. Japanese women do not fall over Carver as happens in other films with a western hero, nor is he shown to be bigoted. The Japanese are not portrayed in a particularly negative light; quite the opposite, in fact. When Carver finds out that the oldest daughter of his sensei, whom he secretly married just before the war, was killed by her brother because of the shame a mixed union would bring, the sensei sides with Carver against his own son, and demands that his son kill himself to preserve the family honor.

Carver wraps up the mystery, finding the missing platinum, though he almost loses his life in the process. He also finds that his lover is not alive, and that the woman he sees is her younger sister, who is her spitting image. Defying conventional Hollywood happy endings, Carver does not stay in Japan with his sensei and his daughter, though they ask him to. He has seen too much. As he gets into a cab bound for the airport, we know he will never come back.

Ian Fleming's MI 6 super spy James Bond began his long cinematic run in the 1962 release *Dr. No. Goldfinger,* the third feature, sported Olympic weightlifting medalist and professional wrestler Harold Sakata as Odd Job, Goldfinger's hulking bodyguard and assassin. Sakata is probably best remembered for his deadly hat, a derby that, when thrown, slices through concrete, rather than his martial arts prowess. Bond, meanwhile, preferred to make love not war, but as played by the ruggedly handsome Sean Connery, did both well. The Bond fight scenes were well choreographed and fit the character to a tee: they were both deadly and humorous, with Bond mixing judo and boxing to overcome his opponents.

In *You Only Live Twice* (1967), SPECTRE is hired by certain radical elements to capture American and Soviet spacecraft for the purpose of starting a war between the superpowers that would destroy them and allow other nations, like China, to take their place. The spacecraft are kept in a secret base hollowed out of a giant volcano in the southern Japanese Islands. For some reason, MI 6 knows about the plan but Washington and Moscow do not. And of course they send their best man to crack the case: Bond. Only Bond is "dead."

The film opens with a burial at sea for Naval Commander James Bond, who died under mysterious circumstances. As SPECTRE agents watch, his body is lowered into

Sean Connery as James Bond in MGM's *You Only Live Twice* (1967). Bond launches a kick against an assassin.

the sea by a British naval vessel. However, divers immediately swim to the body, which has settled to the ocean floor, and remove a very living Bond and take him back to a submarine waiting to pick him up.

Bond immediately heads for Japan, where he teams up with Japanese agents also looking for the secret installation. While in Japan, Bond is accosted by SPEC-TRE agents trying to eliminate him but he gets away in typical 007 fashion, with little damage to himself and a whole lot to the other fellows. Bond and his Japanese partners eventually find the base and, in a razzle dazzle raid, destroy it and SPECTRE, thereby saving the world. Again.

In preparing himself for the mission at hand, Bond is sent to a martial arts training camp, where Japanese agents practice in the ancient samurai arts. While there is no logical justification for the camp, or Bond's presence in it, since using swords and sticks are not the most efficient way of fighting in the twentieth century, he nonetheless learns to fight samurai style—in only a few days!

You Only Live Twice is unique in one respect and repugnant in another. The film is offensive, even for its own time, in its portrayal of Japanese women as sexual playthings for western men, unable to resist the charms of the visiting occidental. Bond first hooks up with one Japanese agent, who, despite supposedly being a professional, falls madly in bed with—and then in love with—007. In one scene where Bond is told he must masquerade as a Japanese man and marry a local island woman, 007 is upset that the woman is reportedly unattractive, all the while his current lover, the Japanese agent, is walking next to him, admiring Bond. When she is killed in an assassination attempt on Bond's life, he shows little sadness as he immediately warms up to the next agent he is teamed with, the "unattractive" woman he must marry.

The movie's uniqueness comes in its influence on set design in future martial arts films. Many films showing martial arts training camps, whether they be ninja- or terrorist-oriented, would feature similar iconography as displayed here, including rudimentary housing, ancient or non-modern facilities, and intense discipline, often with trainees broken down into small groups where they acquire various fighting skills. Bond is shown the camp by his Japanese associate, then is rotated through, learning what he needs to know. The signal that 007 has mastered the curriculum comes when one of SPECTRE's agents blends in with the other martial arts fighters and unsuccessfully attempts to kill Bond in a stick fight, losing the fight and his life.

A seminal film that fell more into the popular motorcycle gang genre than martial arts, but which featured a smattering of the latter, was Tom Laughlin's *Born Loser*s (1967). Laughlin wrote, directed and produced the film, as well as taking the starring role of a loner who goes up against a gang of violent, outlaw bikers. The film was based upon two real life incidents:

> [T]he ex–Marine from Philadelphia who was fined $1400 and sentenced to 180 days in jail for wounding two of the hoodlums who were molesting three ladies (the assailants were fined $50 apiece and set free); and Kitty Genovese who was repeatedly stabbed in front of dozens of apathetic onlookers.[1]

The film was a hit for AIP, which stressed its exploitation aspects—teenage girls being raped and tortured, vigilantism and a skewed sense of liberalism—and cleaned up at the box office. This film marked the first appearance of Billy Jack, Laughlin's ex–Green Beret, half–Indian counterculture hero that would skyrocket him to fame during the early 70s. Jane Russell nearly stole the show as a waitress whose daughter is molested. When the bikers return to scare the girl into silence, Russell speaks for all fed-up, middle-aged Americans tired of crime when she blasts the police and DA as worthless.

The film's title refers to both Billy's and the biker gang's position with regard to the society at large, and the fact that, while fighting one another, they both still have one thing in common: Neither of them can ever win against the establishment. Billy is an outsider, a half Indian who lives alone in the mountains above the town, subsisting off the land by hunting and fishing. Before the war he trained horses, but times have changed and the town has modernized to the point that Billy's services are no longer needed.

The bikers live in the town, but are just as isolated as Billy, not accepting the mores of the community. They race up and down the streets, none of them holding a job, and many wear all manner of offensive tattoos and buttons, including swastikas. Their clubhouse is more a snake pit, where the bikers party, abuse drugs and kidnap women for "initiations" (gang rapes).

When the bikers attack a driver who accidentally hits one their bikes, none of the townspeople will help. One store owner even kicks the boy out of his place, saying he doesn't want trouble. The bikers pull the boy into an alley, and only Billy Jack comes to his aid, using his rifle to keep the attackers at bay. When the police arrive, they arrest Billy Jack for being a vigilante, and he actually gets a stiffer sentence than the bikers.

Out on bail, Billy must raise a thousand dollars for his fine, but the bank refuses to loan him the money. Burned by both the justice and financial systems, Billy finds the social order is blind to the plight of people like him, good folks trying to do the right thing. As he withdraws to the forest, the bikers become more aggressive in their behavior, threatening the rape victims and their families one by one until there is no one left to testify against them.

Billy Jack represents a number of the decade's predominant images, or themes. He is a man who prefers solitude and peace. He communes with nature, living free in the outdoors with no ties or responsibilities. Billy cares about the wellbeing of people, and will make the effort to help someone when others won't. Unsullied by the greed of the banker and the closed minds of the police, he avoids the pitfalls of capitalism and its adoration of riches, instead settling for just getting by. At heart Billy is something of a mystic, believing that each person must find their own answers in their heart.

Though much of the film is drama, when Billy does fight it is clearly an extension of his character and not an aberration. After deciding to mind his own business and stay out of trouble, Billy still manages to find adversity when the bikers kidnap visiting college girl Vicky out from under police custody. Witnessing the act, Billy confronts the three bikers who have her. When he cannot talk the bikers into relinquishing the girl without a fight, Billy unleashes his rage in an abrupt and deadly display of hapkido, felling the biggest man with chops, punches and a number of bone-crushing arm locks. After the bikers raid Billy's trailer looking for Vicky, they find Billy's fine money hidden under a couch sofa and steal it. The next day Billy confronts the bikers at a gas station, and he is attacked by the biggest one. Billy fends off the man's clumsy attack by remaining perfectly balanced, then knocks him out with some well-placed chops and punches.

A number of stock institutions and characters round out the story, personifying the various difficulties facing the youth of that period. The police are ineffectual, and rather than being something to look up to, are either cowards (the sheriff) or prone to brutality (the main deputy). Bankers and business are only interested in the profit line. The older generation either does not understand, or is hostile to society's young people. When Vicky is escaping from the bikers, an old lady refuses to let her hide in the house or call the police. Bigotry is still an issue, as Billy is continually harassed by the bikers for being part–Indian.

Though Billy recovers from his beating at the hands of the gang, he cannot even spur the police to help him get Vicky back. Again taking the law into his own hands, he burns up their bikes and kills Daniel with a well-placed shot between the eyes. When the police finally get the courage to raid the biker clubhouse, Billy has finished the job for them, but his reward is to be shot himself. However, the wound is not fatal, leaving the door open for the eventual return of Billy Jack.

John Wayne's *The Green Berets* (1968), an "A"-level film from Warner Bros., was the only pro–Vietnam war film made during the actual conflict, and starred the Duke as a Special Forces colonel assigned to a high-risk fire base. The film featured a spectacular night battle sequence in which Vietcong troops storm the base. The Green Berets manage to hold the fort, before Wayne and a hand-picked crew are off to spirit away a VC general.

While the movie was as popular with fans as the war was unpopular with critics, it did feature an interesting martial arts sequence worth noting, if, for nothing else, its logical motivation. Ex–football star Mike Henry, also known for his Tarzan incarnation, played one of the Green Berets in the Duke's team. Scouting ahead of the main party, he is ambushed by five or six Vietcong. Unlike many fights that would be seen in subsequent martial arts films, which had no rational basis, the nature of this fight was clearly motivated by the need for silence. The VC, planning to lure the squad into an ambush, couldn't shoot Henry without giving away their position. Instead they attack him with knives and other weapons. Henry fends off the attack using judo, killing all the assailants though dying in the process.

Two films were released at the end of the decade that, while dissimilar in content, were alike in their portent of stars to come. *Marlowe* (1969) tossed up for our viewing pleasure an updated version of Raymond Chandler's tough but intelligent private eye Philip Marlowe. Only now, Marlowe, as played by the easygoing James Garner, is more laid back than world weary as he wends his way through a mystery based loosely on Chandler's *The Little Sister.* When an enforcer comes to warn Marlowe off the case, the detective is mildly amused when the diminutive figure of Bruce Lee pays a visit to his office. The smiles fade, however, when Lee kicks his office to smithereens. The next year would find Lee in Hong Kong starring in his own films.

The Wrecking Crew (1969), one of the four Matt Helm super-spy films starring Dean Martin, was a serio-comic burlesque of the Bond films. Ostensibly Helm was a CIA-type spy who, like Bond, found sex a more pleasant outlet for his energies than violence. However, for Helm, sex became as much the goal as the actual mission, though Martin, nearing his mid-fifties, preferred double entendres and risqué banter to any actual assignations. Every now and then Helm actually had to fight, and would execute some martial arts moves, again, in a light manner as befitting to comedy as to drama. As he struggles to complete his mission, karate champion Chuck Norris (who up to that point had worked as a stuntman) confronts him. Norris has one line before Helm goes on to save the world. Norris, meanwhile, also moved on: to bigger parts and eventual stardom.

Shaw Brothers Productions

Hong Kong, a British Colony during the 60s*, was a major production center for martial arts films. The majority of these films celebrated what could be called "homespun" Chinese values such as familial piety, discipline and loyalty, abstention from immoral behavior and, of course, fighting the Japanese. Shaw Brothers Productions was the first, biggest and most profitable of the studios churning out these films, which were especially popular in the Orient, particularly where there were large Chinese populations.

---

* Hong Kong was remanded back to Mainland Chinese rule in 1998.

Run Run Shaw began his ascent as film mogul via the theater—as an owner, that is. Shaw rented out his theaters for opera performances as well as the exhibition of old black-and-white Shanghai films. Shaw, ever the businessman, decided that it made much more sense to produce the films he planned to show. At first, from the early 60s on, Shaw Brothers made all types of films, but martial arts remained a favorite. *The Chinese Boxer* (1969), one of their most successful releases, shifted its emphasis from weapon and swordplay to man-to-man combat, thereby paving the way for modern martial arts cinema.

Lo Leih became one of Shaw's biggest stars, and his 1970 film *King Boxer* was among the top-grossing kung fu films ever. It was released in the U.S. as *Five Fingers of Death*, and a measure of its success here was doubtless attributed to its connection to the American Western, with Leih's character having the "fastest hands in the east" as opposed to the Western hero blessed (or cursed some would say) with the fastest gun in the West.

Eventually, the Shaw Brothers became a dynasty, and from 1970 forward focused almost exclusively on kung fu films. Their studio was located in the Clearwater Bay area and boasted a number of sound stages, huge sets depicting old Chinese locations, full editing bays, and post production facilities. By most accounts, Run Run Shaw was a latter-day Harry Cohn who controlled his studio, actors and films with a tight fist. Actors were signed to contracts that paid them literal peanuts. Most complained that they couldn't live on the salary, while others who broke their contracts with Shaw found themselves in court. Many actors went in a different direction: some got second jobs while others involved themselves with the triads (organized Chinese gangs), a situation touched upon in Bruce Lee's posthumous *Game of Death* (1977). Bey Logan, in his *Hong Kong Action Cinema* notes, "Many actors and stuntmen became active members of Hong Kong's powerful triad societies, causing the massive infiltration of Chinese show business by organized crime that still remains a problem today."[2]

The Shaw Brothers' studio operated much the way Monogram, PRC and other "B" studios had during the 30s and 40s: Their films were manufactured in an assembly-like manner, one after another, using the same casts, crews, writers and directors. Chang Cheh, a veteran director of Cantonese swordplay cinema, joined the studio in 1962, initially as a screenwriter, but by the middle of the decade was directing. His films, low-budget or not, exhibited a frenetic, bloody pace that has influenced, among others, John Woo, and during a 15-year period Chang directed 75 of them!

By the 1980s, economic changes and competition from other film studios like Golden Harvest Productions cut into the studio's profit margin. Shaw, sensing a decline in fortunes, shifted into television production, churning out period piece costume dramas. Always looking for a way to corner the market, Shaw bought a television station just to make sure his shows would have a guaranteed outlet. Though no longer making martial arts cinema, the Shaw Brothers Productions remain an important pioneer in the development of kung fu films as a whole, and an integral factor in the evolution of American martial arts cinema.

V

The 1970s: Martial Arts and American Cinema

The 1970s saw the birth of an American martial arts cinema, manifested in the appearance of scores of martial arts films, particularly *Enter the Dragon*, and the rise to superstardom of Bruce Lee. Television blazed the trail, popularizing the genre for mass consumption, while new heroes were waiting to emerge from Lee's long shadow. The hero paradigm from the western movies of old came full circle, and were visible in these new films, just as the "B" genres provided narrative frameworks within which the martial arts films could operate. While major studios, particularly Warner Bros., continued to make martial arts films on a low-budget basis, the independents got into the fray as well, and would one day take over most productions.

On the Small Screen

The television series *Kung Fu* debuted in 1973, featuring (soon-to-be) "B" superstar David Carradine as Caine, an Amerasian Shaolin monk wondering the Old West in search of his half brother, a white man. Caine was born in China, his father an American missionary, his mother a Chinese woman. When they are killed, the orphan is left at a Buddhist temple where he is accepted as an apprentice to the monks. He spends years perfecting his martial arts skills through rigorous training, and is eventually released from the shelter of the temple to serve the outside world.

Some stories say that the idea originated with Bruce Lee; others that he was merely involved as a potential star. But, whatever the case, the popularity of *Enter the Dragon* and other import kung fu movies certainly played an important role in getting ABC to air the hour-long show. Another factor in the show's popularity was its generic quality: In many respects it is a reworking of the very popular *The Fugitive*. Caine arrives in a America with just the clothes on his back, and a price on his head, wanted in China for the murder of the Emperor's nephew, whom he killed

defending another monk.
Each week finds Caine in
another location, always moving, inevitably having to use
his martial arts prowess to
either save himself or protect
others. In essence, as he tracks
down his brother, the law
tracks him.

The high quality of the
stories certainly contributed
to the series' modest success.
Caine's world was one of constant bigotry, where he was
usually judged immediately by
his appearance, something
easily related to by many segments of American society
during the 70s, be they minorities, long hairs, bikers,
even truckers. But the narratives often eschewed the simplicity of white versus other,
and examined the many faces
of racism. In one episode,
Caine assists some Chinese
migrants in their fight against
a brutal rancher who wants to

David Carradine as Kwai Chang Caine in ABC Television's *Kung Fu*. The show often examined racial
and social justice as Caine wandered the southwest.

destroy them because his son wants to marry a Chinese woman. Initially the Chinese are as bigoted as the whites about the relationship. In another story, Caine
must fight an Indian scalp hunter who despises other tribes so much that he hunts
them for bounty.

One of the most interesting episodes of the series revolved around a Brazilian black man, a former slave, looking for a hidden bounty. When whites attack
him, Caine helps out, and is surprised to see that the man is accomplished in a
form of martial arts that he had never seen. The black man tells him that it is a
combination of dance and fighting which the slaves had developed to protect themselves. But prejudice comes in many forms, as the black man then attacks Caine,
whom he believes to be a thief. The two men cross paths a number of times, the
black man goading Caine to fight. Only after the Shaolin defeats him does he realize that he is being consumed by his own hatred of others.

Kung Fu was unique in the sense that it provided no simple answers to the
racial strife that marked the Old West, a situation which viewers could certainly
identify with some hundred years later. Mexicans, blacks, whites, Asians and Indians all coexist uneasily, and no one group is good or bad all the time. In fact, if
anything, it is refreshing in the sense that for every bad person Caine came across,
he also touches the lives of one or more good people. If there were any overarching

message to the series, it was "deeds not words." Caine changed people, even bigots, by his actions, the way he lived his life and the way he treated others, not by talking about it.

The martial arts sequences in *Kung Fu* were unique from the standpoint that they appeared "slowed down," which was just the opposite of Bruce Lee's kinetic energy and rapid-fire blows. Whether this was because of Carradine's lack of ability or an intended effect, the fight scenes had a realistic quality to them that the average viewer, who didn't live and breathe martial arts, seemed to appreciate. Gone were the exaggerated noises the martial artist would make when punching and kicking, or the almost impossibly high jumps and somersaults that characterized any number of Chinese import films. Caine could take on any number of opponents, but he also got hit and hurt, and would attempt to avoid a fight whenever possible.

Carradine reprises his role as Caine's great grandson in *Kung Fu: The Legend Continues*. The show had potential but was not given enough time to find an audience.

The series ended in 1976, but remained a fan favorite; in fact, Carradine made a *Kung Fu* television movie a decade or so later, updating us on the further adventures of the Shaolin monk. The telefilm co-starred Brandon Lee, Bruce Lee's son, as the son Caine never knew he had. Carradine then went on to star in a number of martial arts and action films, mostly low-budget, and some of them for Roger Corman, who capitalized on Carradine's television martial arts prowess.

But it remains the Caine character that is tied to so closely to Carradine. The character's popularity remained so high that almost 20 years later a new, syndicated television show was launched: *Kung Fu:The Legend Continues*. In this version, Carradine returns, again as a Shaolin monk, but now the great grandson of the original character. The show, while good, was pulled from the schedule after a couple of years on the air.

The Influence of Bruce Lee

Though Bruce Lee's filmography is unfortunately short, his effect on the genre remains powerful, and it is certainly arguable that without him martial arts films would have remained fringe import movies in the United States. One question will forever remain unanswered, yet begs asking: Was Lee more of an influence alive or dead? There can be no doubt had Lee lived* he would have continued to make films, but what kind? Up to this point, all of his martial arts films were of the "pure" variety discussed earlier: very light on story and quite heavy on action. As the 70s progressed, American martial arts films increasingly became a cinema of the "story" variety. Would Lee have adapted his work? Or would his continued presence in the industry have skewed the direction of these films toward the pure variety he seemed to favor?

On the other hand, his death, like that of Valentino, raised him to the status of a popular culture icon. T-shirts emblazoned with his picture became requisite dress for junior high and high school boys; posters featuring scenes from his films were selling like the proverbial hotcakes, a particular favorite being the hall of mirrors fight from *Enter the Dragon*. Of course, where there's money to be made, there's someone to make it. Books, comics, even supposed "autographed" pictures of the late martial artist flooded the marketplace, usually in flea markets or swap meets.†

But retail merchandise wasn't the only by-product of Lee's death. Lee's brother released a folk album dedicated to him; it featured soft ballads regaling martial arts in general and Lee in particular. Carl Douglas' *Kung Fu Fighting*, a Top 40 pop music song, hit the charts in the summer of 1974 and went straight to number one, as they say, like a bullet!

An entire cottage industry of Bruce Lee look-and-sound-alikes was formed almost overnight. Bruce Li, Bruce Le, Bruce Leung and Dragon Lee all played the real-life actor in either uncompleted films of Lee's or in sequels to his previous works, causing some astonishment. After all, since acting is a make-believe world to begin with, the notion of pretending to be someone who was pretending, well....

The entertainment arena wasn't the only area affected. Enrollment at karate studios, like those established by Chuck Norris, went through the roof. The elite Hollywood clients that Lee had taught, including Steve McQueen and James Coburn, were now being joined en masse by the middle class as well as the middle-aged. Karate, kung fu or any of the other martial arts forms were being sold as a panacea to parents who wanted to find a painless way to provide their children with discipline and respect for authority. Lee, quite the iconoclast, would have been turning in his grave. His own fighting style was synthesized from a number of martial arts forms, which he called Jeet kune do, so the idea of confining one's self to a particular fighting style would have seemed like folly.

Whenever anyone dies a tragic or untimely death, there is a natural tendency to try to assign some kind of meaning to it. Lee's cerebral hemorrhage cut short the life of a rising star. Conspiracy theories surfaced: Lee was planning to take on the Chinese mobsters in Hong Kong, so they rubbed him out. Lee was training for a secret mission and pushed himself to the point of death. One of the most bizarre involved his old studio, Golden Harvest. Word circulated that Lee's jumping ship from the Hong Kong studio caused innumerable financial problems. The studio was angry at Lee's ingratitude, since they were the ones that made him a star. When

*He would today only be in his sixties, roughly the same age as Chuck Norris, and certainly still a viable star.
† At any given time, eBay features hundreds of photographs and other memorabilia associated with Bruce Lee.

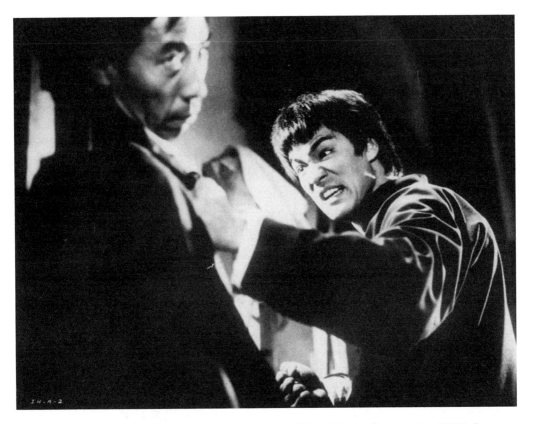

Lee finishes off an attacker in Golden Harvest's *The Chinese Connection* (1972). Lee was about to become a superstar.

Lee refused to come back after *Enter the Dragon*, they put out a hit and had him eliminated.

Conversely, whenever a star dies, an opposite tendency also arises, that is to deny his or her demise, which manifests itself right away. When Janis Joplin and Jimi Hendrix died of drug overdoses, many fans refused to believe it. Stories circulated that the two ran off to be together. A story swirling around Jim Morrison's death in France said it was faked, just so that he could get out from under American obscenity charges that were pending. Lee's death was no different. One story that was particularly resonant was that Lee had gone undercover, to work for the government, like a one-man army taking on crime.*

All this controversy, rumor and innuendo over the death of Bruce Lee contributed to a climate that brought favorable attention to the world of martial arts in general, and martial arts films in particular. Whether Lee would have been more or less influential alive is impossible to answer. What is clear, however, is that in death he became an enormous power, a driving force for the success of martial arts cinema in America. A testament to that influence comes in Lee's last picture, *Game of Death* (1977), which he had been shooting at the time of his death and

* *Many Elvis fans who believe he is still alive maintain an almost similar position, that the King was working undercover and then went into the Witness Protection Program.*

Lee pummels Chuck Norris in the Coliseum sequence of *Return of the Dragon* (1972). The film was shot before *Enter the Dragon* but was released after Lee's death, resulting in confusion for many fans who mistakenly thought it was a sequel.

which, based on his popularity, was completed posthumously. The studio added footage of American stars Hugh O'Brian and Dean Jagger so that it appeared as if they were part of the original film (they weren't), and played on the conspiratorial notions that had swept the country, positing Lee as the victim of an evil cabal.

Billy Jack

Another seminal figure in the pop culture of the 70s was that of actor-director Tom Laughlin's character Billy Jack, the half–Indian war vet who made his first appearance in *Born Losers*. In *Billy Jack* (1971), the title character defends an ultraliberal "Freedom School" for American Indians, against who else?, white bigots. Like the previous entry in the series, this film is more drama interspersed with bursts of martial arts action, and fits into the vigilante pattern that seemed to take hold during the decade, whereby a basically decent guy is pushed too far, and has to open up a can of whoop ass to rectify the situation.

Much of the picture is predicated on a succession of aggravating incidents against the Indians, one worse than the next, which culminates in the gang rape of the schoolteacher Billy Jack loves. The in-between time is dominated by contrasts between the good Indian culture and the bad white one. Though Billy Jack has been trained by the military to fight, he puts his hapkido skills to good use much less than in the true martial arts films which would follow.

Probably the most memorable scene in the film comes when the hero confronts Posner, the white big shot responsible for giving the Indians so much grief. Billy Jack tells the villain that he is about to place his foot against the man's jaw; the latter scoffs, until Billy Jack does just that with an awesome sweeping kick. He then proceeds to fight off dozens of racists, until he is finally overpowered and beaten to a pulp. After recovering, Billy Jack kills Posner's vile son and is hauled off to jail by the police, a martyr for Indian justice.

Throughout the film, Billy is told over and again by Jean, the director of the Freedom School, that his fierce temper is the major problem he must somehow get over. But is it? While Jean may not be a Christian, she is certainly a pacifist, and by her standards any display of violence is wrong, even defending oneself. But for most everyone else, Billy's actions are logical and justified, wherein lies the rub. If, as Billy told Posner and the deputy as they were illegally hunting mustangs on

Chuck Norris finds Bruce Lee too hard to handle in *Return of the Dragon* (1972).

Indian land, when the police break the laws then there is no law, then Billy's actions were certainly justified, if not a required response to the violence being levied against the Indians and the school.

Both *Born Losers* and *Billy Jack*, the two Laughlin films with which this study is most concerned, pivot on the idea of men having the right, if not obligation, to take the law into their own hands when the system has failed. While certainly not a new idea, vigilante action achieved new justification with these films, not to be surpassed except, perhaps, by the *Death Wish* cycle put out a few years later. The film's narratives follow a set blueprint which includes:

1. *Both films feature villainous sons of overbearing fathers.*

Daniel, the leader of the motorcycle gang that Billy Jack fights, has an abusive father who beats Daniel's younger brother.

Bruce Lee in *Game of Death* (1977). Lee's last film, it relied upon a number of doubles to fill in for the actor, who had died four years before. Only a few minutes of the real Lee is in the film, including this shot.

While the film does not say so, it is implied that the father did the same to Daniel, providing rationale for why Daniel turned out the way he did. Bernard, Posner's son, is weak-willed and bullied by his father into becoming a monster, which he readily does.

2. *Billy has to face increasingly violent provocations from the villains.*

In *Born Losers*, the biker gang beats a young man, flattens Billy's tires, rapes some local girls and then threatens them with death if they testify, steals Billy's money, then pummels the girl he is falling in love with. *Billy Jack* featured the attempted slaughter of wild horses, the humiliation of the Indian children in the ice cream parlor and the continued harassment of the Freedom School, not to mention the murder of one of the Indian students, all by Posner and his men.

3. *In both films, the women Billy loves are raped.*

In *Born Losers*, Vicky, the rich college girl on vacation in town, is terrorized and molested by the biker gang. In *Billy Jack*, Jean, who runs the Freedom School, is tied spread-eagle to poles in the ground while Bernard and his friend take turns raping her.

4. *Law enforcement is ineffectual or powerless to stop the violence.*

The sheriff in *Born Losers* is acknowledged by the DA and everyone else as the weakest man ever elected to the position. He is unable to protect the rape victims from the bikers and only at the last minute does he act to help Billy take on the gang. Sheriff Cole in *Billy Jack* is an honest lawman who respects the rights of all people. However, Posner runs the town, and Cole is unable to muster the support to effectively oppose him.

5. *Billy Jack is continually harassed or ridiculed by those who hate Indians.*

Billy is usually referred to derogatorily as "Indian" by the biker gang, even though it is clear that Daniel, the leader, grew up with Billy. Posner and the others consider Billy a half breed and troublemaker, and do everything they can to rid the area of his influence.

6. *Billy's final outburst of violence leads to serious consequences for him.*

Billy is forced to take on the bikers by himself after they hold Vicky in their clubhouse and beat her senseless because she won't strip. After he frees her, a deputy shoots him in the back as he makes his escape. In *Billy Jack*, he bursts in on Bernard after finding out about the rape of Jean and murder of Martin and kills him with a vicious chop to the throat. The police then trap him in a church, after which he gives up and goes to prison.

By today's standards, the fights in *Billy Jack* are crude, if not effective. Billy only engages in one major fight, but it is a doozey, when he takes on Posner and his gang of hooligans in a park. Billy fights a running battle against them, flipping, kicking, chopping and punching, but is finally overcome when one of the men hits him from behind with a weapon of some kind.

The locus of many of the problems between the Indians and the townspeople is the Freedom School, where self-expression and independence appear to be the only things being taught. Conventional learning does not seem to be addressed. For a conservative town, such a concept in the worst seems criminal and at best, wrong. Complicating things is the daughter of the deputy who is hiding out at the school to avoid the wrath of her father, (he beat her almost to death when he found out that she was pregnant and didn't know who the father was).

Billy Jack does not stand the test of time as well as *Born Losers*, mostly because the political and philosophical sentiments it expresses are indelibly rooted in the causes of the early 70s, which had already began to fade by the end of the decade. Its fanatic anti-war stance would not play well in the following years, with Reagan at the helm, nor the period after that as the United States was attacked by terrorists and had to fight a war in Afghanistan and Iraq.

Its emphasis on cultural diversity was ahead of its time, however, as well as prophetic. All manner of races are represented at the Freedom School, living peacefully together, yet the only thing they seem to have in common is contempt for traditional social institutions and a bitter dislike of European culture, regardless of their skin color. This seems to be a continuing characteristic in the social push for contemporary cultural diversity today.

On the other hand, with the benefit of time and distance from the 70s, a clearer, more balanced view of *Billy Jack* is possible. It is quite apparent that the townspeople are spoiling for a fight, in some ways because of their own racial narrow-mindedness, in others because of their ignorance. They do not question the status quo, nor are they necessarily against the war. They don't like non-whites, but since the only non whites we see are from the school, we don't know if their dislike and bigotry stems from the school's political agenda or if they are truly prejudiced by the color of the children's skin.

Either way, the intolerance is not justified, but since it is just as clear that adults and children of the school wish to provoke trouble with their leftist positions, the former position is both understandable and probably inevitable. The inhabitants of the school mock and reject much of what middle-class America supports or believes in. During a skit where a group sings the national anthem and one man won't stand, they beat him senseless, equating violence to patriotism. However, the biggest hypocrisy is that the school is actually funded by the very government the adults and children reject. It is clear that they don't mind receiving the largess of what they consider a corrupt system so long as it fosters their ability to clap, sing songs and hold hands, and voice opinions that offend the very people who are paying their bills. So, with reactionary and radical factions facing one another, it is no wonder that violence would somehow surface.

Viewed some three decades later, the film's major claim to fame is twofold. First, it serves as an eternal document of the left wing, youth-oriented counter culture percolating in the United States in the late 60s and early 70s. The adults and kids of the Freedom School present it as a model for the future, where peace and mutual respect can be achieved. Second, and more importantly for this study, it spurred interest in martial arts, both on and off the screen.

Billy Jack was a monster hit for both Laughlin and Warner Bros., which had picked up this independent production.[1] The debate over art influencing life or life influencing art took center stage as the film either exerted a significant pull on hip fashion and counter-culture attitudes or merely reflected them. Cowboy hats similar to the style worn by the character suddenly became popular, and jean jackets were the rage for a while. Many people suddenly became "native American" to varying degrees, while similar numbers claimed to "know martial arts!" A pressbook release from Warner Bros., *two years after the film was released*, points up its continuing popularity:

> "Billy Jack" has played longer in hundreds of cities and towns in America than probably any picture in recent times. The film has garnered over $30,000,000 in box office receipts to date, making "Billy Jack" one of the greatest phenomena of recent times.[2]

Laughlin followed up with two more Billy Jack opuses, *The Trial of Billy Jack* (1974) and *Billy Jack Goes to Washington* (1977), the former drawing comparisons on relative guilt, between that of Nixon and Watergate, and Billy Jack's justifiable homicides of the racists, while the latter saw the hero as a politician out to tame the Senate. Both films were short on action and long on melodrama.

Other Films

Call Him Mr. Shatter (1974) was an interesting martial arts production putout by Hammer Films, the British company most famous for their horror flicks. Stuart Whitman stars as Shatter, an international hit man hired to assassinate a corrupt African dictator. Shatter completes the job and then flies to Hong Kong to collect his fee—$100,000. Unfortunately for Shatter, those who hired him have no intention of paying and instead try to kill him. The city becomes a no-man's land for him, with the mob and police hounding him every step of his way. Shatter has the good fortune to be saved by a martial arts champion named Tai Pah, and he hires him to keep him alive while he chases down his money. The result is a bone-splitting ordeal for whoever gets in their way.

Shatter is the consummate professional, cold but fair, with his mind on business. When he kills the African dictator, he leaves the man's girlfriend alone, though he could just as well have taken her out too. But that isn't in the contract. Shatter easily smuggles his gun into Hong Kong, fooling the customs people, and then while taking a cab to his motel is always watchful if being followed. After he checks in, he purposefully bumps into another guest and exchanges keys with him, thereby confusing anyone coming to find him, a move which eventually saves his life. He's also as good with a gun as he is with his fists, and both come in handy as he and Tai Pah engage the mob in a number of confrontations.

Tai Pah, on the other hand, is the kung fu champion of Hong Kong, no mean feat in a land where everyone seems to know martial arts. He is the master of his own school when he is not tending bar, which is where he first meets Shatter after seeing the latter beaten in the alley by special service Hong Kong police who want Shatter out of the city. Tai Pah, like Shatter, isn't much on words, and lets his fist and feet do the talking when he has to. In a superior display of his prowess, Tai Pah engages in an exhibition at a night club which pits him against the tae kwon do champion of Korea, the karate champion of Japan, and the kickboxing champion of Thailand. Tai Pah beats them all in a not-so-subtle symbol of Chinese martial arts superiority. In agreeing to protect Shatter, who cuts him in for half the take, Tai Pah becomes in essence a professional bodyguard with the hottest client in the city.

Call Him Mr. Shatter is pure 70s cinema, from the character's long hair and flair pants, to the music and rock posters which adorn the wall of a massage parlor that Shatter visits. Even more in tune with that decade is the film's political allusions to black nationalism in Africa, which was on the rise at the time. The opening scenes of the film show riots and civil unrest in the African nation which Shatter comes to ply his trade. We later find that the drug cartel wanted the dictator removed because he was able to get his weapons and armaments from Communist China at bargain prices, something occurring with great regularity at the time, so he no longer needed the mobsters.

As in a long line of 70s films, Shatter is not a typical hero but rather fits the bill of the anti-hero. However, as the story moves along, Shatter becomes a more traditional protagonist, much the way Tai Pah is. First we learn that Shatter usually operates for the CIA, which means he has a government sanction for his work. Later we find that not only is the dictator he killed a ruthless despot, but he is also a drug supplier in league with European Cartels. When the mob kills Mai Mee, the woman Shatter was beginning to love, Shatter is no longer operating solely for money but is now out to avenge the death of someone close to him. When the smoke clears, Shatter has finished the job he set out to do, and he and Tai Pah walk away a little wealthier, and perhaps with a better future ahead of them both.

Another 1974 martial arts film, *Golden Needles*, was produced by AIP, a first for them, and (like *Call Him Mr. Shatter*) featured a white, two-fisted expatriate American running afoul of gangs in Hong Kong. The film starred Joe Don Baker, fresh off roles in *The Getaway* and *Walking Tall*, as Mason, a gambling adventurer living in Hong Kong and partnered in an antique business with Kwan, an elderly Chinese man. When Kwan brokers a deal with mobster Lin Toia to sell a mystery woman named Felicity a golden statue containing special acupuncture needles whose effects can stimulate a man's sex drive—or lead to a horrible death—and Lin Toia backs out of the agreement, Kwan enlists the aid of his partner Mason to steal it.

Golden Needles is as much a period piece as *Call Him Mr. Shatter*, appearing on the surface to be invested with the norms and sexual freedoms of the 70s which followed the discord and upheaval of the 60s. However, while the story takes place in Hong Kong, it is less Asian than western in nature, and can just as easily be read as a strongly conservative tale linking American puritanical social strictures against sex to female deceit, and ultimately death.

Felicity is the locus for the betrayal and double-dealing which occurs in the story. She makes a deal with Lin Toia to buy the statue for $100,000. When Lin Toia changes the deal and ups the price to 250, Felicity balks and instead chooses

In *Golden Needles* (1974), Western inhibition clashes with Eastern sensibilities. Jim Kelly smashes an opponent's face with an elbow.

to have the statue stolen, which leads to a chain of killings, beginning with Kwan, following through to an American antique dealer named Bobby, and ending with the millionaire's bodyguard, Claude, whom the millionaire tests the needles on. We later find that the millionaire had originally given Felicity $300,000, more than enough to pay for the statue, and that she was just being greedy in wanting to keep the left over cash.

In the film's opening scenes, an elderly man with a harem of young women possesses the statue and needles. As the old man lies down, a skilled acupuncturist inserts the needles into the designated nerve points, and suddenly the man comes alive, is able to walk unassisted and is full of vitality. As the old man and his women head toward the bedroom, men armed with flame throwers suddenly break into the house and scorch all of them, then take the statue.

Later, when Kwan and Felicity approach Mason with the proposal to steal the statue, Mason makes it abundantly clear that spending the night with Felicity is also part of the bargain. After breaking into Lin Toia's safe and removing the prize, Mason delivers it to Kwan, who plans to smuggle it back to the States for Felicity by putting it in a case of rubbing oil. Mason then takes Felicity back to her hotel room, where he obtains both his monetary payment and his sexual payoff. However, while the two engage in sex, crosscut with the love scenes are Lin Toia's men breaking into Kwan's warehouse and killing the old man.

At the film's conclusion, after battling to find the golden needles with a seemingly insane millionaire (Burgess Meredith), Mason approaches Kwan's young girl-

Jim Kelly (left) in action in *Golden Needles* (1974).

friend, Lotus, and finds that Kwan had kept the real statue and made a duplicate of it to send to the States, hoping the real one would reinvigorate his sexual relationship with the much younger girl. In double-crossing everyone for the chance at sexual vigor, Kwan instead found himself thrown headfirst through a skylight, plunging to his death far below.

Jim Kelly co-starred in the film, and his role was one of his least provocative: a businessman contently engaged in the system and not rebelling against it. As an antiquities dealer, Kelly represents the more refined aspects of capitalism, marketing the very historical artifacts that reinforce the status quo. As Mason's best friend and partner, Kelly engages in most of the martial arts sequences in the film, though he is helped from time to time by Mason, who fights mostly with his fists, and a beautiful, high-kicking Chinese police detective who is also after the statue. Kelly choreographed his fight scenes as well, something that would begin occurring more often as his film output grew.

In 1976 Columbia picked up *The Stranger and the Gunfighter*, a 1974 Shaw Brothers co-production. An east-meets-west spaghetti Western crossed with a Hong Kong–style kung fu film, the result was pure entertainment, as stars Lee Van Cleef (the gunfighter) and Lo Lieh (the stranger) team to find a treasure belonging to a Chinese warlord that had been entrusted to Lieh's uncle in America. Van Cleef and Lieh ride the countryside searching out four women, each of whom bears a tattoo on her backside. When the message on all four backsides is put together, it reveals the location of the treasure! Along the way, the two encounter a series of adventures, and adversaries, including a town that wants Van Cleef hanged, a gang of Mexican bandits and Hobbit, a psychotic preacher-gunfighter who is also after the treasure.

Both Lieh and Van Cleef come with credentials. Lieh is the ablest of kung fu fighters, which he proves to everyone in a number of battles, while Van Cleef is the fastest of the gunfighters. Both get ample time to demonstrate their prowess—in fact, at times, one upping each other. As Van Cleef is being hanged, Lieh throws his knives into the rope, literally saving Van Cleef's neck. Van Cleef returns the favor when the two are escaping, using some fancy shooting to ward off the posse. When Lieh fights off a saloon owner's gang, Van Cleef helps by shooting various fixtures to knock out the men. In the final assault on Hobbit, who is holed up with the Mexican bandits, Lieh picks off the bad guys one at a time while Van Cleef grabs a Gattling gun and wipes them out in droves.

The Stranger and the Gunfighter was released toward the closing stages of the Western cycle, and squarely at the tail end of the spaghetti Western series, and as such bordered on parody. Sight gags and jokes fill the story. In one scene, Lieh, with a dog on a leash, purposefully enters an establishment whose sign posts the warning that Chinese and unaccompanied dogs are not allowed. When Lieh is told to leave, he begs that he cannot because the dog would then be unaccompanied! The film was a natural for a sequel, with Van Cleef accompanying Lieh back to China to give back the warlord's fortune. Sad to report, none was forthcoming.

Race and Martial Arts Cinema

Race relations and the problems of stereotypes have been problems confronting this country since its inception, though a great deal of progress has been made during the last 30 years to eliminate much of the strife and inequality. The treatment of race and ethnicity in film has been no exception. In *The Chicken Thief* (1904), a comedy from Biograph, a carefree Negro steals a chicken from a white neighbor and is shown devouring it, smiling all the while from ear to ear. When the whites decide to stop the poaching, they plant a bear trap in the chicken coop, catching the crook in a "humorous" manner. The narrative leaves no room for doubt that blacks are lazy and shiftless, willing to steal their dinners whenever hungry. Such attitudes continued to predominate for decades in the cinema.

In the 1906 film *Skyscrapers*, Dago Pete and others are constructing the tallest building in the city. When Dago Pete steals some money, he blames it on the foreman. The foreman is tried in court and, fortunately for him, his daughter exposes Dago Pete for the thief and rascal he is. All is well now that the owner of the property (the upper class) and the foreman (the working class) are reconciled.

The film was shot in New York City, which was experiencing large-scale immigration, with many of the newcomers being Italian. The implicit message of *Skyscrapers* is that because of Dago Pete's thievery, and by extension that of all immigrants, misunderstandings can arise between native-born Americans that must be dealt with. The film was obviously anti-immigrant, and certainly anti–Italian, with Dago Pete's motivation to steal solely being that he was from an onerous group.[3]

The year 1916 saw the release of D.W. Griffith's *Birth of a Nation*, which was a landmark film and one of the most important events in cinema history. The story, about the Civil War and its aftermath, used thousands of extras and was considered a budgetary extravaganza. However, Griffith's portrayal of blacks as happy slaves, and the Ku Klux Klan as guardians of virtue who keep the criminal tendencies of freed blacks in check, was as controversial then as it is now, and caused riots in some cities when first shown.

As cinema advanced from silence to sound, the same thing could not be said about the treatment of minorities, with Native Americans usually portrayed as bloodthirsty savages out to stop the spread of civilizing forces in most Western films. The Japanese and Germans took it on the chin during World War II, the former as a devious and conniving enemy, the latter often represented as a race which knew no bounds to its cruelty and degeneracy.

With the passage of the Civil Rights Act of 1964 and the Voting Act of 1965, which put a stop to various tricks that some states were using to prevent minority voting, new registration drives were conducted to move blacks into the political mainstream and get them to vote.[4] Demonstrations and riots wracked the decade, as did assassinations, while a number of political measures advocated by the President and Congress caused disagreement and sometimes violence. Integration, or desegregation as it was sometimes called, led to the forced bussing of children from one school to another. Affirmative Action is still being debated today and has been the subject of much litigation.

With such controversy swirling throughout American society, it is not surprising to find it reflected in cinema, and martial arts films were not exempt from such a movement. While the decades of the 80s, 90s and the new millennium have seen martial arts cinema largely shying away from racial issues,* the 70s were a different story, with the political, racial, social and economic tempests occasionally spilling over into the narratives of the period.

In *Enter the Dragon*, Jim Kelly is preparing to leave for the tournament, but before he can get to where he has to go, he is stopped by two white policemen, who taunt him. When they draw their batons and confront Kelly, he knocks them both out, then steals their police car and drives off to the airport. In *Billy Jack*, peaceful Indian children are humiliated in a store by white bullies, and in *Kung Fu*, Caine is often the target of anti–Chinese prejudice.

One of the most provocative films of the decade, though, has to be *Three the Hard Way* (1974), which co-starred Jim Kelly. *Three the Hard Way* is prime mix of "black exploitation"—a popular action subgenre of the time that paid lip service to the socio-economic plight of African Americans by featuring primarily black casts in gritty urban settings, generally as hip protagonists who not only operated on both sides of the law, often against white institutions like the police or the mob, but who were also dandies with the ladies, black and otherwise—and practiced martial arts. The nexus of black exploitation and martial arts is usually found in the films of Jim Kelly, and this is a key example.

The story is about a group of white supremacists who have discovered a formula that can kill black people but is harmless to everyone else. A millionaire, Feather, has invoked the services of a doctor, allowing him to test his experiments with live blacks on a secret compound. Feather's goal is the racial purification of America, and he will stop at nothing to achieve that purpose. When one of Feather's prisoners escapes and alerts his running buddy Jimmy of the plot, the supremacists kill the prisoner and take Jimmy's girlfriend Wendy hostage. Jimmy saddles up for action, enlisting two other pals, lady's man Jagger (Fred Williamson) and karate expert Mr. Keyes (Jim Kelly).

The first shots in the movie establish the tone: A raggedy-looking black man in blue prison-like dungarees is handing out slop to feed other, mostly faceless black prisoners. All we see is their hands. Behind the black man is a guard—a white man in a uniform, wearing sunglasses at night, a rifle in his hand. He is larger than the black man and faces the camera, establishing a controlling position as he brusquely prods the black man to hurry up. The background music is fast and incites suspense, while the lighting is dark and grainy, accenting the prisoner's deplorable condition. By the positioning of the characters and their relation to one another, white domination is clearly the image projected, but the black response is initially ambiguous as the black man merely dishes out the slop, saying nothing.

Later, when the black man escapes, we find he is not in a prison but some kind of compound, and the guards are not working for the government but are a type of paramilitary force. Either way the implication is apparent: The government must not care about what is going on because it allows the paramilitary group to operate in the open; or the government is unable or unwilling to stop the racists because they have become too powerful. As the black man flees, he takes refuge in a large

---

Martial arts philosophical teachings have largely been accepting of all races within their fold. Supremacy of race has usually not been an issue during the last decades, though there have been occasional films which tend to promote a certain discipline as being superior to that of others.

shed, where we see scores of dead black people laying in a pile like a sort of modern-day Auschwitz. He hides under a blanket in the pile, then kills the white guard with a crowbar, takes his machine gun and shoots his way out of the complex. Now the black response is clear: violent resistance to racial oppression and brutality.

This theme repeats itself throughout the movie, as time and again Jimmy, Jagger and Mr. Keyes are attacked by massive numbers of white supremacists, only to beat the racists back with superior fighting skills and firepower. When Jimmy and Jagger meet up in Chicago, Jagger is not convinced the problem is serious enough that he needs to get involved. As they talk about the situation, two white men follow them and try to push them into the E-train. Jimmy kills one man and the two chase the other into a carnival, but lose him. Suddenly, a dozen or so paramilitary supremacists converge on the pinball gallery where Jimmy and Jagger are and direct a great number of shots into the establishment. The two men return fire, killing most of their enemies and sending the rest running.

Now convinced of the seriousness of the threat, Jagger accompanies Jimmy to find Mr. Keyes, who is preparing to drive away from his home. He is confronted by a white policemen who demands to see his license (even though he is not driving yet). Mr. Keyes complies, but then the policeman pulls his gun and tries to arrest Keyes for some drugs they planted in his car. Keyes kicks the gun out of the policeman's hand. From out of nowhere, white policemen descend on the area, mimicking the scene at the pinball gallery. Keyes systematically destroys the entire lot of them, kicking, flipping and punching his way through half a precinct, until all the cops are sprawled on the ground. It is obvious now that the police will not help either, and in fact may be aligned with the white supremacists. The three men must handle the situation themselves, with all the force they can muster.

A third encounter quickly follows, with the supremacists tailing Jimmy and the others to a car wash, where another shootout begins. As Jimmy and Jagger exchange rounds with their enemies, Keyes uses his martial arts to debilitate everyone he comes into contact with. Glaring differences between the black men and their white opponents become apparent: The blacks have a sense of honor when fighting, while the whites do not. When Jimmy comes up on some supremacists from behind, he calls out to them before opening fire, giving them a chance. When one of the whites comes up on Jimmy from behind, he shoots, wounding him. When Mr. Keyes is fighting a supremacist, and has him in a lock from behind, another supremacist shoots his partner in cold blood trying to get a shot at Keyes.

Once the three men have figured out Feather's plans, they each head to a different city to stop the supremacists from planting the toxins in the water: Jimmy to Los Angeles; Jagger to Chicago; Mr. Keyes to Detroit. Jimmy and Jagger have a relatively easy time stopping their opponents, either killing the racists themselves or causing their vehicles to blow up—with them inside. Mr. Keyes heads to his martial arts school, where there are no white students, and elicits the help of his assistant, an Asian karate master, symbolically linking another minority to their cause. The two men chop and kick their way through the supremacists and save the water supply.

The three men get together again and head for Feather's compound, to cut the head off the snake as it were. Though outnumbered and outgunned, they assault the place with firebombs, blazing guns and Mr. Keyes' karate, killing most of the white supremacists in the process. Jimmy finds Wendy, his girlfriend, in the burning complex and rescues her. Now reunited, the four finish the job they started, bombing everything in sight and saving the black race from extinction.

Viewed almost 30 years later, the plot of *Three the Hard Way* is in the least ridiculous, while at most is slighting to anyone firmly committed to racial equality. However, at the time of its release, it was sure to have fanned some flames of distrust in the inner city communities where many of these movies were popular. On the other hand, black exploitation was not the only contentious type of film. In *Death Machines* (1976), we have a complete reversal of *Three the Hard Way*, proving again that weak writing and the urge to make a quick buck by pigeonholing the usual stereotypes are universal.

The plot of *Death Machines*, what can be fathomed at any rate, follows three martial arts killers, supposedly highly trained, who have somehow been taken over by a mysterious big shot we never see, and directed by Madame Lee, an Asian woman with a horrible accent. The woman's stated goal is to take over all contract killings in the area, and she begins by killing the hit men of "Mr. G," the city's mob leader. Eventually, Mr. G is forced into using the services of Madame Lee's men to off some competitors.

The opening credits of the film feature an obelisk with two faces: one black; one white. The features of the black face seem exaggerated, as if to suggest a wide aesthetic chasm between how blacks look and how whites do. The opening scenes place the martial arts killers in an Asian-style manor, complete with pond and bridge. Two Asian men fight on the bridge, brandishing swords. Down by the water, two black men duel with sticks. Across the way, two white men fight in unarmed struggle, immediately positioning them as the more appealing of the combatants since western values favor such conflict.

Madame Lee's black and Asian martial arts killers finish off their opponents routinely, but her white martial arts killer is double crossed by his nemesis, who pulls some knives out of his socks. The "white death machine" backs off and pulls a snub nose .38 from his sock and shoots the knife wielder, proving the old adage that you never bring a knife to a gun fight. The white martial arts killer has established his ability to think, to improvise, which seems lacking in his Asian and black counterparts. He is clearly the killer to watch.

It is unclear how Madame Lee controls her death machines, but they never speak, only do as they are commanded. Their first test is to eliminate Mr. G's hit men. When the three killers confront a hit man on the roof of a building, the black one gets shot (miraculously, whenever the men get shot they never die) so it is up to the white one to finish the job. When the trio attacks the second hit man, the white death machine fires the bazooka that blows him up; the others stand behind him. The third hit man is entrusted to the white killer alone, and is murdered rather gruesomely. Later, when the death machines are sent after Mr. G's driver, the white killer again takes control, crashing a truck into the restaurant where the driver is eating. While it is clear that all three martial arts killers are pawns, it is also apparent that the white killer has taken on the head, or guiding role, something taken for granted in American society at the time.

Other stereotypes are played upon as well: When the death machines accost the daughter of a banker that Mr. G wants to leave town, she is thrown to the ground and the men stand over her. Another of Madame Lee's associates removes a camera and begins to take pictures of the girl and the killers. Later, he meets the banker in his office and shows him the pictures, trying to blackmail him into leaving town. While the photographs are not shown, Madame Lee's associate makes it known that society would not think highly of the girl if they saw her copulating with one of the death machines—a clear reference to her having sex with the black martial arts killer.

The projection of blacks being oversexed continues. In one scene, Madame Lee finds the black death machine sitting in a special room that only she is authorized to be in. When she commands him to leave, he merely stares at her. Finally she gets the "message" and smiles, then turns off the lights. Even though his mind has been taken over somehow, it obviously hasn't been taken over enough in some regards.

For that matter, women and Italians fare little better. Women are portrayed as either sex objects, as evidenced by the first time we see Mr. G, who has a poolside full of beautiful topless women, or scheming and conniving, which Madame Lee certainly characterizes as she plots double crosses and brutal murders. In a later scene that takes place in a bar, and which has almost nothing to do with the arc of the film's story, we see a partially nude girl dancing on a tiny platform. Distinguished from the dancer is a "good girl," a nurse who is waiting to talk to her boyfriend who works in the bar. She is visibly uncomfortable with the dancer's activity, maintaining her virtue in the eyes of society at the expense of the dancer.

The scene in the Italian restaurant could almost be funny (which was certainly the intention) were it not for the memory of "Dago Pete" in *Skyscraper*. The restaurant's owner provides Mr. G's driver with a spaghetti dinner, and boasts about its freshness and great taste. His accent is so thick and obviously phony that it could be cut with the knife the driver is using to eat with. The owner's facial features are also exaggerated, like that of the black death machine on the obelisk, with huge thick eyebrows and an unkempt moustache. The exclamation point to this typecasting levity comes when Mr. G's driver cuts into his spaghetti and finds some type of rodent buried in the meat sauce, much to his (and the viewer's) chagrin.

If *Three the Hard Way* was playing on racial dissension to guarantee a good box office draw, then it is just as apparent that *Death Machines* relied on socially expected stereotypes to advance its thin plot. However, as the black exploitation phenomena petered out, and the nation's commitment to racial equality continued, such stories were the exception in martial arts cinema, especially as other concerns, political and domestic, took center stage during the Reagan years.

However, a contrast of these two films with two unique entries which were South Africa's first venture into martial arts cinema: *Kill or Be Killed* (1980?) and *Kill and Kill Again* (1981?), prove interesting and insightful.[5] The movies were modest successes at the box office, but the stigma of Apartheid cast its ugly shadow over the films, and provides a glimpse of how race was treated in a country with an even worse record than the United States. At the time, South Africa was a racially divided country, with whites controlling the government, while blacks and other minorities served as the labor forces the country needed. From the time the Dutch East India Company landed there in the seventeenth century until 1948, race relations between the Dutch, or Afrikaners, and blacks were generally one of supremacy and inferiority, with whites on top and blacks, Indians and mixed races below them.

After 1948, when the Nationalists came to power, Apartheid, or "apartness," became the official policy of the land, written into law. Interracial marriage or sexual relations were outlawed, and in the Population Registration Act of 1950, which is sometimes called the cornerstone of Apartheid, races were classified into three groups: "white, Coloured, or African."[6] Parliament, which was the supreme legislative power, was chosen by whites and restricted to whites. Segregation became the byword and Africans were forced to carry passes, ID–like reference books that would tell the police who they were, and they were restricted from entering certain areas.

During this time, South Africa was considered a rogue nation by most countries, but in many cases that did not stop those nations from investing in South Africa's infrastructure or doing business with them. The IDAF, in its study *Aparthied: The Facts*, cites that by 1979, "between 2,000 and 2,500 transnational corporations had been identified as having subsidiaries or associated companies, or other investments in South Africa."[7] Major among the investors was the United States, Great Britain and Germany. And despite UN sanctions against South Africa, including an arms embargo, the South Africans mobilized and trained one of the best militaries in the world, with some of the best weaponry. By 1982, the South Africans were actually looking to become major players in the exportation of armaments.

For its part, South Africa liked to portray itself as the continent's only democracy, with free elections, freedom of religion and freedom of the press. A sunny, friendly place on a barbarous continent. However, such freedoms were only guaranteed to roughly 20 percent of the population. Everyone else was considered less than a person, whose only use being that of cheap labor to keep the regime going. With this in mind, *Kill or Be Killed*, and to a lesser extent *Kill and Kill Again*, are not merely martial arts films, but cultural reflections of the socio-political anomaly that Apartheid was.

One of the first shots in *Kill or Be Killed* is that of a Nazi flag. When one considers that the German National Socialists supported racial supremacy and anti–Semitism, a policy which appealed to many Afrikaners during the 1930s,[8] the symbol seemed appropriate. The story was as simple as it was preposterous. A Nazi general wants to assemble the greatest karate team the world has ever known, made up from fighters around the world, to take on a similar team fielded by the Japanese master Miyagi. Why? Because some 40 years earlier, the general was disgraced in front of Hitler when his German karate team was beaten by Miyagi's Japanese karate team, so the general wants revenge.

Both sides want Steve Chase (James Ryan), who initially is fighting for the Nazi squad. However, Chase and his girlfriend want to leave, but they and the other tournament fighters are trapped in the general's castle, which is hundreds of miles removed in the Namibian desert. They finally do escape, and make it back to civilization, but Chase's girlfriend is kidnapped by the general to force Chase to come back and fight for the Nazis. Instead, Chase fights for Miyagi's team, hoping for a chance to rescue her.

As a mirror image of the "apartness" of South Africa, *Kill or Be Killed* has no equal. Namibia, where the film takes place, was occupied illegally by the South Africans and was a launching pad for their military raids in Angola. So what is a

Nazi general doing there, with his own castle and private army? Is he a symbol of the South African regime? The world's greatest fighters assembled by both teams are all white save one. In lands where Africans make up almost 80 percent of the population, only two blacks are seen in the film. One is a worker on a surveying expedition in the desert; the other a fighter who is only briefly shown. Miyagi is the only other minority seen, while the philosophical aspects of the martial arts, which are so important in Asia, have been openly replaced by the western revelry in the sheer force and violence the forms are capable of producing. In short, the film is a microcosm of what Apartheid intends: the marginalizing of minorities to the point they seem an afterthought, and the justification of a white supremacy, as evidenced by the "world's greatest" karatekas, who are mostly European and American.

The fight scenes in *Kill or Be Killed* are of the Hong Kong variety, with thudding, snapping effects for punches and kicks, and a lot of slow motion somersaults and back flipping during the combat. In the end, Chase defeats the Nazi fighters, but the win is certainly not representative of some victory over the South African political system. Chase originally fought for the Nazi side because of the money they paid him. His reason for fighting for Miyagi was merely an excuse to get back into the castle to rescue his girlfriend.

Kill and Kill Again featured Ryan reprising his Steve Chase role, only this time Chase is a high-living martial artist for hire. He is approached by a beautiful woman who wants him to rescue her kidnapped father, a research doctor. Chase agrees, of course, with the stipulation that he is paid handsomely. Where the Chase character in *Kill or Be Killed* was paid in the thousands to fight, the Chase character in this film is paid in the millions. Without a doubt, Chase is a poster boy for capitalist ethic.[9] He finishes what he sets out to do, and while this film was less insensitive than its predecessor, a third film to complete a trilogy was not produced.

Like its predecessor *Kill or Be Killed*, the opening shots of *Kill and Kill Again* focus on a particularly controversial subject, in this case Sun City, where Steve Chase is being awarded a trophy for businessman of the year. During the 70s and 80s, Sun City was a provocative symbol of Apartheid, a glamorous resort community cut out of an African Homeland where wealthy South Africans could go to gamble, carouse and pretty much do all the things they prohibited in their own country. A number of resorts there attempted to bring in big name acts to perform shows at their hotels, attempting to pass themselves off as a Las Vegas–like community, even though racial separation and animus was still present, and a number of rocks stars did play. However, even more rockers banded together not to, and released songs and videos advocating a boycott of Sun City.

As the master of ceremonies ticks off Chase's accomplishments in the business community, and the fact that he is the four-time world martial arts champion, Chase is attacked by a group of karate chopping men, most of whom he disposes of in a running battle through an ornate casino (which is devoid of any black faces). Chase later learns that the men were employed to test his skill by the agency who wants to hire him to find the doctor. Chase names his terms and then goes off to build up his rescue team, most of whom are white karatekas. Wherever he travels, be it to trailer parks or karate schools, almost everyone is white. The one exception is "Gorilla," a very dark-skinned black whom Chase wants on his squad. Unlike the karetekas, who are shown to be smart, skilled fighters, Gorilla is first seen in a tug of war contest, an activity that takes no brains, only brawn.

Gorilla is the only significant minority presence in the film, and while he is treated as an equal, it seems more out of neglect than recognition. Chase and the others do most of the important work. When the team has a briefing by the men employing them, Chase does all the talking. When the team is attacked by Marduk's forces, Gorilla relies mostly on brute strength in his fights, not skill like the other men. Even in the bar scene, where the group goes for information, despite a huge Confederate battle flag prominently displayed, the raucous patrons pick a fight with Chase and don't even acknowledge Gorilla, their prejudice and bigotry being unbelievably displaced upon the whites, who are strangers to the area.

Chase eventually makes it to the town where the doctor is being held against his will, and finds that Marduk, the billionaire, has used the by-products of the doctor's potato-fuel experiments to produce a mind-altering drug that can make a slave out of anyone taking it. Marduk's plan is to produce a new civilization, one that obeys only him, and like with the first film, the allusions to fascism are apparent, with Marduk's group, who have special uniforms and salutes, using force to keep rigid separation between various elements of the new society.

Chase and his team break into the town and meet up with the doctor, but are caught by Marduk's men and forced to fight in the ring, where they vanquish Marduk's best men in superior displays of karate. However, Chase is forced to fight Marduk's behemoth champion, who has never been defeated. Chase eventually prevails and sets the town free, destroying the doctor's work on the mind-controlling serum. Once again, on a continent almost entirely black, Chase and his fellow Afrikaners have saved the day, and the world.

Looking back with older eyes, three decades of experience and (one hopes) steady progress towards racial parity, critics would have to judge most of these stories as dated reflections of more extreme viewpoints that most Americans don't share now, and probably didn't share then. A modern viewer with no understanding of the workings of South Africa two generations ago would probably completely miss the racial disregard of *Kill or Be Killed*. Similarly, someone without knowledge of 70s black exploitation films might be offended by the narrative of *Three the Hard Way*. Now that Apartheid is gone, replaced by representative government in South Africa, and the strident black power message of the early 70s has been exchanged for legitimate political activism, radical or insulting film narratives are almost unheard of, particularly in martial arts films, where racism goes directly against the spiritual teachings of the various martial disciplines.

Old Stars and New Faces

Despite, or perhaps because of Jim Kelly's appearance in *Three the Hard Way*, he was chosen by Warner Bros. to be the next martial arts superstar. To that end they hired *Enter the Dragon* veteran Robert Clouse to direct and hoped to catch lightning in a bottle with their 1974 release *Black Belt Jones*. They didn't. The film tanked for a number of reasons, foremost among them that Warners forgot the lessons they learned regarding the importance of widening the film's appeal to a mainstream audience.

The resulting film was of the pure martial arts variety, its thin plot a mere excuse to highlight Kelly's fighting ability. Kelly plays the title character, a secret agent who is also a community activist. When the local martial arts studio is threatened by the mob, which wants to sell the property, Kelly has to swing into action to stop them, putting his martial arts prowess to good use. Unfortunately for all involved, the film comes across not as martial arts but rather as another black exploitation flick.

Since the genre was never really popular with mainstream white viewers, or large groups of blacks for that matter, it precluded vast segments of the audience from even thinking of seeing the film. The movie itself bordered on the ridiculous, with the implied class consciousness of Bruce Lee's early films, which Warner Bros. wisely elided in his American debut, becoming overt Marxist statements in this one, that were then contradicted by the very characters mouthing them. College students and karate apprentices alike spout off about "capitalist pigs" when confronting the businessman villain, while Toppy, one of the karate masters at the studio, is reminded that he quit a good job to teach the kids, and that the money isn't the important thing.

Money, literally, becomes the root of all evil, and business becomes analogous to corruption, the bigger the business the more corrupt. The mob operates a wine factory that fronts for its dope peddling; the pool room owner's establishment also serves as the community hot spot for dealers; the gangsters wants to take possession of the karate studio because they learn the city is going to redevelop the area and will buy the property from them at a premium rate. Contrasted with this is the presentation of the have-nots. Those who are poor or without large sums of money are shown in a positive light, as decent folks committed to their neighborhoods, while the wealthy or well-to-do are depicted as criminals who prey on the people. All, that is, except Kelly.

Kelly is a secret agent with a million dollar house on the beach, plushly furnished right down to the beautiful woman who caters to him. He drives a fancy sports car and wears the hippest threads in town. Kelly is clearly a raconteur, not a proletarian working man, and spends his time at political gatherings that promote Third World affairs. His occupation leaves him long amounts of idle time, some of which he spends training a group of women in gymnastics. In fact, Kelly has so much money that he actually turns down missions from the government.

Such transparent (and at times hypocritically humorous) contrasts marginalized the drawing power of the film, not to mention turning off martial arts enthusiasts by its irreverent if not disrespectful treatment of the discipline. The dojo that Kelly was fighting to save was operated not by a venerated master, like the Shaolin priests of the Temple where Bruce Lee taught, but rather by a lazy, shuffling pimp with a horrendous toupee. Where the Shaolins stressed discipline and training, the pimp–studio master couldn't even take the time to fill out the paperwork to renew the studio's lease, instead wiling away his hours in back room poker games. The karate students are almost as pathetic, their militant attitudes far outweighing their ability to fight. The climactic fight scene, where Kelly engages the mob and the pool room owner, takes place in a car wash full of rising, foaming soap, and is played for laughs rather than for real.

Though Robert Clouse was gone, Warner Bros. tried again two years later with *Hot Potato*. Jim Kelly reprised his role as Jones, and the film is interesting for being everything that *Black Belt Jones* was not. This film, like the first, was pure style martial arts, but the black exploitation angle was gone, left back in Los Angeles, while this one moved to the jungles of Asia. Again the plot is skimpy: Jones is sent to rescue the daughter of a US Senator, kidnapped by a warlord who wants the Senator to change his vote on a foreign aid deal. And while the film did not take itself too seriously, this was a refreshing change in light of the first one, which attempted to be earnest but was anything but.

Two white men and a female Asian police detective assist Kelly's character this time around. The two sidekicks provide the comic relief with their bantering and arguing, while Kelly and the detective remain deliberate and committed to the mission. As the group makes their way through the jungle to the fortress of the evil warlord, it is clear that this Jones is a much more conservative hero than the previous incantation. He nixes the proposition of sex with local women to concentrate on matters at hand and, after rescuing the Senator's daughter, continues to remain unconvinced that the mission was a success. His caution saves the group's life, as the daughter is really a doppelganger hired by the warlord.

Along the way, the group picks up a native woman whose tribe has disowned her. The two sidekicks fall in love with the native woman and the Senator's daughter, while Kelly tries to remain aloof from the detective, not wanting to complicate the mission by allowing emotion to cloud his judgment. Both the Jones films have a courtship scene that contrasts the characters change well. In the first, Kelly and the pimp–studio master's daughter frolic around the beach. As a precursor to sex, their foreplay consists of a martial arts fight in the sand; in the second film, Kelly courts the detective on a beach, only the banter is innocent and playful—and they don't have sex.

Hot Potato ends with the warlord and his minions destroyed, the real Senator's daughter safe and the two sidekicks ready to settle down with their respective women. Kelly prepares to leave for home without saying goodbye to the detective, figuring she wouldn't want anything to do with someone like him. One of the sidekicks persuades him otherwise, takes him to her house, where she greets him in native dress, and invites him for dinner *and* breakfast. The implication is clear: The cool polyester threads may remain, but the super stud has now been domesticated, replaced by a thoughtful man serving his country. Compared with the earlier Jones persona, this Jones could be a middle-class guy who just happens to be a secret agent.

Though the fight scenes (choreographed by Kelly) sometimes appear unmotivated—only one gun appears in the entire movie—they are serious and deadly, and the quartet acquits themselves well, much better than in the first movie. Martial arts fans, if disappointed by the way the discipline was portrayed in *Black Belt Jones*, had nothing to complain about with this film. Kelly leaves the humor to his sidekicks, where it belonged, and engages in a number of thrilling unarmed encounters. He also ratchets up the excitement with a Thai-style stick match, and holds his own in a kendo-style sword fight against a number of the warlord's men.

Black Belt Jones, *Hot Potato* and *Enter the Dragon* share a number of similarities, which is not surprising since they emanated from the same studio and shared a combination of cast, crew and director. In all three films, established authority is inefficient and must instead rely on agents working outside the system to get the job done. The films all contain a set piece assault on a guarded stronghold, and feature strong women martial artists in supporting roles. *Hot Potato* even features the same character breakdown as *Enter the Dragon*, with Kelly taking up the Lee role as the disciplined, no-nonsense agent, while the two sidekicks branch off as the egotistical lady's man and the libidinal force.

Hot Potato was not a box office smash, though it was head and shoulders better than *Black Belt Jones*, leaving one to wonder what would have been the result had the second film preceded the first. Admittedly, Kelly's acting was raw, but there was a certain professional quality visible in this film that signalled that he was maturing as an actor. The year 1976 also saw the release of *Black Samurai*, which was directed by cult favorite Al Adamson,★ and which again showcased Kelly's martial arts abilities, although the budget on this film was deplorably low.

Black Samurai could have been a continuation of the *Black Belt Jones* saga, since once again Kelly stars as a secret agent in the employ of a mysterious government agency, this one called D.R.A.G.O.N.† Kelly plays Robert Sand, a reluctant black James Bond who bristles at working for the "white man." When a diplomat's daughter is kidnapped, Sand refuses to take on the rescue mission until he learns the victim is an old girlfriend of his. His nemesis is a devil worshipper who runs dope out of Hong Kong, and has a private army at his disposal. With the assistance of another agent, Kelly defeats the devil worshipper and rescues his girlfriend, but not before having to fight off an array of thugs, some African warriors, deadly midgets, a vulture and a room full of snakes. Kelly choreographed his own fight scenes, but they were not as impressive as those in *Hot Potato*, at least until the end, when he and his partner Pines battle an entire army all by their lonesome.

Again, the influence of the black exploitation film genre that was sweeping some parts of the country was somewhat apparent in *Black Samurai*. However, since for the most part black exploitation films briefly acknowledged the social-economic plight of African Americans and then quickly careened into excessive violence and sexuality, whatever political elements might be present in other black exploitation films had been displaced in *Black Samurai* by a concentration on social deviance, that of the Occult and drugs.

Racial and sexual slurs abound in the film, and unfortunately for Kelly, he comes off as the biggest bigot of all, quite unintentionally I'm sure. The devil worshipper and his followers are multi-racial—equal opportunity evildoers, it would seem—and they are not particularly concerned about Kelly's race. Kelly, on the other hand, does not trust his white partner Pines, and makes a number of comments that indicate whites and homosexuals are not high on his list of favorite people. In one unintentionally funny moment, Kelly rescues a devil worshipper from rape. When she tells him that she likes to think of him as her "White Knight," Kelly replies to the effect that he doesn't want her to think of him as *anything* white!

Kelly's last major role was in 1982's *One Down, Two to Go*. Kelly plays Chuck,

---

★ *Adamson was best-known for his cheapie horror and sexploitation flicks. He was murdered in 1995.*
† *The acronym is never explained in the film.*

a martial arts master from Los Angeles who brings his team over to compete against the local New York team. Almost half a million dollars is riding on the event, which Kelly's team wins. But after Kelly finds out that the locals were cheating, they shoot him and keep the money. Kelly manages to contact his friends Jim Brown and Fred Williamson, and they shoot up the town, rescue Chuck and get his money back.

One Down, Two to Go features a number of Kelly fights and a face-off between his character, wounded in the shoulder, and the local master; Kelly gets the best of his opponent. Unfortunately, the film suffers from a time warp, and much the way Lee Van Cleef rode the spaghetti Western well into the 70s, this is an example of a black exploitation film shot long past the genre's prime. By 1982 most audiences wanted more from a film than all whites = bad and all blacks = good, which was pretty much the case in *One Down, Two to Go.* The film boasted the usual black exploitation iconography of the black stud (Kelly bedding a woman while he was wounded; Williamson having a sexual romp with one of the locals); the impotent or crooked law (the sheriff looks to be in his eighties and can't do anything right); the town full of white hooligans; and massive black firepower. The only thing missing was more of Kelly, who had matured as an actor, and his florid style of martial arts.

On the other hand, John Saxon and Chuck Norris were opposite sides of the proverbial coin. Saxon was an actor who learned martial arts; Norris was a martial arts champion who learned to act. Saxon began his career in a number of "A" level productions; Norris started out as a stuntman. Though indelibly tied to the most influential martial arts film ever, Saxon's subsequent films veered away from that arena; Norris, conversely, stayed the course and has remained a fixture in the martial arts scene, on film and television. Where Saxon's fight scenes stressed force, particularly punching power, Norris relied on tremendous speed, especially with his spinning kicks. Late in his career, Saxon would relish his place in martial arts cinema, narrating documentaries on the genre; Norris, secure of his credentials, would move behind the camera, becoming a producer. Both men were in remarkable physical shape, and both projected confidence and poise in the characters they portrayed.

After the release and success of *Enter the Dragon,* it would have seemed a given that John Saxon would have either reprised his role as Roper in another film, or followed up with a new martial arts film. Neither happened, at least right away. Saxon, a popular actor abroad as well as at home, worked in a number of films in Europe as well as doing some television here. However, in 1978 Saxon starred in *The Glove,* the closest thing to a martial arts film he would ever again make. Saxon plays Sam Kellough, a burned-out, seen-too-much bounty hunter who accepts an assignment to capture a behemoth ex-con who is exacting revenge on the people who wronged him. Complicating matters for Saxon is not only the size of his prey, played by gigantic ex–football star Rosey Grier, but the fact that the con uses a lethal metal glove to bust up his victims.

Saxon again gave the character a Roper-like appeal, and an excellent supporting cast (which included Joanna Cassidy and Keenan Wynn) made the film enjoyable. Saxon's few action scenes showcased his martial arts skills, but were obviously secondary to the story, which, despite its violent tagline of "Wanted Dead

NOT Alive,"[10] bore some elements of narrative subtlety. Saxon's character is offered a mere $20,000 to stop the raging killer, hardly worth his time it would seem, and an indication of just how low the man has sunk. Though Saxon triumphs in the end, at what cost to himself? The con had good cause for his vengeance and, though he could have killed Saxon earlier, allows him to live for the final showdown, in which he gives Saxon the lethal glove to use for their fight. The bounty hunter will indeed collect his money, but we finally understand just why he is such a world-weary man.

Saxon's career was diverse, if nothing else. But he never starred in a martial arts film again, at least as an active combatant, though in his later years he played supporting roles in a number of them, often as a police chief, detective or other authority figure. Chuck Norris, on the other hand, hardly deviated from the western hero paradigm and was a defining force in popularizing the American martial arts cinema with the public. Norris was a six-time karate champion who, after serving a stint in the Air Force, settled down in Torrance, California, where he worked at Northrop aircraft by day and taught karate by night.

Norris' first starring role was *Breaker! Breaker!* (1977), the ultimate in "B" exploitation that featured the martial arts sensation as a J.C. Doss, a truck driving karate expert. Satisfying both the CB radio trucker frenzy created by C.W. McCall's *Convoy* song (a huge hit) as well as the martial arts crowd's need for violence, the film featured character actor George Murdock in a major supporting role as a corrupt judge ruling over an evil town.

The film, while not a major success, accented story as much as fighting, and was interesting for its reworking of the Western genre. Norris is the latter day cowboy who, like Spencer Tracy's *Bad Day at Black Rock* character, is a stranger in a town that clearly doesn't want him around. The government and people are all debased, while the numerous background shots of the American flag contrasted with scenes of political and moral malfeasance suggest the correlation between established politics and corruption.

The distinction between tyranny and freedom becomes almost an over-determined theme, as it would in a good number of films during the decade. The film's opening marks the town's celebration at being granted a city charter from the state of California. Subsequent scenes show the police beating passerbys, luring truckers into the town so as to steal their rigs and loads, and gathering at the courthouse to discuss the amount of money coming into municipal coffers from various illegal operations.

Contrasted with the moral decay of the city is the independence of the truckers and the autonomy of the open road. The men come and go as they please, working hard and playing rough. Norris' character has just returned from Alaska and, like the Western hero of old, carries a reputation that is recognized among his peers far and wide. Where the truckers form an extended family based on mutual respect and camaraderie, the secrecy and isolation of the townspeople has produced a number of mentally defective persons, the implied product of in-breeding.

The film's end is a clear inversion on the classic norm: Norris, finally captured by the town, is about to be shot. The truckers, more like the Indians than the cavalry, ride to the rescue and destroy the town, while Norris faces off with a vicious bottle-wielding deputy in a corral. To make sure we don't miss the point, the director uses an obvious metaphor for freedom: a black horse, also in the pen, runs around and around, becoming more agitated as the fight reaches a crescendo. After Norris beats the villain to a pulp, the horse jumps the rail and escapes.

While a forgettable film by anyone's standards, *Breaker! Breaker!* was most significant in its portent of things to follow. In *Good Guys Wear Black* (1978), Norris played ex–CIA and military officer John T. Booker, who uncovers a plot to kill the former members of his special ops unit, the Black Tigers, five years after the war has ended. The film opened with a spectacular night battle sequence, gritty and almost drained of color, in which Norris' team is decimated.

The film's overt politicism was vintage post–Watergate; Norris, like all Americans, was betrayed in Southeast Asia by calculating politicians and heartless diplomats, a notion that would be further explored by Sylvester Stallone in *Rambo II* (1985). Norris soon finds that he is in a new, "American" Vietnam: The enemy is unseen, a shadowy force he cannot get to. No one can be trusted, and the bodies of his compadres pile up. As Norris and his partner Murray, a CIA operative, fight their way to the truth, they trace the conspiracy to the new Secretary of State designee, who sold out the Black Tigers as a condition of peace. The Secretary's reasoning was expedience: The elimination of the unit was demanded by the vengeful Vietnamese and was a small price to pay to end the war.

Norris finds that he is just as powerless now as he was in Vietnam, unable to reach the enemy who threatens him. When the Secretary blithely argues that politics is a matter of the ends justifying the means, a condition that has built the nation, Norris avers in principle and leaves, only to return later. He kills the Secretary and dumps his body in the ocean, where presumably it will never be found. Norris, in taking such action, betrays his own beliefs. As he and Murray drive away, a news bulletin reveals that the Secretary designee had withdrawn his name from consideration for the job and has left Washington D.C., making it clear that not only has the CIA has covered up the murder, but that apparently the ends *do* justify the means.

The film's controversial ending notwithstanding, *Good Guys Wear Black* was a hit whose political nihilism was probably lost on most viewers, buried beneath a number of first-rate martial arts sequences that were choreographed by Norris himself. Of particular note was a spectacular fight at a small airport, where Norris kicks in the windshield of a moving vehicle, killing the driver who was trying to run him down. Mar Vista, who produced the film, followed the venerated "B" movie route by surrounding Norris with a first-rate cast which included Lloyd Hanes, Anne Archer and James Franciscus. The story stands up well almost a quarter of a century later.

Norris was clearly emerging as the new American martial arts hero, a status that would be cemented by his next film, *A Force of One* (1979). Norris plays a martial arts instructor hired to teach a narcotics squad self-defense. As a killer picks off the detectives one by one, someone is stealing drugs from the department's lock-up. Norris ends up battling both the drug ring and his friend, a karate champion who is involved with the cartel.

The theme of institutional corruption, so evident in Norris' first two starring roles, is continued in this one. Not only are the authorities unable to stem the tide of drugs, they can't even protect themselves. The film's title tells it all: Norris *is* a

Karate champion Matt Logan (Chuck Norris—top center, bottom left) battles various opponents in the ring in *A Force of One* (American Cinema Productions, 1979).

force of one, the outsider who has to both destroy the drug dealers and save the police. Society is depicted as sick, the urban sprawl of the city a vast wasteland of victims, as contrasted with Norris' idyllic suburban compound, a place of security and strength, where he trains with his adopted son and students. The police department itself is decaying from the inside, with one of the narcotics detectives actually supplying the drug dealers contraband stolen from police lock up that has been designated for destruction.

Force of One built on the success of *Good Guys Wear Black* by repeating the casting formula. Once again Norris was surrounded with top talent like former model Jennifer O'Neil, veteran character actor Clu Gulager and black exploitation star Ron O'Neal, who was best known as "Superfly." The film's climax featured a riveting showdown between ex–middleweight karate champ Norris and then–current karate champion Bill "Superfoot" Wallace.

The two men had never met during their time in the ring, and the celluloid fight gave martial arts enthusiasts just as many thrills as if they had; it was one of the best ever shot. Although both champions were in the same weight class, Norris was retiring as Wallace was coming up.[11] Though such a match-up between real martial arts fighters and the martial arts film star was an unusual, if not rare occurrence in American martial arts films of the 70s and 80s, it would become a common occurrence in the 90s, with the advent of home video and the new breed of martial arts heroes. However, this would be among the few times Norris would share screen fight time with a current champion and he makes the most of it.

The decade ended with two martial arts films with virtually diametrically opposite points of view. *The Jaguar Lives!* (1979) featured karate champion Joe Lewis doing battle with international drug dealers. However, unlike Norris (who battled them in *A Force of One*), Lewis's character, the Jaguar, is a jet-setting secret agent. This film and others following it started a trend which glamorized the martial arts protagonist. Rather than the proletariat hero of *Fists of Fury*, or even *Breaker! Breaker!*, this hero was impeccably dressed, felt equally at home in the capitol cities of Europe or his beach estate in California, and liked fast cars and beautiful women. In other words, he willingly embraces material goods and (like Steve Chase from *Kill and Kill Again*) venerates the capitalist ideals.[12]

Circle of Iron, released the same year, was a mystical look at the nature of life that became a surprise box office hit—and a cult favorite. Relative unknown Jeff Cooper plays the young martial arts hero on a mythical quest to find a book of knowledge. In a Campbellian-like journey, he faces temptation, tribulation and tests of strength. David Carradine stars as the wise, mysterious chameleon figure who appears throughout the story in many guises—a clear play on his Caine character—as either a helper or a hindrance to the stalwart Cooper. The martial arts sequences were first-rate, as was the cast, which featured the likes of Eli Wallach and Christopher Lee in supporting or cameo appearances.

Unlike the worldly glorification of *The Jaguar Lives!* or the overtly political *Good Guys Wear Black*, this film not only debunked the pursuit of wealth but that of political power as well, and harkened back to a simpler world which probably never existed but which nonetheless appealed to male viewers in much the same way that *Enter the Dragon* did: by presenting a self-enclosed world where a man was the master of his own destiny, free from all social encumbrances. Jobs, bosses, pensions and retirement were no longer significant when all a man needed was a good quest and the requisite fighting skills to make his way through life.

The characters in *Circle of Iron* are searching for something that would never interest the Jaguar, or which the Booker character would only pay lip service to: personal growth. Where, at the end of *Good Guys Wear Black*, Booker's character has become as corrupt as the enemy he was trying to defeat, and the Jaguar is so busy looking cool he never bothers to delve beyond sensory motivation, the Cooper and Carradine characters withdraw to a personal sanctum to gather strength from within. Philosophy, not politics or materialism, is the message, while the hero's struggle becomes one of freeing himself from the bonds of his ego, of rejecting the cynicism and selfishness that the other two characters willingly embrace. The spoils this world has to offer (wealth, sexual bliss, power—sought after by Booker and Jaguar in relative degrees) are rejected by the hero of this film for what is revealed to be the ultimate treasure: the peace that comes from being one with himself.

The Martial Arts Hero Revisited

Martial arts films were firmly established as their own genre by the time the decade wound down. Almost without exception, the hero paradigm of the martial arts protagonist followed the "B" models developed in Westerns and action-thrillers during the 30s: tough men, usually loners, who swung first and never worried about asking questions until the fight was over. If then.

Unlike some of the anti-heroes that had become popular in mainstream movies, there was rarely if ever a problem of figuring out where the martial arts hero stood. They might be establishment types; then again, they might be anti-establishment types. One thing was sure: They were never ambiguous. Force was always an option, and no matter how much they tried to avoid it, they always ended up using it—and well. Invariably the plots worked along the same lines. Some of the pure martial arts films and almost all of the hybrid story variety based their narratives on the "B" genres that we noted earlier: Western; action-thriller; sci-fi; and, to a lesser extent, horror and war.

The screen persona of Norris was beginning to take shape, and of all martial arts heroes, he would be the most directly related to the "B" cowboy hero of yesteryear. Rugged individualism was its most identifiable trait. The Norris hero was usually a loner, often an outsider, but never to the point of being an anti-hero. He is not only single, but usually unattached. J.C. Doss was a long haul trucker, while John T. Booker was a bachelor professor whose favorite hobby was racing cars. Matt Logan was a karate instructor who owned his own school. Solitude was an important aspect of these men's lives, yet significantly, all three work for a living, so while they may be disaffected by the system, they have not abandoned it.

Where "A" movie Western heroes might be outlaws, the same could usually not be said for their low-budget counterparts. The "B" cowboy hero always fought for what was right and just, and the Norris protagonist never deviated from that paradigm, even when he was a reluctant participant. Norris had to be pushed into a fight—he rarely ever started one—but like his predecessors (John Wayne, Don "Red" Barry, Tom Mix et al.)—he took care of business when the time came. If the Norris hero had an identifiable partner (as opposed to just a best friend), he was usually employed as comic relief, while the best friend was often killed as the catalyst to launch Norris into action.

Contrasts between Lee, Kelly and Norris revealed subtle differences. Lee's initial roles posited him as a student or worker. Kelly's early screen appearances showcased his militant stance and more often than not Norris would be a teacher or professional person. Kelly came closest to being an anti-hero, Lee to a reluctant one, while Norris was the most conventional. Where Lee worked within the system, to the point of surrendering to the authorities after killing his Japanese opponent in *The Chinese Connection*, Norris often worked from the outside to save the system. Kelly worked both sides against the middle.

Martial arts styles were also at odds, and go a long way in explaining Norris' relative success. While all three men would at times choreograph their own fight sequences, Lee favored high-pitched screams when engaged in battle, and the Hong Kong style dubbing of heavy punching sounds when he landed a blow. Kelly's battle scenes generally accented his speed and grace, yet he continued Lee's use of noises and screams when fighting as well as the dubbed punching sounds. Norris broke with these established conventions, instead developing a fight mannerism that appeared more conventional to western audiences.

Norris rarely engaged an overwhelming number of opponents like both Lee and Kelly would. When he did, like in *Breaker! Breaker!*, he fought a running battle to escape. Norris refrained from loud or unusual noises when fighting, ratcheted down the sound effects of punches and kicks landing on opponent's jaws, and not only allowed himself to be knocked down when hit by a good punch or kick, but rather than "kip" up to his feet, would get up like the average Joe on the street. While future Norris films might feature a scene or two showcasing his ability with a sword, nunchukus, or other martial arts weapons, depending on the story, he usually stuck to hand-to-hand combat. When Norris did have need of a weapon, he had no problem using the latest array of firearms to solve problem at hand. Like most Americans, Norris saw no sense in bringing a knife to a gunfight.

The decade of the 70s ended with the firm establishment of an American martial arts cinema, replete with its own conventions and heroes, as well as featuring a number of well-made martial arts films. The "karate movie" was here, as was the karate hero, and these early films paved the way for what would be the golden age of American martial arts cinema in the 1980s.

VI

The 1980s: The Reagan Years and the Ascent of Martial Arts Cinema

Martial arts cinema in America prospered during the 80s, as much from the popularity of Chuck Norris as the nation's evident swing towards conservatism, which was manifested in the election of former "B" movie actor and one-time Republican California Governor Ronald Reagan as President. Reagan, immensely popular with many segments of society, exacerbated Cold War tensions with the USSR through his antagonistic speeches and apparent willingness to confront the Soviets wherever and whenever American interests—as defined by Reagan—were threatened.

Cinema in general, and martial arts films in particular, reflected this conservative trend, particularly those of Norris, and to a lesser extent those of Japanese import Sho Kosugi, who found brief popularity in a number of American films that established the "Ninja" subgenre. New stars were rising as well, men who would not only help keep the genre fresh but take it to new heights. However, like with its "B" predecessors of a half century earlier, martial arts cinema would be profoundly affected by studio marketing shifts and the advent of the VCR, which would virtually spell the end of low-budget martial arts theatrical releases.

The Reagan Years

In the fall of 1980, incumbent president Jimmy Carter found himself locked in a tight race with Republican challenger Ronald Reagan. A television commercial run by the Republicans crystallized the fear, frustration and anxiety felt by many Americans at the beginning of the new decade: A hunter, alone but not afraid, walks through the forest. The narrator intones that there is a bear in the woods; some think he is harmless, others are not so sure. Suddenly there is some rustling noises and the hunter coolly brings up his shotgun and takes aim. The narrator then asks if we shouldn't be ready....

The Cold War had suddenly heated up, and there was no question that by the end of President Carter's first term the nation's military readiness had lapsed to a point that alarmed most Americans. Adding to the perceived menace of the Soviet Union was the humiliation of having American embassy workers taken hostage by the radical fundamentalist government of Iran. As these victims were paraded over television each day by their captors, some news shows, such as Ted Koppel's *Nightline*, began their programs with words to the effect of "America held hostage. Day 112." Carter's almost cartoon-like attempt to launch a secret rescue mission ended in unmitigated disaster, with a number of American servicemen dead as a result of poor planning and avoidable errors.

Reagan played on these feelings of insecurity, promising there would be "Morning in America" when he took office. He did not disappoint. During his eight years in office, he presided over the biggest arms and weapons buildup since the Korean War, boosting defense spending by 59 percent,[1] while dividing the world into a virtual chessboard, where he confronted the Soviets over and again, from Africa to Central America, and assailed them as an "evil empire that would end up on the ash heap of history."

More than any other president or individual, Ronald Reagan forced the Soviet Union into the one war they could not win: technology and spending. Congressional Quarterly's U.S. Defense Policy notes, "The Reagan Administration viewed the existing nuclear balance generally as much more favorable to Moscow than did Carter and his defense advisors."[2] Citing a window of vulnerability, whereby the Soviets could theoretically launch their missiles and destroy us, Reagan favored the deployment of a powerful MX missile, originally touted as being shuttled on an underground railway between silos, so that the Communists would never know where they were. He leaned toward a counter-force defense doctrine, which targeted the enemy's military complexes rather than the counter-valence doctrine advocated by the previous administration, a cheaper strategy that targeted civilian and industrial centers in the hope of dissuading an attack. His defense posture increasingly became that of a "war-fighting deterrence," a position advanced by a number of conservative military experts which advocated the United States have superior firepower and weaponry at every level, from ground forces to ICBMs, so that any potential enemy realizes they can never win by escalating a confrontation. And most controversially, he embraced the development of a ballistic nuclear missile defense system, the Strategic Defense Initiative, or SDI, which would free the United States from the Mutual Assured Destruction (MAD) doctrine by creating "a series of defensive systems layered together in such a way as to create a protective shield."[3] Nicknamed "Star Wars" by the press, the plan appeared to directly violate the ABM treaty with Moscow.*

Reagan's massive military build-up could not be matched by the Soviets, and eventually, after the country imploded from (among other things) the arms race, the non–Communist Russian Federation rose from the ash heap Reagan had so eloquently predicted, under the leadership of Moscow mayor and reformer Boris Yeltsin, the hero who helped thwart a military coup which had threatened to halt

*Many of Reagan's positions either prove untenable or misguided, yet by the very fact that he advanced them he put the Soviet's on the defensive, especially the prospect of the SDI. Development of the SDI has been left to the George W. Bush administration, which withdrew from the 1972 ABM treaty and announced deployment of a missile shield starting in 2004.

then Soviet leader Mikhail Gorbachev's plans to dismantle Communism. But Reagan's saber rattling had a price: massive deficits, which were exacerbated by the supply side economics of huge tax cuts designed to spur growth in the private sector. These deficits, along with huge trade imbalances and the Persian Gulf War, resulted in a recession that brought the Democrats back to power in 1992, four years after Vice-President Bush succeeded Reagan as President.

While the long-term significance of Ronald Reagan's presidency must be left to future historians, a more immediate influence was felt in the area of film, somewhat appropriately considering the President's origins as a "B" movie lead. Cinema, as a popular art form, has always been particularly reflective of socio-political change. Reagan's eternal optimism and easygoing confidence presented a welcome alternative for many Americans exhausted after two decades of cultural upheaval, from the changing sexual mores, violent anti-war protests and the Civil Rights movement of the 60s, to the Watergate era of the 70s, where the specter of government conspiracy and corruption led to a suspicion of authority and an overblown fear of crime. Belton writes,

> If the low-budget exploitation films of the late 1960s and early 1970s capture the chaotic temper of the times, then the big-budget exploitation films of the 1980s reflect the new conservatism of Reaganite America. A handful of films and filmmakers resist this reactionary tide, but ... they fail to match the success of the more conservative, mainstream films at the box office.[4]

Hollywood reacted to this rightward tilt in a number of ways. "A" level films lightened up: Anti-heroes were in less demand, as was a good deal of cynicism, replaced by the new corporate values of hard work, loyalty and the desirability of material success. In films like *Fame* (1980), young men and women, many of them lower or working class, don't reject the system but rather exalt it, competing to be the best in their fields, and of course to one day reap the riches and celebrity that come with it. The kids are all lumped together into a special high school, where they are worked harder because they are considered "talents." Critics adored the film, which was nominated for six Academy Awards and won two. Roger Ebert gushed that "the movie had the kind of sensitivity to the real lives of real people that we don't get much in Hollywood productions anymore."[5]

Flashdance (1983) was a box office smash that featured newcomer Jennifer Beals as a welder who dreams of being a ballet dancer. The setting is a gritty working class Pittsburgh neighborhood where hope dies hard and dreams are best left unspoken. She moonlights at a go-go club, where an understanding boyfriend encourages her to pursue her goals. Eventually, after hours of training and much hard work, she succeeds, and is accepted at a prestigious ballet school.

Dirty Dancing (1987), a period piece starring action hero Patrick Swayze as a dance instructor at a Catskills resort, mined much the same terrain. Stuck in a job that goes nowhere, Swayze falls in love with a rich girl whom he is tutoring for a "big dance." Both work hard and prosper from the relationship: Swayze loses his cynicism and finds a sense of direction for his talent while the girl gains a feeling of confidence and esteem. *Flashdance* started a craze of sorts among young girls, who began patterning their dress after the Beals character, while *Dirty Dancing*, also a box office smash, started an oldies music revival.

Rocky III (1982) featured a new and improved Rocky Balboa. The working class underdog was now a svelte, successful heavyweight champion, rich beyond his wildest dreams. However, he slacks off, trains sporadically or in an uncommitted fashion, and learns that his opponents had all been handpicked by his manager because they weren't good enough to beat him. Rocky is decimated in his next fight, but finds the determination to work his way back into shape. He trains day and night, lives in a flea bag to get his mind "hungry" for victory, and faces his fears. After he knocks out his opponent in the rematch and is champion once again, the moral of the story becomes clear: Anyone willing to struggle hard enough for it can find prosperity and riches.

The Reaganesque paradigm for material success was balanced by a similar trend in action films, one that emphasized respect for authority, the family and the country. *Sudden Impact* (1983) saw the return of Clint Eastwood's "Dirty" Harry Callahan but, just like Rocky Balboa, in a new and improved version. This Harry is still conservative, albeit hardly the iconoclast he was during the 70s, instead working within the system to solve some vigilante murders. The film spawned one of the most famous one liners ever: "Go ahead, make my day."[6] Reagan used the line when threatening to veto congressional legislation.

Even Paul Kersey, the architect-turned-vigilante made famous by Charles Bronson in the *Death Wish* films, becomes an agent for the police in *Death Wish III* (1985), taking on a gang which is terrorizing a neighborhood. At the film's climax, the neighbors follow Bronson into the streets to fight the criminals, while the police, like the cavalry, arrive to save the day. Bronson, who had indicated he was not interested in continuing the series, had a change of heart following the shooting of four gang members by one Bernhard Goetz, a mild mannered suburbanite who was threatened by the toughs while riding the New York City subway. The groundswell of support from mostly white, middle-class America caused Bronson to change his mind.

Of course, there was unfinished business in Vietnam. America's only military defeat had to be reconciled somehow, and film was as good a place as any. When the President spoke of the war he called "ours a noble cause." In *Uncommon Valor* (1984), such nobility was made explicit, as Academy Award winner Gene Hackman leads a mission to rescue POWs still being held by the Communists. The film featured a short but excellent martial arts fight between Tex Cobb and Patrick Swayze. Stallone would follow up the next year in *Rambo II* (1985), not only rescuing the POWs but single-handedly wiping out a Russian Speznatz team in the process. As famous as Eastwood's line was Stallone's, when he wondered aloud whether we, meaning America, would get to win this time.

Arguably the most conservative film of the time was John Milius's *Red Dawn* (1984), which featured an invasion of the United States by Russian, Cuban and Nicaraguan forces. A group of boys from a small Colorado town take to the hills and fight the Communists guerrilla-style, turning the Rocky Mountains into an American Vietnam for the overmatched Russians. First runner-up would go to *Rocky IV* (1985), where the unstoppable dynamo has to fight a huge, drug-enhanced Soviet boxer. Of course the overmatched Rocky succeeds in due time and, after a good pummeling, causes the Russian people to cheer, much to the chagrin of the Party stalwarts in Moscow.

Martial Arts Heroes: Right, Left and Straight Down the Middle

The conservative tilt of mainstream films during the Reagan years was particularly evident within the martial arts genre. Big and buffed equated to success, both at home and abroad. Sylvester Stallone and Arnold Schwarzenegger bared their muscles as they battled all manner of vermin. Even Chuck Norris began muscling up, and as the 80s wore on, he became a veritable one-man army, fighting drug dealers, terrorists and Communists, sometimes all in the same film. Norris' roles became increasingly conventional after starting work with Cannon Films in 1984. Cannon, an Israeli company, saw a well-liked president in Ronald Reagan, and to the extent that the Great Communicator's anti–Communist rhetoric was popular with a majority of Americans, it should make for good business as well.

Originally, Cannon was a purveyor of B movies during the 70s, but by the end of the decade was teetering toward insolvency. Two Israeli cousins, Menahem Golan and Yoram Globas, moved to the United States and bought a controlling interest in the company for about 20 cents a share.[7] While the two men had been heavily involved in the Israeli film industry, once here they didn't miss a step as they quickly landed a film distribution deal with MGM. Most of Cannon's fare was exploitational, whether it was starting a trend like the ninja cycle or following one, like the break dance craze that began in the early 80s. However, they made a bid for respectability by signing big stars like Charles Bronson, and even landed Sylvester Stallone for *Cobra* (1986) and *Over the Top* (1987), neither of which was very successful.

Though their mid- and lower-budget films continued to be the bread and butter, Cannon also branched out to larger budgeted films like *Superman IV* (1987) and *Masters of the Universe* (1987), both of which were utter failures, as well as critical favorites and art films like *Runaway Train* (1985) and *Barfly* (1987), which starred Mickey Rourke. The combination of huge losses from the big-budget films and no money incoming from the art films put enormous financial stress on the company which its exploitation fare could not make up. By 1989 Cannon was at the end of its tether and found itself in bankruptcy proceedings. MGM picked up Cannon and ran it under Pathe Communications, though the Cannon name still was used. However, by 1994 Cannon had hit the end of the trail, and its last theatrical release was *American Cyborg: Steel Warrior*.

Probably the most profitable films for Cannon, and perhaps even the company's best remembered, will be those starring Chuck Norris, whom they had signed to a multi-picture deal which lasted almost ten years. Norris was their most reliable draw, even though they had other martial artists in their stable of actors, and he continued to carry himself well no matter how bad the script was. With the folding of Cannon, the cousins went their separate ways but continued to remain in the film business. Golan, in fact, restarted Cannon under the banner "New Cannon Films," which completed its first film, *Death Game*, in 2001.

Chuck Norris

Norris continued to make films in the early 80s before hooking up with Cannon. The titles tell all in Norris' action-thrillers *Eye for an Eye* (1981) and *Forced*

Norris defends against a kick in *Forced Vengeance* (MGM, 1982).

Vengeance (1982). In the former, Norris plays Sean Kane, a San Francisco police detective whose partner is murdered in a set-up; the partner's girlfriend is later killed by the same people, setting Norris into action. He uncovers a drug smuggling ring about to make a substantial delivery and ties the organization to a media head for whom his partner's girlfriend worked. In the latter film, Norris is Josh Randall, a casino security expert whose boss is killed after refusing to sell his gambling parlor to a local rival. Chuck declines an offer to work for the killers and eventually finds that the man behind the murders is a reclusive businessman long thought retired.

No new ground was broken here, but the films had good supporting casts, were well-made, and began a trend which showcased Norris as a highly paid professional, usually in law enforcement or with prior military service. Both *Eye for an Eye* and *Forced Vengeance* turned on the idea of retribution, hardly a novelty in this type of fare, but the two films followed a strict pattern that would manifest itself in future martial arts films, both Norris' and others, in the years to come:

1. *The protagonist's friend or partner is killed, often by someone acting duplicitously.*
Sean Kane and his partner are involved in a drug sting, but their informant has been bought out by the drug dealer, they are ambushed, and Kane's partner killed. Randall escorts his boss to meet with a gaming rival, only to find later that the boss has been killed when he refused to sell out. In the one instance, members

of the police department were on the take; in the other, the boss' son was working with his father's rival.

2. *The police are of no assistance so the protagonist must solve the crime himself.*

Kane quits the force because he suspects that he and his partner were set up. He later finds that another detective had been feeding information to the drug dealers. Randall goes to the police but is handcuffed, beaten and jailed by cops on the take.

3. *The protagonist often walks the streets, searching for the answers or leads he needs.*

Both Kane and Randall must navigate their terrain looking for clues, Kane in San Francisco and Randall in Hong Kong. Sometimes the scenes are shown in montage, other instances in real time, but almost always the hero finds something he can use to trace the location or identity of the antagonist.

4. *During his search for the truth, the protagonist must face off with a gauntlet of men.*

Kane boards a ship and finds the hold loaded with fireworks that are filled with heroin. He is discovered and battles a whole slew of men until he can get to the bow and jump into the ocean. With a bounty on his head, Josh Randall is on the run with his girlfriend and his boss' daughter. From hooker hotels to train stations and stairwells, Randall must fight a host of men out to collect the money.

5. *The protagonist often has the help of a sympathetic female.*

Kane teams up with a colleague of his partner's murdered girlfriend, and it is she who finds the final piece of the puzzle that helps Kane solve the mystery. Randall's quest for answers is aided by a friendly hooker who points him toward the right people to talk to.

6. *To catch the antagonist, the protagonist must assault a well-guarded home or hideout.*

Sean Kane finds that the men who killed his partner are clustered in a palatial mansion overlooking the San Francisco Bay. He scales the hill, picks off the guards and finally gets his chance at some payback. Randall pilots a small rubber boat to an isolated island, also scales a hill and picks off the guards.

7. *The protagonist must face off with a hulking foe, often the antagonist's bodyguard.*

Kane makes it into the mansion, only to have to deal with the "professor," a huge behemoth strong enough to lift a car! Kane overcomes the man, but not before taking a severe beating and having to call upon all the anger welling up inside of him. Likewise for Randall, who cannot get the upper hand over his opponent until he concentrates on the pain the man caused him and his loved ones.

8. *The final antagonist that the protagonist wants is often a millionaire or businessman.*

Both Kane and Randall find that their ultimate enemy, the man who called the shots and murdered their friends, was a rich businessman, someone neither the police nor society would ever expect to be the engineer of such violence.

While this organizational structure will be present in a large number of martial arts films, the iconography is not mandatory. In other words, some films will manifest more of the traits than others, some will manifest less. There will also be subdivisions of the various characteristics, such as the helpful female being kidnapped or killed; the final antagonist being a friend or someone trusted by the protagonist; or the protagonist being caught and held at the antagonists' fortress, from which he must then wreak his havoc. Whatever the case, the guide provides an outline from which most martial arts films can be better understood, and a tool for dissecting the various plot structures that follow.

In the same year that *Forced Vengeance* was released, Norris was involved in an unusual undertaking that combined martial arts with elements of the teen-slasher horror trend that was popular at the time, all in the framework of a contemporary western. In *Silent Rage* (1982), Norris played the sheriff of a small city in Texas who has to combat a hulking psychopath brought back from the dead by an amoral doctor out for money and fame. In this combination *Frankenstein*, *Halloween* (1979) and *Rio Bravo*, the psychopath turns on the doctor and then society, while Norris,

Norris takes his first turn as a Texas Ranger in *Lone Wolf McQuade* (Orion, 1983). Ten years later he would return on the small screen in the CBS series *Walker, Texas Ranger*.

Colonel James Braddock returns to Vietnam to find some soldiers who are *Missing in Action.* When the Vietnamese won't cooperate, Norris makes things personal (1984).

like the Duke, refuses help in dealing with situation, preferring to kick the monster's ass all by his lonesome.

By 1983 Norris was intimating that he was no longer interested in making martial arts films.[8] *Lone Wolf McQuade* (1983) returned Norris to Texas, again as a lawman, only this time as a Ranger, and with more accent on story than martial arts. Narco-terrorists are the subject of Norris' ire, particularly David Carradine, a jet-setting kickboxing champion who runs drugs along the border. Norris is paired with a Hispanic deputy and a black FBI agent, neither of whom are very effective, and lives up to his name by breaking up the drug ring almost single-handedly. The film's most interesting aspect was the climactic fight between Norris and Carradine, a battle really between the martial arts *film* hero and the martial arts *television* hero. Norris easily outclassed his small screen opponent and appeared ready for bigger, more mainstream movies.

The following year Norris began making films for Cannon, and veered hard to the right. Banking on the success of *Uncommon Valor*, Cannon shot *Missing in Action* (1984), casting Norris as Cnl. James Braddock, an ex–POW who returns to Vietnam as part of a commission to investigate the possibilities of other prisoners still being held in Southeast Asia. On the first night in the country, Norris escapes through a hotel window and tracks down evidence that there are still POWs in the country. The Vietnamese can't prove it was Norris scouting around, but they evict him from the country anyway.

Norris goes to Thailand, where he does a little fighting, then finds an old buddy who has access to various weapons. Norris and the buddy return to Vietnam with enough firepower to defeat a battalion, which is fortunate because that's about what he has to fight off to rescue the POWs. This film, as in other back-to-Vietnam flicks, stressed a distrust of politics and negotiation, preferring direct action, i.e. an extreme application of force, to remedy the situation. There is also a latent notion that creeps through the film that the government knows about the MIAs but is afraid to rock the boat.

Norris returned to Vietnam twice more. *Missing in Action 2—The Beginning* (1985) was a prequel that told the story of Braddock's own torture at the hands of the Vietnamese during the war. It featured Japanese and Korean villains and was shot on location in the Philippines. Cannon was doubtless banking on the audience being more interested in the heroic colonel and his men resisting their horrific treatment than noticing there were no real Vietnamese to be found. Highlights, or lowlights if you will, include Norris being hung upside down, with a bag over his

In *Missing in Action II*, a prequel, Colonel Braddock's time in a POW cam is relived. In this scene, the traitor Nestor (Steven Williams) takes on a chained Norris, much to his misfortune.

head containing a giant, angry rat; the killing of one soldier's pet chicken; and the blowing off of a reporter's head at point blank range. *Missing in Action I* and *II* were filmed at the same time, saving Cannon a bundle of money, which easily translated to mega profits.

In *Braddock: Missing in Action III* (1988), Norris learns that his Vietnamese wife and son, whom he believed dead, are still alive. He mounts a rescue mission, only to find the Vietnamese are waiting for him. They kill Norris' wife and torture Norris, although no rats in bags this time. They do, however, mount a shotgun pointed at Norris' son's head, and force Norris to stand on his toes for hours to keep the gun from going off. Norris eventually escapes and leads his son and a group of Amerasian children through the jungle on a long and arduous trek to freedom.

Like the other *Missing in Action*s, this film raises certain issues about politics, war and the aftermath, only to skirt by them as many genre films do. Specifically, what obligations does this country owe to the children of American servicemen left behind? Norris' solution is clear: He takes the children home to America, but such an answer clearly ruptures the conservative fabric of his audience, who may root for Norris as he fights off the barbaric Vietnamese, but at the same time prefer a halt to immigration, especially from third world countries.

With the nation's loss in Southeast Asia now properly avenged, Norris and Cannon aimed their firepower at terrorists. However, before taking care of that nasty piece of business, Norris made for Orion Pictures what was arguably the most critically acclaimed of all his films: *Code of Silence* (1985). In it Norris plays a detective

Colonel Braddock (Norris) evens the score with Colonel Yin (Soon-Tek Oh) in *Missing in Action II.*

caught up in a mob war between two gangs, not to mention battling the cops on his own department. In the opening sequence, Norris' team sets up on a drug deal, only to find themselves involved in a three-way shoot-out when the Italian Mafia tries to rip off the Columbian cartel.

Norris tries to stop the impending war between the factions, but at the same time there is growing animosity against him in his department because he is vocal in his opposition to one member of his team whom Norris suspects is a bad cop. The Columbians wipe out the Italians except for the daughter of the Don, who is not involved in the Mafia. Norris rescues the woman before they can kill her, then spends the remainder of the film trying to protect her while dealing with the antagonism from other officers.

The film's title has a duel meaning: Not only won't the crime syndicates cooperate with the police to stop the bloodshed wracking their organizations, but the police themselves mirror the criminals, turning on the Norris character who breaks the code of silence to testify against a fellow officer who wrongly killed an innocent bystander. The film boasted first rate direction by Andrew Davis, a number of well-choreographed fights (including Norris taking on an entire gang in a poolroom) and some exciting scenes on Chicago's el train.

Norris followed this watershed with *Invasion USA* (1985), from a script he co-wrote, which found terrorists invading Florida, planting bombs everywhere, or dressing up like the police and killing various minority groups. Society is on the verge of collapse until loner Norris, the government's secret weapon, comes out of retirement and dispatches the cretins in a variety of gruesome ways. Rightfully forgettable in its time, the film is intriguing to watch a generation or so later in light of America's war on terror.

In the film's high or low point, depending on one's view, landing craft hit the beaches of Florida, depositing hundreds of terrorists representing America's enemies at the time: Russian; Eastern European; Cuban; even some Arabs, all speaking different languages, all fanning out to different cities to cause their mayhem, echoing the periodic ethnic phobias that have swept through the nation since its inception. If the film has any significance now, it is in demonstrating the remarkable ease in which these terrorist gained entry to the country, and the reminder that freedom is not without a certain level of vulnerability.

Norris in his "classic" pose from *Invasion USA* (Cannon Films, 1985). While the plot of the film seemed over the top at the time, events of 9/11 have shown that the country's porous borders remain a problem.

Delta Force (1986) was the closest to a prestige release that Cannon could muster, and featured an all-star cast which included Lee Marvin, Shelley Winters, Robert Forster and a host of other name attractions. Forster leads a group of Arab hijackers in the commandeering of an American jetliner in the Mideast. Based loosely on an earlier hijacking of a TWA plane, the terrorists ruthlessly murder an American soldier and hold the remaining passengers hostage. Marvin and Norris lead the Delta Force commandos, a highly trained military team that specializes in hostage situations. The hijackers are shown to be the cowards they are, with Norris easily dispatching a number of them in various fights while the world-weary Marvin executes the rescue operation flawlessly.

In *Firewalker* (1986), Norris took the Indiana Jones route as a freewheeling adventurer looking for ancient treasure. It was the closest thing that Norris would do to comedy, unfortunately some of it unintended, and Cannon again surrounded Norris with great actors, which included Academy Award winner Lou Gossett, Jr., Sonny Landham, Will Sampson and John Rhys-Davies.

The story didn't match the cast and what could have been magic deteriorated into some good fights surrounded by a lot of clichéd events in which Norris and Gossett reaffirm their male bond and find some treasure. Norris picks up Melody Anderson as an afterthought; however, it is clear that she's worth more than the booty. Look for a memorable Central American bar fight and a showdown between Norris and the "thing" guarding the treasure.

Norris, Melody Anderson, and Lou Gossett in Cannon's *Firewalker* (1986). This was Norris' first attempt at *intentional* comedy.

Delta Force 2 (1990) *sans* Marvin, who had died in 1988, was a scaled-down version of the original, which pitted Norris, now leading the commandos, against narco-terrorists in South America. The film received more attention than usual due to the Iraqi invasion of Kuwait and the American military build-up in preparation for Desert Storm. The Iraqis were known to be developing bio-chemical weapons, and in *Delta Force 2*, a number of scenes involve chemical weapons, which the terrorists use to kill some American agents. A marginal box office draw, the film was marred by a tragic accident involving actor John P. Ryan, who was almost killed in a helicopter crash while shooting a scene.

Norris' screen success seemed more coupled to Reaganism than any other action or martial arts hero. This was, in part, a result of the exploitational nature of Cannon's output. Norris's films and characters directly linked him to a number of right wing fantasies: re-winning the Vietnam War; glorifying military action; fighting terrorists and drug dealers. However, as the Cold War cooled down, and the war on drugs failed abysmally, so too did Norris's popularity. His films seemed tired and clichéd, and as Cannon's financial fortunes flagged, so too did the quality of his films.

Norris as Major Scott McCoy in Cannon Films' *The Delta Force* (1986). The film was well-made and boasted a number of big stars, including Lee Marvin, but Norris' rocket-shooting motorcycle during the big battle took away credibility from an otherwise fine movie.

The Hero and the Terror (1988) was an exception, however, and brought Norris back to the world of horror. In it he plays a detective suffering from post-traumatic stress after single-handedly bringing in Simon Moon, one of the worst serial killer imaginable. When Moon, played by ex-boxer Jack O'Halloran, escapes from an institute for the criminally insane, Norris must track him down and stop the killings, which have begun all over again. The film, while gruesome in many places, had some nice character touches, such as Norris' psychiatrist-girlfriend giving birth to their baby, as well as some humorous moments as well.

Norris looking solemn as he prepares to ride his rocket-shooting motorcycle in *The Delta Force*. Does Harley Davidson offer a version of this bike?

Norris' next venture into horror–martial arts was *Hellbound* (1993), a decidedly lower-budget tale which relied almost entirely on Norris' built-in following to draw an audience. The film's opening sequence, involving crusaders fighting off an evil force, was its best moment, and it was all downhill from there. *The Hit Man* (1991) was a departure for Norris in that he appeared to be a villain, only to find that he was working deep undercover for a government agency fighting drug lords. These two films were the last that Norris would make for Cannon, which had filed for bankruptcy earlier and was operating under a new name.

Sidekicks (1992) brought Norris into the family film venue, in this instance playing himself as he helps an asthma-stricken boy in a martial arts tournament. The film relied heavily on scenes from other Norris movies as the boy imagines that he is "helping" Norris take on the bad guys. The film ends on a high note with Norris coming out of "retirement" to fight a bragging karate instructor, thereby helping the boy and his team win the tournament.

By the middle of the decade, however, Norris' concentration was on the small screen, where he starred in the very successful *Walker, Texas Ranger* for CBS. Norris plays the title character, who along with his partner Trivette takes care of crime throughout the great state of Texas, usually peacefully—but when that doesn't work, fists and feet will. The show

You can't keep a good man down. Norris returns as Scott McCoy, leader of the Delta Force, in *Delta Force 2* (1990). Norris battles narco-terrorists who use chemical weapons while, eerily enough, American troops were about to fight Iraqi troops who were armed with the same weapons.

remained fresh by continually bringing in new characters and ran for eight seasons, anchoring CBS's Saturday night lineup. The show was also a family affair for Norris, featuring his brother Aaron and both his sons, Eric and Mike, as sometime directors. As *Walker, Texas Ranger* ran down, Norris starred in the television film *The President's Man* (2000), playing a top secret operative given all the difficult covert operations by the President. A sequel followed. While Norris remains busy, he has not done a theatrically released film in over eight years.

Sho Kosugi

Sho Kosugi was a Japanese martial artist purportedly trained in ninjutsu, a centuries-old combat form that stresses secrecy, invisibility and the art of assassination. Kosugi initiated the ninja sub genre with *Enter the Ninja* (1981), where he played a bad ninja hired to kill a good ninja, played by Italian superstar Franco Nero. The film was essentially a reworking of a spaghetti Western, with Nero called to help a friend fight a ruthless tycoon who is trying to force the friend off his plantation.

Chuck Norris's *Octagon* (1980) actually preceded Kosugi's film and presented Norris as the reluctant hero dragged into a fight he would rather avoid, but which the audience was just itching to see. Terrorists in Central America are being trained in ninjutsu by Norris' Japanese adopted brother; Norris, also a trained ninja, must confront him. Both films contain climactic confrontations between good and bad ninjas who have trained together in the past, and both portray women as deceptive and untrustworthy.

In *The Octagon*, Norris encounters three women in the course of the film, one pretending to be an artist but really working for a terrorist organization; a second who lies to try to persuade Norris to kill his ninja brother; and a third who actually trained as a terrorist. In *Enter the Ninja*, the wife of Nero's friend seduces him while her husband lie drunk in their bedroom.

Kosugi's success led to a succession of ninja films: In *Revenge of the Ninja* (1982) he plays a Japanese businessman who is forced to use his ninjutsu skills against his partner, also a ninja, when he finds the man is dealing drugs. The film provides a clear link between the hard work and material success of business to the discipline aesthetic of martial arts, and condones the use of direct action to eliminate criminal activity. *Ninja III: The Domination* (1983) bordered on the absurd, and is most noted as a lame attempt to introduce break-dance sensation Lucinda Dickey into the world of the ninja. The opening sequence featured a ninja who was killed more times than a cat has lives but would not die, while the story, what there is, follows Dickey, who is possessed by the spirit of an evil ninja. Kosugi, as a good ninja, must defeat it.

Kosugi followed up with *9 Deaths of the Ninja* and *Pray for Death* (both 1986) and *Rage of Honor* (1987), in which he fought to protect his adopted country and/or his family against criminals. In *9 Deaths* Kosugi is a ninjutsu-trained member of an elite U.S. military team sent into the Philippines to rescue a busload of tourists held captive by Arab terrorists. The film borders on a James Bond spoof, with deadly women, outlandish weapons and an opening credit sequence (clearly borrowed from 007) that features scantily clad women dancing as Kosugi brandishes his sword. Yet, the humor is interrupted by some vicious killings, giving the movie a jarring effect. The story, weak as it is, provides Kosugi a whole litany of problems to fight (drugs, homosexuality, feminism, terrorism), and he is more than up to the task. However, the recent slate of kidnappings of foreign tourists by Muslim extremists in the Philippines makes the viewer wonder about the old maxim "Does life imitate art, or vice versa?"

Pray for Death presents Kosugi as a recent immigrant victimized by thugs and criminals. After his wife is killed and children threatened, Kosugi finally swings into action, and his enemies find themselves literally praying for death. The two films crystallize the Reagan era perfectly: *9 Deaths* advocates the use of force whenever and wherever American lives are threatened, while *Pray for Death* upholds the protection of the family at any cost.

Rage of Honor showcased Kosugi's unique talents as a drug enforcement agent who has to take the law into his own hands when bureaucratic red tape stifles his pursuit of an international drug dealing syndicate. Part of a three-man team, both his partners are killed and his girlfriend taken hostage, giving Kosugi a whole lot to rage about. Much of the filming takes place in South America, where the drug trade booms. Like in *Rambo II*, the implication is that the battle can be won if only the politicians will stay out of the fray.

Unlike the conservatism of Norris' films, which exhibited overt political strains, the conservatism in Kosugi's films could be viewed in a cultural context. While Norris was always a man of his era, a professional in some field or another, Kosugi was generally the practitioner of an ancient, arcane martial art, and as such was a man either out of step or uncomfortable with modern Japan. Where Norris was at ease as an all–American avenger, taking on the battles of the working and middle classes, the men Kosugi played were often more complex, plagued by trouble or sorrow. Unlike Norris, who was almost never married, Kosugi usually was, or was a widower, or in a stable relationship.

In some cases, the trajectory of Kosugi's character takes him on a quest to America, where he hopes to build a new life, only to find a clash between his ancestral values and that of his adopted homeland. That the grass is greener somewhere else is an issue never directly raised but, rather, where to find it and what price to pay is. The violence Kosugi seemed to reject when leaving Japan merely follows him abroad, though ironically it is only by the very martial skills that he has called into question that he is ultimately able to survive.

Where the narrative in Chuck Norris' films usually reinforce the heterosexual paradigm, with him finding love—and sex—during the course of his adventure, Sho Kosugi's films usually shied away from such activity. In *Revenge of the Ninja*, the widowed Kosugi explicitly rejects the sexual advance of a beautiful friend and student, instead channeling her attention to her martial arts training. In *Pray for Death*, there is little or no overt affection displayed between Kosugi and his wife, though it is clear he loves her.

In fact, for Kosugi, sex is often linked to decadence and death. The corporate villains in *Enter the Ninja* live in a modern high-rise building, complete with beautiful young women at their beck and call, while the rest of the city lives in poverty. They all meet a rather gruesome end. In *Revenge of the Ninja*, the evil ninja, Kosugi's partner Braeden, murders a Mafioso and a young woman having sex in a hot tub, while Braeden's henchman is garroted as he tries to rape Kosugi's young student. The mobsters in *Pray for Death* live high on the hog, particularly the brutal Limehouse, who likes sadistic killing and loose women but not necessarily in that order. At the film's end, Kosugi ties him to a saw and he is cut in two from the crotch up. In *Rage of Honor*, a boat party features bikini-clad women everywhere—until Kosugi and his partners break up the reverie to bust up a drug smuggling ring.

Black Eagle (1988) was an exception in Kosugi's *oeuvre* as its blatant politicism boiled down to an "us against them" attitude regarding the Cold War. Kosugi plays an American CIA agent code named "Black Eagle." When he reluctantly accepts a mission to retrieve a top secret laser-guided weapons system from an American fighter jet downed in the sea off Malta, Kosugi finds himself up to his ears in Soviet agents and adventure. The film's overarching message, that of good versus evil, or the U.S. versus the Soviets, is mirrored by Kosugi's private battle with Andrei, the Soviet's top agent.

Kosugi's ninja background is played down in this film, and most of his fighting is hand-to-hand, including a number of sequences against Jean-Claude Van Damme, who plays Andrei. *Black Eagle*, while appearing outdated in today's post–Cold War era, touched on a number of conservative topics of its time, including aid to Afghani rebels fighting the Soviets (Kosugi is first seen operating with the guerrillas against the Red Army) and, in light of recent terrorist attacks emanating from those very same elements we helped a generation ago, bears important witness to the political adage that today's friends might be tomorrow's enemies.

Aloha Summer (1988), a film about a group of teens coming of age during a Hawaiian vacation in the mid–50s, was Kosugi's best role, and clearly a summation of his screen persona. While hardly a kung fu movie, it did feature a number of martial arts sequences, and Kosugi had a key supporting part as an embittered Japanese veteran still upset over the loss of the war. Unhappy at the social and cultural changes around him, and unwilling to change, Kosugi is literally a man trapped between worlds. The demons tormenting him become apparent during a dinner party scene where the American and Japanese friends bring their parents to sit at the same table, and there is an embarrassing silence among the adults.

Eventually Kosugi's rage spills over when his son, whom he is teaching in the martial arts, brings the American friend over to watch him train with his father. Kosugi goads the American boy into a Kendo lesson and then beats the unsuspecting teen almost senseless. At the film's climax, a huge storm blankets the island and Kosugi's son, who is surfing in the huge waves, is knocked from his board unconscious. The American rescues him, causing Kosugi to have a change of heart. He presents his son and the friend the two Samurai swords that he had won for bravery during the war, thereby coming to terms with both his old enemy and the new world.

Kosugi's last major English-speaking role was in 1992's *Journey of Honor*, in which he played Mayeda, the most trusted and able samurai of Lord Ieyasu, leader of Japan's eastern army during its sixteenth century civil war. The eastern army is losing the war because it does not have firearms, so Ieyasu sends Mayeda to Spain to buy the weapons, and entrusts his son Yorimune to Mayeda's care. The trip is fraught with danger, including a bitter storm which almost sinks the ship, treachery in which Yorimune is almost killed, and the loss of the money Ieyasu sent to pay for the weapons.

Once in Spain, Mayeda must navigate the often treacherous ways of court life in his attempt to get the Spanish king to give him the guns he needs. Opposing Mayeda's mission are Don Pedro, a court noble, and Father Vasco, a Jesuit Priest looking to gain a foothold in Japan for his order. However, Mayeda prevails at court and gains the weapons, though on the way back to Japan the ship is taken by pirates and Mayeda, Yorimune and the rest of the crew are all enslaved by Moroccans.

Like other Kosugi films, the notion of honor and duty is the underlying tenet of the story. Mayeda has surrendered his own life to serve his liege, Lord Ieyasu, and whatever personal pain and tribulation he goes through he must suppress. In the film's opening battle sequence, Mayeda blindly leads his cavalry in a suicidal charge against muskets, which accounts for him losing over half his men. Only the sudden appearance of rain, which causes the muskets to malfunction, allows Mayeda to win the day for Ieyasu. After the battle, assassins attack Mayeda's home, killing his wife and son who were helping Yorimune to escape.

Mayeda buries his grief behind a stone face. Like so many of Kosugi's other characters, Mayeda is a man marked by personal tragedy; however, he takes on Ieyasu's latest assignment to go to Spain without question. When King Philip of Spain grants Mayeda's request and gives him the guns he needs, he makes Mayeda swear never to use the guns outside of Japan. Later, as Mayeda and the crew escape the Moroccans, Yorimune turns the guns on them, but Mayeda stops him from using them because he had given his word.

Since much of the film turns on Mayeda's heroics, he is in almost every scene. He charges muskets without question when Ieyasu commands it. He fights off assassins to protect Yorimune, sacrificing his own family in the process. In King Philip's court, assassins attack but not only does Mayeda save Philip, he charges the assailants and single-handedly beats them off. In return, Philip gives him the weapons he has requested. When the crew is captured by the Moroccans, Mayeda escapes the dungeon and then saves the Moroccan King. In return, the King

Sho Kosugi battles David Essex in *Journey of Honor* (Universal, 1992). Kosugi's characters were the most conservative of the 1980s, though for the most part they eschewed politics.

allows Mayeda to fight Don Pedro for the right to free himself and the crew.

The Japanese civil war between east and west is mirrored in the culture clash between east and west that Mayeda and Yorimune face in Spain. While King Philip is an honorable man who treats Mayeda and Yorimune like the royalty they are, Don Pedro looks at the Japanese as little better than monkeys, while the Japanese belittle the Europeans as uncivilized. The Japanese believe the food the Europeans eat is not fit for a dog, while the Europeans mock the way the Japanese dress. Don Pedro boasts that Toledo steel is the finest and sharpest in the world, and puts it to the test against Mayeda's sword, which in the end cuts the Toledo sword in two. Only when confronted by the Arabs do the Japanese and Europeans come together, but the film leaves little doubt that Japanese ways are superior.

This was Kosugi's one and only high-budget epic, and he makes the most of it. The swordplay is first rate, with Kosugi and his son Kane, who plays Yorimune, taking on all comers in lightning fashion. The fight within the hold of the ship is a major highlight, as Mayeda and Yorimune battle traitors working for the western forces. With water bursting into holes in the ship, and the ship being tossed around by a fierce storm, Mayeda wields a dangerous sword, able to kill impassively while keeping an eye on Yorimune, who has his hands full with a western army samurai. Kosugi mixes in some ninjutsu with the sword fighting and, in the last scene on the beach, fights without weapons, dispatching a number of assassins who are attempting to prevent Kosugi and the crew from sailing by using kicks and punches.

Kosugi wrote the story for *Journey of Honor* and produced it through his own company, the Sho Kosugi Corporation. The film was shot in Japan and Yugoslavia, and for the first time Kosugi had an excellent supporting cast, which included Christopher Lee, rock star David Essex, Polly Walker, John Rhys-Davies and the impeccable Toshiro Mifune, who played Lord Ieyasu. The last two were veterans of the *Shogun* miniseries that aired on American television is 1980.

The Ninja Craze

Kosugi cut back on filmmaking after this, though his name was used to hype a number of "Ninja Theater" videos that featured ultra low-budget films of that ilk. However, other ninja films followed, including a whole series by Cannon that introduced Michael Dudikoff and David Bradley to martial arts cinema. Dudikoff started his career as a professional model.[9] While not a martial artist per se, he is a fitness buff, having competed in a number of Iron Man contests.

The first film, *American Ninja* (1985), starred Dudikoff as an orphan trained by a Japanese soldier on a deserted island, who is now grown up and in the army. He rescues the colonel's daughter from ninja terrorists, unaware that her father is in league with them, selling arms to raise money for anti–Communist rebels. The film has an uncomfortable ambiguity about it: On the one hand, pictures of President Reagan and John Wayne, the terrorist's constant referral to Dudikoff as "the

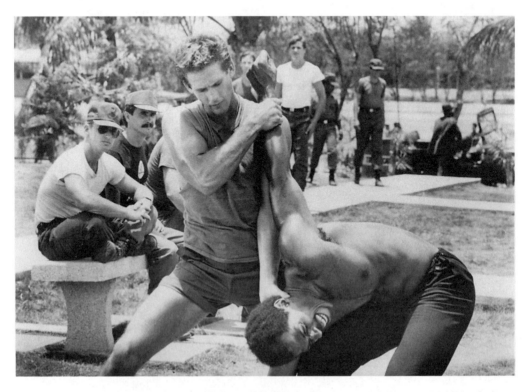

Michael Dudikoff is the "American Ninja" in Cannon's *American Ninja* (1985). Dudikoff shows Jackson (Steve James), the self-defense instructor, what he has.

Joe Armstrong (Michael Dudikoff) defends against an unseen antagonist in 1987's *American Ninja 2*.

Sgt. Jackson (Steve James) takes on (what else?) a ninja in *American Ninja 2*.

American" and the military's violent response to the terrorists at the end of the story auger a conservative perspective. Yet, the view that segments of the military would sell arms to rebels after Congress denied them aid was painfully close to the shameful events that actually occurred in Reagan's administration.

In *American Ninja 2* (1987), Dudikoff returns as an Army Ranger, investigating the disappearance of Marines from an embassy attachment. In this installment of the series, it turns out the island's authorities are involved in drug trafficking, and Dudikoff and partner Steve James have to battle ninjas who are protecting the drug lord.

American Ninja 3 (1989) saw James returning in his role as Curtis Jackson, but Dudikoff was gone. James was now paired with David Bradley, who plays a karate champion who was trained as a ninja after the death of his father. The two men are on a Caribbean Island for a martial arts tournament when they find that a master criminal is attempting to use biological and genetic engineering to create perfect ninja terrorists. The usual assortment of stereotypes were present to buy these unstoppable assassins: Arab terrorists, African terrorists, South American strongmen, etc. This installment had more humor than most of the others, with James almost caricaturing his role, at one point shaking his head at the prospect of having to deal with ninjas again.

American Ninja 4 (1991) lost Steve James, and any potential humor the film might possess, but brought back David Bradley and Michael Dudikoff (the latter's appearance at best was little more than a lengthy cameo). The grimmest of the series,

Joe Armstrong (Michael Dudikoff, center) returns to action in *American Ninja 4* after sitting out the third film. On the right is David Bradley, who would go on to star in a number of martial arts films during the 90s.

this time Bradley is captured trying to rescue Delta Force personnel from an Arab terrorist and his ninja army. Dudikoff must come out of retirement to save the entire lot. The film sports some good fight scenes and an exciting cross cut between Bradley taking on one of the bad guys and Dudikoff locking up with the head ninja. It is not for the squeamish: A number of scenes show the Arabs burning American soldiers alive.

The *American Ninja* series featured a number of similarities that ran throughout the various installments. In all cases, an Anglo hero was teamed with a minority sidekick, usually black. Both heroes had to fight in exotic, out-of-the-way locations, often on an island. A pretty girl always helps the American ninja defeat the evildoers; sometimes her father is involved with the criminals/terrorists, other times she is but has a change of heart. As a white man trained in ninjutsu, the American ninja is naturally an outsider. This carries over into his personal life: In *American Ninja*, Dudikoff is an outcast among his fellow troops; in *American Ninja 2* he is an army ranger in a marine outfit. *American Ninja 4* finds Dudikoff in the Peace Corps, alone and far from home.

In all cases there is a conspiracy among the authorities that forces Dudikoff, James and Bradley to handle the dangerous situations themselves. It might be their commanding officer involved (*American Ninja*), or the ambassador (*American Ninja 2*). It could be the chief of police (*American Ninja 3*) or even the head of state (*American Ninja 4*) who is in league with the terrorists. Dudikoff always faces off with the head evil ninja in the final confrontation, and the last sequences are of a military-style assault on the ninja's fortress in which the good guys prevail. Every *American Ninja* film previewed a different threat to American national security, be it drugs, biological and chemical weapons, even nuclear weapons in the hands of madmen, all problems still in the new millennium.

American Ninja 5 (1993) was a completely different animal, more or less a children's movie in which David Bradley starred as a ninja who must train a boy to take his place as a ninja, the last of his clan. There is a side plot about a scientist's daughter who is kidnapped to force the scientist to develop nerve gas, but all in all the focus is on Bradley and the boy. Of all the installments, this one features the worst fight scenes, though it does have its humorous moments. The ninja trend continued throughout the decade of the 80s, even manifesting itself in the martial arts television series *The Master*, which featured none other than Lee Van Cleef, who in *The Octagon* was a ninja hunter, now playing a master ninja being hunted by an evil ninja, played by none other than Sho Kosugi. The series lasted a year.

Other Films

Other martial arts films, some with big stars, some with very minor martial arts stars, or none at all, continued to exhibit the decade's conservative trends. *Force: Five* (1981) featured Joe Lewis, who never caught the public's fancy as a martial arts hero, as the leader of an elite team of mercenaries who agree to take on a cult leader brainwashing American college students. The film is both a thinly veiled volley at Korean cult leader Sun Yung Moon and his Unification Church, which has been periodically accused of various crimes against the young people it recruits, as well as a reminder of the Jonestown massacre, in which crazed cult leader Jim Jones ordered the suicides of his entire congregation after assassinating a United States Congressmen. The success of the film's heroes in destroying the cult argues for the application of force against those corrupting our young with foreign values.

Kill Squad (1981) was an ultra low-budget flick that followed an ex-soldier gathering together his war-time squad to avenge an attack on another of their ilk. The fighting scenes were so-so and the plot, nearly incomprehensible, had something to do with Vietnam. Cameron Mitchell made a cameo appearance as one of the bad guys but even an actor of his abilities was unable to salvage this film.

As bad as *Kill Squad* was, *Bionic Ninja* (1986) was a thousand times worse, if that is possible. A top secret tape is stolen in Hong Kong and the KGB hires ninjas to retrieve it. The Americans send CIA agent Foster to get the tape back. According to one character, the information on the tape could be used by terrorists to destroy world peace. A score of competing plot lines complicate the story beyond understanding, but of interest here is the Cold War plot, and the positive light in which Foster is portrayed. In keeping with the conventions of the decade, Foster overcomes the head ninja by hard work and training, not to mention a guide on how to be a ninja.*

On a higher note, *The Challenge* (1982) starred Scott Glenn as a journeyman boxer who is chosen by a wheelchair-bound Japanese man and his beautiful sister to smuggle a sword back to Japan. Glenn is almost killed in the process, and becomes involved in a bitter feud between two brothers who cherish the sword and who are allegories of modern Japan. One is a traditional samurai played by Toshiro Mifune, the other a heartless businessman. Glenn tries to steal the sword for the businessman but then has a change of heart, deciding to stay and learn with the samurai. Eventually the businessman attacks the samurai's fortress and obtains the sword. As the outsider, it falls to Glenn to save it for Mifune and uphold the old ways of the masters.

The film boasted a superior script written by John Sayles and great performances by Glenn and newcomer Donna Kei Benz. This marked Steven Seagal's first foray into Hollywood, in this instance as fight choreographer, and he did a fantastic job. Both Glenn and Benz, who plays Akiko, the very independent and headstrong daughter of Mifune, trained at Seagal's Osaka Dojo to prepare for their roles.[10]

Gymkata (1985) marked director Robert Clouse's return to the cinematic world of martial arts. The feature starred none other than Olympic gold medalist Kurt Thomas as Cabot, a world-class gymnast trained by the CIA to compete in the Game (a tournament mixing martial arts and survival), held in the mythical country of Parmistan (which is somewhere close to the Soviet Union but which looks a lot like Yugoslavia). Other nations are also training fighters to compete in the Game but, as the CIA informs Thomas, there can be but one winner, and his reward is to be granted a single request: Everyone else will be killed during the tribulations of the Game.

---

*Bionic Ninja *was a borderline choice to be included in this history since its language was Cantonese. However, it used a number of American and Chinese actors who spoke English so it got the nod.*

Thomas' gymnastic skills are superb, but they don't necessarily translate to combat aptitude. Many of his fights are forced and not motivated by reality, such as when he and the Princess Ribali are running from enemy agents and Thomas just happens to find a gymnastic type parallel bar in the alley! Doing giant swings from it, he kayoes the agents as they come around the corner. A similar weakness occurs in the style of fighting that Thomas employs. Because of his gymnastic background, he is limber and able to deliver a number of different style kicks, from spinning to front and side ones. However, as almost all martial arts forms employ some type of grappling or hold techniques in the event an opponent gets in too close, Thomas has none to use, so his fights are mostly conducted at long range, and leave a lot to be desired.

On accepting the mission, Thomas undergoes three tests. First, he must be trained for the Game, which entails the eager gymnast running for miles on end to prepare for the endurance aspect of it, and then learning how to fight from a Japanese master and an American master. He is taught to kick and punch, and to avoid being hit. As is common with these type films (and as would be seen in *Rocky IV*, released the same year), Thomas's training is conducted in a natural environment. There are no large Everlast heavy punching bags, no speed bags, no weights to bulk up Thomas. He doesn't train in the big city. Instead he is tucked away at a quiet cabin and strengthens himself by walking up a flight of stairs on his hands, or learns proper breathing by chopping wood.

When Thomas is ready for his mission, he leaves for Parmistan, but on the way, enemy agents kidnap Princess Ribali, Thomas's ally as well as his guide into her native country. Thomas is told to leave for Parmistan without Ribali because she is being held in a terrorist camp but he refuses, and instead barges into a large mansion, where he fights off a slew of terrorists, killing most of them. He grabs Ribali and they wend their way through the Byzantine streets of an ancient city, all the while being chased by some nasty guys with machine guns. They finally escape, but not before discovering their native contact had betrayed them.

Thomas' final test is the Game itself. Not merely a martial arts tournament, the event is mostly a survival trek, with the martial artists being hunted as they make their way through unfamiliar and hostile terrain. Thomas and the others are given a head start, and then are chased by hunters on horseback. One by one the martial artists are killed in a gruesome fashion, by spear or arrow, or even by pitchforks. Only Thomas makes it to the final stage, which is a nightmarish journey through a village populated by violent, criminally insane people. He endures, wins the Game and gets his request.

Gymkata resembled Clouse's masterpiece *Enter the Dragon* in a number of superficial ways: Thomas is recruited by a government agency to infiltrate a tournament like setting for the national good; fighters from around the world compete; firearms are prohibited and result in instant death to anyone caught with them; and Thomas' one friend, Gomez, played by John Barrett, is hideously murdered.

More noteworthy is the political milieu in which the film takes place. Most of it occurs in third world countries that appear, if not Arab, than Muslim, and the main division in Parmistan is between those elements who want to keep the country in the Middle Ages and the king, who wants to modernize and bring the people into the twentieth century. This outlook was as optimistic as it was unrealistic, for just the opposite was occurring at the time: Islamic Fundamentalism was sweeping across most of the Middle East, wiping out almost all attempts at democratic innovation.

An air of anti–American sentiment is also strong within the film. In one scene, Thomas is accosted by a market place seller who throws water in his face when he learns that Thomas is an American.[11] But probably the most interesting aspect of the film is the request the CIA wants Thomas to make: allow the United States to build a tracking station to assist in its Star Wars ABM capabilities. At the time, President Reagan's Strategic Defense Initiative was a very controversial plan, popular with some elements of the public and not with others. The support for SDI put *Gymkata* near the top of the conservative pantheon of martial arts films of the decade.

No Retreat, No Surrender (1986) is a cross between Bruce Lee's *The Chinese Connection* and *Rocky IV* (1985). A young man trains at a martial arts studio which thugs attempt to take over. He resists, and eventually must fight their champion, referred to only as "the Russian," to free the gym from their clutches. Like Rocky, he is smaller than his opponent, and less skilled. He trains hard with make shift equipment, and is helped by the spirit of Lee, who guides him through his paces. The young man's victory is the same as Rocky Balboa's, a symbolic defeat of Communism, herein linked explicitly to criminality, and the assurance that individual discipline, hard work and moxie can overcome any challenge facing the nation.

Karate Warrior (1987) was a decidedly low-budget affair that seemed to piece together various parts of the *Karate Kid* saga. A boy visits the Philippines to see his long-absent father. He runs afoul of a local gang who beat him unmercifully and leave him for dead. He is found in the forest by an ancient martial arts master who nurses him back to health and trains him to defend himself. The boy returns to town a man and rescues his girlfriend's little brother from a fire started by the gang. He then takes on the gang leader at the local tournament, and beats him decisively.

Karate Warrior offered nothing new to the genre, but it was so low-budget that there's a good chance it flew under most viewers' radar. The fights were well choreographed, though, and little asides, such as the boy and his girlfriend bartering for a necklace with an old woman in the marketplace, or the father asking the son in a roundabout way how his mother is doing, lent some nice touches to the story. Hard work, personal achievement and the triumph of the individual are epitomized in the film, as is the notion that Americans can do whatever it is the natives can, only better.

Released in 1988, *Day of the Panther* is an Australian martial arts film that features a James Bond–like character, Jason Blade, a graduate of the "Panther School," a super-secretive martial arts academy. Blade works for the Hong Kong police, special service branch, and is most comfortable wearing fabulous suits, staying in five-star hotels and driving only the swankiest cars. When Blade's partner is killed by a Perth drug lord, he swings into action, infiltrating the organization, chopping and kicking his way to the truth—and a knock-down, drag-out brawl with the drug lord's bodyguard.

Day of the Panther featured a number of first-rate fight scenes, including an entire sequence filmed in a series of broken-down buildings, where Blade's partner

Lucy is killed obtaining evidence against the drug lord. The running battle (which follows Lucy up and down a number of flights of stairs and in and out of abandoned rooms, on roofs and landings, and across a footbridge) took up half of the first act of the film, and set the stage for Blade's obsession with avenging her murder. A later, similar sequence finds Blade, now working for the drug lord, taking on some thugs in a warehouse after a drug deal goes sour; this fight is played more for humor. The film's star, Edward John Stazak, a fresh face and an excellent martial artist, made a sequel to this film and then disappeared.

Patrick Swayze starred in two martial arts–flavored films toward

Patrick Swayze practices his kata in *Road House* (MGM, 1989). Swayze's character exemplified the notions of tradition, loyalty and rugged individualism that were popular during the Reagan years.

the end of the decade. *Steel Dawn* (1987) was a post-apocalyptic story about a nomad who was once a soldier before the end of civilization. He wanders into a small desert community and becomes a bodyguard for a widow whose farm hides a vast pool of underground water. Swayze gets in some action, both with weapons as well as fists and feet, in saving the community from a warlord who wants the water.

In 1989's *Road House*, Swayze starred as Dalton, a bouncer for hire with a reputation for being the best. The film is almost a copy of *Steel Dawn* placed in the contemporary U.S.: Dalton is hired by an honest club owner to fend off the attacks of a big shot who wants to own the town. Pretty soon it becomes Dalton vs. every bad guy the big shot can rustle up. They present no problem to Swayze. Finally, the big shot gets his own karate man to take on Swayze, and then the sparks fly. The film showcased Swayze at his action best, and featured the hard-rocking music of the Jeff Healy Band as a backdrop. In both films, old-fashioned values such as loyalty and tradition were exemplified.

Steven Seagal

Much of left-wing martial arts star Steven Seagal's initial popularity resided in the confusion regarding his past, and the apparent link between his screen personas and his real life. Seagal is the highest ranking non–Japanese Aikido expert, and the only American to ever run his own dojo in Japan. Though accounts of Seagal's life differ, it is apparent that he traveled to Japan at the age of 17 to better learn the martial art of Aikido, a non-aggressive style of combat whereby the opponent's force is turned against him. While in Japan, Seagal taught English, studied Zen, perfected his martial arts and, as Chris Betros reported in JapanToday.com, "he was [even] rumored to have been a bounty hunter."[12]

Seagal has denied in interviews that he was recruited by the United States for secret missions in Indo-China during the war, and the government has denied he was ever on the payroll in any capacity. Whatever the truth, *Baseline's Encyclopedia of Film* sums it up best:

> Seagal cemented his popularity as an avenging action hero ... in which his larger-than-life persona alternates between meditative serenity and vigilante violence. The pony-tailed actor has enhanced his mystique by creating a public persona shrouded in mystery and surrounded by speculation about his possible past as a CIA operative.[13]

While in Japan, Seagal dreamed of returning to America to become a film star. When he eventually returned to the United States, he settled in Los Angeles, where he taught Aikido, often to connected Hollywood players. Producer-agent Michael Ovitz, one of Seagal's students, arranged a screen test for Seagal but the executives were not overly impressed. He came back to the studio and performed a live Aikido demonstration, which did the trick. In March 1987, he signed a deal with Warner Bros.,[14] which produced *Above the Law* (1988)—story by Seagal—that featured him as an ex–CIA agent turned Chicago cop who uncovers government corruption.

Seagal's brand of gritty, urban populism ran contrary to the Reaganesque times, and was at clear odds with Norris' marked conservatism. Reagan supported, illegally at times, the Contra rebels in Nicaragua against the Marxist Sandinista government, and was backing the right-wing governments of Guatemala and El Salvador, despite growing evidence of rampant human rights abuses, including the rape and murder of four Catholic nuns and lay workers by Salvadoran militia. In *Above the Law*, Seagal offered a stinging indictment of the administration's policy when he presented in a positive light the controversial Sanctuary Movement, which was formed to aid undocumented aliens who (supposedly) have been politically persecuted in their homelands by the very people Reagan was backing, and are now hiding in the United States.

Seagal takes on almost single-handedly a number of CIA hired killers associated with Central American death squads, who blow up a church sheltering the aliens. The labyrinth which Seagal must traverse to find the truth becomes a revealing look at the base nature of American covert interference in other countries, and what happens when our own nation subverts the rights of those abroad to supposedly protect those at home. The film's title is a clear jab at the President and his policies: Reagan himself was linked to illegal arms trafficking involving Iran and Nicaragua. Though a direct involvement could not be proved, the implication remained that the President had broken his trust with the American people, and escaped punishment because he was, inevitably, above the law.

The dirty tactics of the government and politicians continued to be a major theme in Seagal's films. In *Hard to Kill* (1990), Seagal plays Mason Storm, an honest undercover cop trailing the Mafia. When he makes a videotape of a politician paying the mob to bump off a Senator so that he, the politician, can be appointed to the Senator's seat, dirty cops working for the politician kill him and his family, and frame him for being a cop in the drug trade. But Seagal is hard to kill, and remains in a coma for seven years. When he suddenly emerges from unconsciousness, the killers are back on his trail. Seagal not only has to shake them, but find the tape he made to prove his innocence.

The marriage between politics and organized crime, the presence of conspiracy, police corruption, military–CIA duplicity and corporate malfeasance were themes that would permeate almost all of Seagal's future films in some form or another. *Hard to Kill* is a prime example, but it separates itself from other films in the genre by an accent on detail and characterization that is missing from many martial arts flicks. For example, when Storm awakens, he is weak, his muscles almost

Left-wing karate gets its chance: Steven Seagal takes aim in *Hard to Kill* (Warner Bros., 1990). Seagal brought a fresh, urban approach to his movies that was popular with the public, particularly in the cities.

useless from years of inactivity. He can barely speak. After he and his nurse escape the dirty cops sent to kill him, his recovery is slow and realistic. Later, after he makes love to the nurse, he sits by himself and stares at his wedding ring, clearly confused and guilty over his actions.

Storm is clearly meant to be a Christ-like figure, complete with long hair and beard, who is resurrected to right a wrong, in this case bringing down a false god—the Senator. However, as the body count rises, we see that turning the other cheek is not in this messiah's vocabulary. Seagal kills at least a dozen men, and that's just with a gun. He disables even more in hand-to-hand combat. The fight scenes are well done, but there are fewer of them than in most films of this ilk.

Like *Above the Law*, *Hard to Kill* made money and set the stage for Seagal's next film, *Marked for Death* (1990), in which he plays John Hatcher, an ex–DEA agent who returns home from working abroad, only to find more drugs here than overseas. After Hatcher returns to his hometown of Chicago, he immediately runs into trouble with a Jamaican posse dealing drugs at the high school. The Jamaicans try to kill Seagal's sister and niece, which only serves to piss him off. Seagal busts up the posse by (among other things) throwing members out the windows of high buildings.

The film (which also throws in some voodoo and sacrifices) co-stars Joanna Pacula as an occult expert who advises Hatcher on what he is up against. Hatcher follows the posse to Jamaica, where he kills a bunch of them after cutting the power to their mansion and using night vision to ferret them out. The implicit message of *Marked for Death* is that the Reagan-Bush war on drugs is a failure, but the only solution Seagal offers is vigilante violence, which in fact might be the only thing the government hasn't tried.

Out for Justice (1991) was among the least political of films of Seagal's *oeuvre* but, conversely, among the most violent. He plays a New York cop, Gino Felino, who spends a night searching the city for Ritchie Madrano, the murderer of his best friend Bobby. Seagal's quest is complicated by the local Mafia, which wants Ritchie dead because he has brought the heat down on their business. Ritchie is a full-blown, drug-addicted psychopath who, after killing Bobby, shoots a woman point blank in the head for honking her horn at him.

The stretch patrolling the street allows Seagal time to ruminate about various things, which tends to slow the film down whenever he was not fighting. However, Seagal does get down and dirty, and one particularly brutal clash comes in a market, where a group of butchers—on Ritchie's orders—attacks Seagal with knives. Seagal takes out the henchmen, pinning one man's hand to the wall with a cleaver! A later fight in a bar owned by Ritchie's brother pits Seagal against a whole crowd of cue stick–wielding bad guys whom Seagal dispatches handily by using a pool ball wrapped in a bar towel. The film's violence quotient was facilitated by the use of special prosthetic devices which made it appear that Seagal "broke" one adversaries arm at the elbow.[15]

Out for Justice was a letdown in many ways, particularly the final fight, where Seagal goes up against William Forsythe (who played Ritchie), an excellent actor but certainly not a hardcase tough guy of Seagal's quality. Unlike Norris, Van Damme or most other martial artists who usually fought formidable opponents at the climax of their movies, much of Seagal's appeal comes from the fact that the characters he plays are almost invincible. By pitting him against one man (Ritchie) who was not even close to Seagal's equal, the slack had to be picked up somewhere else. In this case it was in the level of violence that Seagal uses to dispatch Ritchie. Every time the bloodied and battered Ritchie rises from the floor, he grabs a weapon, which Seagal turns against him. In the end, it takes a corkscrew in the forehead and six shots from a revolver to do Ritchie in.

While there was nothing special about the story, *Out for Justice* did allow Seagal the opportunity to test his artistic abilities. For one, he has to master his character's Italian Brooklyn accent; for another, he must occasionally speak both Spanish and Italian. But perhaps most importantly, at least for Seagal, was his musical connection. Seagal co-wrote many of the songs featured in the film, including the final track, which was sung by Greg Allman.

In 1992 came Seagal's only true blockbuster, *Under Siege*. Seagal is Casey Ryback, a Navy cook who was once a SEAL. Says Seagal of Ryback:

> Ryback has lived his whole adult life in the Navy, and he's best at covert combat operations; but he's seen and done some things he'd rather not recall—things that have disillusioned him even though they've been heroic.[16]

During the night, a renegade American CIA agent named Strannix (Tommy Lee Jones) takes control of the battleship that Seagal is on and, using a stolen North Korean submarine, plans to offload nuclear missiles. Seagal has to swing into action to prevent the crew from being slaughtered and the ship's weapons from being launched. He leads a ragtag bunch of sailors to fight the terrorists and, in the finale, engages in a knife fight with Strannix, who is really a mirror image of Ryback save one important thing: Ryback still has values and Strannix does not. He no longer believes in his country while Ryback, disillusioned as he is, still does.

The film was exciting from beginning to end, boasted excellent production values and showcased Seagal at his best. Much of the filming took place in Mobile, Alabama, where the decommissioned battleship USS *Alabama* is now serving as a museum. Since the *Alabama* resembled the USS *Missouri*, which is the ship the action is supposed to take place on, it was a natural replacement. The film broke $100,000,000 and set the stage for a sequel, *Under Siege 2* (1995), in which Seagal, now out of the Navy and running his own restaurant, has to battle terrorists who take over a train.

Under Siege 2 was an interesting film about a secret, illegal U.S. killer satellite which can target anything on the Earth for destruction, and was vintage Seagal. The government has hidden all knowledge about the satellite, which can also be used for hi-tech spying, and now that terrorists have control of it, the powers that be have

Seagal's films usually boasted the latest firepower and weapons.

to rely on Ryback to save their bacon. The film continued the family angle that many of Seagal's films featured, in this instance, Ryback having to care for his late

Casey Ryback (Steven Seagal) leads his ragtag group against American terrorists trying to take over the U.S.S. *Missouri* in *Under Seige* (Warner Bros., 1992). This was Seagal's only blockbuster.

brother's daughter, who is bitter toward Ryback because of a feud between her father and uncle. *Under Siege 2* sported helicopter stunts, train crashes, tons of terrible terrorists and enough shooting to qualify for a small war. Seagal's fights were on target, including a couple of moves he shows to his niece that come in handy later. Unfortunately, the film did not make the money its predecessor did, and Seagal's theatrical decline began.

Seagal's politics also came across in his support for the environment. In *On Deadly Ground* (1994), he plays an oil rig troubleshooter who uncovers, what else?, a corporate cover-up involving pollution in Alaska. The usual message of peace through violence, so prevalent in many of Seagal's films, rears up its head right away. In one of the first scenes, an Inuit native is wandering through an oilman's hangout, begging for money to get a drink. One of the oilman humiliates the native, which upsets Seagal so much that he in turn humiliates the oilman. As the bully stands bloody and dazed, Seagal then preaches to the bar about respecting people's dignity!

After Seagal uncovers some shady business by his employers, he is whacked and left for dead in the tundra by the corporation's hit men. However, he is taken in by Inuits and nursed back to health, undergoing a rebirth during a dream sequence where his character resists temptations of the flesh. Once well and in fighting shape, Seagal goes after the corporation with a vengeance, much to the chagrin of the boss and his hit men, who hire a mercenary firm to stop Seagal. They chase Seagal and his female Inuit partner across Alaska. With an accent on mechanization vs. nature, Seagal and his partner travel by horseback, doing battle with the mercenaries, who use cars and helicopters.

From the opening credits, Seagal sets up the dichotomy of what's to come: the beauty of nature, as seen through the shots of nature and wildlife, vs. the destructive character of man, as seen through a flaming oil rig spilling thousands of barrels of oil into the environment. Seagal's character of Forrest Taft is the ultimate metaphor throughout the story: the troubleshooter ostensibly hired to put out oil fires turning his unique talents to snuffing out the oil company causing all the problems in the first place.

The better part of the film's last act takes place in the Aegis-1 oil rig, which the company must get on-line immediately or they will lose the land rights to the Inuits. To knock out the plant, Seagal must not only get by a phalanx of FBI antiterrorist agents, but the mercenaries the oil company has hired. With Joan Chen (the daughter of the chief who rescued Seagal) in tow, mostly to look awestruck and astonished at Seagal's derring do, he picks off the mercenaries using explosives, guns and a number of hand-to-hand battles as fires and explosions rage all about.

When the smoke begins to clear, Seagal has not only knocked the oil rig off-line, thereby enabling the Inuits to take back the land, but he has completely destroyed the entire complex! However, the film does not end there, but continues with a tag that finds Seagal addressing a press conference on behalf of the Inuit tribes in particular, and all Native Americans in general. He rails against the conspiracies of oil companies to keep the world dependent on gasoline, and repressing the development of alternative engines to power motor vehicles, both of which contribute to the poisoning of the air and environment. Filmclips of oil spills, dead and dying animals, exhaust fumes billowing up into the atmosphere all underscore Seagal's points as he speaks.

The final shot shows Seagal being accepted by Native Americans as one of their own, a champion of their cause, and harkens back to the film's opening shots of the beauty of nature, bringing the story full circle. In this instance, Seagal and the environmentalists have won, but Seagal's final diatribe reminds us that there are many battles to be fought—and a whole war to win. Judging from the Earth's changing climates and the effects of global warming, it is a battle we are losing.

Seagal not only starred in, but produced and directed *On Deadly Ground*, though the final product did not meet box office expectations,* perhaps because its preachy nature did not generate the word of mouth that less politically motivated stories of his did. It's not that what Seagal is saying is wrong or misleading. Rather, it is probably true in most cases. The rub comes in the audience that Seagal's films appeal to: mostly action fans who look for an extreme measure of violence aimed at an appropriately villainous target, to produce a catharsis of sorts, not overt politicism, from either the left or the right.

Undaunted, Seagal carried on. In *The Glimmer Man* (1996), Seagal plays LAPD detective Jack Cole, who is investigating a serial killer who crucifies his victims. Tagged as "The Family Man," the killer targets Cole's ex-wife, casting the suspicion on him. The plot was more complex than most Seagal films, with a dual storyline running for most of the movie, the story of the serial killer and that of some Russian mobsters doing business with the CIA. In the end, the two threads come together and Seagal solves the case, but not before beating a whole slew of Russian gangsters, busting up a restaurant filled with CIA operatives, and surviving a number of attempts on his life.

Like *Above the Law*, Seagal returns to familiar territory, that of government conspiracy, but the film was a first for the actor in a number of ways. It was the only time (to date) that Seagal was actually investigating a local crime where the perpetrator was unknown to the audience; and secondly, Seagal had a cohort who played a primary role in the film. Keenan Ivory Wayans lends an excellent touch of comic relief as Seagal's partner, and the two could not be more different. Seagal is a Buddhist clad in eastern dress, complete with beads, who can be liberal and at times compassionate toward not only other people but criminals, too. Wayans is more conservative, wears western suits and has a screw-'em-all attitude.

The film mimics the pattern of many action-cop narratives, with an older, wiser cop who knows what he is doing teamed with a younger partner who learns from him. In the beginning, after the two are paired, Wayans wants nothing to do with Seagal, which is a role reversal for the usual loner Seagal, who in this instance is solicitous and friendly. From the outset it becomes obvious that Seagal is clearly more observant and learned: He finds a breast implant in an unknown victim, thereby giving them a way of identifying her; he can speak Chinese and is culturally aware. Seagal takes his partner to an Asian market where he introduces him to herbal medicine; he is also the much better fighter. The differences between partners like these Seagal and Wayans form a cornerstone of detective stories.[17]

---

* *A trend for most theatrically released martial arts films during the decade.*

Seagal places some joint locks on two crooked cops in *Fire Down Below* (Warner Bros., 1997). Seagal's concern for the environment was more evident than his skill in fighting.

Fire Down Below (1997) covered environmental disaster at the hands of big business, with Seagal as an EPA super agent who infiltrates a backwoods Kentucky community to find out who is polluting the water supply. During his investigation, he observes first hand the effects of the pollution, as scores of deformed or malnourished children wither away. The polluter turns out to be the local big shot (Kris Kristofferson), and Seagal has to take on a number of his hillbilly goons before finally busting the big shot in his own casino. Seagal also plays a little guitar at a local dance as he romances the town's outcast, played by Marge Helgenberger. Director Felix Enriquez Alcala filled the cast out with a number of country music legends such as Randy Travis, and likened the film to a classic Western:

> A small town is controlled by big money. And our hero, this outsider from the big city, comes to town and makes the citizens realize what they're doing is wrong. He rallies them and then it is time to fight back.[18]

The Patriot (1999) featured Seagal as a martial artist–scientist–Eastern medical practitioner fighting a bio-chemical plague in the Northwest. The disease, launched by some anti-government militia types, is spread through the air and eventually is beyond control. Soon the entire area is quarantined and it is up to Seagal to find a cure, when he's not beating up militia men. In keeping with Seagal's commitment to nature and his identification with Native Americans, Seagal discovers the cure in flower petals, which the Indians had been using all the time. After no studio wanted to give the independently produced film a theatrical opening, it was picked up by HBO and then went straight to video.[19]

Seagal hit pay dirt again, however, in 2001's *Exit Wounds*, in which he played Orin Boyd, a beat cop in Detroit's toughest precinct. Boyd, a detective, is fired after fending off an attack on the Vice President by—you guessed it—another right wing militia group! He gets his job back, but this time he has to go back to uniform, where he finds that a cabal of crooked cops are dealing drugs. Says director Andrzej Bartkowiak of Boyd:

> Orin Boyd is the ultimate underdog. He may have been demoted from detective to crossing guard, but he's not going to let that break his spirit— he's going to do whatever it takes to bring down the bad guys.[20]

With only his partner to back him, Boyd exposes the corrupt faction, busting up a bar and some other folks in the process. The film racked up over $50,000,000 but the question remained did the audience come to see Seagal or the rap stars like DMX who co-starred with Seagal?

To get the cast in shape for the film, fight coordinator Dion Lam worked with the actors long hours so that nothing looked rehearsed, and the actors were flexible and at the top of their game.[21] Seagal's expertise in Aikido was complemented by Chinese-style kung fu, while a whole group of stunt people focused on the more

Seagal was back on top after a great performance as a beat cop uncovering corruption at the highest levels in Warners' *Exit Wounds* **(2001).**

mundane but expected tasks, such as devising breakaway chairs and exploding windows. The result was an entertaining film, if not a dated one, with Seagal still harkening back to his *Above the Law*–type conspiracies.

An odd discrepancy in star appeal occurred in Seagal's next film, *Tickers* (2002), which featured him with third billing and went straight to video, though it is apparent the producers were hoping for a theatrical release. Tom Sizemore and Dennis Hopper, who usually are supporting characters in "A" films, are placed ahead of Seagal, who is usually the star of his films. Seagal shares equal time with Sizemore, while the screen heroics are skewed mostly toward Seagal, a bomb expert taken to spouting Zen-like sayings at crucial times, like when a bomb is about to blow up. This celluloid schizophrenia may point to the producers attempting to sell the story as a thriller, veering the production away from a strictly martial arts film and toward a more broadly based audience. The film itself is book-ended by massive police sieges of buildings wired with explosives. Seagal is mostly filmed at close range and hardly in full shot, unless it is night and dark, undoubtedly because of his weight gain. He only engages in one or two fights, and these are grainy, chopped edited affairs.

Seagal's 2002 film *Half Past Dead* made it to the theaters but didn't stick around long, despite the fact that, like *Exit Wounds*, it featured a number of rap stars in supporting roles and had an interesting scenario. Seagal plays an FBI agent in deep cover, infiltrating a prison to get leads on a Russian mob leader. In a first, a paramilitary criminal group breaks *in*to the penitentiary to take hostage a criminal scheduled to be executed so that they can find where he hid $200,000,000 in gold stolen from the treasury. Unfortunately for the criminals, they didn't count on having to deal with Seagal or the "good" cons that help him out.

Half Past Dead featured some first-rate stunts, including some fancy driving in between and around big rigs, as well as a skydiving scene lifted straight from James Bond, where Seagal jumps from a helicopter to save a judge who has no parachute. The shootouts were noisy and flashy. For the most part the film veered away from any messages and allowed Seagal to play a man plagued by the death of his wife, who has to carry on regardless.

Seagal's next film, *The Foreigner* (2002), went straight to video with no publicity at all. The story was muddled and bewildering, with hit men killing each other all over the place while buildings explode every so often to make sure that the viewers were awake despite their confusion. Again, like in the other films, Seagal's fight scenes are sparse and choppy. It seems clear that, as he ages, Seagal is steering his career into the realm of thrillers and not martial arts films.

Still, while Seagal's politics ran counter to the conservative trends of the time, he became popular nonetheless and, as noted, his initial films were modest box office successes. In large part this was due to the fact that while his causes were overtly liberal, his characters remained socially conservative, much like Kosugi's. Seagal almost always played a committed family man, sometimes married and a churchgoer, which was unusual for action heroes. Protecting, reuniting and, failing that, avenging the family became an important goal of his characters.

Seagal's appeal also transcended race and ethnicity, much more so than Norris, Kosugi and other martial artists. Blacks and other minorities tended to view Seagal as harder and more streetwise, ready to mete out revenge in a moment's notice, while the narratives of his films tended to feed into an anti–establishment mood. Casting played into this as much as anything else. In *Above the Law* Seagal teamed with black exploitation icon Pam Grier, while *Marked for Death,* in which Seagal takes on a Jamaican mob, features a predominantly black cast. The extent of Seagal's popularity with minority viewers is remarked upon in the gritty urban gangster film *Menace II Society,* wherein one of the teenage killers compares himself to Steven Seagal while preparing for a drive-by shooting.

Another element in Seagal's success was the freshness of his style of martial arts, which relied on overcoming his opponent with twists, holds and locks, or flinging them across the room, something radically different than the kicks and punches seen in most martial arts films.[22] A third factor was Seagal's natural ease before the camera, which translated into hip, wisecracking cops or steely-eyed veteran-types— cool, sometimes cynical, but always trustworthy. Not surprisingly, however, his most successful films have been those where the political content is overshadowed by the action.

Jean-Claude Van Damme

Jean-Claude Van Damme is a Belgian-born martial arts star who skyrocketed to fame in Cannon's *Bloodsport* (1988), a low-budget karate tale that cost a little over a million to make but which grossed over 30 times that amount. Van Damme arrived in the United States when he was 21, hoping to become a movie star. He began studying the martial arts when he was 11, and won his first starring Hollywood role as the Russian villain opposing an American karate student in *No Retreat, No Surrender* (1986).[23]

Best known for his muscular physique and gymnast-like flexibility, Van Damme was a European karate champion who, as legend has it, auditioned for Cannon studio brass by doing splits. Friend and fellow martial artist Michel Qissi, who had come to America with Van Damme, noted that no one at Cannon was really impressed with Van Damme—that is, until they mentioned that he was playing the part of the villain in Arnold Schwarzenegger's film *Predator.*[24] That got the film ball rolling. However, unlike both Norris and Seagal, Van Damme's films have remained largely apolitical, instead featuring him as a man plagued by personal loss and inner demons, while playing up his sex appeal to the ladies.

Bloodsport was a variation of *Enter the Dragon* with Van Damme's character, a military man, going AWOL to fight in the kumite—a secret tournament where martial artists gather from around the world to crown the best among them. The film was of the pure variety, with Van Damme, fighting for his master's honor just as Lee was fighting for his Shaolin Temple, befriended by another fighter and a newspaper reporter, again repeating the trifecta of Lee's masterpiece. *Bloodsport* featured top-notch martial arts sequences, showcasing a number of styles, from tae kwon do to judo, to lima lama and jujutsu. Van Damme's ultimate victory was made more exciting by director Newt Arnold's use of slow motion at crucial times, fanning viewer anticipation.

Bloodsport's success led to a slew of quickly released, low-budget martial arts flicks. The 1989 release *Cyborg* was a post-apocalyptic nightmare in which humanity

武德乗倩
下天覇雄　四震威

JV1

Jean-Claude Van Damme burst onto the scene with his performance in *Bloodsport* (1988), playing American airman and marital artist Frank Dux, who competes in the kumite to honor his dying sensei. Superb fight scenes and an excellent supporting cast enhance a great story.

has been virtually wiped out by a plague. Van Damme, whose family has been slaughtered by renegades, is the "slinger," or mercenary, who agrees to escort a woman cybernetically engineered to save mankind to a medical facility across dangerous terrain. The film featured a number of martial arts sequences, including a running battle (encompassing almost an entire act) which pits the Belgian against a large number of opponents.

The generic oppositions set up by the story almost read like a Western in postmodern reverse. The city is no longer the home of civilization and culture but rather its nightmarish opposite; the countryside is seen as a paradise. Technology is not the hope of the future but rather the cause of the past holocaust. The law is non-existent. The fact that only highly mobile, well-armed, well-trained individuals can survive for any length of time is a Darwinian argument against the forming of any established society.

Below the surface, *Cyborg* seems to be less about martial arts than about the price we pay for progress. Its ultimate message, that in offering up our humanity on the altar of scientific progression we have become a purely dehumanized species, is clearly underscored by the film's last scene: Van Damme, having successfully completed his mission at great personal cost, is offered refuge in the scientific haven of what was once the Center for Disease Control (CDC) in Atlanta. He refuses, preferring to return to the miseries of the only social order he knows, where, as he says, he is needed most. The last shot is not of Van Damme but, tellingly, of the scientists with their cybernetic savior. As the heavy, mechanical door that safely separates them from the squalor of the real world clangs shut, it begs the question of what new horrors they will cook up in trying to save mankind.

Kickboxer (1989) featured Van Damme as the brother of a martial arts champion who trains to avenge his brother's crippling. The action takes place in Thailand, where Van Damme and his brother are for a fight against the unbeatable Tong Po. After his brother is mauled brutally in the ring and put in a wheelchair by the Thai champ, Van Damme wants revenge, and journeys to the jungle to work with a mysterious mentor to get in shape for the revenge match. Of course, complications ensue, such as the rape of the girl Van Damme loves, but the scrappy

Van Damme demonstrates his kicking and stretching ability.

Belgian perseveres and in the end beats Tong Po to a pulp.

While *Kickboxer* offered nothing new, it did showcase Van Damme's physicality and awesome martial arts talents. It also was the first time Van Damme provided a storyline for a film and it became an archetype for certain future films of the genre, those where an underdog hero must fight an unbeatable foe and, to do so, must rely on the advice and training of a wise master. One of the plusses of the film is that it was not overly pretentious, allowing Van Damme to concentrate on what he did best—fight. The film, like *Enter the Ninja*, spawned all manner of sequels, as well as films playing on the "Kickboxer" name, and along with *Bloodsport* paved the way to energizing the martial arts tournament film.[25]

Death Warrant (1990) had Van Damme in the role of a cop who, after the murder of his partner, goes undercover in prison to investigate the mysterious murders of inmates. With the help of a pretty assistant on the outside (posing as Van Damme's wife) and a boy computer genius, Van Damme uncovers an organ theft ring that uses prisoners' body parts. The warden, the guards and the man who recruited Van Damme to go undercover are all in the conspiracy up to their necks, and allow the isolated Belgian to be brutalized by the prisoners. The last act of the movie is almost a total fight as Van Damme battles rampaging prisoners as well as the Sandman, the brutal psychotic who murdered Van Damme's partner.

In *Lionheart* (1990), Van Damme played a Foreign Legionnaire who deserts to help his brother's family after his brother is murdered. He stumbles onto an illegal street fighting racket and wins money by taking on all comers. As he tracks down his brother's killer, he himself is being tracked by the Legion, who don't take kindly to deserters. Though Van Damme manages to win the final match against a brutal opponent, he is eventually caught by the Legionnaires and finds that his partner bet all the money on the other guy.

With the 1991 release *Double Impact*, Van Damme had broken out of the low-budget arena into higher-budgeted studio films. The story highlighted his acting ability: He plays twins separated at birth after their parents are murdered. One is a street hustler in Hong Kong, the other a martial arts instructor in the States. The bodyguard of the parents reunites the brothers, and the three of them track down the killers. The production values on this film were markedly better, and it was the first where Van Damme received not only screenplay credit but was able to choreograph the fight scenes, which were extremely complicated since some involved Van Damme fighting himself.

In *Universal Soldier* (1992) he played an already dead soldier who is kept "alive" artificially as a member of a secret government anti-terrorist unit. Van Damme begins having flashbacks of something in his past, and eventually comes out of his trance. With the help of a reporter, he investigates what happened to him, learning he was killed in Vietnam and reanimated to fight for the government. Hunted, he ultimately squares off against his former partner, played by the massive Dolph Lundgren. The opening sequence, where terrorists have captured a dam, is most memorable as the Universal Soldiers repel down the sides and storm the complex.

Hard Target, a reworking of *The Most Dangerous Game*, followed the next year. Van Damme plays a tough, out-of-work merchant seaman who investigates the disappearance and murder of some homeless people. He teams up with the daughter of one of the victims to discover that a maniac is staging human hunts while the police are walking the picket lines on strike. Van Damme was at his fighting best in this film, notable as Hong Kong director John Woo's American debut.

Released in the same year as *Hard Target*, *Nowhere to Run* (1993) combined a little of *Shane* and *Hondo*, with Van Damme as an escaped con who helps a widow fight off greedy land developers. The story's themes of redemption as well as progress vs. nature seemed at best a weak endorsement of individualism at the expense of the common good. Van Damme's character is given a choice by the local sheriff, to leave before he is caught—but he chooses to stay and help the widow save her farm. Yet his sacrifice is a dubious one: the widow's farm in this rural community stands in the way of a billion dollar building project that stands to enrich everyone. As Van Damme is carted away back to prison, the viewer can't help but ponder what happens to the scores of other people who lose out because of one person's stubbornness.

Street Fighter (1994), based on a videogame, bombed at the box office. It was an ill-conceived venture that at times seemed like an over-the-top parody, and just plain made Van Damme, who played Colonel William Guile, look silly. The opening credits revealed problems from the beginning: five different editors were used, which may account for the choppy, almost incoherent storyline. Guile is the commander of the "AN," which are trying to free a Southeast Asian country from the grip of Bison, the brutal general and egomaniacal psychopath who rules with an iron fist. A mix of Saddam Hussein and Darth Vader, the general is holding relief workers for ransom.

From this point, the plot deteriorates markedly. Three groups are angling for the general: Guile; two adventurers recruited by Guile; and a news crew headed by a karate-kicking reporter and her two assistants, a sumo and a boxer. Raul Julia, in his last role, plays the general, and clearly deserved a much better part to be remembered by. As the groups target Bison, he in turn is developing a super creature—a perfect fighting machine that can help him control the world.

Van Damme does little fighting in the first half of the film, leaving the fisticuffs to the other folks. Because the film was based on the popular video game of the same name, lip service was paid early in the film to the fighting aspect by showing no-holds-barred cage matches run by the vile Sugat, a gunrunner in league with the general. When Guile and his troops attack Bison, the real fireworks begin, and the film actually begins to look like the videogame. Guile busts into the fortress and battles with the super creature, whom it turns out was his best friend before Bison captured him. The plucky news reporter battles Bison, while the sumo fights a strongman. In all the cases, the dress of the combatants, from Guile on down, resemble somewhat those shown in the video game.

In the end, the troops arrive, both sides do battle and, with explosions everywhere, Guile and Bison face off. However, Raul Julia, who was suffering from cancer at the time, is hardly a match for Van Damme, so (like the final battle in Seagal's *Out for Justice*) the results are disappointing, despite the use of a double in the kicking scenes. However, Bison does possess the power of electro-magnetism, or some such nonsense, which he shoots at Guile to disable him, much the way the Emperor disables Luke Skywalker in *Return of the Jedi*.

There is little positive that can be said about *Street Fighter* except that Ming Na, who played the reporter, looked good in traditional Chinese dress, and that perhaps Van Damme was beginning to get down the finer aspects of acting by understanding and playing along with the goofiness of the film. The fact that so much money could be spent for such a poor product bolstered many critics' opinions that Van Damme's best movies were made on the cheap. Whatever the case, the fight scenes were poor and, without a proper villain for Van Damme to fight, seemed boring.

Time Cop (1994), made the same year, featured Van Damme as a special agent, haunted by his wife's murder, who patrols the past to prevent criminals from going back and changing history. He is able to thwart the politician who is out to control the time control device and actually save his wife, though not before being betrayed by a fellow agent. Like *Street Fighter*, the film was not a hit, and began the decline of Van Damme as a major box office draw.

Sudden Death (1995) was a *Die Hard*–style thriller that follows stressed out fireman Van Damme as he tries to save the Vice President of the United States from terrorists who capture him at a hockey game. While the martial arts sequences, as in almost all of Van Damme's films, were excellent, the story was weakened not only by the fact that fans were coming and going into the stadium, thereby undercutting the urgency of Van Damme's heroics, but that no one but Van Damme knew what was going on. Complicating things for Van Damme was his son, who is in the arena watching the game.

Van Damme bounced back artistically with *The Quest* (1996), which led to a lawsuit by Frank Dux, the man Van Damme played in *Bloodsport*, who says he co-wrote the story for the film.[26] Dux lost the lawsuit, and the film didn't do as well as expected, but it was a major step for Van Damme, who ended up pulling dual duties of star and director. It was Van Damme's first time behind the camera, and the film was sweeping and solid and at times exciting, with pirate battles, police chases and plenty of fights.

Van Damme plays Chris, a Fagin-like character who operates a criminal gang using street urchins in 1925 New York City. After a big score against the mob, he and the children are targeted and he must leave New York. Stowing away on a Turkish steamer, he is captured and forced into slavery. He is then captured by the pirate Dobbs, played royally by Roger Moore, and turned over to Thai kick boxers, who train him to be one of them. He becomes a fighter, and is then ransomed back by Dobbs, who wants to use Chris to gain entry into a fabulous tournament of all the great fighters in the world, so that he can steal the treasure promised to the victor.

The film is a satisfying adventure, in part because it faithfully followed the Campbellian "hero quest" almost to the letter, and is worth briefly comparing to *On Deadly Ground*, fellow martial arts star Steven Seagal's directorial debut, which also stuck closely to the same type of hero quest. Campbell, a noted mythologist and author, is best known for his book *The Hero with a Thousand Faces*, which traced and examined universal myths present throughout the world's cultures, as well as for the influence he exerted on filmmakers like George Lucas and his *Star Wars* films.

In the first stage of Campbell's quest, "The Call," the hero finds himself on the brink of enormous change and embarks on a great adventure. For Chris, life is unfulfilling and at times dangerous. He is a street thief whose only redeeming feature is that he is loyal to his kids. Most of the time the hero answers the call, but sometimes, and in Chris' case, he blunders into it. Such blunders can expose an unknown or unrevealed world to the blunderer, and bring him face to face with forces that are not rightly identified. Campbell notes, "The blunder may amount to the opening of a destiny."[27] When the mob and police come after him, Chris has no alternative but to run, and it is by mere chance that he is able to stow away on the steamer. Yet, this is the first step into his becoming a new man.

Forrest Taft, Seagal's character in *On Deadly Ground*, receives the call from his friend Hugh, the oil rig foreman, who points out that the oil company is using inferior products and that's what's causing the fires and pollution. Forrest rejects the call, noting that his pay of $350,000 is enough to make him the whore that Hugh calls him. So where Chris falls into his call, Forrest initially rejects his. Only later, when Hugh approaches him again, does Forrest investigate and accept the task ahead of him.

"The Other" is a figure who possesses the exact opposite characteristics of the hero. He can be friend or foe or, like the pirate Dobbs, who is Chris' other, a little of both. Dobbs is gregarious and scheming and, while likable, is amoral and at times a killer. Chris is quiet and loyal, and only uses violence to protect himself. Through the experience of life, both men have become thieves, but it is Chris who learns from Dobbs' lesson to strive for something more.

Forrest's other is Michael Jennings, a one-time pal who owns the oil company that Forrest works for. He has utterly no redeeming values, which contrasts him to

Forrest, who cares for a lot of things and is willing to stand up for them. However, a glimpse of Jennings' dark side can be seen in Forrest, particularly in the violence he so readily uses to solve problems. When faced with the choice of going to the authorities and media, as Masu, Forrest's Inuit partner suggests, Forrest declines, preferring to mete out the justice himself. Unlike Chris, Forrest has not learned anything from his other and in fact may now be even more violent.

Van Damme did double duty as director and star of *The Quest* (Universal, 1996).

"The Journey" is the difficult and often hazardous enterprise the hero must undertake to achieve his goal. In this instance, Chris survives slavery, pirates and the Thai kick boxers, then allies himself with Dobbs to steal the treasure. He wants to return to America, but not empty-handed. His excursion takes them through jungles and deserts, on elephant and horse, until they arrive in Tibet. Once there, Chris risks life and limb to face the best fighters in the world.

Forrest's journey is also one of survival. He barely escapes the explosives-rigged oil substation that Jennings uses to get rid of him. Once back in good health, he takes to the road to return to the oil town where his weapons are. Along the way he must fight scores of Jennings' hired goons, until he can unleash his pen-up rage on the Aegis–1 oil rig, and Jennings himself.

"Helpers" are those who guide the hero through his quest and help him along the way. The assistance can be supernatural, as when Chris prays to the Buddha for help, or it can be material. Maxie, the heavyweight champion of the world, relinquishes his belt and invitation to the tournament to Chris because he has discovered that Chris is the better fighter. He takes it upon himself to help train Chris for the grueling fights that are ahead of him.

Inuit Chief Silook is Forrest's helper. He has a vision that says Forrest will be the "bear" which stands up to those who would destroy the land. He leads Forrest through a mystic vision, which purifies him and refines his intent. Unlike Chris, whose help comes physically, Forrest's assistance is purely spiritual. Forrest needs no training—he is already a killing machine. What he needs is the mystical depth of real purpose.

A treasure awaits the man who wins the tournament that Chris will fight in— a solid gold dragon. But the "Treasure" aspect of the hero quest can be material, as it is here, or spiritual, such as great knowledge or the like. Chris has come to get the treasure, but not by winning it. Yet in the midst of the fighting, he has a change of heart. This is the "Transformation"—the stage where the heroes life is "transfigured by the quest they have undertaken and completed.[28] For Chris, the experiences he has gone through have made him a different person, one who sees the world through new eyes. Though he wins the tournament, he does not receive the golden dragon, having given it up to save Dobbs, who tried to steal it without Chris.

There is no tangible treasure associated with Forrest's quest, no gold or money. But there is the chance to stop the oil company and save the land for the Inuits, which could be considered a higher or more noble cause. Forrest's transformation comes when he changes from "oil company whore" to devoted environmentalist and champion of Native Americans. He and Chris share the same fate: to become different, better persons and bring their knowledge back to share with the world.

As noted previously, neither *On Deadly Ground* or *The Quest* were box office successes, yet though they shared a similar narrative pattern, Seagal's film was heavily message-laden. Van Damme's film was a simple movie that mixed entertainment with the notion that people can change, which in the end made it a more pleasurable story that people could identify with. In an interview with the *Toronto Sun*, Van Damme stated that he wanted Oliver Stone to direct the movie, but Stone suggested that Van Damme should

Van Damme plays Alain Moreau, a French police officer investigating the murder of a twin brother he never knew, in Columbia Pictures' *Maximum Risk* (1996).

do it himself. Van Damme held out the hope that future directorial efforts would result in "more deep and less adventuresome movies."[29] To this point it hasn't happened.

Maximum Risk (1996) followed *The Quest* and harkened back to *Double Impact*, Van Damme's first major film, where the Belgian played twin brothers. In this story, Van Damme is a former French Army sniper turned police officer who discovers that he had a twin brother he never knew, whom his mother abandoned as a baby. The brother, raised as a Russian in America, was involved with their mob, but somehow found out about his French sibling. In the opening sequence, the Russian brother is killed in France while trying to escape from the FBI. Van Damme spends the rest of the film trying to unravel the who's and why's of his brother's murder, not to mention learn a little about him.

What Van Damme finds is a mixed bag: a boy who was abandoned to live on the streets in his teens; a gangster, completely submerged in the Russian Mafia but desperately wanting out; and a man who was brave enough to gather evidence to not only shut down the mob, but bring to justice the FBI agents on the mob's payroll. He also finds his brother's attractive girlfriend (Natasha Henstridge), who was helping the brother to bring down the Mafia.

To get to the truth, Van Damme becomes his brother and is hunted every step of the way, from a Russian nightclub, where he fights off a group of Mafia thugs in an alley brawl, to a stunning nighttime chase across New York rooftops, where fists, feet and bullets fly. Van Damme is in top fighting form, and the film features a number of highlights, mostly comic or downright bizarre, including a blabber-mouth cab driver who tags along to help Van Damme; an accordion player belting out tunes in a steam room; and a knock-down, drag-out brawl in the sauna between Van Damme and the Russian's top assassin, both men clad only in towels!

Double Team (1997) was a complete turnaround from *Maximum Risk* but, like the latter, spared no expense, with Van Damme as a secret agent considered "soft" by his employers, in this instance the CIA, who is sent into forced retirement on an island populated by other retired agents. Of course Van Damme promptly escapes and is on the trail of the master terrorist who has kidnapped his wife and baby. The film features a James Bond–like opening with futuristic vehicles and machine gun–toting motorcycle riders, along with an odd group of pairings that lent new meaning to the title word "Double": Basketball bad boy Dennis Rodman as Van Damme's sometime partner; a wild shootout pitting the various intelligence agencies in the world against one another; Van Damme holding off a rampaging tiger; and Van Damme pitted against Mickey Roarke in a violent showdown in a coliseum (reminiscent of Bruce Lee and Chuck Norris getting it on in *Return of the Dragon*).

In 1998, Van Damme returned to Hong Kong and re-teamed with *Double Team* director Hark Tsui for *Knock Off*, a tortuous tale that at times made little sense, but which was almost redeemed by Tsui's high speed, frenetic direction and Van Damme's high-flying martial arts. The story, what there was, concerned the "king" of the Hong Kong "knock offs" Marcus Ray, played by Van Damme. ("Knock offs" are imitations of recognized brands of clothing, watches and the like.)

Ray has finally gone legit, partnered up with comic relief Rob Schneider, but someone has knocked off the jeans that Ray and his company are making, which leads to a clash with the Russian Mafia, who have developed something called nanobombs, battery-sized explosives they intend to use in the United States. The CIA moves in and uses Ray to break up the plot, yet Ray finds they are in the scheme with the Russians up to their eyeballs. The film is book-ended by breathtaking sequences. The opening finds Hong Kong police chasing the Russians through the harbor in speedboats, while the finale pits Van Damme against the Russians and CIA on a cargo ship steaming out of the bay. Add to the mix the fact that Hong Kong is about to be turned back over to China by Britain and you have an explosive brew.

Van Damme appears prematurely aged in this film, and while his martial arts prowess certainly had not diminished, featuring him as a raconteur was a bit of a stretch. At times he appears flat and tired, hardly the playboy he is supposed to be. Arguably the best performances were turned in by Schneider, whose acerbic observations punctuated the film, and Lela Rochon as the sexy, savvy woman who is not what she first appears to be. Paul Sorvino, who played Harry, the CIA station chief, spent most of his time grimacing.

In many ways this film was a Jackie Chan movie without Chan: a story that did not take itself too seriously; a hesitant, unlikely hero; large opening and closing set pieces followed by a series of high-energy sequences showcasing the director's ability and the star's physicality; and lots of gags and humor. *Knock Off* was not a hit, but with its weak plot it was surely not going to get the word-of-mouth business so important to films like these.

Van Damme bounced back with 1999's *Desert Heat*, a tongue-in-cheek version of Clint Eastwood's *A Fistful of Dollars* set in modern times. Van Damme stars as Eddie Lomax, a decorated military veteran who is wracked with guilt from all the killing he has done. He rides a 1949 Indian motorcycle out to the desert, where he intends to present it as a gift for his Native American buddy, before committing suicide. However, before he can do all that, he is beaten and left for dead by the Hogan clan, white trash who control a small town. Van Damme, saved by his buddy who finds him in the desert, is determined to recover the motorcycle.

Desert Heat was one of Van Damme's best performances and recalled the innocent humor of *Bloodsport*. Sporting a scraggly beard, a cowboy hat and .45 pistol, Van Damme sets out to divide and conquer the Hogans and their fair weather partners The Heathens, a biker gang who sell the Hogan's methamphetamine. Like "The Man with No Name," Van Damme first plays one side off the other until the two groups almost blow each other to smithereens. When they finally realize they've been duped and come together to hunt Van Damme, he and the town are ready for them.

Desert Heat is filled with odd and eccentric characters, such as the elderly Japanese man waiting for a wife who left years ago; an old man who needs oxygen but smokes like a chimney; the half-senile owner of the local cafe; a snake-charming religious motel owner fascinated by both the Lord and sex, although not necessarily in that order; two women from Cleveland who Van Damme "services"; and of course the Indian, Van Damme's buddy who lives in a shack with a coyote for company. Combine these characters with the various white trash and you have a film as funny as it is deadly, and as likable a hero as Van Damme has ever played.

Unfortunately, the film went direct-to-video, which is a shame, because it showcased the kind of breezy, tormented but lovable hero that Van Damme plays so well. The martial arts sequences are fewer than in most of his movies, but they are done well. In the first, when he is left for dead, he tries to take on the Hogans while drunk, and is beaten to a pulp. Of interest here is watching Van Damme purposefully be bad, which is harder than it looks. He later fights a couple of in-breds running a gun store as well as taking on the Hogans' leader in the film's final fight, where his patented spin kick is put to good use.

Universal Soldier: The Return (1999) was released the same year as *Desert Heat* and did go to theaters, but it was a major disappointment. Van Damme reprises his role as Luc Devereaux, one of the original Universal Soldiers from the initial experimental program who now works for the government improving the *new* Universal Soldiers program. (Universal Soldiers are dead military men whom the government reanimates, improves upon, and then turns loose to fight terrorists and other threats to the United States.)

Unfortunately for Devereaux, and everyone else involved, the military decides to cut the program, citing costs, but SETH, the supercomputer which helps run the program and feeds the Universal Soldiers their orders, finds out. Not wishing to be terminated, it kills the program's mentor and takes control of all the Universal Soldiers, prompting Van Damme to swing into action to stop it, which turns out to be damn near impossible since the Universal Soldiers are already dead.

Universal Soldier: The Return was more or less an amalgam of better films like *2001: A Space Odyssey* and *The Terminator*. SETH is merely HAL 9000 in the pumped-up body of Michael Jai White while the Universal Soldiers, almost impossible to defeat, are killed only to get back up again. Professional wrestler Bill Goldberg, star of the now defunct WCW and now one of the top WWE ring warriors, plays one of the Universal Soldiers who fights Van Damme continually, coming back to life over and over again. As such, Van Damme's fight scenes are without any urgency or excitement, considering the "things" he is fighting are stronger, faster and feel no pain.

Aside from Van Damme's fights, which are many and mostly futile—witness SETH throwing the Belgian through countless plate glass windows—the film raises moral questions that its authors probably never considered: Is a regenerated life really sentient? And if we have the technology to reanimate the dead and make them normal like Luc, why not do that? By developing the technology to reanimate life, have we not conquered our own mortality and placed our selves in the position of God? And by not using such power to restore the person to what he was, like Luc was restored, are we not fated, like Dr. Frankenstein, to see our own creations come back to destroy us?

The film made no attempt to address these issues, instead concentrating on explosions, shootouts and fights. A brawl in a high-class strip bar with naked women everywhere seems to be an afterthought that was added in as filler. (The film only runs 82 minutes, which is quite short for a theatrical release.) Considering that the original *Universal Soldier* was not an overwhelming success, one wonders why a sequel was even contemplated, let alone produced. *Universal Soldier: The Return* quickly folded. To date, none of Van Damme's subsequent films has rekindled his box office drawing power.

Lorenzo Lamas

Lorenzo Lamas came from an acting family. His father was actor Fernando Lamas, his mom was actress-model Arlene Dahl and he was the stepson of musical swimming star Esther Williams.[30] He is an actor with a background in the martial arts who segued from musical films like *Grease* (1978) and television shows like *Falcon Crest* into action-packed, martial arts–flavored films at the end of the decade. In *SnakeEater* (1989), Lamas plays Soldier Kelly, a veteran of a special marine outfit called Snake Eaters, men trained to handle any situation, the more violently the better. *SnakeEater* offered a little martial arts, mostly Lamas punching and flipping opponents, and a lot of action, not to mention some broad humor. The sequels that followed, *SnakeEater II: Drug Buster* (1990) and *SnakeEater III: His Law* (1992), displayed Lamas' abilities in martial arts, but future films would better define him as a martial arts hero.

Like Norris, Lamas' characters are often loners who buck the system, and they are proficient with all manner of weapons, particularly edged ones, a la Kosugi. Like Seagal, they are often anti-authority, even when they are law enforcement officers. Soldier Kelly continually gets suspended from his department for bucking his bosses. Andrew Barrett in *The Swordsman* (1993) is continually on the wrong side of his NYPD superiors. Unlike most of his martial arts cinema peers, Lamas has a talent for broad humor, whether it be sight gags or flip sayings.

Lamas' long hair and penchant for riding Harleys establishes his characters with a certain "outlaw" persona, and while he could be the one hunting the criminals, as in *SnakeEater II*, where he tangles with drug dealers and their gangs of killers, he could just as easily be the hunted one, as in the television series *Renegade*, in which he played Reno Raines, a wrongly accused cop on the run for murder. Two films ideally showcase the dimensions of the Lamas' "character." In Image Organization's *Bounty Trackers* (1993), bounty hunter Jonathan Damone operates outside the limits of the law. Not a cop and not a civilian, he forever straddles the middle zone, continually meeting hostility from all sides.

In Vidmark's *Night of the Warrior* (1991), Miles Keane is an enigmatic bar owner who just wants to be left alone

Lorenzo Lamas starred in the syndicated television series *Renegade*, about a wrongly accused cop on the run. His long hair and penchant for motorcycles enhanced his bad boy image, though for the most part he has played heroes.

to live his life in peace. While he rides a Harley and fights in illegal no-holds-barred matches to help pay the bills, he is also a photographer with a sensitive side. Where the former film was shot with bright light and colors to emphasize Damone's breezy nature, the latter film was lensed mostly at night, using washed-out colors to convey the sense of dread and depression of Kean's world, while linking the realm of fine art (music, dance, photography) to the physical splendor of the fighting arts.

During the early part of the decade, Lamas hit his stride, with not only his television series but a slew of exceptionally well-choreographed martial arts films. *Final Round* (1993) was another updated version of *The Most Dangerous Game*, with Lamas as a martial artist–biker trapped in a warehouse complex, hunted by mercenary killers while bettors from all over the world place wages on the outcome. When Lamas uses his fighting abilities to turn the tables on his stalkers and becomes a betting favorite, the firm holding the event becomes desperate and pulls out all the stops to kill him. The type of violence featured herein was the usual good guy vs. bad guy stuff, with the lines clearly drawn. But midway through the film, Lamas finds that his love interest has betrayed him and uses force against her. Such a display is unsettling but also provocative: Is one type of violence inherently better, or more justified, than another, particularly when both are clearly provoked?

The Swordsman, a metaphysical tale about reincarnation and Alexander the Great, allowed Lamas to demonstrate his abilities with edged weapons. As detective Andrew Barrett, Lamas is investigating a number of mysterious deaths, all by sword. As he gets deeper into the case, he finds that all the murdered men have all competed in death matches involving swordplay. Lamas enters into the matches hoping to bust up the ring behind them, all the while trying to deal with an ESP dream phenomena that has been plaguing him. The story is more complicated than most films of this nature and runs a dual trajectory: As Lamas unwinds the mystery of the death matches, he also learns the meaning of his dreams and his ultimate destiny.

Gladiator Cop (1994) finds Barrett re-investigating the swordplay murders and once again taken off the case by his superiors. The film's muddled plot is about a reincarnated general who wants revenge on Barrett for killing him some 2,000 years before. The confusion results from the producers trying patch a movie around out takes of Lamas from the first film. However, the matches are excellent, better than in the *The Swordsman*, with the fighters combining kicking and punching to accentuate their swordplay prowess.

One of the most unusual films put out by Lamas was *Final Impact* (1992), which was as much a character study as it was a martial arts film. Lamas plays Nick Taylor, a former light heavyweight kickboxing champion who now owns a nightclub. Nick lost not only his wife but his title a few years before to Jake, who beat him mercilessly. When Jake meets Danny, an aspiring kick boxer with tons of talent and speed, he trains the young man hoping to get vengeance against Jake through Danny.

Measured through Danny's eyes, Nick is but a shadow of his old self. Where Nick was once proud, patient, talented and in shape, a man who valued self respect, he is now impulsive, jaded, untrustworthy and a chain smoker who drowns himself in booze and self-pity. In short, Nick's a loser who can't get over the beating he took at the hands of Jake. Danny idealizes Nick, and compared to the young man, who came from a poor background, Nick has it made: successful business; fantastic house with a pool; and a great girlfriend who loves him.

Time and again Nick is his own worst enemy, first using Danny to get to Jake, which leads to their ill-fated trip to Vegas for the championship tournament; getting drunk and cheating on his girlfriend Maggie with a Vegas whore, which prompts Maggie to leave him; and insulting his ex-wife and Jake's current wife, which results in an illegal showdown between the two men in Las Vegas' famous neon graveyard. Only on his deathbed in the hospital does Nick understand what he has become and realize that he must change—only then it is too late. Nick's death spurs Danny to beat Jake and win the championship, but he is sure not to repeat the same mistakes as the man he once idolized.

Final Impact succeeded on a number of levels where lesser martial arts films had not. The fighting sequences were fine but they never overshadowed the relationship between Nick, Maggie and Danny, nor did they ever appear "staged," or placed in the story merely for the sake of displaying some action. In portraying a character like Nick, who not only loses in the ring but in his grudge match against Jake, Lamas conveyed a maturity that many martial arts film stars could not. Few if any could imagine Steven Segal or Chuck Norris losing a fight. Lamas appeared comfortable with the character and the story, and his performance showed it.

The year 1994 was a busy one for Lamas, who completed four films, one of which he directed (*CIA II: Target Alexa*). In *Blood for Blood*, Lamas plays John Kang, an LAPD cop assigned to work youth services. When the Russian and Cambodian Mafias go to war, Kang is pressed into service because he speaks Cambodian. As he monitors a clandestine meeting of Mafia leaders, translating for his partners, the Cambodians discover that one of their own is a police informer and kill him. Kang and the other cops bust in on the meeting, killing a number of the gang members, but the leader and his henchmen get away. The Cambodians call a truce with the Russians so they can target Kang and the other cops in the unit for revenge, providing the meaning of the film's title.

Like his character Andrew in *The Swordsman*, Lamas again plays a cop with extra sensory perception, in this case being able to sense things through dreams. His first real taste of police work comes when he and the team shoot it out with the Cambodians. That same night, as he sleeps, he visualizes the revenge plans being laid against them, only he is slow to figure out the meaning of the dream. Later, after the Cambodians have killed everyone in the unit but Kang and his partner Paddy, the two men and their families are moved to a hotel and put under police protection. Kang suddenly wakes up in the middle of the night and knows that Paddy is dead. He gives his wife his gun to protect herself and then confronts the mysterious hit man.

In some ways, *Blood for Blood* represents the country's hardening feeling toward immigration, legal or otherwise. Both the Cambodians and the Russians are transplants, having immigrated here from their respective countries, and both have brought with them the scourge of crime. Stereotypes of both groups are presented: The Cambodians say the Russians have no honor or decency and that their personal hygiene is less than adequate. Kang makes a similar observation when he confronts the Russian mob boss at a soccer field. The Russians feel the Cambodians are inferior. Even the police chief gets into the act, labeling the Cambodians "barbarians" after they kill Paddy.

The one thing both groups have in common is that they are using America to profit from their illegal activities. The Russians view the Americans as a people who can be bribed or bought to do anything; the Cambodians don't look at America as a home, just as a place to continue their corrupting behavior. In one scene, a Cambodian master tells Kang that a secret warrior society to which he, Kang, belongs often sent their members abroad in the event they would one day be needed to come back and save "our country," meaning Cambodia. There is certainly no uncertainty as to where this character's loyalty lies.

Clearly neither group has any regard for America, except as a place where the laws are easily broken because of our "lax" system. When Kang and his team are preparing to spy on the Cambodian meeting, one of the team seems more concerned with whether they have a court order to do what they are assigned to do than the dangers inherent in the mission. After the raid, when Kang goes to question the Russian boss, the man demands to know if Kang has a warrant, certainly inflammatory behavior by someone who spent their whole life in a totalitarian society. In fact, it becomes quite clear that the police are ineffective. Not only can't they bust the respective Mafias, they can't even protect themselves. The only way to deal with such a plague is to take the law into one's own hands, which is precisely what Kang does. He ambushes the two gangs when they have a meeting and blows them all away, including dispatching the mysterious Cambodian hit man in a slam-bam affair involving swords, ropes and one very sharp cape. The film ends with Lamas rescuing his family and promising them a vacation. Whether he will go back to the calm of youth services or stay with the action of the organized crime detail remains ambiguous.

Lamas continued his winning ways with 1995's *Bad Blood*, a hard-hitting tale of two brothers, one woman and a whole lot of trouble. Lamas plays Travis, an ex-cop who was imprisoned after destroying evidence that would have put his brother John away for life. While Travis was in prison, John repaid his brother's magnanimity by running off with his girlfriend Rhonda. Travis stays apart from his father and brother now, working as welder–tow truck driver. When John gets involved in a money-laundering operation, then skims millions off the top, the cartel comes after him, and Travis has to decide whether to help his little brother one more time.

Bad Blood is a good example of character contrast. Travis is a hard worker, honest and blue collar at heart. John likes easy money, is a shyster with a perpetual scheme and pretends to have a million even if he doesn't have a dime in his pocket. Travis threw away his career and livelihood to save his brother, and now lives in an old trailer with no air conditioning. John spends little time dwelling on his brother's sacrifice, instead living the highlife on dirty money. Even their dress is radically different. Travis wears jeans, T-shirts and boots. John wears sport suits and leisure attire fitted for the country club. Besides being brothers, the two men have little in common, save for Rhonda.

Opposing Travis and John are Mr. Chang, a.k.a. "Buddha," a sadistic fireplug of a man who heads a merciless crew of hired killers. Chang is an indiscriminate murderer, targeting children and adults alike. Travis takes the fight to Chang, excelling with both his fists and feet in a number of encounters with Chang's men, a good many of whom represent themselves as martial artists. In the grand finale, Travis beards the lion in his den and attacks Chang at his warehouse, unleashing a massive display of firepower to rescue John and Rhonda.

Bad Blood broke no new ground but, like Lamas' previous outings, it continued to showcase his intense physical prowess and easygoing nature. Like in many films of this sort, women are shown to be duplicitous and untrustworthy. Rhonda dumped Travis when he was in prison, and when Travis returns to help John, she attempts to get back with him behind John's back. Lindy, Travis's girlfriend, is so jealous that she follows him to his family's house, where she runs into Chang and has to help him find Travis in order to save her own skin.

Mask of Death (1996) was an important film for Lamas as it marked a turning point in his career. Not only did the story accent character, but it shied away from overt martial arts and pointed Lamas in the direction of more conventional heroes. Lamas plays McKenna, a detective whose wife is murdered by a mobster on the run from the FBI. The mobster is attempting to sell a top secret micro chip to the Russian Mafia when the FBI tries to bust them. Lamas, who is also shot in the raid, bears an uncanny resemblance to the Russian's go-between Mason, and the FBI convinces Lamas to undergo plastic surgery to take the deceased Mason's place.

Lamas undertakes only one serious fight in the entire film, most appropriately in a strip bar, which seems to be a conventional place for these types of showdowns.

He also embarks upon a quick one-two in a tattoo shop, convincing the proprietor that it would be best to cooperate with him. The rest of the action is of the shoot-'em-up variety, with car chases, explosions and, of course, gunplay. McKenna's partner on the force, Cass, gets in a number of licks herself as the mobster comes after her, believing she was the one who fingered them for the FBI raid. Ironically, it is Cass' face that gets continually bruised and shattered as the story wears on, while McKenna-Mason's mug remains pristine and handsome.

The character that McKenna becomes to catch the mobster was a pathological murderer. With the FBI's encouragement, and his own driving need for revenge, McKenna slowly becomes Mason, transforming from a caring cop to relentless killer. When McKenna-Mason finally meets the mobster to arrange the sale of the microchip, the police bust in on them and McKenna actually shoots one in the heat of battle. Later, when the mobster discovers that his cousin is the one who fingered him to the FBI, the mobster tortures him first, then gives McKenna the gun to kill him. Though McKenna hesitates, he finally pumps the informer full of rounds.

Having crossed the line of no return, McKenna "becomes" Mason and his face is indeed a mask of death. Forced to drive around with the mobster's hit men, McKenna figures out a way to get loose and subsequently picks a fight with a local gang that almost gets all of them (not to mention a load of innocent people) killed in a diner. McKenna takes the remaining hit man and strings him up high over a building under construction. When the man doesn't answer the questions to McKenna's liking, he cuts the rope holding the man up. When he and Cass are finally reunited, he tells her that he has already gone too far to come back, and warns her that he will kill her if he has to. It is clear that the only thing that matters to McKenna is killing the mobster who murdered his wife.

The story ends with "Mason" being uncovered as McKenna. With the mask of death finally removed from him, McKenna returns to his old self, saving his partner and wiping out the mobster and his associates. As he and Cass walk off, it is apparent that he is ready to become a cop again, but considering the amount of murder and mayhem he has already committed, one has to ask, is he fit?

In *The Rage* (1997), Lamas completely disregards his martial arts persona and immerses himself in the role of a tortured FBI agent who smokes too much and trusts too little, although there may be good reason. Nick Travis is a psychological profiler up to his chin in dead bodies as he tracks a roving band of serial rapists–killers roaming the countryside. When a rival at the Bureau, played by a very devious Roy Scheider, partners him with an untested agent, Nick is sure that Scheider is out to botch his investigation and get him fired.

While *The Rage* had all the earmarks of a big-budget film, with a superb supporting cast including Gary Busey and David Carradine in a cameo, the story was confusing at times as the ostensible storyline, that of former military men turned militia men turned serial killers, clashed with the theme of government duplicity and cover-up, with the latter being the more fascinating topic; this was surely not the way it was planned. At the time the film was shot, Ruby Ridge and Waco were in the news, as was the involvement of the FBI in covering up their duplicitous actions in the shootouts there. (Both disasters are mentioned by Lamas in the film.) However, a scenario of 12 psych ward patients from a VA hospital coming together under their old leader and allowing him to rape and murder on the way to some kind of revolutionary action was preposterous at best.

Where the film did excel is examining the way government entities like the FBI not only corrupt local investigations with their political maneuvering, but how the blame game becomes a national pastime in the ranks of government service. Scheider, Lamas' superior, wants Lamas out of the Bureau because he blames him for ruining his career by not playing along after a team of agents, under Scheider's command, botched a hostage incident, which Scheider then said was Nick's mistake. It becomes apparent that whenever federal agents mess up, culpability is passed around to everyone but the person responsible. When Nick and his partner at the time are chasing one of the militia men, the partner shoots after Nick tells him not to, and kills the man, whom the police needed alive. When the local sheriff becomes irate, the agent responsible blames Nick for not knowing how to drive right.

As the investigation progresses, and nothing seems to get done, Scheider arrests Nick's new partner after a raid on the militia doesn't pan out and some innocent people sustain minor injuries. He tells Nick that the Bureau has to hold someone responsible. Nick busts her out (after a pathetic fight with Scheider which Nick should have easily won) and they go on the run, eventually solving the case, but not before more blame is passed around and Nick has to work his way around criminal charges filed by Scheider. The final shootout seems almost anti-climactic as it really makes no sense, but it is well staged and Lamas does get his man.

By 1998's *Good Cop Bad Cop*, Lamas seemed to have completely forgone his earlier ass-kicking image to concentrate on regular action films, leaving most of his martial arts moves at home. Lamas plays Jake, a retired San Diego cop who is summoned out of retirement to track down a wealthy man taken hostage by a drug lord south of the border. Accompanied by the wealthy man's young wife, Jake hunts both sides of the border, eventually pinpointing a likely location where the man is being held.

The film's title refers in part to the lengths that Jake and other will go to do their duty. When Jake was/is on the U.S. side of the border, he acts as the proverbial good cop, following the law and honoring the rights of people he comes into contact with. However, whenever he crosses onto the Mexican side, rules and rights go out the door, and Jake becomes as ruthless as the people he is dealing with. In fact, the drug lord that Jake is after was at one time a San Diego cop working with Jake in a secret task force on the Mexican side of the border. The task force was assembled with the Mexican police because U.S. laws were too restrictive and did not allow the police the authority they needed to act, which was not the case in Mexico.

Good Cop Bad Cop reinforces the traditional notion that south-of-the-border law enforcement is non-existent, and that Mexican cops are either on the take of drug cartels or so woefully trained and paid as to be completely useless. The second half of that notion, that overwhelming brute force on the part of Americans is what is needed to solve the drug smuggling–dealing problem, is also advocated, with Lamas and a few honest Mexican cops destroying the drug lord's organization. However, the idea of stopping *demand* along with supply is never touched upon, not here in this film nor others like it, as the notion of using devastating power against the middle class and American elite who casually use cocaine and other drugs would be unthinkable.

Like Norris, Van Damme and the others, Lamas slowed his filmmaking output as the decade wore on. He starred in two ill-fated television series after *Renegade*: *Air America* (1998) and *The Immortal* (2000), a *Highlander*-like show which featured him as an immortal martial artist fighting for good. However, later films have continued to be of the thriller or straight action variety, although Lamas still gets his kicks and chops in when necessary.

Brandon Lee

Brandon Lee, like his father Bruce, had infinite possibilities in both the world of martial arts and film. Ironically, his first film involved the TV series his father originally

Brandon Lee, son of Bruce, battles David Carradine (off-screen) in the Warner Bros. television movie *Kung Fu: The Movie* (1986).

thought up. *Kung Fu: The Movie* was made for television and Lee was cast as the illegitimate son of Buddhist monk Kwai Chang Caine, played again by David Carradine. Caine's character is confronted by the father of the man he killed in China, and he uses Lee to get at him. Of course, Caine triumphs in the end and Lee sees the error of his ways. The same year Lee followed his father's path and went to Hong Kong, where he made a movie, then returned to the United States to make a *Kung Fu* movie pilot.

In 1990, Lee went to South Africa to film the low-budget *Laser Mission*, playing a mercenary employed by the CIA to spirit a scientist back to the United States. Academy Award winner Ernest Borgnine played the scientist, bringing some much-needed credibility to the film, which was laced with broad humor, sometimes bordering on slapstick. The film did not highlight Lee's martial arts skills as much as it could have, though he did get in a few licks here and there, particularly in an opening scene escape from prison. Firepower was omnipresent, however, and of particular note was a running gun battle between Lee in a VW van and scores of African troops.

In 1991 Lee got his first theatrical break: *Showdown in Little Tokyo* was produced by Warners and boasted a decent budget. Lee co-starred with Dolph Lundgren, the two actors playing cops after a Japanese drug lord. The film had some minor gaffes, mostly involving sexual innuendo. In the hot tub scene it is clear the measurements of Tia Carrere's body double are much larger than Tia's, while later on, when Lundgren and Lee are surrounded by the drug lord's henchmen, Lee comments on the size of Lundgren's well, you figure it out. The fight scenes were plentiful and decent, however, and Lee gave a good accounting of himself.

Rapid Fire (1992) cemented Lee's role as a martial arts film star, featuring him as a young man being pursued by both the mob and the feds, which in this case seem to be one and the same. Father figure Powers Booth plays a renegade cop who helps save Lee and bring down the mobsters. Lee choreographed the fight scenes himself, and his speed and lightning-like reflexes seem at times to rival his father's. In 1994 Lee starred in his first non–martial arts film, what many thought was his breakout role, *The Crow*.

Tragically, it was to be Lee's last movie as he was accidentally killed while shooting his character's death scene. Had Brandon Lee lived, there is no question of his superstar status in the martial arts film world. However, unlike his father Bruce, who was clearly tied to the world

Brandon Lee fights his way through the kitchen in *Rapid Fire* (Twentieth Century Fox, 1992). Lee would meet a tragic death during the filming of his next movie, the non-martial arts *The Crow*.

of martial arts films, Brandon Lee had the ability to break out, to venture beyond into other genres of film, an ability that, alas, we will never witness.

Ron Marchini

Ron Marchini was a martial arts champion during the late 60s early 70s who segued into films during the middle of the decade. In many ways he is the reverse of Chuck Norris: While both men are talented fighters–martial artists who came up at the same time, and while both men moved from in front of the camera to other facets of production, like producing and writing, and in Marchini's case directing, only Norris caught on with the public. Many of Marchini's films are obscure or difficult to find. And from the 90s on, most of them went directly to video.

Marchini's first role was in a Philippines production entitled *Murder in the Orient* (1974), in which he plays a white man living in the Philippines who runs afoul of a murderous gang trying to find a hidden $10,000,000 stash of gold. After he rescues a woman who is being chased by the gang, he is dragged into the mess. When the woman is murdered by the gang despite Marchini's attempts to protect her, the woman's brother, a martial arts master, is also drawn into the affair. Together, the two men work to unravel the mystery of where the gold is hidden, teaming with a beautiful police detective assigned to the case.

The film's fight scenes are rudimentary at best, but Marchini shows some presence on camera and his acting skills are as good, if not better, than other martial artists turned actors. The film's drawback is budget—the sound quality is horrible and it seems clear that lack of money not only prevented the story from being told in a coherent fashion but it also meant the supporting cast around Marchini was amateurish. The exception was Leo Fong, a good fighter who spoke clearly and carried himself well on screen. Fong would go on to make a number of films as actor, producer, director and writer; many of them starred Cynthia Rothrock and/or Richard Norton.

Murder in the Orient parallels *Call Him Mr. Shatter*, (released the same year) in a number of ways. The two films teamed white and Asian males as leads, with the former being some type of professional* and the latter being martial arts masters. In both films, the men have to take on a criminal gang, and both films cater to the stereotypical image that white male characters are irresistible to the Asian females who fall all over them, while their Asian counterparts appear asexual. Mai Mee professes her love for Shatter after knowing him for only a couple of days, even though she has had some type of relationship with Tai Pah, the martial artist protecting Shatter. The opening scene of *Murder in the Orient* finds Marchini in bed with a married woman and having to easily beat down the offended husband, who is shown to be completely inadequate in comparison to his white counterpart. Later Monica, the police detective working with Marchini, falls in love with him, and into his bed, which is implied when the two are walking on the beach together.

In 1976 Marchini followed up with *Death Machines*, another low-budget tale that defied credulity and kept him silent for the entire film! In essence he played a killer zombie under the influence of a serum that takes away his and other killers' willpower. They spend the rest of the movie going around murdering people in the most gruesome ways imaginable. The fight scenes were a notch better than in his last film, though (with the exception of a brawl in a martial arts studio) none lasted all that long.

Almost ten years passed before Marchini made his next film, *Ninja Warriors* (1985), which came at the height of the ninja craze. The story, what there is, follows Steve, a friend of a police detective who is investigating the theft of top secret documents from a government facility. Steve has spent some time in Japan and, unknown to anyone, is a ninja. When the police detective asks Steve to help him solve the case, the two men are constantly attacked by ninjas out to stop them, until Steve heads up the mountain to confront the entire ninja clan and get back the stolen documents.

Though not from Cannon Films, *Ninja Warriors* is another derivative of their *Ninja* series that features white men trained in the Orient in the art of ninjutsu who return home ninjas, only to find their skills needed to fight some evildoers. The film is actually a model of the postmodern experience on celluloid, as characters engage in tried-and-true, or perhaps clichéd, actions with no real connection to any plot or story. *Ninja Warriors* was supposed to take place in the States, but suspiciously looks like the Philippines, while the actors, white and otherwise, have

---

* *The Marchini character's job is not mentioned in the film, but the videobox labels him as a secret agent of some type, which is as good as any job under the circumstances.*

accents that identify them as other than Americans. With no narrative balance to this film, generic aspects of the ninja pictures are met without any type of meaning.

A number of examples stand out: Steve has no last name and no visible means of income, but he does have a nice home at the base of the mountain from which the ninjas emanate. He possesses a sixth sense that allows him to sense other ninjas and, upon being brought into the case, immediately finds a bug in the commanding officer's office. Why the bug is there or who put it there is never explained or followed up on.

The ninjas' movement is synchronized as they go about their business (such as stealing the top secret documents); however, there appears to be no tangible reason for it except that such synchronicity is common in all ninja films. In fact, after stealing the secrets they go to a beach and then bury themselves in the sand but no one knows why. The documents that the ninja stole were to be used by doctors hired by the master ninja for some great experiment, which of course is never adequately explained. And in the finale, Steve goes up the mountain for a showdown with the master ninja and his warriors. As the wind blows like in an old Western shootout sequence, Steve dispatches all concerned and saves humanity from whatever evil the master ninja had planned.

The Forgotten Warrior (1986) was just as derivative, following the Rambo scenario. Marchini plays Parrish, a Vietnam vet being held in a prisoner of war camp along with two other men. Parrish leads an escape but is betrayed by his cage mate Thompson and left for dead. When villagers discover Parrish, they nurse him back to health, and eventually he becomes an important part of the village, teaching the men self defense and protecting them against Communist troops who continue to steal their food. Parrish marries the village elder's daughter and they have a son, but trouble is on the horizon. Not only are the North Vietnamese tired of Parrish's guerrilla activity but so are American politicians, who are being bombarded in the press with allegations of POWs being left behind. In the ultimate betrayal, the American government sends Thompson back to Vietnam to work with the Communists to find and terminate Parrish.

The Forgotten Warrior takes the "Will they let us win this time?" attitude of Sylvester Stallone to new extremes, with Parrish as a killing machine so thorough no one can touch him. Like its predecessors *Uncommon Valor, Missing in Action* and *Rambo II*, this film turns on the notion that the American government is more interested in forgetting the war and its humiliating defeat than trying to discover its POWs and MIAs. However, *The Forgotten Warrior* takes it one step further, making the politicians active participants in the cover-up and attempted eradication of MIAs as opposed to merely the governmental neglect of MIA issues posited in the other films.

The Forgotten Warrior spends the last third of its running time in a continual series of fights pitting the lightly armed Parrish against his American and Vietnamese stalkers. After the troops burn and massacre all his village, and Thompson rapes and kills his wife, Parrish devises gruesome ways to kill his adversaries, including being chopped up by a sword, blown up by explosive charges, stabbed and gutted by knives, neck breakings and, of course, shooting.

Parrish eventually saves the day, but not before another clichéd group of Asian women sacrifice themselves for him. His future wife was the person who originally found him and convinced her father to take him in. The daughter of the Vietnamese commander who is tracking Parrish sets him free at the cost of her own life, while a friend of Parrish's wife gives her life holding onto Parrish's son, whom Parrish believed to be dead. Parrish succeeds in the end, wiping out the entire North Vietnamese base along with Thompson, the American turncoat. As he disappears into the jungle, with his baby son strapped to his back, the future is uncertain, as he has no home anywhere.

In 1990, Marchini starred in *Omega Cop* as one of the last law enforcers in a post-apocalyptic earth. Holes in the ozone, a catastrophic Greenhouse Effect and huge solar flares that burn the flesh and cause madness are the origins of the complete breakdown of society. The police are holed up in an underground bunker; they come out to patrol, and to try to keep back the advancing gangs of scavengers that have been destroying the city. When John Travis and his team take on a slave trader named Raith, all but Travis are killed, and he's on the run. Unable to get back to the compound, which is under siege by the gangs, he must guard three women he's rescued until he can find a safe place to take them. However, the scavengers know he has the women, so a deadly game of cat and mouse begins as Raith does everything he can to kill Travis and get the women for his slave trade.

Travis is a pragmatic man who doesn't spend a lot of time worrying about the reasons the world went to seed; it won't help or change anything. He just knows it has. The consummate professional, he keeps his nose to the grindstone, taking on each assignment as if it is his last. His main focus is to hold back the gangs for as long as possible and to keep his team alive, though he knows he will eventually fail in both. The gangs are growing too strong, and fan out across what is left of the city like a plague. The police are running short on rations, and the military has disintegrated except in Washington D.C. and New York, which is where the women talk about going. When his friends are killed, and the compound is being overrun, the only validity that Travis can assign to his life is the elimination of Raith and his followers, something easier said than done.

Omega Cop, which was produced by Romarc, was Marchini's first film with decent production values and a good supporting cast. Troy Donahue, the teen heartthrob from the 60s, and Stuart Whitman, the rugged leading man from the same period, have cameo roles, and Adam West of *Batman* fame plays Marchini's superior, a hard-nosed man with little patience and, when that familiar substance hits the fan, a tiny sense of levity. After Raith and the scavengers finally break into the compound, West pulls the pin on a grenade and exchanges wedding vows with a police dispatcher, putting the grenade ring over her finger.

Even the level of combat is a notch better than other Marchini films, as Travis shoots, punches and kicks his way across the city, an ever-reluctant knight in tarnished armor. Standout scenes include Marchini wiping out the slave auction with awesome firepower, using his fists and feet on a gang of scavengers for stealing his hat and, in the funniest moment of the film, facing off with some gang members in a Wild West showdown, complete with spaghetti Western type music as he draws his revolver and shoots them dead!

Where the film was dead serious and ahead of its time is in its identification of the Greenhouse Effect as a major cause for concern. Presently, some 14 years later, the second Bush Administration, which is heavily dependent on the use of fossil fuels, continues to deny the validity of the Effect, even as the ozone grows thinner and weather patterns continue to manifest bizarre shifts and substantial droughts in various parts of the world, including the United States.

Travis eventually traps Raith and his scavengers in the compound and blows them to smithereens, but now he is alone. The final scene shows him up in the mountains with the girls, swimming in a beautiful lake. The implication is that he will live quite nicely with the three women to take care of him, most every man's dream. Only he is still a cop, perhaps the only cop left anywhere, so whether he will stay or not is anyone's guess.

Return Fire (1991) saw Marchini reprising his role as Steve Parrish, the Vietnam vet forsaken by his country but who has now returned home to spend some quality time with his son after undertaking a dangerous mission for the CIA. Immediately upon arriving in San Francisco, Parrish is followed by hit men who want him dead. His son's caretaker is murdered, his son is taken captive and Parrish is forced to flee in a police car, chased by a van full of killers, whom Parrish eventually finishes off one by one in a truck depot.

Similar to *The Forgotten Warrior,* this film speaks to government duplicity and the above-the-law attitude of many people in it. On his mission in South America, Parrish literally destroys a drug base, killing scores of criminals and rescuing a hostage that the CIA wanted back. However, when the hostage makes it to the waiting helicopter, the pilot takes off, leaving a limping Parrish to be captured by the cartel. Upon arriving back in the States, Parrish's boss CIA Chief Caruthers orders that he be killed so that he, Caruthers, can do business with a drug dealer running narcotics through the city. It seems that no matter how many sacrifices Parrish, and by extension all veterans, make for their country, they are always used, and in the end discarded.

While Marchini does engage in some martial arts, primarily in the first few minutes of the film, most of his time is spent shooting and blowing people up. Taking his son along for the ride, Parrish wastes scores of men and, in the final shootout, wipes out what seems to be a whole platoon of bad guys. The film wasn't as poorly produced as Marchini's past films, but considering the amount of gratuitous violence present in the story, it seems somewhat provocative for the Parrish character to bring his son along for the killing.

Marchini followed *Return Fire* the same year with what could arguably be considered his best work, *Karate Cop* (1991). Action-packed and humorous, the film does not take itself too seriously as it brings back John Travis, the last cop in the world. This outing, Travis is heading for Washington State when he saves Rachel, a young woman taking care of about two dozen children in an electrified compound that is surrounded by scavengers—mutilated, radiation scarred menaces who work for Lincoln, the commander of the reunification troops.

Marchini lends a sense of world weariness to his role as Travis, a man proud of what he used to be and not afraid to still wear the uniform. His gear is clean, and he even has a functioning police car, an older model but one that still runs. In fact, no matter what pinch Travis gets in, whether he is driving a motorcycle and wearing a helmet or wearing the helmet of a unification soldier to infiltrate their hideout, he always takes the time to put on his baseball cap, the one with the patch reading "Special Police," when he is ready for action.

Rachel asks Travis to brave the scavenger's zone and find a certain crystal which she can use in a government experimental transporter, a device which will send her and the kids to safety thousands of miles away. Travis reluctantly agrees and, using a motorcycle Rachel has stashed in the compound, escapes to steal the device. He is forced to fight every inch of the way, but eventually makes it to the laboratory, where he is able to obtain the crystal, but not as easily as Rachel insisted. He runs another gauntlet of scavengers on his way back, and they destroy his motorcycle, but he makes it into the compound safely. Once there, the kids tell him Rachel has been captured by Lincoln, so Travis is off again to the rescue.

Karate Cop presents a serious dilemma in a sometimes humorous manner. With a number of nuclear nations poised to destroy one another and the Earth, what would happen to the world if there were no police, no law enforcement? The society that Travis, Rachel and the kids inhabit is dystopic to say the least. Force is the sole arbiter of everything, and law is judged and enforced by whomever has the most power. Women, even scientists like Rachel, are relegated to positions of sexual adornment to aggrandize the position of dominant men, either warriors or leaders like Lincoln, who is rarely seen without his snake woman by his side.

During the course of the story, the film comments on a number of pressing environmental or social issues in a roundabout or funny way. When Rachel is knocked unconscious by the scavengers and is saved by Travis, she wakes up covered in only a blanket. Upset and wondering where her clothes are, Travis deadpans that he had to wash them or the acid rain on them would have burned holes in her. When Rachel is showing Travis the transporter, she explains that Lincoln is after her because he wants to use it to distribute drugs. Even in a society already destroyed, the urge to sell drugs and do more damage is irresistible. And later, when trying to retrieve the crystal that Rachel needs, Travis has to go up against a religious cult that idolizes the thing, once again confirming that the weirder something is, the more likely it is to be fetishized to some degree.

Travis finally rescues Rachel and brings her back to the compound, where she is able to transport herself and the kids away. Unfortunately, Travis has to stay behind to fight off Lincoln and his henchmen, which he does in first-rate style. Up to this point, many of Marchini's fight scenes were lackluster, not due to any fault on his part but mostly because of budget restraints. In this film he is able to show what he can do, and it is quite impressive. *Karate Cop* ends with Travis and his dog setting out north, to find Rachel and the kids. The set up for a sequel was obvious, but none was coming.

James Ryan

Ryan is a South African martial artist who broke big on the scene at the beginning of the decade in *Kill or Be Killed* and *Kill and Kill Again*, standard drive-in fare that was popular enough to actually gain Ryan an American fan club based in Encino. Unlike a lot of karatekas, Ryan did at times incorporate the spiritual aspects of the martial arts into his characters, and yet the low-budget nature of his films did not dull his obvious screen presence, which exuded a certain European persona missing from American martial arts stars.

With his unkempt, shoulder-length hair and slight accent, Ryan seemed destined to play karateka mystics, fighting men who understood the greater picture of things, and knew that any variance or misstep on their part could cost them their life. In *Kill or Be Killed*, Ryan engineers his and his girlfriend's escape from the Nazi general he was supposed to fight for, and then has to will his way through a parched, barren desert. In *Kill and Kill Again*, Ryan has to levitate in midair to impress one man to join his rescue team.

Ryan was fairly busy in the latter half of the 80s; however, there were often long lapses between films. After his first two films, it was five years before his next major role. In 1987 Ryan starred in *Rage to Kill*, a military adventure set on the imaginary Caribbean island of St. Heron. Ryan plays Blaine Striker, a successful race car driver and bon vivant whose brother is held hostage when a military coup on the island by a psychotic, renegade general establishes a total dictatorship. Striker finds a way to sneak aboard an aircraft delivering parts to the island and finds his brother, who is among the medical students being watched. Striker leads the students out of their college dormitory and into the mountains, where they hook up with rebel leaders and await rescue, all the while planning on destroying a missile factory being built by the Russians.

If the scenario sounds familiar, it is. In October 1983, Marxists took over the Caribbean island government of Grenada, backed by Cuban and Russian advisors. The fact that American medical students going to college in Saint George's were possibly in danger was used as a pretext for an American invasion almost a week later. The operation was wrapped up in a short period of time, and democracy restored to the country, though the actual peril faced by the students is still a matter of debate today.

In carrying on the conservative tendencies of the Reagan years, *Rage to Kill* makes no such bones about the menace facing the students by the military on the island. Guards roam the college campus, bursting into dorm rooms whenever they want and even going into the showers to watch female students bathing. In fact, the military plans to massacre the students and blame it on the opposition group fighting the coup. Only the timely arrival of Striker and CIA operative Bill Miller, played by Cameron Mitchell, prevent the slaughter.

The film marked a departure for Ryan in that he used his considerable martial arts skills quite sparingly, first in a battle with soldiers at the airport where he is caught, and then later in an interrogation room. Both times he scores some knockdowns but is eventually overtaken by his numerous opponents. Ryan's major effort was dedicated to exercising extreme firepower to kill his enemies. To that extent he becomes a low-budget Rambo, complete with the same combat fatigues and ribbon around his bicep. Leading the students on a breakout from the campus, Ryan grabs a large-caliber machine gun similar to the one that Stallone used to shoot up everything, and blows away countless soldiers during their escape. During a torture scene, a shirtless Ryan is strapped to a wire mattress frame, hands out from his side, like Rambo, and beaten with a truncheon and shocked with an electric cable.

The insidious presence and influence of the Soviet Union is stressed, with reminders every so often that not only are they on the island, but they are up to no good. One of the medical students steals a Jeep, goes for a drive to look around and finds a secret testing facility. He gains entry and finds a number of huge missiles being developed, all with Russian writing on them. When Striker arrives at the airport, he fumbles through a darkened warehouse and stops at some boxes to look around. While the viewer can easily see they are marked "USSR," Striker has to make sure everyone sees by lighting the boxes up with his flashlight. Later, he is questioned by a Soviet officer and beaten for refusing to answer. Miller, undercover as a Soviet non-commissioned officer, lays on a thick Russian accent and beats Striker senseless to stop the officer from shooting Striker.

Opposing the Communists are Wally Arn and his peasants, who live in the more rural regions of the island. The CIA tells the American President that Arn is a pro-democracy, pro-capitalist leader, one that the U.S. can get along with. To bolster his credentials as a western favorite, a reporter tells Striker that Arn used to walk to school six miles one way just to get an education, something a lot of older Americans can certainly relate to in a time before busses. However, Arn's movement needs weapons and ammunition, but Washington is slow to react, forcing a split between Striker and Miller.

Striker, younger and more active, is alleged to have been a mercenary before becoming a race car driver, which would explain his martial arts background and his familiarity with weapons. He is hot-headed and impulsive, though not without the ability to plan ahead. Miller on the other hand is an old CIA hand who has been around a long time. He is cool-headed, pragmatic and by-the-book. The two disagree on how to proceed with their operation against the Communist, but through the intercession of Arn, they come together again and then reach the same conclusion: With or without Washington's help, they will destroy the missile base before it becomes operational.

Opposing the forces of freedom is General Turner, a vile man who loves drinking, killing and women, though not necessarily in that order. Arn, Turner's main rival, is everything that the general isn't: honest, brave, morally upright and committed to a free society. Though the differences between the men are black and white, so are the men, with Arn being a black man indigenous to the island while the white Turner, played by Oliver Reed, appears to be from England.

With time running out, Arn and his men attack the missile factory, creating a diversion so that Striker can get in and plant some bombs. Though Striker gets the job done and blows the place sky high, reinforcements from Turner's army arrive and threaten to overwhelm the rebels. Just when all seems hopeless, the Marines parachute onto the island, saving the day. As Arn closes in on Turner, the general takes the easy way out by putting a revolver to his head.

By 1988, Ryan moved further away from straight kung fu and co-starred in *Space Mutiny*, a thoroughly derivative film that borrowed quite heavily from the American television series *Battlestar Galactica*, a late 70s sci-fi show that itself was inspired by the overwhelming success of *Star Wars*. In *Battlestar Galactica* a rag-tag fleet of space vehicles and the sole remaining battlestar of the human race head through uncharted space looking for Earth, all the while pursued by the Cylon Empire, a race of robots who hate mankind. In *Space Mutiny*, the Southern Sun, a battlestar housing thousands of humans, travels through space, looking for a home planet they can one day colonize. When the "Enforcers," an interior police unit, decide to take over the ship and head into pirate territory, where they believe it will be easier to find a home planet, the remaining crew, led by visiting pilot Reb Brown, fights back.

Space Mutiny went so far as to employ stock footage from the television series, mostly of the battlestar and its fighter ships, and used it to show shooting and fighting breaking out every few minutes in the reaches of deep space. The few martial arts scenes in the film were not done well, possibly because Ryan, who played the duplicitous chief engineer, was a villain and a cripple in the movie. Reb Brown, as the invincible hero leading the defense of the ship, gets in most of the hand-to-hand licks, and is not exactly convincing, in part because of the film's low budget.

After Reb and the others eventually beat back the mutiny, he and the commander's daughter are to be married. The Enforcers do not fare so well. Many of their men are blown to bits; a number of them appeared effeminate or posturing, with bizarre haircuts or bondage-like uniforms. One such individual follows the head enforcer around everywhere, clad in tight-fitting muscle shirts. Unfortunately for the character and the viewers, he has no muscles to show off. Another is buffoonish, and easily tricked by the commander's daughter into taking off his clothes, after which the latter promptly escapes from the Enforcer's clutches.

Visually, *Space Mutiny* constitutes an homage to 30s art deco science fiction serials like *Buck Rogers*, with many of the crew dressed in padded, wide-shouldered uniforms and, in the case of the commander's daughter, hot pants and a low-cut zipper top. Reb Brown's outfit places him in the high-flying adventure world of *Flash Gordon*, with white pants and white flowing sleeveless shirt. The combatants on both sides use ray guns that shoot out plenty of light but don't seem to hit much, as well as small bazooka-like weapons that aren't very effective but cause a lot of explosions.

Cameron Mitchell, who plays the Southern Sun's commander and wears a preposterous, ill-fitting beard, could be likened to a postmodern Moses leading his people across the wilderness of space to the Promised Land. He makes a number of noble statements refuting violence, while his ship is armed to the teeth. Yet the film's pastiche plot, which cannibalizes other stories, can't hide the fact that not much violence is really necessary since the Enforcers only comprise a minuscule portion of the crew. In going through the motions of displaying bold action, Reb and the others become mock heroes.

Reb, upon landing on the ship, is immediately recognized as a superior man of action, despite having not engaged in much activity. He becomes the commander's Joshua, leading the crew into the picturesque battles. In following the pattern of the past serials, Reb engages the Enforcers in a number of battles, then retires to be lauded or asked to do something else even more challenging that only one man—he—can do.

Much of the acting in *Space Mutiny* is over-the-top, with the treasonous villain Kalgon breaking into a sinister laugh every few minutes, or staring ominously in the distance when he is ordering someone killed. Brown doesn't fare much better. In many action scenes, he yells and hoots as if to reinforce to the viewer that the activity on screen is really exciting. Only Ryan's performance as the duplicitous chief engineer merits any praise.

Unintentional humor abounds. When the commander orders a computer check on Reb Brown's crash, we see a 386 model with a floppy disk drive. In the last battle,

Reb picks up the latest model flame thrower—a propane tank with a hose attached to it. However, *Space Mutiny* takes itself just seriously enough to play it straight. Just whom the film was geared toward is difficult to imagine. The *Star Wars* craze of the late 70s launched a number of inferior space films, but they eventually petered out, and this one was shot long after the others had all faded away.

Ryan next co-starred in *Code Name Vengeance*, sharing top billing with B movie icon Robert Ginty, ex–*Playboy* sensation Shannon Tweed and Cameron Mitchell, who steals the show as "Dutch," an eccentric, retired CIA operative running a general store in the middle of the African bush. Ryan plays Tabrak, an Arab★ terrorist in a mythical African country called Katar (?) who raids the king's palace and kidnaps the queen and their son. Tabrak's goal is to break the alliance between Katar and the United States, which is keeping the king in power. The king appears ready to placate the terrorists when the American embassy puts together an emergency rescue operation led by Ginty, who at one time was their best operative.

Comparing this film with Ryan's earlier martial arts efforts is like comparing night to day. *Code Name Vengeance* features a much better cast, story and a larger budget, not to mention a lot more action. However, most of it is in the form of explosions and shootouts, not hand-to-hand fighting, which is a trade-off of debatable value. Ryan, who is the expert karateka, again has no opportunity to show off his skills, while Ginty, who does do some fighting, is horribly inadequate. In fact, the first shots of Ginty are as a prisoner, engaged in a fight with another prisoner, and getting the worst of it. If Ginty is supposedly the best hope to save the queen, he is not very reassuring.

Probably the most interesting facet of *Code Name Vengeance* is that it bucks the conservative trends of the 80s. Ginty was betrayed by the CIA and sent to a foreign prison because he knew too much and was going to expose their dirty, covert actions around the world, especially in third world countries. When the CIA breaks him out of the prison to handle the mission, they arrange for one of their own to accompany him and, in the end, to double-cross and kill him.

In contrast to *Gymkata*, which placed Americans in a similar situation (a third world country of great importance to the United States wavering in its alliance), *Code Name Vengeance*'s left wing stance is patently evident. Where the former film presented an honest and patriotic CIA operative winning over the support of a somewhat backward but strategically valuable country, the king being propped up by the U.S. in the latter film is no more than a dictator in a military uniform, one who talks about freedom for the masses but never delivers. In fact, many of the king's speeches sound nonsensical, as much because he's an idiot as because what he is saying doesn't really matter. There will never be democracy in the country so long as the king and the CIA can work out a mutually beneficial deal.

While the king and his family live in a palatial estate, most of the country seems mired in poverty. In a symbolic gesture of class warfare, Tabrak machine guns to bits the giant chandelier hanging in the king's palace as he makes off with the queen and her son. Make no mistake, Tabrak is certainly not a good guy. He is a psychotic maniac who cuts off the head of the queen's friend and mails it back

---

★ *It is difficult to say with certainty what Ryan's character or his followers are. Most of them appear African but like Tabrak, dress like Arabs. Ryan's accent places him as a European or Afrikaner.*

to the king to let him know that he means business. Later, in a fit of rage after hearing that Ginty, his sworn enemy, has escaped from prison, he shoots up a hospital, murders the staff, then firebombs the building, killing all the sick and injured. Yet despite this, and in the estimations of other characters in the film, Tabrak has the support of perhaps more than half the country, obviously not because he is good but rather because the king is so bad.

Like the conservative films that wave the flag every so often to remind everyone of Mom and apple pie, *Code Name Vengeance* wears its left-leaning colors on its sleeve, its ham-handed approach only slightly more conspicuous than that of the previous year's *Above the Law*. President Reagan's picture adorns the walls of the embassy, fingering who is ultimately responsible for the covert actions being undertaken in the name of national security. Applegate, the CIA bigwig who recruits Ginty for the mission, turns out to be the man who had framed him years ago and sent him to prison, not Tabrak, hence the film's title. When Applegate tries to kill Ginty, the latter shoots him at the top of the staircase, and Applegate falls into a flag and rolls down the stairs, his body coming to rest draped in red, white, and blue.

The Last Samurai (1990) returned Ryan to a form of martial arts, in this instance kendo, the art of Japanese swordplay. Ryan plays Miyagawa, the assistant to Mr. Endo, a powerful Japanese conglomerate owner who returns to Southern Africa on a business trip, but is really there to reckon himself with the restless spirit of a Japanese samurai. The story itself is hard to follow, at least Mr. Endo's portion of it, while that involving the other characters is more straightforward.

Endo hires American Johnny Congo and his girlfriend to pilot him to the opposite end of the country, where he wishes to meet an old friend, Hakim, a self-tortured gun dealer who lives luxuriously in the bush. Once there, the group is taken hostage by an African rebel leader and held for ransom. When Mr. Endo refuses to call his company to pay, the rebels prepare to hang him and his assistant Miyagawa, thereby setting the stage for all the major players to come to terms with their lives.

Johnny, played by Lance Henriksen, is an ex–Vietnam vet who is slowly unraveling before our eyes. He drinks too much, gambles too much and has no plans for the future. When the rebels take the group hostage, Johnny escapes by swimming across a river, then picks off a few rebels so that he can arm himself. As Johnny prepares to raid the camp to rescue the hostages, it becomes clear he is not doing it so much to save his girlfriend or the others but rather for a last thrill before he dies.

Mr. Endo and Miyagawa continue to practice their kendo skills in their cage, Mr. Endo somehow sensing that the spirit he seeks is in rebel leader. Hakim, meanwhile, attempts to get the hostages released, since it turns out he was the one who arranged for the kidnappings in the first place as a cover for his gunrunning operation. When Johnny launches his suicide attack, Miyagawa uses his bow to fell rebels while Mr. Endo battles the rebel leader, his sword against the rebel's machine gun, and prevails. The hostages can now leave, but Johnny, Hakim and the rebel leader lay dead, their restless spirits finally free.

As a martial arts film, *The Last Samurai* leaves a lot to be desired. There is no hand-to-hand combat and the actual kendo scenes are short. Also, as mentioned, the story sometimes makes no sense, and a cause-and-effect pattern is not always present, especially with regard to Endo, who says and knows things yet we don't know why. Then there's the notion of cultural superiority that manifests itself so subtly. In the bush, Hakim, Endo and the others dine around a fancy table, dress fashionably and drink the best liquors, just as if they were in Europe. Hakim's tent is a testament to decadence, with fine rugs and linens and a bath where the women can luxuriate.

Contrasted with this grouping of Asian, American, European and Arab civilization is the rebel's way of life. Brutal and dirty, the Africans are shown to be thieves when they rob and destroy Hakim's camp. Upon arrival at the camp, the rebel leader tortures some of his men by beating them on the soles of their feet. Even the inside of the rebel leader's house is scary, with war masks and animal skins lying everywhere. City-dwelling Africans fare no better. When Johnny and his girlfriend enter the country, a customs officer searches the latter, running his hands all over her body, including a lengthy grope of her breasts. In the end, whatever it was the rebels were fighting for now appears a lost cause, as Johnny and the others have devastated the camp. However, considering how the Africans were depicted, this is of little importance anyway.

In 1991, Ryan starred in *Pursuit*, an action film taking place in southern Africa. He plays Cody, a retired mercenary living a monk-like existence in the bush, away from the distractions of man. When a rogue general kills the president of a small African nation and steals its gold, representatives of the nation contact Cody, hoping to lure him out of retirement with a job to retrieve the bullion. He accepts the mission and puts together his team, which include a couple of mercenaries he had served with in the past. Cody and his team easily dispatch the general, wipe out his camp and take possession of the gold, only to have his partners get greedy and steal it, leaving Cody to die with a gunshot wound to the shoulder.

Ryan does practically no martial arts in *Pursuit*, though the film starts out promisingly. The first shots of Cody are at his hideaway, doing his kata high above a stream that runs beneath the cave he lives in. His body is muscular, though not bulked up like Chuck Norris or Jean-Claude Van Damme, but rather cut and lean, like an Anglo Bruce Lee. When the government representatives come to talk with him, he serves them tea Japanese-style at a small table, reinforcing the image of a man at home with both the spiritual and cultural aspects of karate as well as the combat ones. Unfortunately, except for a quick head butt and gun takeaway early in the film, Cody performs no other martial arts, letting his guns do the talking for him.

Cody is clearly a rare type of mercenary—one with a sense of honor and integrity. The very word "mercenary" conjures up pictures of venality and faithlessness, of someone whose services are sold to the highest bidder. In fact, Lucky and Doyle, two mercenaries who are working for the general who stole the bullion, immediately change sides when Cody and his team arrive. Cody, however, is different. Money is not his sole motivation. In fact, he only takes the job because the government administrator promises him that the gold will be used to alleviate some of the poverty facing the nation. Later, when his fellow team members have retrieved the bullion and decided they want to keep it, Cody opposes them, and in a scene reminiscent of Joel McCrea and Randolph Scott in *Ride the High*

Country,* tells the group they had contracted out to do a job, not steal the government's assets. After his partners leave him for dead, Cody recovers and follows them, hoping to complete his mission, even though David, his African tracker, tells him he is crazy.

Pursuit, while bereft of any martial arts, is certainly not lacking in action. A highlight is the destruction of the general's camp, which is shown as high-octane guitar rock 'n' roll is heard on the soundtrack. The characterization of the mercenaries is excellent, white faces on a black continent whose only real talent is to keep the flames of war stoked high. None of the men have anything to show for their years of fighting except, perhaps, old stories and bad attitudes.

The situation in southern Africa is also addressed, at least indirectly, as we see the various groups vying to control the power structure on the continent. The general who stole the gold is Cuban, while the Anglo mercenaries come from South Africa, Rhodesia (now Zimbabwe), Ireland and possibly England. Blacks play a marginal role, as subordinates, both for the general, who needs white men to train his black troops, and for the mercenaries, who use Abu, the African mercenary, to carry the gold. The Seduka, a tribe of cannibals, is almost portrayed as silly and childlike, stereotypically dancing by the fire as they prepare to cook Samantha, the journalist they have captured.

Cody and his African tracker David eventually catch up to the mercenaries, but not through their own doing. The gold the group carries is a Pandora's Box, weighted down with the men's dreams as well as greed. They slow considerably, get sloppy and leave behind tracks, and eventually begin fighting among themselves. By the time Cody finds them, only his friend Matthews is left, and he is so blinded by avarice that, even after Cody saves him from the Seduka, he turns on him. Fortunately for Cody, he has Samantha watching his back.

Ryan has been inactive in films since 1995, his last being *Kickboxer 5: The Redemption* (1995). More so than other martial arts stars', Ryan's movies often seemed linked to the dark shadow of totalitarianism. In *Kill or Be Killed*, Steve Chase fights in a tournament run by a Nazi general who has his own compound in the middle of the desert. In *Kill and Kill Again*, Chase battles a megalomaniacal tyrant who plans to rule the world with mind-controlled slaves. *Space Mutiny* finds Ryan betraying the Southern Sun into the hands of Kalgon, the mad Enforcer with designs on ruling his own world. In *Code Name Vengeance* he plays the psychotic terrorist who leads his army with an iron fist. *Rage to Kill* matches him against Communist soldiers taking over an island, while *The Last Samurai* pits him against African rebels.

By the time of *Kickboxer 5*, Ryan had come full circle, in this instance playing his own version of the Nazi general—a tyrannical ex–martial arts champion–millionaire who will do anything to control the world of martial arts fighting. This film showcased Ryan's martial arts abilities better than any of his previous films, and was certainly his best performance all around.

As Mr. Negaal, Ryan exudes a slick charm. Obsessed with extending his oppressive dominion over all martial arts, he kills anyone who stands in his way,

---

McCrea and Scott play a couple of aging ex-lawmen, down on their luck, who take a job transporting gold from a mining camp to the bank. Scott wants to keep the money and McCrea reckons on keeping his word to the bank and miners.

usually in the most brutal manner imaginable. Even his palatial estate is reminiscent of that of the Nazi general in *Kill or Be Killed*, far away from civilization; it is from there he intends to run his empire.

Only Matt, played by Mark Dacascos, stands in his way. Matt, a famous martial arts champ, won't play ball with Mr. Negaal, so the battle is on. Matt finds an unlikely ally in Paul, a world-class martial artist set up by Mr. Negaal and doing prison time in Los Angeles. Mr. Negaal pays for Paul's freedom, the trade-off being he has to murder Matt. Instead, Paul warns Matt and then both men are on Mr. Negaal's enemies list. Fighting together, they overpower Mr. Negaal's men and then, in the finale, Matt and Mr. Negaal go at it, fists and feet a blur. Matt eventually wins, destroying Mr. Negaal and his hopes for a martial arts empire.

The Theatrical Demise of Martial Arts Films

By the end of the 90s, most martial arts films had run their course in the theaters. Except for Jackie Chan's movies (which appeal mostly to kids and not adults as do the American style martial arts films), few American-style martial arts films have been released theatrically in the U.S. since 1999. Seagal is still churning out pictures, while Van Damme worked a deal with Nu Image/Millennium; the films have gone straight to video. *Replicant* (2001) returned Van Damme to the theme of twins (first explored in *Double Impact* and *Maximum Risk*), or in this case the *doppelganger*, in which a "good" replicated Van Damme squares off against his evil self.

The film was something of a departure for Van Damme in that the martial artist had to make his character relate to the viewer not through talk, or even action, but rather reaction, that is, watching his fellow actors and then using facial expressions and eye movement to interact with them. Van Damme plays a clone, or replicant as the Feds like to say, made from the DNA of a serial killer's hair follicle which was left at the scene of a gruesome murder. The killer, known as "the Torch," stalks, kills and then burns single mothers. Because the replicant is thought to be psychically linked to the Torch, it is hoped he can lead the police to the killer. However, though the replicant is "born" a full-grown man, he must be taught as a child, learning how to walk, sit, stand, etc., from television tutors. This leads to some rather humorous situations, for instance, when the replicant runs into a hooker and has to figure out what to do by watching the porno film running on her TV.

To accomplish this sense of child-like innocence, Van Damme rarely speaks in full sentences, and expresses a sense of wide-eyed surprise at everything. For most of the film he walks over hunched slightly, as if afraid, and is clad in an oversized jacket and a large baseball cap, which conveys the sense of a big kid. The Torch, also played by Van Damme, is the complete opposite, a man twisted from years of child abuse who vents his pain on the symbol of his tormentor: mothers.

Caught between these two extremes is Riley, the retired detective still tracking the Torch. Played to great effect by Michael Rooker, Riley is a good man with a bad streak. He is too quick to use force and can be brutal at times, but he can also be caring. Riley's own mother cautions him, after seeing the beating he administered to the replicant, that if you treat people like a criminal, that's exactly what they will become. These words almost come true as the Torch tries to drive a wedge between the replicant and Riley.

What the replicant finally realizes is that he is expendable: the Feds could not care less about the Torch—they merely want to see how their billion dollar experiment is functioning. Riley initially is using him to get to the Torch, and treats him like a dog most of the time. The Torch wants to recruit the replicant as an additional killer. The murdered women are afterthoughts—for the Torch they are fodder and for Riley the hunt has long ago become personal; the women mean nothing. The only one who has a sense of compassion and treats the replicant decently is the hooker, and the replicant is not quite sure what to do with her.

In the end, the replicant, who has psychically experienced the murders committed by the Torch, and felt the physical brutality of Riley, must choose between the men. He fights the Torch, not because Riley is good, but because he recognizes that the Torch is bad. The martial arts fight between the two men is intense and, because the replicant can read the Torch's thoughts, each man blocks the others blow perfectly. Director Ringo Lam does an excellent job of making it appear that Van Damme is fighting himself. It is a shame the film did not make it to the big screen.

In *The Order* (2001), Van Damme plays an artifact thief whose father is kidnapped by a fanatical religious group called "The Order" in Israel. The group seeks to set off a religious conflagration between Christians, Muslims and Jews by detonating a bomb under a mosque. The film's story hinges on a number of pursuits: The Order chasing a map belonging to Van Damme's father, Van Damme chasing the Order, and the police chasing Van Damme, all of which allow Van Damme plenty of opportunities to exercise his martial arts prowess. Highlights include a cameo of Charlton Heston as Van Damme's father's old friend, and a chase on the airport tarmac which destroys a 747!

The Order cost about $25,000,000, and included an excellent supporting cast, including Ben Cross as a double-dealing police inspector and Brian Thompson as the violence-obsessed leader of the Order. The film's opening sequence consisted of a voiceover which explained the origins of the Order as the Crusaders fought to take the city of Jerusalem. It then cuts to the present, and Van Damme ripping off of the Russian Mafia. Van Damme was quoted as saying their film was the first to allow an international crew to work on the roofs of the holy city.[31] Reportedly Palestinian bystanders were cheering Van Damme, posing as a Hasidic Jew, as he fought a running battle against actors dressed as Israeli police.

The 2002 release *Derailed* places secret agent–courier Van Damme in harm's way aboard a train taken over by terrorists trying to steal some smallpox virus. Van Damme fights the killers car to car, and even has to chase the train by motorcycle, until he finally gets them all. Van Damme gave a credible performance but unfortunately the special effects were not; in many instances it was obvious that models were used (for example, when two trains collided).

Jet Li, a mainland Chinese dynamo, has released a few American films showcasing his martial arts prowess, but none has been a blockbuster at the box office. (Nor were they particularly aimed at a martial arts audience.) Li, a child prodigy in Wushu, which is the Chinese term for a variety of martial arts, won his first "championship" at the age of nine with an award for Excellence.[32] He retired from

Jet Li, a mainland Chinese dynamo, has made a number of solid martial arts films, though none has caught fire at the box office. Here in *Kiss of the Dragon*, he battles a number of opponents.

the sport at 17 and instantly began getting movie offers. His first film was entitled *Shaolin Temple*, which catapulted him to stardom.[33]

Li appeared in a number of Chinese films before making his American debut in *Lethal Weapon 4*, in which he was a lethal weapon in the Chinese Triads. Li seems to have found a niche, like Seagal of late, working with rap stars such as DMX, though in *Kiss of the Dragon* (2001) he teams with Bridget Fonda to play a Chinese agent framed for murder by a drug lord. The original story is credited to Li and features the first-rate action sequences that Li is famous for, including a stick fight against an entire French dojo.

With the older, veteran martial artists fading fast, and Li's films not catching fire with the public, one would think martial arts films, like the Western, had run their course. Yet that is not the case. The genre is still around, as evidenced by Norris' long-running television show *Walker, Texas Ranger* and its former companion series *Martial Law*, both onetime Saturday night hits on CBS. So why did these martial arts films disappear from the theaters? The answer lies back in the late 70s, with a small device that revolutionized home entertainment, much like television did in the late 40s.

The Videocassette Player

By 1975, Sony had developed its Betamax, a half-inch videotape that could be played on a recorder hooked up to a television set. Matsushita followed suit in 1977 with its VHS format. Beta was smaller and more compact, so (like the battle between 8 track and cassette) common sense would dictate that the smaller Beta tape, easily stored without taking up so much room, to be the practical choice. It also presented a better picture. However, while both systems cost a bunch, the VHS was cheaper by about a third, and in the long run its lesser cost contributed to it outselling its chief competitor two-to-one, thereby ensuring that VHS would become the industry standard.

As they did with television, entertainment executives initially viewed the new device as a threat: Viewers could theoretically pile up films and shows that they taped, even create their own "libraries" which could be sold or viewed by others, thereby cutting into studio revenues and the talent's residuals. Lawsuits to stop the new technology wended their way through the court system, until the United States Supreme Court ruled in 1984 that taping programs for home use was allowed because it was merely a form of "time-shifting," a way of allowing viewers to decide when they wanted to watch a program, and therefore not a copyright infringement.

A new phenomenon coincided with the VCR's increased popularity: the video outlets. Almost overnight, "mom and pop" stores appeared, shelves stocked full of whatever films they could find, to rent to customers. Some even rented the VCRs themselves. Pornography became a popular (some would say pernicious) favorite among viewers.★

★ *PT Anderson's 1998 film* Boogie Nights *savagely chronicled the effect that video had on the pornography industry in the early 80s. During the previous decade, some X-rated films had taken a stab at artistic respectability, moving from the Pussy Cat Theatres to the mall quadriplexes. The* Story of O *(1975), and the* Emmanuelle *films were all "dirty" movies which sported a "story" and high production values. In Anderson's film, Burt Reynolds plays a porno director who aspires to make real films, just with sex in them (well, a lot of sex). The advent of video spelled the end of this movement as customers began renting videos, made cheaply and often with "amateurs," in front of the camera. "B" theatrical releases would soon meet the same fate.*

Older studio films and "B" theatrical releases competed on the same footing in these early days. A video store window might feature posters for both Paramount's *The Godfather* (1972) and New World's *Big Bad Mama* (1974). The entertainment industry's initial fears about lost revenue were largely unfounded. While video piracy was and is a concern, studios made small fortunes selling the video-cassette tapes of their films for rentals. Older movies, which had until that point just taken up space in studio vaults, were once again turning profits. Entire film libraries, from Warner Bros. to AIP, found their way to the video shelves. Low-budget producer Zane Levit (*Fist of the North Star* 1996) notes,

> At this time [1988], everybody in the world was buying video machines. Video stores were being opened at a rapid pace and they needed product to fill the shelves. A lot of films hadn't been transferred to video yet, and stores were just trying to fill this void.[34]

So, as the 80s drew to a close, large nationwide video outlets like Blockbuster, which was initially based in Florida, grew into a significant force in the industry. Blockbuster Video began in 1986, with 17 stores. By 1988 it had increased to 300; it doubled after buying the Major Video Chain and by 1990 it had more than a thousand stores across the U.S.[35] Regional chains like Hollywood Video, National Video and the Wherehouse also competed for customers, eventually driving the smaller stores, which increasingly had to rely on rentals of pornography to make money, out of business. (Blockbuster and Hollywood Video do not rent pornographic tapes.)

Up to this point, a number of independent studios—Crown, New World Pictures, AIP, Cannon and Corman's new company Concorde, among others—routinely released their "B" grade films, including their martial arts films, at local theaters and drive-ins. And some scored huge hits. New World's *Death Race 2000* (1975) starred David Carradine, and gave the world its first glimpse of a snarling Sylvester Stallone. It made money and inspired a video arcade game, eventually banned, where the players try to hit pedestrians to score points. *Rolling Thunder* (1977), written by Paul Schrader, was in some ways more gory than his *Taxi Driver* and fetched AIP a pretty penny (or two). *Ator, the Invincible* (1983), which showcased Bo Derek's *Tarzan* leading man Miles O'Keeffe, and *Yor, Hunter of the Future* (1982), which featured stalwart "B" and sometime "A" player Reb Brown, both did reasonably well, anticipating the anti-nuclear movement that would and was sweeping across Europe.

Norris' films of the 80s, particularly those produced by Cannon, continued to make money, too, though in large part that was due to the fact that their budgets were shrinking. By this time Norris had a built-in audience and was still a top martial arts draw, so the studio could gamble on keeping the budgets low, relying on his fan base here, in Europe and Israel, where Norris was quite popular, to squeeze blood from a turnip. Van Damme temporarily invigorated the genre, his early films lining Cannon's pockets. However, the writing was on the wall, and as other changes loomed in the shadows, B films were eventually crowded out, bringing an end to the martial arts theatrical release.

The Cinema BLOCKBUSTER

From the mid–60s on, the relative homogeneity of the viewing public that classical cinema depended upon during its heyday was gone. In its stead was continued pressure from television, the growth of cable and a diversifying culture. Fracturing any sense of the universal for the movie makers was the variety of systemic convulsions that had erupted throughout the world: the aftermath of the riotous 60s; the increase in third world debt; Japan and the European Common Market moving up to economic super states; the fall of Communism; and the re-emergence of America as a worldwide enforcer. Frederick Jameson identifies such chaos as "postmodernity," or the late stage of capitalism.[36]

The studios ensuing difficulties in finding a concrete viewing audience resulted in an almost frantic search for something that would "work." As big-budget musicals and location-based epics failed one after the other, the postmodern fissures identified by Jameson began to be manifested, both textually, as in *Bonnie and Clyde* (1967) and *The Wild Bunch* (1969), which featured an alternate universe where the outlaws were bad but traditional authority figures were even worse, and subtextually, like in Wim Wender's *Paris, Texas* (1984), where European doctors practice medicine in Mexican border towns, where French women are L.A. housewives, and German girls are Texas peepshow dancers.

Timothy Corrigan echoes Jameson in his *Cinema Without Walls*, arguing that the instability facing the American film industry is the direct result of too many audiences or too vague an audience:

> In an important sense, that audience and the blurry conception of it will invariably produce contemporary films such as Ishtar. Like Heaven's Gate, its financial voices ... seem largely about the hysteria of production for an audience fragmented beyond any controllable identity.[37]

To stem any further deterioration of its viewing base, Hollywood finally countered in the early 70s with the "Blockbuster," a mega-expensive film designed for mass consumption. A superficial throwback to the epics of the 50s and 60s, such films combined big stars like Tom Cruise, Mel Gibson and Harrison Ford with visual spectacle, amazing special effects and fast-paced action. These movies aimed for the broadest possible appeal, which inevitably entailed the dumbing-down of the story and character to the lowest common denominator, to be replaced by fast music, stunning cinematography and a plethora of loud explosions and/or sexual situations ... or, better yet, both.

A film like *Top Gun* sports only the barest of storylines—a pilot training to be the best at the Navy's top aviation facility simultaneously romances an astrophysicist—yet its driving rock score and superb photography made it a huge hit in the summer of 1986. With "something" for everyone and "nothing" really for anyone, *Top Gun* is merely one among many possible examples that exhibit the primacy of spectacle over all else. Spielberg's *Close Encounters of the Third Kind* (1977) was a huge hit that featured an ultra-slim plot (a loose story about some people affected by the appearance of UFOs), but which was buoyed by a quarter to third of its running time sporting state-of-the-art visual effects.

So cobbling together an audience these days costs money—lots of it. Can this approach work consistently? Probably not over the long run. Since the late 70s, the price of the average motion picture has risen sharply. Studios live and die by the success of these blockbusters, and in an ever-spiraling inflationary cycle, everything from union labor to talent salary has skyrocketed, with "A" list stars such Sylvester Stallone, Tom Hanks, and even Jim Carrey now receiving upwards of $20,000,000 per film! Benjamin Svetkey of *Entertainment Weekly* points out,

> But there is a flaw to this logic: Big stars bomb all the time. There is simply no such thing as guaranteed box office draw, no matter how much the studios are willing to pay for one.... Another problem with these jumbo salaries: they explode the cost of making movies.[37]

To find some common denominator for an audience to support these mega-films, then, plots can become so simple as to be incomprehensible, *Mission Impossible* (1998) being a good example. Others include pastiche, that is, clipping together pieces or examples of other films to hold together a narrative (*Pulp Fiction* 1995), parody (*Scary Movie* 2000), and genre-crossing (*Time Cop*—martial arts-science fiction; *Shanghai Noon* [2000]—martial arts–Western), all of which are methods of broadening the audience base.

Similarly, in a reverse of the *Death Race* formula, where a popular movie spawned a video game, Hollywood has turned to kid's games for narratives: Wing Commander the popular video game became *Wing Commander* (1999) the box office flop. Television shows are also not immune from such poaching. *Batman* (1989) and its two sequels did well in the theaters; *Batman and Robin* (1997), which made a fraction of what had been expected, was a case of going to the well once too often. Even old cartoons like *Rocky and Bullwinkle* have been brought to the big screen on a large budget—and have failed utterly. Comic book adaptations have had mixed results: *Spiderman* (2002) was a huge smash; *The Hulk* (2003), *Spawn* (1997) and *X Men* (2000) did reasonably well; *The Fantastic Four* died in pre-production, a victim of its overwhelming cost.

And while blockbusters like these would anchor the studio's yearly releases, both at summer and Christmas, the studio's schedule would also include some lower budgeted movies. But the latter would still be ten or more times a "B" release's cost. With the escalation of such prices across the board, then, it comes as no surprise that the "B" would eventually be pushed out of theatrical exhibition. For example, Clint Eastwood's production company Malpaso's films for Warners—hardly "B" movies but still low for a Hollywood "A"—average around $30,000,000, half to a third as much as a major blockbuster like *Rambo III* (1988) or *Independence Day* (1996), and a fifth of Universal's *Waterworld* (1995). Faced with the choice of *Heartbreak Ridge* (1986) or New World's same-year release *POW: The Escape*, theater chains, and viewers, not surprisingly opted for Clint and not Carradine.

Along the same lines, the major studios began seeing video release as a way to recoup losses on box office flops. A disaster like *Hudson Hawk* (1991) that tanked immediately in theaters could be rushed to video, thereby recouping some of its costs. Early video release became a basic Hollywood strategy. A new stratification of film gross thus emerged for the "A" feature: Its theatrical release would be the

Steve James (left) and David Carradine (second from left) star in Cannon Films'
POW: The Escape (1986). Audiences were beginning to prefer big-budgeted films to
"B" films like this one, spelling an end to low-budget theatrical releases by the end
of the decade.

primary market, but it would next be followed by video release anywhere from four
to six months later. Weeks to months after that, the film would be available to cable
and pay TV. Barnouw notes,

> Through this strategy, home owners might be induced to buy or rent the
> video before having a chance to tape the film off-air. After HBO or other
> premium channels would come sales to the old mainstays—NBC, CBS,
> ABC—for sponsored broadcast revenue Then would come syndication,
> domestic and foreign—first run, second run, third run, ad infinitum.[38]

According to Pricewaterhouse-Coopers, the major studio's revenues can be
broken down as follows:

1. Theatrical box office (for films released) 24.6 percent
2. Television 28.8 percent
3. Home Video 46.6 percent[75]

With finite amounts of shelf space available to video outlets, "A"s got the lion's
share. "B" theatrical films, particularly martial arts ones, could not hope to compete against such releases, even flops, with their name stars and high production

values. As the 90s approached its midpoint, Cannon Films, the ultimate modern "B" theatrical purveyor, which had filed bankruptcy in the late 80s, disappeared, and the "B" theatrical release, including the martial arts film, faced its dusk, only to be resurrected in the 90s by a new paradigm called the "direct-to-video" release, of which the American-style martial arts movie was an important element.

VII

The 1990s: DTVs—Martial Arts Films Find a New Outlet

With an American theatrical release no longer a viable outlet for martial arts films in the 1990s, independent studios scrambled to come up with new ways to market their product. And they did. Like the "B" releases of the 30s and 40s, which were replaced by the exploitation features of the 50s and 60s, low-budget American martial arts films got down-and-dirty to survive, the producers dropping their budgets even further and finding other outlets for their product.

Direct-to-video (DTV) films emerged, movies made on extremely low budgets with no theatrical release. However, once completed, the DTV still had to be sold, usually at major film markets like Cannes or the AFM. Along with this new type of film, new stars emerged, a significant number of them martial arts champions, or at least hardcore practitioners who were martial artists before turning to acting. Hollywood's classic age came full circle as these martial arts films found homes in the Western, action-thriller, sci-fi/horror and war genres, while the pure martial arts story also made a comeback with the drop in budgets, usually manifested in the "tournament" stories, wherein the hero exacts revenge for some past transgression by fighting in a kumite.

A New Paradigm Emerges: Direct-to-Video Films

As "A" features dominated the box office, low-budget, independent production companies, ever the survivors, adapted to the changing economic climate. Rather than aim for a theatrical release, they cut their film costs even more and concentrated on a twofold attack: whatever they could muster from video sales and cable releases in the United States, plus foreign sales to Europe, Asia and the rest of the world. The Cannes and Milan film festivals, along with the American Film Market (AFM) in Santa Monica, provided these companies (and the major studios) delineated distribution areas in which they could sell their product.*

Of course, there were ways around this structure for the enterprising company, too. Since a theatrical release raises the fetching price of a film overseas,[1] some independents actually rent a theater, advertise the film in the newspaper and then subsequently claim their product is a "theatrical release!"

The direct-to-video (DTV) model was as simple as it was profitable: a very low budget, a recognizable genre, usually erotic, horror/sci-fi, children's or action, one, two or three "name" stars, preferably one of whom had "A" recognition, and a short film shoot (increasingly) overseas, in Europe, Canada, Mexico or the Philippines, where costs are lower.

Fred Olen Ray, a veteran producer-director who has churned out more low-budget films then just about anyone, successfully transitioned from theatrical "B" releases like *Armed Response* and *Commando Squad* (1987) to the DTV environment of the 90s. Ray's mantra is as simple as it is unpretentious: complete the film quickly and inexpensively—"Six days, no waiting."[2] Filming *Operation Cobra* (1996) in India, Ray put his mantra into practice, continuing shooting even after one of his extras was bitten by a cobra during the climactic fight scene![3]

One of the most important means used to garner interest in a film is to employ poster art. The posters can often carry a dual purpose: obviously underscoring the highpoints of an existing film, but also generating enthusiasm for future films. Like AIP and the other exploitation companies that came before, DTV producers can use posters to obtain advance monetary allocations from various buyers *before* the film is even made. For example, an imaginary film entitled *Recon Force* might be touted as a revenge story, with a retired Marine hunting the urban gang bangers who killed his family, chasing them from the city streets through the Florida Everglades. The poster might display the Marine in camouflage gear, concealed in the swamp; the gang members terrorizing his wife and daughter; police cars with lights flashing; the Marine dispatching a group of the gangsters in a karate fight, etc. With commitment from a known DTV star, buyers may ante up the cash before the first scene is shot.

When these DTV films are finally released in the stores, the cover art on the video and DVD boxes become like mini-posters, displaying the highlights of the film, either with pictures from the movie or drawings. Van Damme's *Cyborg* is in the former category, featuring still photographs of various fight scenes; however, what you see is not always what you get. While Chuck Norris' likeness graces the video of his *An Eye for an Eye*, it shows him rappelling from a helicopter—which never occurrs in the movie. *Kickboxing Academy*'s (1997) video box cover features a cute little boy who is not even in the film!

A variation of this formula is found in the distribution route of the B's artistic cousin, the low-budget "indie" film. These movies, as often as not made by outsiders looking to break into the film industry, usually feature no stars, are scraped together in financially unorthodox ways, and can deal seriously with trivial matters (The Blair Witch Project), trivially with serious matters (Clerks) or highlight other, more controversial topics that major studios shy away from (Boys Don't Cry). The films are showcased in film festivals, from the most famous event, Sundance, to lesser known ones such as Telluride, New York, Berlin—even Temecula (a small city in Southern California's Mojave desert)! Studios looking for additional product quite often pick up some of these films for theatrical distribution. The Blair Witch Project (1999), made for approximately $35,000, grossed over $100,000,000 for Artisan Entertainment.

Similarly, in *Cyborg 2* (1993), which sounds like a sequel to the Van Damme film but is not, a drawing of Academy Award winner Jack Palance is prominently featured on the box, when in reality he makes what amounts to be a cameo appearance. *Open Fire* (1994), starring Jeff Wincott as an embittered ex–FBI agent, is shown on the cover of his film climbing a wall with the city around him. In the film, he was fighting terrorists in a chemical plant. The back cover shows him holding a "streetsweeper"-like shotgun in one hand and a semi-automatic pistol in the other. No such event occurred. As they say, let the buyer—or in this case the renter—beware.

The Talent: New Stars

Under such tight budgetary formulas, the American-style martial arts film became a natural staple for the low-budget producers, much like the Western had been in the 30s,* due not only to its popularity in the Asian market—always a factor—but its inherently inexpensive nature. Kung fu costs much less to shoot than plummeting meteors or huge monsters; and top-quality martial artists, while a rare commodity, *can* be found.

Don Wilson

Roger Corman was among the first to start up production, using relatively unknown Amerasion fighter-actor Don "The Dragon" Wilson as his star. I say "relatively" because Wilson was a professional kickboxing champion widely respected in the martial arts community. He grew up in Cocoa Beach, Florida, where his father worked as a NASA engineer. Started in the martial arts by his brother, he moved into professional kickboxing in 1974.[4] Wilson was one of the greatest fighters ever, having amassed "11 World Titles, in 3 different weight classes under 6 different sanctioning organizations."[5] Wilson remained world champion for an unprecedented 11 years running.

Wilson tried his hand at Hollywood at the suggestion of friend Chuck Norris and eventually auditioned for Roger Corman, who was impressed with the young fighter. He signed a seven-picture deal with Corman and their first was 1988's *Bloodfist*. Because Wilson was still fighting professionally at the time, Corman reportedly insured Wilson's face "for $10 million dollars with Lloyds of London."[6] The film's credits indicated Wilson's professional titles—which included a score of championships—that bolstered Wilson's reputation as one tough hombre. This trend would follow in most of Concorde–New Horizon's subsequent martial arts films.

Bloodfist took place in the Philippines, not surprisingly since it is a cheap place to film and Concorde–New Horizons has a production facility there. Jake Raye, a

---

* *I think a valid argument could be made that the martial arts films were just as responsible for the ultimate demise of the Western as was the sci-fi* Star Wars–*type movies. Most, particularly those of the right, featured heroes with many of the same views as those espoused in the Monogram quickies a half-century earlier. Exit* John Wayne *and enter Chuck Norris; the six-shooter is replaced by a karate chop, and the horse by an SUV, but the themes and values remain similar.*

former kickboxing champion, scours the streets of Manila to locate his brother's murderer. He finds that not only was his brother *not* well-liked, but no one really wants to cooperate with him. He finally hooks up with his brother's trainer, begins working out and meets a fellow fighter whose sister is gorgeous. The two fall in love and Raye finally finds his brother's killer, though it is the person he would have least expected.

Like the B series entries of the 30s and 40s, from George Sanders' *The Falcon* to Ronald Reagan's *Secret Service of the Air*, this film set the pattern for its numerous and profitable sequels. Wilson, a peaceable man, finds himself in situations where he must fight to survive. *Bloodfist II*, released a year later, was much the same—Wilson journeys to the Philippines to help a friend and is taken captive to fight in an illegal tournament. However, this film boasted an interesting albeit well-known message: Drugs are bad! Wilson is teamed with other champions and pitted against the villain's cadre of drug-enhanced fighters. Needless to say, the champions prove their worth, and make mincemeat of the drug abusers.

Bloodfist III: Forced to Fight (1991) was filmed in an actual prison, boasted increased production values and surrounded Wilson with a supporting cast of such veteran actors as Richard Roundtree (*Shaft*, 1971) and Richard Paul (*The People vs. Larry Flynt*, 1997). Corman's proclivity toward left-of-center narratives is evident as the Amerasian Wilson, railroaded into a prison for a crime he (naturally) didn't commit, becomes the protector of a group of decent prisoners, most of them

Don "The Dragon" Wilson battles the Aryan Brotherhood in Concorde–New Horizon's *Bloodfist III: Forced to Fight* (1990). This was the first of Wilson's films where he was surrounded with a top-notch supporting cast.

where they are because of racism and prejudice, save a child molester whom Wilson nevertheless takes under his wing. In the end, Wilson must fight off both the Aryan Brotherhood and Black Guerrilla Family to save his new friends.

In *Bloodfist IV: Die Trying* (1992), the series reached a high point, with an intelligent, complex narrative and an excellent supporting cast. Wilson portrays a car repo-man and single father. He's an average guy who loves his small daughter and struggles to make ends meet, but because of his past, repossessing cars is the only work he can find. And it's not easy. Time and again Wilson has to duke it out with irate owners or chauffeurs, including a hilarious fight with Judo Gene LeBell over his car. But when Wilson repossesses the wrong car, his entire work place is massacred by a terrorist group exporting illegal nuclear material to Middle East nations. Wilson goes on the run, helped only by his babysitter, who is herself suspicious of him.

Chasing Wilson are the local police and the terrorists, the former for murders committed by the latter. The FBI intercedes, but by this point Wilson can trust no one. He keeps what the terrorists want to himself, bargaining with them to save his daughter. In the film's climax, he destroys the terrorists, only to find that he was a pawn in a much larger game: The CIA was using the terrorists to provide an un named Middle East country (read Israel) with nuclear triggers.

Factor out the martial arts scenes in *Bloodfist IV: Die Trying* and what are you left with? A very compelling story, finely told, about weapons of mass destruction; the frantic, deadly search for them by terrorists and government agents alike; the blur between who's who; and the endless maze of conspiracies which all point to a time of extreme social and economic anxiety as the world faces a new millennium. In essence, *Die Trying* can be read as a cultural reflection of America in the 90s: prosperous for some, not for others, a bubbling cauldron of fears over terrorism, nuclear proliferation and economic uncertainty.

The *Bloodfist* series which paved the way to Wilson's success is one of the most popular martial arts series ever made, in part because of the various characteristics which constitute the "Bloodfist" hero:

1. *The Bloodfist hero is a lone wolf.*

"Wolf" because his martial arts skills make him very dangerous. "Lone" because circumstances have set him apart from other men. In *Bloodfist VI*, Nick finds himself alone and outgunned in a nuclear missile silo, fighting off terrorists as he tries to prevent a nuclear launch. Jimmy Boland in *Bloodfist III* just wants to do his prison time in peace, left alone by everyone, but in the end is forced to fight.

2. *The Bloodfist hero is marked by some trauma or injustice.*

Jake Raye in *Bloodfist* loses his brother to a vengeful murderer. In *Bloodfist II* he is taken captive and forced to duke it out with drug-enhanced fighters. Jimmy Boland in *Bloodfist III* has been victimized by guards and prisoners alike. In *Bloodfist VII*, Jim Trudell tries to help a lady in distress and winds up being chased by cops and crooks. Danny Holt in *Bloodfist IV* is a single father who has lost his wife. In *Bloodfist V*, Jimmy has lost his memory.

3. *The Bloodfist hero must deal with authorities who are crooked or duplicitous— or both.*

In *Bloodfist III*, the prison guards condone and provoke much of the violence in the institution, while in *Bloodfist IV*, the CIA knows all along what is going on and uses Danny to further their aims. In *Bloodfist VI*, while Nick is fighting for his life in the missile silo, the Air Force plans to destroy it and everyone inside.

4. *The Bloodfist hero finds himself either on the run, or a target for others.*

In *Bloodfist VIII* Rick/George is in the bullseye of the CIA. In *Bloodfist IV*, Danny is on the move, hunted by terrorists who want the nuclear triggers he has in his possession, while in *Bloodfist III*, both prison gangs want Jimmy Boland dead. In *Bloodfist VII*, Jim Trudell is chased across the city of Los Angeles by mobsters who want the tape they think he possesses.

5. *The Bloodfist hero prevails in the end, despite the odds, but only by his own ingenuity and fighting prowess.*

In *Bloodfist*, Jake wins the tournament, but then must fight his coach, who is the murderer he has been searching for. In *Bloodfist II*, Jake and the other champions outclass their opponents and take down the drug kingpin. Nick outsmarts the terrorists in *Bloodfist VI*, using his martial arts abilities to wear them down. In *Bloodfist IV*, Danny bargains with the terrorists for the life of his daughter, then eventually beats them with his fists and feet, while the CIA and FBI stand back and monitor the situation.

Wilson continues to remain among the most bankable low-budget commodities, not only for the story quality of his films, but in large part because of a style or pattern that seems to manifest itself in many of his movies. In his early days,

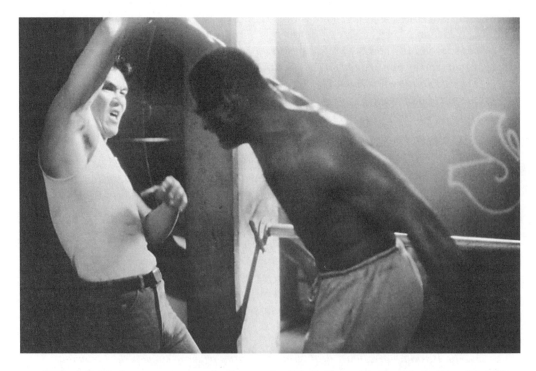

Wilson (left) changes gears and takes on the Black Guerrilla Family in *Bloodfist III: Forced to Fight.*

Wilson rarely played a cop or a law enforcement agent, but rather was often hostile to authority because the system had burned him one too many times. In *Black-belt* (1992), Wilson plays an ex-cop run off the force who now works as a private eye. When he's hired to protect a singer from a fanatical hit man–fan, action explodes everywhere as Wilson fights an entire biker bar and later the hit man, played by Mathias Hues.

In *Ring of Fire I* and *II,* he is a martial arts expert–doctor, but not exactly cordial to the police. In the former film, Wilson handles the stresses of the emergency room at work, while at home counseling Chinese youth who are battling white youth for turf. Wilson's advice backfires when he suggests that the gang's two leaders duke it out using broken glass tarred onto their fists: one of the boys dies. In the latter film, Wilson's girl is kidnapped by some freaks. Not trusting the cops, he enters a bizarre underworld of tunnels and caves that criss-cross the city, fighting his way to her.

When Wilson *is* a cop, he is usually an outsider, as in *Red Sun Rising* (1993), where he plays a Japanese policeman in the States. In *Terminal Rush* (1995) he plays a half–Indian deputy sheriff, the victim of bigotry and a conspiracy within his own department as he battles some terrorists taking over the Hoover Dam. Roddy Piper plays Wilson's chief opponent but the two never get it on, and the bizarre eye gear that Piper uses distracts from his menacing figure.

Often Wilson can be viewed as the lone man looking in, but remains an ethically balanced character in a world where morals shift like sand in a desert wind, even when he has lost his memory (*Bloodfist V* 1993), or he is not human (*Future-kick* 1993). Many of his films take on a "Hitchcockian" twist and feature him as an innocent man victimized by both organized crime and the police out to stop the criminals (*Bloodfist VII: Manhunt,* 1995). Who's who becomes difficult to determine until Wilson "chops" his way through the chaos to unravel the mystery.

When Corman signed a deal with Cinemax to produce a batch of low-budget action-thriller films for the cable channel's Saturday late-night action slot, *Bloodfist VI: Ground Zero* (1994) was among the first releases. While fast-paced and action-packed, with Wilson defending a nuclear silo against terrorists, it lacked some of the bite of *Die Trying,* but nonetheless was an excellent example of solid, low-budget filmmaking.

Wilson plays Nick Corrigan, an Air Force courier who makes a delivery to a silo. He gets himself locked in by terrorists who are busy obtaining the missile launch codes. They figure he's no big deal, but he turns out to be ex–Special Forces, and as they hunt him, he turns the tables and begins to hunt *them.* Complicating things are the military, which is preparing a nuclear strike on the silo to prevent any launches. Wilson saves the day, but not until fighting almost every guy in the place, not to mention gals (Wilson is reunited with one of his nemesis' from *Bloodfist IV,* Catya Sassoon, who plays a treacherous femme fatale).

More films followed: *Operation Cobra* (1997) and *The Prophet* (1999) were directed by old hand Fred Olen Ray and featured Wilson at the top of his game. In the former, filmed on location in India, Wilson plays an American cop out for revenge. *Redemption* (2002), a gem of a film and arguably Wilson's best role, features him as a disgraced police officer working on the other side of the law. After being fired from the force, Wilson finds himself facing tough times. He needs money to buy a house that he promised for his son, and to pay for the summer that the son will stay with him. After some soul-searching, Wilson crosses the line, but finds it is very different being a crook as opposed to a cop.

Part of *Redemption*'s appeal is that it presents situations and events not in terms of black-and-white but gray, which is often how it is in police work. Wilson's character "Johnny Boy" is going through a divorce, but clearly still has feelings for his wife, who has taken up with a professional baseball player. But what does she feel toward Johnny? We never learn. Wilson's decisions are also suspect, which prompts his team to desert him. During the film's opening (the raid of a drug dealer's house), the villains discover that an undercover cop is among them. Rather than immediately going in, Wilson waits because a child is in the house. The cop is stabbed. Later, Wilson's team prepare to bust up a drug sale. His second-in-command urges that they call for back up but Wilson attacks. One of his team is killed.

Redemption clearly marks a turn toward more character-driven roles for Wilson. The fights are good, but seeing Wilson as Johnny Boy, the down-and-almost-out ex-cop is better. The film's title sets the point of the story: Before Wilson is sacked, he tells a prostitute that life is about choices, making the right ones over the wrong ones. With no money and his back against the wall, Wilson takes a job with a drug dealer. As he ponders his decision, a bundle of cash is laid on the table and one of the drug dealer's associates tells him that if he picks the money up, there's no turning back. Wilson pockets the cash, then spends the rest of the story looking for a redemption that doesn't come easily.

Cynthia Rothrock

If Wilson was the first low-budget martial arts superstar, others quickly followed. Cynthia Rothrock is arguably the most recognizable female martial arts star in the world. A spot in a Kentucky Fried Chicken commercial launched her career. She apprenticed in Hong Kong, where her agility and extreme flexibility was put to use in such films as *Fu gui lic che* (1986) and *Zhong jian ren* (1987), among others. These Hong Kong films were good training for Rothrock, who noted in a Martial Arts Network interview with Ben Smith that the fight scenes there were brutal, and that the directors were continually expecting more from her with each film.[7]

In 1986, Rothrock paired with Michelle Khan in *Yes, Madam*, which is the honorific title given police women in Hong Kong; in America, where *Madam* has a slightly different meaning, the title was changed to *Supercops*. Rothrock certainly lent a unique presence to these films, where she was often not only the sole Anglo but a woman to boot. *Prince of the Sun* (1990) again featured Rothrock as the only Anglo in what was clearly an import film. She spends most of her time protecting a precocious little boy from harm, which means plenty of signature-style Cynthia action.

Rothrock later signed with Golden Harvest Productions, which teamed her with *Enter the Dragon* director Robert Clouse. The result was *China O'Brien* (1990) and *China O'Brien II* (1991), which co-starred Richard Norton. The films were shot back-to-back in Utah, and featured Rothrock as the spunky daughter of a sheriff—murdered by corrupt politicos—who battles the gangsters tooth and nail in this female version of *Walking Tall*. The two films were successful with audiences and immediately established Rothrock as a bankable figure in the action industry.[8]

Other roles followed, including a television spot in *The Dukes of Hazzard Reunion* (1997). In *Sworn to Justice* (1996), one Rothrock's best films, she plays a Jekyll and Hyde–like psychiatrist who by day counsels troubled children and at night battles criminals. The film boasted good production values, and director Paul Maslak underscored the Dionysian aspects of her character by specifically choreographing her fight scenes to classical and other types of music. *Night Vision* (1997) teamed her with Fred "The Hammer" Williamson as the two search for a serial killer. Nice touches, such as the Hammer going to an AA meeting, add to the story.

Irresistible Force (1993) paired Rothrock with Stacy Keach in a breezy, action-packed story about a female cop on her first day on the force. She's partnered with Keach, a detective looking for a woman partner since his male partners always end up getting him shot, beat up or worse. He finds that he is in for the shock of his life. The two immediately have to break up an armed robbery but they demolish a car dealership in the process. Both are suspended, but then have to contend with an armed takeover of a mall by a militia movement while the SWAT team cowers outside. The chemistry between the leads was good and the film's production values fair. It was designed to be the pilot for a television show. Unfortunately it was not picked up by CBS and a sequel was never commissioned.[9] However, Rothrock's martial arts moves never looked better, and from the film's opening she proved she was indeed an irresistible force.

Like with Wilson, much of Rothrock's appeal comes from an on-screen persona that follows her from film to film. Though a ferocious fighter, more than able to hold her own against any martial artist, let alone any man, she remains lady-like and gracious, never emasculating. Many of her characters are up-and-comers, professional women in a man's world who have to earn the respect of their male counterparts. In *Guardian Angel* (1994) she is a widowed police officer–turned–bodyguard who protects her wealthy client while unraveling the mystery behind his predicament. In *Rage and Honor* (1992), in which she plays the master of her own martial arts studio, she aids the police in finding a vicious murderer. The follow-up, *Rage and Honor II* (1993), featured Rothrock as a federal undercover operative infiltrating a gang for the government.

Of Rothrock's many films, *Tiger Claws* (1992) provides a typical delineation of both her character and predicament. "The Death-Dealer," a dreaded killer preying on the martial arts community, is murdering prominent fighters with a little-known technique called "Tiger Claw"—a devastating punch that destroys the victim's insides while leaving only a paw-like scratch on the victim's face or body. Rothrock plays detective Linda Masterson, who is going nowhere in the vice unit. Her days consist of dressing up like a hooker to be propositioned by perverts. After one john attacks her with a knife, she takes him into custody with a devastating array of kicks and punches, appearing as such a perfect mix of beauty and savagery that the suspect exclaims, "She's a cop...?"

Rothrock longs to get out of vice, so she takes the initiative and investigates the Death-Dealer case on her own. She is finally assigned to the case by her supervisor, who is impressed with her hard work and knowledge of the martial arts. Initially she is rejected by her partner, who would rather work alone, but eventually

Cynthia Rothrock doing what she does best in this scene from *Tiger Claws* **(SGE, 1992).**

he and the others come to respect her for her effort and abilities as they not only find the killer but then have to fight to bring him to justice.

Rothrock's character is the exact opposite of her partner and, ironically, in some ways more akin to the killer. The Death-Dealer, while a madman, is one bound by certain traditions. He despises the martial arts champions whom he has killed because they are boastful types or "celebrities" who are rebels for abandoning the established ways of their disciplines, thereby aligning him more with Rothrock than her partner. Where Rothrock works hard and relies on established methods of investigation, her partner, also an accomplished martial artist, is lazier and tends to improvise. Where Rothrock follows procedures and goes by the book, her partner makes up the rules as he goes along. When the duo find some possible suspects, it is Rothrock who argues for calm, that they take pictures before physically confronting the suspects. While it is the Rothrock photos that provide the leads to the Death-Dealer, she takes a proverbial back seat as her partner eventually overcomes the killer in the final showdown.

Rothrock's charm come from her ability to prove herself without detracting from her male counterparts. She is not a revolutionary out to destroy the system, nor a strident feminist out to make waves, but rather a self-assured woman who merely expects the same respect that others in her profession receive. *Tiger Claws II* (1997) underscores Rothrock's persona. Now a detective, she and her partner must once again overcome the Death-Dealer, who has escaped from prison and headed to San Francisco, where he links up with his gang. Rothrock's character has now matured as a detective, and though there is some gruesomely realistic violence, including the execution of two unsuspecting state troopers, she fights more as an equal than a subordinate, giving as good as she gets. The year 1999 saw her in *Tiger Claws 3; Manhattan Chase* followed in 2000 and *Never Say Die* in 2001. In 2002 she was cast in *Redemption,* her first pairing with Don Wilson, and a reunion with previous co-stars Richard Norton and Sam J. Jones.

Jeff Wincott

For a number of years Jeff Wincott honed his acting skills by playing a kickboxing police officer on *Night Heat,* a late night television series that followed the adventures of some AM watch detectives. All the action took place during evening hours, facilitating a sense of foreboding as the officer's prey stalked the night. Wincott grew up in Toronto, Canada, where he competed in a number of sports "as well as training in the martial arts such as kung fu, karate, and tae kwon do."[10]

Wincott segued into low-budget martial arts films when the series was cancelled, and as much as anyone has consistently tried to improve the quality of his films as well as his fighting skills, appearing in movies other than martial arts. In 1992 Wincott starred in one of his best films, *Deadly Bet,* for Pepin-Merhi Entertainment. He plays an alcoholic gambler who loses his girlfriend in a bet with an underground fight promoter. He spends the rest of the story trying to overcome his addictions while getting his girl back. Of course, that means winning the *big* match in the underground tournament. Top-of-the-line fight scenes and a welcome accent on character distinguish this film from others of its ilk.

In *Last Man Standing* (1996), Wincott gives another outstanding performance as a cop trying to figure out who murdered his partner and why. Good chemistry between Wincott and veteran character actor Jonathan Banks distinguish this film, also from Pepin-Merhi Entertainment, while in *Open Fire,* Wincott plays a hotheaded ex–FBI agent who fights terrorists in a chemical plant. Since they hold his dad prisoner, Wincott gets involved despite warnings by the authorities. With the police and FBI portrayed as incompetent, it becomes clear to the audience that Wincott's brand of vigilantism is the only way to solve the problem.

When the Bullet Hits the Bone (1995) features Wincott as an emergency room doctor pushed to the edge by the criminal violence he encounters, while in *No Exit* (1995) he plays a college professor whose martial arts abilities come into play when his wife is almost killed and he is forced into an illegal tournament which broadcasts the fights on closed circuit television to gambling parlors in Asia. The fights here are extremely well choreographed, with the northern tundra serving as a backdrop for the combat, and a metaphor for the hopelessness of the fighters trapped in this endless cycle of violence.

In an unusual turn, Wincott played a scientist in *Future Fear* (1997) and eschewed any form of martial arts, instead relying on his screen wife and nemesis Maria Ford to do all the chopping, kicking and punching. The film was confusing at best, and the sound quality was poor, yet there was a creepy reality to it that stuck with viewers who could remain attentive. The story concerns a virus that was unleashed on Earth when a space transport crashed. Wincott learns that the crash was planned by the military for the purpose of ethnic cleansing, but by then it is too late. However, the themes of individual thought vs. authoritarian rule, and civilian control vs. military regime, weren't thoroughly sketched out, so a good premise ended up being just another low-budget film.

Jalal Merhi

Jalal Merhi is an expert martial artist and jack-of-all-trades behind the camera. He has appeared in a dozen or so pictures, produced at least that many, and directed six films. He has also been a fight coordinator, second unit director and camera operator—not to mention one extremely talented fighter. In many of his pictures he is paired with other famous martial artists, among them Billy Blanks and Cynthia Rothrock. Arguably his best performance is in *G.O.D.* (2000), in which he plays an ex-cop who works as a security guard. He gets fired from that job after a bank heist in which his wife is killed. Olivier Gruner plays his adversary, and David Carradine takes a break from his usual role as the heavy to play a salty, retired cop who helps Merhi rescue a kidnapped girl.

In *Operation Golden Phoenix*, Merhi does a dual turn as both star and director, and shows why he is such a talent in martial arts cinema. Merhi plays Assante, an expert security specialist protecting antiquities. Assante's background is mysterious, as is that of Jones, his partner, but it is mentioned that they were at one time government agents. Assante and Jones are assigned to escort a valuable museum exhibit (a pendant) from Lebanon to Canada but, unbeknownst to Assante, Jones has betrayed the mission to Chang, a treasure hunter. The security crew is wiped out and the pendant is stolen. Assante, left alive to take the fall, is arrested and locked up without bail. That is, until he escapes, obtains a false passport from his girl and makes his way back to Lebanon to find out who set him up and why.

Under Merhi's taut direction, *Operation Golden Phoenix* never flags, the action is crisp and fresh and a number of motifs running through the story set it apart from other action flicks: the effects of greed and the seeming liability of trust in a hard world. At the film's outset, Jones is confronted by a man to whom he owes money. Rather than pay, he shoves a pen into the man's gut, then shows him that he had the cash to settle his debt all the time. After Assante is arrested for the theft of the pendant, the police chief grills him, accusing him of the robbery and murders because of his own greed.

Once in Lebanon, Assante learns that the chief was right—greed *was* the driving force behind his troubles and the murders of his security crew. Chang, the mastermind, is obsessed with the mythical treasure of the Ottoman Empire whose location the stolen pendant, along with another matching pendant, is supposed to reveal. Chang will do anything to get the pendants and the treasure, using hit men to kidnap and kill, and then murdering them to cover his tracks. Jones is lured away from his honest work of guarding museum antiquities by the riches promised to him by Chang, enough treasure to make him frame and murder his best friend Assante. Susan, the wife of the professor excavating the antiquities, betrays her husband to partner with Chang, providing him with inside information on what the professor and Assante are doing.

After Chang obtains both pendants and murders the professor, he, Jones and Susan find the ruins where the treasure is hidden, Susan jabbering all the while about how many millions they will have. 100,000,000? 200,000,000? 300,000,000? Chang is not sure, but it will be a lot. When Susan falls down some stairs and breaks her neck, Jones smiles, telling Chang that leaves more money for them. When the two men finally find the treasure, the ruins begin to collapse. Chang is buried alive in a mountain of gold coins.

From the outset of *Operation Golden Phoenix*, Assante is the victim of multiple setups, mostly from people he trusts. He is double-crossed by his partner Jones and left to take the rap. In Lebanon, he steals the second pendant from Princess Angelica and hands it over to Susan, who then arranges for him to be killed. The professor is betrayed by his wife Susan and murdered by Chang, while Princess Angelica is taken in by Assante, who mistakenly steals her pendant. Even Jones, among the most treacherous, is double-crossed by Chang when they find the treasure, giving credence to the old axiom that there's no honor among thieves.

If Assante has any flaws, it is that he was so easily blindsided. A man of integrity, loyal and honest, he is everything that Jones is not. Even after seeing Jones alive, he still has trouble believing his old partner set him up. The final fight between the two men is a running battle which takes place in some old ruins, furnishing a sense of energy and excitement to the combat. Assante engages in two other major fight sequences. One, in jail, pits him against a cell full of rough-and-tumble prisoners who don't like the way he is dressed. The second takes place on a dam, where Assante takes on a gauntlet of men trying to kill him.

The film ends as it began. Assante is cleared of all charges, Jones is in the custody of the Lebanese police and the antiquities stolen from the museum have been returned. Assante is back at his old job, reputation restored, guarding material for the museum, and he is reunited with his girlfriend.

Gary Daniels

Gary Daniels is a hard-hitting kickboxing and karate champion from the UK who landed in the U.S. with about 400 bucks in his pocket, ambition and star aspirations. He studied what he called "Mongolian kung fu for three years and tae kwon do for four to five years."[11] Eventually he got involved with the Professional Karate

Association (PKA). Like Jean-Claude Van Damme, Daniels' chiseled body has made him as much of an action star as a favorite with the females.

Daniels' first starring role was in *Capital Punishment* (1991), a very nebulous story that quickly becomes tiring to follow. Daniels plays Thayer, a kickboxer making money by pit fighting in Asian nightclubs. After convincingly beating the house champion, Thayer is recruited by a secret organization within the DEA and assigned the job of bringing down his old sensei, who is now marketing a very potent new drug in America. As Thayer gets deeper into the investigation, he finds betrayal at every turn, until he is at a point where he can believe nothing and trust no one.

Where the film got the title is a mystery. It seems to have no connection to the actual plot, except for a quick mention by Daniels after one particularly bruising battle. However, if for nothing else, *Capital Punishment* is a worthwhile film just for its fights. Daniels is set upon constantly and the combat is excellently choreographed, with the participants not only engaging in kickboxing and karate but plenty of arm twists and holds, something not always present in these movies.

The level of brutality in *Capital Punishment* is exceedingly high, even for a film of this genre. Many of the fights do not seem motivated by the plot, and weapons of all types except firearms are used to kill and maim. In one fight, Daniels runs a gauntlet of men when trying to escape from the DEA, and smashes one opponent's head into the wall over and over again. In other struggles, he beats his rivals with metal flashlights, a sock full of change and even a flare with which he lights a man on fire. In one scene with apparent homoerotic overtones, Daniels is tied by the arms to a forklift, in a modified crucifixion pose. Men gather all around him; one steps forward, shocking and burning him with an electrical conductor across the chest.

Except for the standard anti-drug message, nothing is exceptional about the narrative, although from Daniels' performance it was clear he was destined for bigger and better films. When Daniels finds out he is the product of a genetic experiment, and that he will not be able to function much longer because of the pain, he consults a sifu who advises him to sweat the drug from his system through meditation and martial arts discipline. After a couple of obligatory scenes showing Daniels concentrating intently with the master, he conquers the drug's effect and is ready to resume unraveling the mystery and living a productive life, clearly an example to addicts everywhere that all it takes to beat a habit is a strong mind and a good sensei.

Daniels continued to work, taking third and fourth billing in a number of films before making an impact as Don Wilson's primary opponent in *Bloodfist IV*. He followed up with the starring role in *American Streetfighter I* (1992), which was somewhat interesting since Daniels is British. Unlike Don Wilson or Cynthia Rothrock, Daniels has not cultivated a particular persona. He has played bit parts, such as a nameless kickboxing fighter in *Final Round*, villains like Scar in *Bloodfist IV*, where he is the terrorist's lead enforcer, or he can play hero, which he now does in most of his films. Early in his career Daniels sported a mane of blonde hair, but was not averse to trimming it to manageable lengths to open up the types of lead roles he can now land. In short, he is willing to make the sacrifice to get the job done.

In 1994, Daniels got a break in the decently budgeted PM Entertainment production *Deadly Target*, a well-plotted, well-acted story that features Daniels as Hong

Kong police sergeant Charles Prince. Prince arrives in Los Angeles to extradite Wang, a drug-dealing killer who is attempting to spread his narcotics business to the United States. Unfortunately for Prince, Wang is not yet in custody, something which the Los Angeles Police Department failed to notify him of. LAPD Detective Jensen, who is assigned to escort Prince, advises him that they intend to pick up Wang that night.

Jensen, Prince and some other officers set up on a high rise building where Wang is supposed to meet other members of the local Chinese Triads to get their approval to deal his narcotics. The members refuse and Wang and his crew murder the bunch in a messy, bloody shootout. Prince and Jensen make their way into the building, Prince fighting a whole slew of men in the stairwell, and then duke it out with some of Wang's killers. Prince eventually captures Wang after an explosive car chase. The next day, Wang is to be brought to the airport for extradition. En route, his convoy is ambushed by his gang and he is freed, setting Prince and Jensen in motion once again.

Deadly Target was the first film to allow Daniels room to focus on his character. Up to this point he had been pretty much a killing machine, taking on all comers and usually winning. Sgt. Prince is not so one-dimensional, and definitely has his own flaws. While he is brave, honest and not without a certain degree of charm, he is also brutal, rash and headstrong. He leaps into situations immediately, often without time for proper reflection, and rarely awaits back-up. When Wang attacks the Triad in the high rise, Prince moves in against Jensen's orders, forcing the rest of the officers to move with him before they are ready. When he interrogates Wang, who taunts him while refusing to answer questions, Prince beats the handcuffed prisoner bloody. In another instance he strings up one of Wang's lieutenants and threatens to draw and quarter him if he doesn't talk. Later, while chasing one of Wang's men (who has his girlfriend Diana), Prince drives right by her after she is thrown from the car into the street, more intent on capturing the suspect than checking on Diana's wellbeing.

Prince's character deficiencies as a man and a cop could be viewed as Wang's strong points as a gang leader. In many ways he and Prince are alike. Wang is vicious and treacherous. He murders his own uncle when the man refuses to get involved in Wang's drug trade. Wang later orders hits on all the Triad leaders, and they are machine gunned down in their nightclubs or, in the case of one leader, while he is giving a campaign speech!

Neither Prince nor Wang care who gets hurt while they pursue their objectives. Prince is indirectly responsible for a number of LAPD deaths his first night in Los Angeles. Afterward, he beats a couple of detectives senseless and steals their police car to continue his search for Wang. On the other hand, Wang, to get at his enemies, guns down whole groups of bystanders and employees who have nothing to do with his narcotics business deals. The ultimate difference between the two men lies in character. Prince learns from his mistakes and, while still headstrong, becomes more sensitive to the involvement of innocent people in his manhunt for Wang, particularly Diana, whom Wang eventually kidnaps as insurance. Wang remains committed to a course of malevolence, going so far as gutting one of his own gang when the man questions his authority. He uses Diana as a human shield when escaping from Prince.

The car chases, shootouts and fights in the film are first-rate, beginning with the knock-down, drag-out brawl–shoot-'em-up in the high rise and ending with the knock-down, drag-out brawl–shoot-'em-up on a ship in the harbor. Daniels' extreme flexibility and high-spinning kicks make for exciting action. Co-star Ken McLeod turns in a fine performance as Jensen, who is also a fairly good martial artist. *Deadly Target* was an excellent vehicle for Daniels to strut his stuff and marked the beginning of a profitable relationship between the actor and PM Entertainment.

While there is no typically recognizable "Gary Daniels film," 1995's *White Tiger* is a fairly representative work that features all of Daniels' strengths, both as an actor and a martial artist. Daniels stars as Mike Ryan, a dedicated DEA agent assigned to bust up a Chinese drug operation in Seattle. Victor Chow, Mike's nemesis, has designed a new drug that is highly addictive and much more profitable than the heroin being imported by the triads he is a part of. When Victor is called on the carpet by the triad for engaging in activities not approved by them, it sets into motion a series of brutal acts of violence, (including the murder of Mike's partner John) which highlights the theme of change vs. tradition that runs throughout the story.

Victor represents the new breed of triad—young, amoral, not bound my any customs. Rather than negotiate with other criminal organizations for turf, Victor blows up their supplies, not caring about the consequences. Bloodshed is always his first option. Even his product, a designer drug, is new—and, as he mentions to the triad elders, improved. Victor prefers chaos to order, because in his view, something better always comes out of the disarray.

The triads are run by elders, men who have worked their way up the criminal ladder to respected positions. Though criminals, they have a code of honor they must obey and rules which must be followed. They are not so much upset about Victor's new drug as they are with Victor for dealing it without their permission. Authority and respect are important to these men. In their eyes, Victor doesn't possess the former, and doesn't give the latter. By killing cops, Victor has upset the delicate balance they have achieved with the police, and by murdering one of the triad, has crossed the point of no return.

The relationship between Mike and John is similarly strained. Mike is a confirmed bachelor while John is a family man with a wife and young son. John shoulders the responsibility of his team and even carries a cell phone with him on his vacation, just in case the department needs him. Mike is more interested in taking out the bad guys than thinking things through clearly.

Mike tracks Victor to the Chinatown area, where his men collect protection money from most of the merchants. However, as Mike's mysterious sometime-ally Jade notes, covering his light skin and fair hair is difficult, hence the film's title "White Tiger," which is what Mike becomes as he ruthlessly stalks his prey through the city streets, engaging in a number of fights along the way. In one instance, Mike takes on a group of Victor's thugs in an alley outside one of his clubs. The fights are exceptional, with Daniels' kicks snapping in rare form. Later, in an even more impressive display of martial prowess, Mike breaks up one of Victor's mah jong clubs, sending his thugs crashing all about and causing Victor to lose face in the community.

At one point, Mike is detained by the police, who are investigating his partner's death and how the arrests went south. The captain in charge sends detectives to escort him to the airport to leave the city; the cops are on Victor's payroll, and they lure Mike to a fake bust. Mike is barely able to avoid the setup, but kills two of the crooked cops in the process. Now there are two hunts in progress: Mike after Victor, and the police after Mike, believed to be a cop killer.

Both Mike and Victor are renegades, in many ways more similar than different. Both men are accomplished martial artists and both like to break the rules. It was Mike who disobeyed orders and moved into a drug deal involving Victor, forcing his partner John to go in after him. When Victor is ordered by the triads to stop his unauthorized drug sales, he rebels and murders one of them. After Victor murders John, Mike feels responsible and, again disobeying orders, goes after Victor himself.

White Tiger was a broad enough story to allow Daniels the ability to exercise more than just his martial arts moves. When his partner is murdered in front of his eyes, Mike breaks down in low sobs. Later, in Victor's club where he meets Jade, he clowns his way through a horrible pick-up attempt, throwing in some heavily accented Chinese to seal his fate with the girl. Eventually he wins Jade over (or does she win him?) and, during a love scene, Daniels shows off his well developed physique, one of the best in the business. Having run the gauntlet from fighting, acting and posing, Daniels gets his man and breaks up Victor's drug ring, bringing order back to the city streets. Mike has learned from his experience and now becomes a more traditional cop, taking John's son out for a vacation in the film's final scene.

In *Hawk's Revenge* (1996), Daniels plays Hawk, a British Royal Marine whose American detective stepbrother is murdered while trying to nail the city's crime lord. Hawk flies across the Atlantic only to find that the police are stymied in their investigation. Though warned *not* to involve himself in the case by his brother's partner, Hawk goes full throttle after the killers, only to find that he's caught in the middle of a three-sided war involving Chinese gangs, skinheads and organized crime.

Daniels looks convincing in his Royal Marine uniform and could easily adorn a recruitment poster. As the odd man out among gangs, criminals and cops, Hawk is the outsider who has come to right the wrongs that the Americans can't. He tells his brother's partner that the cops have a code they have to follow, but that he doesn't. In that spirit, Hawk bruises up the crime lord's hit men and a whole bunch of skinheads, then causes a war between the skinheads and the crime lord by shooting at them both, and eventually blows up the skinhead leader after promising to let him go if he provided information about his brother's murder.

The film's title is not insignificant. A hawk is a bird which is always watching, and Hawk does a lot of that. As an anti-terrorist specialist, he watches out for the people of his country. In America, Hawk watches out for the Chinese gang to which he has allied himself to catch his brother's murderer. A hawk is also a bird of prey, and when Hawk swoops down on those who killed his brother, there is no such thing as mercy.

There are a number of minor inconsistencies that differentiate *Hawk's Revenge* from other Gary Daniels films, and quite possibly from other martial arts films as well. First, Hawk is not above using weapons against a weaponless opponent, something that Chuck Norris and others would never do. In one scene Hawk and his allies are fighting their way out of the crime lord's hideout when he confronts one of the crime lord's men, who is much bigger than he. Hawk uses his martial arts but the big man knows martial arts, too, and gets the better of Hawk, who promptly picks up a drill and sticks it in the big man's eye.

A second discrepancy concerns the skinheads, who seem to be universally reviled by everyone, but appear to be the least racist of all the groups. They don't use any slurs and they pleasantly do business with Blade, the crime lord's black second-in-command. In fact, in one scene, Hawk and his Chinese partner dress as Orthodox Jews and walk past the skinheads, who pay them no mind at all! On the other hand, the Chinese do use slurs such as "round eye," while the crime lord has no problem harvesting the Chinese as human organ donors, apparently believing them to be subhuman.

Hawk's Revenge moves along at a good pace and is another in a long line of superior Daniels efforts. The fights are plentiful, as they should be in this type of film, and there is a sense of broad humor played throughout, mostly involving the crime lord's two chief henchmen, who can't seem to do anything right. Every time they go up against Hawk, one of them loses a piece of his body courtesy of the other henchmen, who cuts off fingers and ears by accident!

Daniels again suited up in uniform for PM Entertainment's *Riot* (1996), playing British SAS Major Shane Alcott, who is in the States to train U.S. soldiers. When a riot breaks out in an unnamed major city, and the daughter of the British Ambassador is kidnapped by a street gang, Shane is called in to deliver the ransom money to the gang. The mission itself seems suicidal as the police and National Guard units have abandoned that area of the city Shane must traverse. Following the kidnappers demands, he must go in alone and unarmed.

The premise of *Riot* promised much more than it ultimately delivered. From the beginning Shane is seen as a physical man, a doer, not a talker. He arrives home at his apartment and immediately begins pumping iron, with karate trophies visible in the background, then works out on the heavy bag. When his neighbor's kids almost start a fire burning a pizza, Shane kicks down the door, puts out the fire, and takes the kids over to his house where, nonplussed, he cooks them Chinese food and teaches them to eat with chopsticks.

Once in the riot zone and on his own, Shane makes his way to the church where the gang is waiting, but first he is attacked by hockey stick–wielding skaters on roller blades. He dispatches the dozen or so players in a number of gruesome ways, including electrocution, while kicking and punching his way through the others. At the church, the gang executes the girlfriend of the Ambassador's daughter for fun, and Shane senses things are going badly. He clobbers a number of gangsters, grabs the girl, then shoots it out with the rest while escaping. Going up a building to catch their helicopter ride out of the riot zone, Shane takes on a gauntlet of gang members in the stairwell, beating to a pulp one especially big man. For the rest of the film, Shane alternates between fleeing with the Ambassador's daughter and stopping to pick off the terrorists who are now hunting them.

All of the fights are exciting; without a doubt, this must have been one of the most physical movies Daniels had made up to that point. Just the battle in the junkyard saw him taking on over a dozen men, alternating between shooting and unarmed combat. The car and motorcycle chases, a specialty of PM, did not disappoint, with Shane having to escape a stalking forklift, a gang of motorcycling pillagers (one of whom he hangs) and the terrorists, who chase him through an abandoned parking garage with their cars. If there were any drawbacks to the action, it was the darkness. The entire film takes place at night, so a number of the scenes involving Shane fighting others, particularly in the stairwell, were a little dark and hard to see.

The story went the route of political correctness: Instead of presenting the riot in a realistic fashion, it degenerated into the usual hodgepodge of balancing out the good and bad of various races so as not to appear racist. Though the movie opens with news footage of rioting in the street, with people destroying police cars and buildings, and groups yelling the infamous mantra "No justice, no peace," realism takes a nose dive from that point on. Racial animus, and responsibility for the riot and kidnapping, assumed to be the work of inner city blacks, is eventually projected onto Irish terrorists, whom we find out bankrolled the gang into kidnapping the Ambassador's daughter.

As the pillagers loot and burn stores where people from the area work, and we see an electronics shop ablaze, the newsman wonders what will become of its employees. Shane, who seems to be the only one with any reason, asks what all the destruction will accomplish. Immediately he and his partner, played by Sugar Ray Leonard, are set upon by redneck softball players angry at the city's blacks for rioting. Again, racial animus is deflected away from the riots and onto socially acceptable targets, in this case fed-up white middle-class men.

Shane eventually accomplishes his mission, bringing the Ambassador's daughter out alive, but not before obliterating the black street gang and then, to be non-biased, all the Irish terrorists to boot. Along the way he is helped by the obligatory struggling black family who take the two strangers in and protect them from the Irish. In a nice gesture, Shane leaves the family with a generous gift. However, as the sun rises and Shane and the woman make their way to safety, the question must arise, what does "No justice, no peace" have to do with stealing television sets?

After putting together a string of explosive, action-packed films, the last couple of which had the strength to be theatrical releases, Daniels starred in *Bloodmoon* (1997), a disappointing effort that neither showcased his acting abilities nor taxed his martial arts prowess. Daniels plays O'Hara, an ex-cop known as a "mind hunter," a tracker of serial killers, who has retired due to the rigors of his last case, in which the killer almost killed *him*. O'Hara is called out of retirement to assist the NYPD in hunting down a monster who has been killing various fighting champions.

O'Hara is teamed with Chuck, a homicide detective who is also an amateur magician and Eddie Murphy impersonator. Chuck doesn't like O'Hara much because he quit under pressure. At first, working alone, the two men get nowhere. In fact, when they both search a crime scene at night without telling each other, they get into a fight—until someone turns on the light and they can see each other. However, the unlikely duo eventually form a partnership and unravel the case, but not before more champions are killed and O'Hara's wife and daughter are held hostage by the madman.

Arguably, in many ways *Bloodmoon* represents some of the worst aspects of martial arts films that continue to plague the genre. The story did not make a lot of sense,★ and was done much better in the earlier *Tiger Claws*, which had a killer stalking high-profile martial artists because they had become celebrities. The murderer in this film, a mysterious superman–martial artist, appeared at various times decked out in a ridiculous costume and mask that made him seem like the Phantom of the Opera on steroids. Since the killer was able to beat a boxing champion, a wrestling champion, a kendo master and, in an unseen engagement, a judo master, one wonders why he would bother with two cops, one of whom spends a lot of his time pulling handkerchiefs from his sleeves.

The action scenes, though exceptionally well choreographed and executed, seemed a bit ridiculous at times, with combatants whirling in and staring at one another after blocking each other's moves, or fighters flying back dozens of feet in the air after being kicked with what appears to be an almost "unworldly" amount of force. In the final fight between O'Hara and the killer, the former scurries straight up a building to save his wife and daughter, and the ropes that allow him to do it are clearly visible.

Daniels continued to make films throughout the remainder of the decade; his best-known film has to be *Fist of the North Star*, based on characters from a Japanese graphic novel. The film had a decent budget and was well cast with excellent supporting actors, including Malcolm McDowell and Chris Penn, while Daniels' fight scenes were fantastically done. While Daniels has averaged a picture or two a year, in 2000 he shot five. One of the younger martial arts stars on the scene, he doubtless has a promising career ahead of him.

Jeff Speakman

Jeff Speakman was chosen to star in the martial arts film *The Perfect Weapon* (1991) for Paramount, in the hope he would become another Chuck Norris or Steven Seagal. Born in Chicago, he practiced American Kenpo karate with Ed Parker. Prior to acting he was an accomplished springboard diver and a college graduate with a degree in psychology. He had taken some acting classes and got his first role in *Side Roads* (1988), encouraged to try his hand at films after seeing the success of Jean-Claude Van Damme.[12] While Speakman's films were not box office hits, he has parlayed them into martial arts DTV success. *The Perfect Weapon* showcased Speakman's Kenpo abilities as he takes on the Korean Mafia. In Cannon's *Street Knight* (1993), he plays an ex-cop suffering from post-traumatic stress who works as a mechanic. Both films were high on action but not at the expense of story.

In these early films, Speakman's persona was that of a man pushed to the fringe by tragedy, an outsider looking in. In *The Perfect Weapon*, Speakman's mother passes away at an early age and he becomes undisciplined and unresponsive to the point that his father, a cop, wants to send him to military school. Instead he sends

★*This depends of course on which side of the fence one sits upon. Viewers who revel in the sheer athleticism of martial arts combat may not care about weak or ridiculous storylines. Others who prefer their martial arts to be functional, to serve the narrative, which is common in most American martial arts films, might be disappointed with films like* Bloodmoon.

Jeff Speakman in Paramount's *The Perfect Weapon* (1991). While Speakman did not catch on in mainstream film, he has amassed a significant body of work in DTVs, not always in martial arts films.

him to a Kenpo master. Speakman learns to fight but not to control his anger. Unwanted by his family, and an Anglo in a Korean area, Speakman is a stranger in a strange and hostile world.

In *Street Knight*, Speakman is a cop trying to save an eight-year-old hostage who is subsequently killed before his eyes. He quits the force and opens a repair shop. No longer a cop, but (in the eyes of the primarily minority community in which he lives) not a civilian either, Speakman straddles the middle ground trying to prevent an all-out gang war while tracking down the paramilitary organization that is trying to start the conflagration as a cover for its criminal activities.

The Expert (1994) found Speakman as a civilian tactics instructor for the police department whose sister is brutally murdered by a serial killer. The *Death Wish*–style plot immediately draws the battle lines between conservative and liberal, between those for prisoner rehabilitation and those for punishment, symbolized by the warden, (James Brolin) who wants all the prisoners to fry, and the assistant warden, a female psychologist who sees good in everyone. Once again Speakman takes the middle path, ready to trust in the justice system until it breaks down—forcing him to swing into action. While the film makes a strong case for capital punishment, its ambivalence toward vigilante justice is unmistakable. After Speakman breaks into the prison and kills the man who murdered his sister, his marshal friend asks him whether the episode was worth it. Speakman tries, but cannot answer.

Later films saw Speakman branching out into sci-fi, horror, even family drama (1997's *Escape from Atlantis*, where he plays a harried, divorced father taking his kids on a cruise—to the Bermuda Triangle!). Like Mark Dacascos, Speakman is not averse to playing non-martial arts roles and will often accept second or third billing. *Timelock* (1996) was *The Expert* in reverse, featuring Speakman in his first heavy role, that of the psychotic criminal McMasters, who leads a breakout from a maximum security prison in the year 2251.

As Speakman's career moved forward, he began taking on more political roles. In 1997's *Land of the Free*, he plays Frank Jennings, the campaign manager for Aidan Carvell, a too-good-to-be-true Senate candidate. When Jennings is tipped by an old military buddy that Carvell is being supported by illegal, extremist militia groups, he experiences a crisis of conscience. Investigating the claim, he finds out more than he ever wanted to know—and puts his family at risk when he agrees to testify against Carvell in court.

Land of the Free was certainly a reflection of the militia fear that swept the country after Timothy McVeigh's bombing of the Oklahoma City Federal Building in April 1995. While the purpose of Carvell, or the militia groups for that matter, are not clearly specified, it is implied through film footage of these units training that they intend to take over the country. Carvell's own campaign slogan, "Free America," begs the question: Free America from *what*? Carvell's own rhetoric is a mix of populist mumbo jumbo that can appeal to both conservatives and liberals and suggests that the nation needs to get rid of self-serving politicians as well as other who put their personal interest over that of the country's, certainly propositions most voters would not argue with.

After Jennings testifies against Carvell in front of the Grand Jury, he and his family are relocated to the Witness Protection Program. However, crooked FBI agents on Carvell's payroll tip Carvell to Jennings' whereabouts and the fight is on. With no one to turn to, Jennings is forced to fight. He bests Carvell's men in a number of battles—including one in a building where Speakman demolishes half the security force—and survives a score of deadly car chases.

When the judge releases Carvell, just as in *The Expert*, Speakman is eventually forced into vigilante action to obtain justice. However, his actions are motivated as much by character as by the need of a cathartic reckoning. Where Carvell is a smooth talker, an amoral man who will stop at nothing to get what he wants, a born propagandizer who speaks in grandiose terms about abstract concepts like freedom and America, Jennings is his polar opposite. He is quiet and idealistic—at first believing in Carvell—and he is highly principled. When he finds the proof that Carvell is involved with the extremist militia groups, he does his duty and testifies against Carvell, at great risk to himself and his family. But perhaps Jennings' most important accomplishment is that of putting Carvell's hollow words into practice: By saving his family, Speakman has done the most American thing possible under the circumstances.

A year later, in *Memorial Day* (1998), Speakman had one of his best roles, that of a Marine Captain and CIA operative who has been brainwashed by a right wing cabal into killing a presidential candidate. In this cross between *Total Recall* and *The Manchurian Candidate*, Speakman uses his brain to get to the truth—saving the kicks and chops to fend off a few bad guys—only to find that the intelligence community for which he worked so diligently is behind a whole slew of unsavory affairs. The title is a play on the fact that Speakman cannot remember, courtesy of years of electroshock treatments, and when his memory does return, in some ways he wishes it hadn't.

Like Norris' *Invasion USA*, *Memorial Day* raised some key concerns that were not considered important at the time, but which became key issues after 9/11. During the Clinton years, CIA and military budgets were slashed to reflect the end of the Cold War. The so-called "dividends of peace" were part and parcel of a breakdown in intelligence that allowed terrorists to strike the country virtually without warning. In the film, Speakman's bosses are part of a group that creates a fictional terrorist group that raises fear across the nation in the hopes that it will force congress and the president to raise the intelligence budget. Throw in a McCarthy-like politician who talks like Goldwater calling for special, almost unlimited government powers to stop the terrorists and one has the Patriot Act, which was passed just a few years later.

Mark Dacascos

A rising star within the ranks is Hawaiian Mark Dacascos. His martial arts training began early, when he was four; three years later he won his first competition. As the years passed his skills grew, and he won a number of European kung fu titles.[13] He is also a martial arts instructor. After turning to acting, he starred in such minor theatrical hits as *Double Dragon* (1993) and *Only the Strong* (1993) before finding steady, starring roles in DTV films.

Only the Strong remains his definitive work, and a very good film. Dacascos stars as Louis Stevens, an Army Special Forces soldier returning back home to Miami after doing his hitch, much of it in Brazil training their troops to fight drug cartels. He returns home to his old neighborhood and school and finds it a complete war zone. After visiting his teacher and mentor Mr. Kerrigan, Louis is forced into a fight and gets the attention of the entire student body. When Louis easily defeats his opponent and friends using capoeira, a Brazilian martial arts form that combines dance and fighting techniques, Mr. Kerrigan arranges for Louis to teach some of the school's most incorrigible kids, hoping that the discipline will turn the students' lives around. Louis soon crosses paths with the local gang leader, and then he finds himself in a battle for his life.

From the opening scenes, the film posits a continual wrench between liberal and conservative influences. Louis stands overlooking a lake in a Brazilian village, dressed in his uniform, a typical American soldier. The villagers working behind him form a circle and perform capoeira with wild abandon. Louis joins them, taking off his uniform and symbolically freeing himself from his duties. As the group "dances" (for lack of a better description), the power and skill of the martial art become evident, and we can see it is a significant force to be reckoned with. Suddenly, down the road, an American military vehicle pulls up and Louis must return to uniform, and to his traditional role.

Later, back home in Miami, he watches a drug dealer beating up his younger brother for not selling the merchandise. The drug dealer mistakes Louis for a teacher, the person responsible for keeping order, but Louis tells him he is not a teacher, implying he is "free" from their rules. The drug dealers accept Louis' challenge but are easily defeated. In the school boardroom, Mr. Kerrigan tells the principal and faculty about his plan for Louis to teach capoeira. One teacher, in vehemently opposing Louis, takes a classic liberal position that violence should not be taught to children. He even goes so far as calling Louis "Mr. Death Squad." The principal and other teachers take the opposite view, that since the children are already immersed in violence, exposing them to a structured program that teaches discipline is useful.

Though supported by the more conservative elements of the faculty, Louis works in a liberal manner, not restrained by any rules of the school. In fact, he lives

Mark Dacascos in scenes from Twentieth Century–Fox's 1993 release *Only the Strong*. The film showcased the Brazilian martial arts form of capoeira, which mixes dance with fighting techniques.

and teaches the kids in an abandoned fire station where he can be free from any interference. He succeeds in his mission, going so far as to bring them on a field trip where they can commune with nature on a deserted stretch of beach and practice capoeira freely like the Brazilians did. However, the local gang leader becomes incensed at Louis' meddling and attacks the school, beating teachers, lighting fires and killing one of Louis' students. At this point, the scales tip conservatively as Louis turns into a soldier again to rescue the neighborhood from the gang. In effect he becomes what the teacher labeled him earlier, a one-man death squad. After destroying the gang's chop shop, Louis fights the gang leader in a to-the-death capoeira match, and wins. Violence is met with violence.

Only the Strong simplifies gang problems. It packs many of the social and economic difficulties plaguing the inner city onto one troublesome and vile individual (Silverio, the gang boss), while ignoring the lack of jobs and hope that kids in this environment have to deal with. That said, it also understates the role that personal responsibility plays in the development of law-abiding and socially responsible people. Louis helps the kids because he believes if he doesn't do something, he will have to live with it because it is his neighborhood. But ultimately, with or without Louis, it is up to the kids to take responsibility for their own lives and actions, not for someone else.

A second conflicting reading comes in the ethnic and racial makeup of the various characters. The gangs, for instance, are for the most part Jamaican and Brazilian immigrants. The teachers, who are chiefly white, appear to be overwhelmingly ineffective in imparting any knowledge to their pupils, who are predominantly minority. Is this typical Hollywood stereotyping? Or an accurate reflection of what teachers have to face in inner city schools? Are third world immigrants a drain on society's resources and responsible for most big city crime? Or is this merely a reactionary viewpoint not backed up by facts?

Like most films, *Only the Strong* doesn't provide any resolution, just a starting point for debate, and only for those scratching beneath the narrative. Most viewers will be content with an exciting tale and some first-class martial arts, not to mention tumbling and gymnastics. As the story closes, Louis' class is graduating from high school, and as a special event, the principal allows the students, and Louis's friends from the Brazilian village, to perform capoeira for the entire audience. Louis joins in, and the film ends in an upbeat and action-packed manner, just the way it started.

One significant difference between Dacascos and most other martial arts luminaries is his willingness to break away from action films. While heading up such low-budget martial arts productions as *Kickboxer 5: The Redemption* and *Sabotage* (1996), he has also played the lead in *DNA* (1997) and *Boogie Boy* (1997), both primarily non-martial arts roles. In 1998, Dacascos starred in the television series *The Crow, Stairway to Heaven*, playing the role which tragically took the life of Brandon Lee. In 2001, he co-starred in the French theatrical release *Brotherhood of the Wolf*, playing a Native American. Whether he will continue to work his way back to theatrical releases remains to be seen. A good start was made in the 2003 release *Cradle 2 the Grave*, where he played the villain opposite Jet Li.

Dacascos (top left, bottom right) in action against Silverio, the neighborhood gang leader in *Only the Strong*. The film, while entertaining, opens itself up to contradictory readings.

Other Stars

Jerry Trimble and Olivier Gruner were martial arts champions who found their way to the video screen. Trimble was offered up by Concorde–New Horizons as an alternative to Wilson, whose price was climbing with his popularity. *Breathing Fire* (1991), one of Trimble's first starring roles, featured him as a heavy, the leader of a gang of bank robbers who must take on his own sons. A man with deadly speed and awesome kicking power, Trimble made his best film, *Live by the Fist* (1993), in the Philippines. Railroaded and imprisoned for the rape and murder of a young woman in a dockside warehouse, Trimble is harassed by white supremacists, who hate him for not joining them, and Filipino gangs, who hate him for being white. The film is ambiguous about finding a means to racial harmony. One character, "Uncle," is a venerated lifer who preaches tolerance and respect, yet only through Trimble's use of force can his message be heard.

Gruner, a French kickboxing champion, debuted in *Angel Town* (1990), which featured him as a kickboxing graduate student learning the ropes at an inner city university. The proverbial fish out of water, Gruner finds his life complicated when gang members begin terrorizing the neighborhood; his indecision whether to move to another area, or stay and fight is indicative of the same quandary facing many good people trapped in bad areas. Gruner followed up with the outstanding *Nemesis* (1993). He was not afraid to mix up the martial arts formulas in his films, going from Westerns (*The Fighter*) to sci-fi (*Automatic*) in the same year (1994). He has even dabbled in family films like *The White Pony* (1999).

Swiss martial artist Daniel Bernhardt, a male model with a finely sculpted physique, signed a contract with FM Entertainment in part based on his resemblance to Jean-Claude Van Damme. Prior to this, he made his debut in *Future War* (1994), an ultra low-budget cheapie put out by Cine Exel that cast him as a "Tool," a slave who escaped from his cyborg captors only to be hunted by "Trackers" across what appears to be Los Angeles. The Tools were humans who were taken from earth thousands of years ago, to be used by a race of cyborgs as workers. The cyborgs also took dinosaurs, which they later trained like hunting dogs, to track runaway slaves like Bernhardt's character. After Bernhardt escapes from a mother ship and lands on Earth, he is taken in by a convent novitiate who helps run a wayward youth home. It doesn't take long for the Trackers and the dinosaurs to find him. Soon the city is besieged by carnivorous monsters lunching on unsuspecting people, and Trackers looking for Bernhardt.

Like many films on this budget level, *Future Wars* has a raw feel to it. A dinosaur could step through the many holes in the story, while the prehistoric monsters and spaceships appear, to put it mildly, cheesy. The dinosaurs are plastic-looking affairs that can only be shown from the neck up; when they chase the cast, it appears that their legs must have somehow evolved into wheels because they roll bumpily rather than run. But Bernhardt and the other actors are quite appealing, so the bottom line is that, like a cult film, viewers will either like it or hate it, and if they like it, they will go along with the story despite its inconsistencies.

From the outset, Bernhardt establishes his presence as a martial artist, fighting a running battle with a cyborg Tracker throughout a meat packing plant, even killing a dinosaur with a sharp cleaver! His spinning kicks and pliable limbs are another reminder of his resemblance to Van Damme. He acquits himself well in a number of fights, all of which he choreographed himself.

The film's character dynamics boil down to the relationship between Bernhardt and Sister Annie, who are alike in many ways and very different in others. Sister Annie is a streetwise, seen-it—done-it-all young woman who, among other things, was a hooker before coming off the streets. She's tough, aggressive and, most importantly, can handle herself in almost any situation. Bernhardt's just the opposite: He knows nothing about Earth, and quotes the Bible (which the slaves somehow had access to) with the strong belief that Sister Annie would like to have. In short, each is what the other should be. Sister Annie is not proud of her past and would like to have the faith and innocence of Bernhardt. Bernhardt is anxious to be a man after being a slave all his life. But the world is hard, and he will need the qualities that Sister Annie possesses to be successful.

Like a whole slew of other science fiction narratives of the decade, *Future War* is probably more interesting for what it implies than for what it presents. With society in an economic downturn and multi-national corporations on the rise, the monsters become a lurking, outside presence which terrorize the community, devouring everything they come into contact with. When a Tracker demolishes a police station filled with officers and CIA agents questioning Bernhardt, it is clear that the law and the government are powerless to stop the onslaught. The final fight between Bernhardt and the Master Cyborg himself, which occurs in a church, takes on a symbolic quality as the machine destroys vestiges of man's faith while Bernhardt struggles to overcome the godless menace attempting to choke the spirituality out of man. Bernhardt ultimately prevails in the battle, but the message is clear: Only the cooperation of all peoples can prevent the dehumanization of Man in an age dominated by machines.

Bernhardt next took Van Damme's place in the *Bloodsport* series, starring in three sequels, and has branched out since. *Perfect Target* (1997), arguably his best film, was the flip side of Seagal's *Above the Law*, featuring him as a mercenary training leftist Central American guerrillas in their fight against a right wing regime propped up by CIA henchmen. The production values and cinematography are first-rate for a low-budget production, as are the martial arts sequences. As 2003 rolls around, Bernhardt has parts in both *Matrix 2* and *3*.

A number of other stars also provide name recognition for the direct-to-video fans, just as their predecessors in the B films did more than a half-century ago. Phillip Rhee has taken the *Best of the Best* series through four films, co-starring with Eric Roberts and Chris Penn in the first two, and going it alone in the last installments. The first two films were released theatrically; the second two went directly to video. All of them feature top-flight martial arts and good supporting casts. The budgets in all the films are higher than most films of this type, and Rhee is a dynamic martial arts star and a natural in front of the camera.

John Barrett was a protégé of Chuck Norris and a superb martial artist who, like Phillip Rhee, is a better actor than most of his fighting peers. In *American Kickboxer* (1991) he co-stars with Keith Vitali as a kickboxing champion embittered and heavily drinking after a stint in prison. Only by training with his former opponent (Vitali) to fight an arch nemesis can Barrett regain his self-respect. While the story itself is average, the fighting scenes pack a wallop, and the movie as a whole is saved by Barrett's performance.

In *To the Death* (1993), Barrett revisits the kickboxing circuit, only this time as a former champion whose wife is killed by a sadistic fight promoter wanting Barrett to appear in his "death matches." The story was above par, as was Barrett's performance. And this was one of the few times the hero (Barrett) loses the ultimate match! In the same year, Barrett had a minor supporting role in *Shoot Fighter* as a down-on-his-luck martial artist reluctantly fighting in a death match tournament. Though his time on screen was short, he was definitely a scene-stealer.

Dale "Apollo" Cook is a multiple martial arts champion who studied tae kwon do and competed at the national and international level. After leaving the fight game, Cook entered the realm of martial arts films, starring in *Fist of Glory* (1991). He was a bit raw in front of the camera in his early roles, but after hitting his stride, he appeared in solid films such as *Triple Impact, Double Blast* (1993), which co-starred Linda Blair, and *American Kickboxer II* (1993), an exceptionally action-packed film in which almost the entire third act was a non-stop fight (guns, fists, knives, sticks and axes).

Bolo Yeung, a Chinese martial artist, has starred with every major player in the game, from Bruce Lee to Cynthia Rothrock and Jean-Claude Van Damme. Usually playing a villain, as in *Tiger Claws*, Yeung is as menacing as he is psychotic-looking in his roles—witness the brutal slaying of two police officers in *Tiger Claws*

The career of Bolo Yeung, one of the most venerated martial arts film actors, dates back decades, to Bruce Lee. While he usually plays a villain, such as in this shot from *Tiger Claws*, he is most effective as a hero.

II. However, Bolo is most effective as a hero. In *TC 2000* he plays a sage-like martial artist who keeps the old ways alive in a post-holocaust world, while in *Shoot Fighter* (1993) and *Shoot Fighter 2* (1996) he plays a venerated master heading the shoot fighters as they do battle against the ruthless overlords who force the pit fighting.

Ron Hall, Billy Blanks and TJ Storm are martial artists known for their speed and intensity. Hall, like Jerry Trimble, has not only made martial arts films but has found small parts in non–martial arts films and has branched out into directing. Some of Hall's best roles come when he is teamed with Dale "Apollo" Cook (*Triple Impact*), while Blanks' finest movies are the ones in which he co-stars with actor-director–martial artist Jalal Merhi or wrestler-turned-actor Roddy Piper. *Talons of the Eagle* (1992), *TC 2000* (1993) and *Expect No Mercy* (1995) team Blanks with Merhi while *Back in Action* (1994) and *Tough and Deadly* (1995) comically pair of Piper and Blanks.

One of Blanks's best roles was as the ex-cop turned school janitor who teaches a boy to protect himself in *Showdown* (1993). Blanks has since hit pay dirt with infomercials touting his workout system *Tae-bo*, a combination of aerobics and martial arts that has become popular (particularly with women) seeking a way to both stay in shape and defend themselves. Storm has starred in the television series *Conan* as well as a slew of other martial arts films, sometimes choreographing the fight scenes as well.

Richard Norton, the Australian sensation, has made over 60 films in a career that stretches back to 1980, where he played numerous masked ninjas in Chuck Norris' *The Octagon*. Before that, in the 70s, Norton was security-bodyguard for some of the biggest rock 'n' roll acts touring Down Under; he managed to teach the Rolling Stones' Mick Jagger a move or two.[14] According to Norton, Linda Rondstadt, whom he was providing security for, encouraged him to try his hand at acting.

Norton found his earliest success in the east, making a number of Chinese martial arts films that highlighted his tall, muscular frame. At the end of the 80s he segued into a number of standard low-budget action martial arts films until he hit pay dirt starring opposite Cynthia Rothrock in *China O'Brien*. The two have been paired a number of times with great results, most recently in *Redemption*. Norton has also done some second unit directing and was stunt coordinator for Warner Bros. syndicated TV series *The New Adventures of Robin Hood*.

If Cynthia Rothrock is the first lady of martial arts, Karen Sheperd is the "Karate Diva." An accomplished gymnast, Sheperd moved into the martial arts and, like Rothrock, was a national forms champion. In her first film, she co-starred with Japanese ninja star Tadeshi Yamashita, *Shinobi* (*Sword of Heaven* in the USA),[15] and from that point work has been steady. Sheperd has appeared in Hong Kong director Cory Yuen's *Righting Wrongs* (1986), Nu Image's *Terminator Woman* (1993) and 13 other films. She was inducted into the Blackbelt Hall of Fame and played a role in the 2000 television series *The Privateers*.

Loren Avedon, an expert in tae kwon do and hapkido, is a seasoned veteran of the martial arts film world. He shot to fame playing Scott Wylde in *No Retreat No Surrender II* (1989) after the actors from the first film did not want to reprise their roles. Jean-Claude Van Damme's part was played by Mathias Hues, while

Avedon replaced the Kurt McKinney character.[16] The film was a Cold War cross between *Rambo II* and *The Searchers*, with Max Thayer playing the grizzled veteran who shepherds Avedon through the jungles of Southeast Asia in search of his kidnapped love, being held by the Soviets. It opened in over 1400 theaters across the country and paved the way for *No Retreat No Surrender III* (1990), where Avedon and Keith Vitali starred as feuding brothers who reunite to avenge the death of their father at the hands of organized crime members. Avedon battled his way through a slate of high-octane flicks, including *King of the Kickboxers* (1991), *Operation Golden Phoenix* and *Virtual Combat* (1996), and was fortunate in the early days to work with good supporting actors, such as Joseph Campanella, James Hong, Luke Askew, Don Stroud and Richard Jaeckel.

In 1997, Avedon co-produced and starred in *Deadly Ransom*, playing Max, a Navy Seal who goes after the kidnappers of his fiancée, Jackie. Avedon also wrote the story for the film, whose great supporting cast included Brion James and Francesco Quinn. The story takes place in Brazil and Venezuela. Jackie and her father, the president of a large international bank, are visiting Rio on a business trip during Carnival when they are kidnapped by masked gunmen and held for a $50,000,000 ransom. Max, something of a hothead, immediately speaks with his father, who is the chief of Naval Intelligence, and receives clearance to mount a rescue effort. The rest of the story follows Max and his team as they track the kidnappers across the South American continent.

Deadly Ransom is not the most convincing of stories, in large part because the character of Max does not covey the sense of physical ability and command presence expected in a Navy Seal. In hand-to-hand combat, Max's fighting skills are suspect. During his key showdown with the villain's hulking henchman, Max is beaten pretty soundly, and only prevails because his girlfriend hits the man with the butt end of a machine gun.

Rash and headstrong, he operates without any thought to the consequences of his actions. Upon learning that Jackie is being held in a mountainous region of Venezuela, Max and his CIA partner Luis fly over the area and spot a compound in the forest. Max immediately suspects this is where Jackie is being held and has the chopper land. When Luis recommends they call for a back-up team, Max storms the compound unarmed, almost getting Luis killed. Later, Max places a tracking bug on a prostitute without her knowledge, then follows her to the kidnappers hideout, only to find the kidnappers have discovered his ruse. Not only is the prostitute sexually tortured but she and half of his team are blown up by explosives rigged to the woman's body.

Far more interesting than the story itself are the topical points the film touches upon, in this instance the 1990s spate of foreign kidnappings in South America, a few of which involved Americans. Some are done by drug cartels, others by movements of a political nature trying to make a statement; almost all demand money for the safe return of the victim. These kidnappers, headed by Rico, a cocaine-addicted American fugitive played by Brion James, move their hideout every day (a common occurrence in real life), which compounds the difficulty the authorities have in tracking them down.

Along the same lines, the perception that the CIA (which has been intricately involved in the domestic affairs of Central and South American countries for decades) is able to immediately field teams for victim rescue and extraction is common; whether or not it is true, it is certainly propagated in *Deadly Ransom*. The view that they are also quite incompetent is also duly reinforced.

Luis, who is a photographer, is also a CIA informant who keeps tabs on local goings-on for the agency. First Communists, he tells Max, and now kidnappers. With a few phone calls, Luis arranges for the assembly of Max's rescue team and taps his system of informants to track down leads while Max and the CIA people train in the mountains. However, Luis is reputed to be a military-trained martial artist, but his skills are even more dubious than Max's, as he is almost strangled to death by one of the kidnappers before Max can save him. The other CIA members, who inspire even less confidence than *Luis*, are killed on their very first outing.

Max eventually succeeds in getting back Jackie, but through no effort of his own, the CIA or that of his SEAL Team, who have joined him in the mountains: Max and the other SEALs, after raiding a cave holding some of the kidnappers, promptly let one of the survivors escape after the man promises to lead them to Jackie and her father. Max is only able to find Jackie by dumb luck. As he walks through town, thinking about Jackie, he spots Rico's henchmen and immediately gives chase in a Jeep with no thought to alerting the others. He is then promptly overcome by the henchman and taken prisoner, joining Jackie in confinement. The film ends with Max and Jackie getting married, but Rico has eluded capture, perhaps setting the stage for another film which has not come.

Subsequent Avedon films did not have the same appeal or quality of cast, and for the most part featured him in supporting roles. In *Tiger Claws 3*, he played Stryker, a martial artist who resurrects the spirit of three warriors in order to become crime lord of the city. Cynthia Rothrock starred. The following year, he and Rothrock re-teamed for *Manhattan Chase*, a Cantonese project. In Avedon's last film to date, *The Circuit* (2001), he has a small role as Sykes, a detective trying to bust up an illegal fight racket. He doesn't fight, though, and is almost unrecognizable behind a full beard.

Behind the Camera

Films don't get made by themselves. Directors play a most crucial role in translating the story to celluloid, and experienced helmsmen can make all the difference between a low-budget film that rises above its station and one that looks like what it cost. The following directors are not "karate specialists" but rather have contributed noteworthy films to the genre. In every respect, they are artists whose vision influences the martial arts films that followed.

Not the most active but perhaps the best-known is Robert Clouse, esteemed director of *Enter the Dragon*. Clouse directed over 20 films in a 30-year career, running the gamut from action to martial arts, from horror to mystery and drama. A writer and a producer, he was just as comfortable working with major stars like Robert Mitchum and Rod Taylor as he was with relative unknowns. He also worked in television, directing the ninja-oriented *The Master* series and cementing the appeal of Cynthia Rothrock in the States with his *China O'Brien* films.

Albert Pyun is among the most prolific directors around and, like Robert Clouse, his body of work is eclectic, though at times hit and miss. He has directed sci-fi, action, adventure, even comedy, but is noted for his hard-hitting martial arts films. His great films like *Cyborg* and *Nemesis* (1993) hold up years later and are finely layered works. His disappointments, like *Nemesis II* (1995), leave the audience wondering, "why?" Lately Pyun has steered in the direction of urban action, working with rap stars like Ice-T and Snoop Doggy Dog.

Writer-director-producer Sheldon Lettich is tied to the martial arts genre, having worked with Mark Dacascos, Daniel Bernhardt and (especially) Jean-Claude Van Damme, with whom he has co-authored a number of scripts. Lettich's flair for action is undeniable. His writing credits include *Bloodsport, Only the Strong* and *Legionnaire* (1998), while he has directed *Double Impact* and *Lionheart*, both starring Van Damme.

Starting out as a cinematographer, David Worth worked as a DP on *Bloodsport*. The next year he directed Van Damme in *Kickboxer,* then went on to helm a slew of martial arts films: *Lady Dragon, Lady Dragon II, American Tigers* (1996) and *True Vengeance* (1997).

Eric Karson's body of work is small but influential. His *The Octagon* started the ninja phenomenon. *Black Eagle* gave us another glimpse at early Van Damme, this time pitted against Sho Kosugi. Karson also directed *Angel Town* (1990), Olivier Gruner's first film, and produced Van Damme's *Lionheart* as well as *Nemesis*.

Sam Firstenberg is an action director who has also dabbled in musicals (*Breakin' 2: Electric Boogaloo*), thrillers (*Motel Blue*), science fiction (*Cyborg Cop*) and even drama (*One More Chance*), but is probably best known for his various ninja films throughout the 80s and his martial arts–flavored action flicks of the 90s. While the stories in some of his films are weak, the action never is. Firstenberg got his start with Cannon, first as an assistant director for Menahem Golan, then later as a director. His first action picture was *Revenge of the Ninja.*

Rick Jacobson's work runs the gamut from television (*Baywatch, Hercules, Xena*) to a string of highly entertaining, action-packed martial arts films, the majority of them starring Don Wilson. In 1994, he directed Wilson in *Ring of Fire III*, then followed up with *Bloodfist VI*, which followed Wilson's exploits as the Air Force messenger in a silo trying to prevent terrorists from launching a missile. The film was another version of *Die Hard*, but Wilson proved to be a much more believable hero than Bruce Willis and the fight sequences were second to none. Jacobson has since branched out to drama and thrillers.

From 1991 to 1995, Richard W. Munchkin reeled off a number superior martial arts films, working with the likes of Cynthia Rothrock, Don Wilson and Michael Worth. His *Out for Blood* (1993) was particularly provocative, updating the *Death Wish* vigilantism of the 70s into the 90s, with Wilson playing the "karate man," a killer taking revenge on all the miscreants society has to offer—with utterly no sense of remorse.

Paul Ziller's career as a director is among the most varied, moving from thriller to family to martial arts without breaking stride. His *Bloodfist IV: Die Trying* is a minor gem in the field. He followed it up with other solid films such as *Shootfighter II* and *Moving Target* (2000).

The Narratives

More so than their 80s theatrical predecessors, which always had the Communists to kick around, post–Cold War, American-style martial arts DTVs targeted new enemies using old genres. Westerns, action-thrillers, sci-fi/horror, even war provided narrative frameworks within which these martial arts films flourished. However, there was an inversion of sorts. Westerns, while the most prolific "B" of the classic era, were the least imitated in this decade. *The Fighter*, starring Olivier Gruner, was one of the exceptions.

Gruner played a French Legionnaire who escapes to Texas from Mexico during the reign of Maximillian (circa 1868). Foreign imperialism is correlated to local greed as Gruner helps a family fight off land grabbers; however, he must also battle French bounty hunters intent on bringing him back. Gruner's predicament, that of an unwilling invader of Mexico, is contrasted nicely with his new status as defender against those invading the family's property. Like most Westerns, the film has a final showdown between Gruner and the villain, another Legionnaire, only it was with fists and feet rather than Colts and Winchesters.

Chuck Norris' last feature film to date, *Forest Warrior* (1996), was a martial arts–family-oriented Western that went direct-to-video. Norris plays McKenna, who, with the help of some youngsters, fights to save a forest from development. *Desert Kickboxer* (1992) was a modern-day Western shot in the desert in which a native American martial artist helps an accountant and her retarded brother escape from a drug lord. After picking off the bad guy's henchmen with his bow and arrow, the hero must face a showdown with the drug lord's bodyguard, also a kickboxer. The story is better than most, and the action is good. In *Cold Harvest* (1998), the Western has been moved to the future: Gary Daniels is a bounty hunter protecting his brother's pregnant wife. Like in *Desert Kickboxer*, Daniels has to face the bad guy in a man-to-man showdown that starts with fists and ends with the two drawing their guns.

Action Thrillers

Action thrillers, which were among the most popular "B" genre framework for martial arts films, boasted a marked predilection toward the gangster and police narratives. Like with their 30s counterparts, the protagonists, good and bad, are extremely tough; misogyny, an implied, always lurking specter for the gangster's moll, becomes explicit in the 90s, with brutality toward women a staple of the genre. Where Cagney used a grapefruit to tame his moll, the drug-dealing gangsters in *Angelfist* (1993) use blocks of ice to freeze the nipples of the heroine. Gang rape, as Cynthia Rothrock finds in *Lady Dragon II* (1993), is an effective means of intimidation, while such misogynic trends reach a gruesome crescendo in *Blackbelt*, when a prostitute is literally ripped into pieces by a psychotic hit man. In *Blood Warriors* (1993), David Bradley's girlfriend is tied to a chair while the bad guys shoot at targets behind her. When she doesn't talk, they use electric shock to get her tell them what they want.

A unique addition to the genre is *Ulterior Motives*, which was released by Imperial Entertainment in 1992. With film noir–ish style the story follows Jake Blalock, played by Thomas Ian Griffith, a private eye hired by a *New York Times* reporter to help her get the goods on a Japanese man suspected of treason. The reporter writes her story on the treason, which serves to influence a strategic Senate vote on banning Japanese import cars; she is then attacked by Yakuza, and the private eye finds himself protecting her. Or is he? As the plot evolves, we find that nothing is what it seems, and that Jake is not what he appears. While *Ulterior Motives* poses a lot of philosophical questions, it provides no substantive answers, letting the viewer decide for himself whether Jake was right in what he did and whether, in cases of national security, the ends justify the means.

Griffith followed up *Ulterior Motives* with New Line Cinema's *Excessive Force* (1993), where he played a cop with a short fuse on the edge of a breakdown. Griffith also wrote the script, which featured Irish cops vs. Italian mobsters, and a conspiracy among the police and the Mafia. Griffith uses his martial arts prowess to break up the cozy relationship between the two, surviving numerous assassination attempts as the body count rises. Like his previous film, this one boasted noirish features, such as a jazz backdrop, canted angles, shadows and light, and an impressive shot of Griffith and his girlfriend running through a snowstorm.

Bloodmatch (1991) was a disappointing film that wasted a unique premise: Brick Bardo tracks down and kidnaps the individuals he thinks responsible for his brother's death, bringing them to an auditorium where they are tied to chairs. One by one Bardo grills them, eventually bringing each into the ring to beat the truth out of them. As all the characters are martial artists, too, the fights are fair, but a muddled script deprives the viewer of any closure. Since it is apparent Bardo knew all along what each character's involvement was in the brother's demise, the questioning seems pointless, and the last fight, where Bardo takes on the supposed "mastermind" of the brother's murder, is substandard to say the least.

While *American Yakuza* (1994) prominently displays a Yakuza member with a sword on the video box cover, martial arts were kept to a bare minimum in the film, which pitted the Japanese Mafia against the Italian mob. With Viggo Mortensen thrown in the mix as an FBI agent who infiltrates the Yakuza, the possibilities for action are endless. Unfortunately, except for a couple of fights and the last ditch assault on the Italian mob by Mortensen and his sword-wielding Yakuza "brother," most of the eye-opening stuff is limited to shootouts.

Ironheart (1992) was director Robert Clouse's last film, and he made the most of it. Britton K. Lee plays Korean-born detective John Keem, an LAPD instructor of the martial arts. He heads to Oregon to track down the killer of his ex-partner, who had transferred to the Portland Police Department. It seems that his friend was onto a white slavery–arms dealing ring when he was shot, and it is up to Keem to uncover the murderers, break up the ring and find the women.

Keem's martial arts skills are put to the test by arms dealer Richard Norton's goons, by a gang of rapists and by Ice (the inimitable Bolo Yeung), Norton's main henchman. Nothing new was explored here, but the production values were good, as was the soundtrack, and the fight scenes were above average, as is to be expected in a Clouse film. Regrettably, Norton plays it straight and does not engage in any fights, leaving the dirty work to his subordinates. The talented Lee has followed up with more films; unfortunately none are available in the video stores.

Martial Law (1992) follows the adventures of two karate-kicking cops, lovers, who go undercover to smash a brutal auto theft ring, only to find that David Carradine, as the crime lord, is using the cars to smuggle precious metals. *Martial Law II* (1992) followed the duo's further adventures, while *Mission of Justice* (1993) showcases Jeff Wincott taking on mayoral candidate Brigitte Nielsen and her evil band of vigilantes. *Martial Outlaw* (1993), another tale of karate cops, pits DEA Agent Wincott against his brother, an LAPD officer gone bad. *New York Cop* (1996) features Japanese actor-director Toru Murakawa as a martial artist policeman after gang leader Chad McQueen. Mira Sorvino has a co-starring role as a girl who helps Murakawa.

Sword of Honor (1994) features Steven Vincent Leigh as an expert martial artist and Vegas cop whose partner is murdered on his last day of work. The killers, employed by a local Mafioso, steal a magnificent sword that has great value, not only monetarily but historically as well. The Mafioso cooks up a scheme to sell the sword to various bidders, collect their cash, then kill them when they come to get their property. Leigh engages in a number of fights, ranging from petty robbers in a liquor store to some punks in a gym, and usually never breaks a sweat. The story is more complex than most in the genre, revealing a number of psychological quirks, and the film is highlighted by good performances all around, particularly by the supporting characters.

In *Immortal Combat*, (1994), cops Roddy Piper and Sonny Chiba investigate murderous ninjas, wreaking havoc on a whole island full of them, while in *Extreme Force* (2000), a martial artist–criminal who was double-crossed by his partner teams up with the Mongolian King's bodyguard to retrieve an ancient stolen seal. The pairing of the two is a humorous one; a fight scene involving the Mongolian and some *Deliverance*-type locals is a hoot.

Imperial Entertainment's 1992 release *My Samurai* was an interesting experiment: part thriller, part family film, and all martial arts. A boy sees a gang dumping a body in the trash behind the dojo where he trains. The gang tries to kill him, but didn't reckon on having to deal with his martial arts instructor, who accidentally kills a crooked cop in the process of defending the boy. The sensei, the boy and Deborah, a woman in charge of the boy, are now on the run, with both the police and the gang after them.

My Samurai engages the viewer on a number of levels. It functions as a father-son story where the two finally come together and work out their problems. It works as a master-student tale, where the boy learns from his sensei the real meaning of tae kwon do—not just its physical aspects but the spiritual ones as well. The good cops vs. bad cops angle keeps the narrative popping, since it becomes apparent from the beginning that finding someone to trust is almost impossible, and it is a love story, as the sensei and Deborah find themselves attracted to one another despite their differences.

The film's martial arts sequences are plentiful and fairly well done, and Julian Lee does a wonderful job as the tae kwon do master who doesn't have all the answers or all the right moves, but does the best he can. This is one of those few precious times when the hero loses a fight: During Lee's initial encounter with the gang in his dojo, one of the hoodlums gets the better of him and he is forced to beat feet. Of course, in the end Lee fights hood again and this time wins, though barely. The film also boasted a number of humorous moments, such as when the three tangle with some street punks who look like Tina Turner and Billy Idol impersonators.

In another mob film, *LA Wars* (1994), Vince Murdocco stars as a disgraced cop caught up in a drug war between rival syndicates. As the bodies pile up, Murdocco finds himself being used by the police and stalked by the mob after he becomes the bodyguard to one kingpin's daughter. The movie boasts two assaults by Murdocco on fortified buildings, where he takes out his assailants one by one, Rambo style. In a similar vein was 2001's *Hard as Nails*, which featured a war between Russian mobsters and Japanese Yakuza. The killings came fast and furious, with swords, knives, guns and, of course, hands and feet. The martial arts sequences were excellent, with people flipping and turning for no apparent reasons other than to create a cool look in front of the camera.

Writer-director David Heavener hit gold with his 1996 release *Fugitive X*, another tale of the human hunt, though this one is fairly exciting and in some ways stands apart from the jillions of other versions floating around. Heavener also stars as ex-cop Adam Trent, who is suffering from post-traumatic stress due to his daughter's death. He has resigned from the force and divorced his wife, and spends most of his time working as an executive in a computer firm. On his birthday, his co-workers arrange for a stripper to pop out of a cake, but she jabs him with a poisoned dart which disorients him. Pretty soon Heavener is "Fugitive X," the designation given to the man being hunted by a team of assassins while wealthy people bet on how long he can survive.

Fugitive X differs from other like movies in a number of ways. First, its production values are better than most films at this level, with a number of exciting chases and explosions. Second, Heavener, a good director, manages to keep the story moving without being dragged down by long periods of sentimentality or exposition. Thirdly, the film boasts some broad humor. For example, Heavener puts some of his blood (which has a tracking agent in it from the poison dart) in a vial and ties it around a stray dog's neck, causing the assassins all manner of problems as the dog leads them everywhere. In another instance, Heavener is in a closet as a woman undresses, calling her boyfriend to come out of the shower. When the boyfriend turns out to be a woman, and the two lesbians begin embracing, Heavener's face belies his eventual decision to interrupt the show before the assassins catch him.

However, perhaps the most important divergence between *Fugitive X* and others like it is the fact that it was shot in the afternoon. Most films of this ilk take place at night, when the notion of danger is at its highest point. In a Hitchcock-like turn, Heavener reverses the situation and has his character being hunted in broad daylight, when one feels the safest. But, because the assassins have threatened to kill Heavener's ex-wife and uncle, he is unable to obtain assistance anywhere. The peculiar feeling of seeing a man running past others, or passing up businesses where someone else needing help would take refuge, throws off the viewer, and makes Heavener seem the ultimate loner.

Richard Norton co-stars as Winters, son of the man running the show and head assassin. While Norton is the true martial arts expert, most of the fighting is left to Heavener, who gives a good account of himself, despite the obvious uses of doubles for some kicks. One of the highlights comes when Norton and Heavener square off on a high parking structure, with the backdrop of the city all around, and the two knock each other back and forth across the lot.

The conservative nature of *Fugitive X* is in many ways a throwback to the 1980s, and something of an anomaly for this decade, in which many martial arts films turned on paranoia, mistrust of authority and fear of the approaching millennium. Lindsay, the game's operator, tells Heavener at the beginning of the hunt that the police have been paid off and that he's on his own. Heavener, the ex-cop, now becomes the law, and the various targets of conservatism are eliminated one by one.

In the opening scene, a yuppie businessman is killed in the most gruesome manner. Later, in an alley, a hooker and her violent black pimp are brutally murdered. When some psychotic characters straight out of Tarentino's *Pulp Fiction* capture Heavener, they meet an equally gruesome fate. A drug dealer is viciously blown away. An assassin posing as a homeless man is blown up by a grenade and, in possibly the most obvious turnaround, a lesbian finds that she has fallen in love with Heavener, thereby rehabilitating her for a return to the heterosexual world.

Fugitive X ends with a whimper, not a bang. The streets are cleaned of society's refuse, Heavener has killed the assassins and shut down the murderous operation and he returns home after a hard day's work. Much to his surprise, his uncle has gathered his friends to celebrate his birthday. Heavener's biggest surprise is his ex-wife, who shows up to give Heavener a chance at reconciliation.

In *Never Say Die* (2001), Cynthia Rothrock stars as Julie Cosgrove, a DEA agent on the run from her own agency after her team is set up and wiped out in Columbia. Among the dead was Julie's fiancé. She makes it back to the States with damaging information that could identify the agent who sold them out. But she doesn't know it. Arriving in a small town, she takes on the local powerbroker who has begun manufacturing designer drugs. The film takes on the "stranger mode" wherein which a newcomer arrives in a small town and finds things amiss. He (or she in this case) must then set things right. Julie blisters the bad guys in a series of high octane fights, until the powerbroker recruits his own martial artist to face off with her. Julie finishes him off—and the drug dealer—yet the story ends not with a smile but a sigh, as Julie heads out again for parts unknown, alone.

If *Fugitive X* argues a certain stereotypical, blue collar conservatism (if the government can't take care of cleaning the streets of predators, the people will), *Never Say Die* takes a different tact (if government has failed to protect society from outside danger, most specifically drugs, vigilante action will do the trick). The two positions are somewhat similar, with this difference: In *Fugitive X*, Adam is motivated by revenge, while in *Never Say Die*, Julie is looking for justice.

In the course of his story, Adam becomes the clear catalyst for eliminating the undesirables, while Julie remains a victim. As Adam is hunted, various elements of society are disposed of—some by him, some by others. As Julie is hunted, she becomes the exclusive eliminator. Both situations lead to the release of pent-up rage at current social trends, but Julie's situation is the more ironic. As a DEA agent in a friendly country,* that is, one in which we are helping to eliminate their drug suppliers, she is betrayed by her government and her team. Once home, she is hunted by the very agency that should be protecting her. Now on the run, she becomes a one-woman wrecking crew in the pursuit of justice, successfully destroying a drug syndicate as a civilian that she had failed to do as a professional. In both films, the application of extreme force without legal constraints is heralded, but only in *Never Say Die* is the notion of government duplicity, so prevalent during the 90s, present.

The Substitute series features mercenaries who find that crime and criminals flourish in the halls of learning, and set out to stop it. In *The Substitute* (1996), Tom Berenger, who plays Shale, visits an old friend, only to find the school where she teaches is a festering pot of violence. After she is attacked, he takes her place as the "substitute" and

Tom Berenger stars as Shale, a tough mercenary who works as a substitute teacher to find out who hurt his friend in *The Substitute* (Live Entertainment, 1996). How does this film compare with *Only the Strong*?

not only teaches his class a few good lessons in history but uses his martial arts skills to "learn" the bad guys that crime doesn't pay. The film, filmed on location in Miami,[16] cost $15,000,000.[2] One of Live Entertainment's first theatrical releases, it did well at the box office but was not a blockbuster. Still, it managed to spawn a whole group of sequels that went direct-to-video.

The Substitute 2 (1998) found mercenary Karl Thomasson, played by Treat Williams looking to find his teacher-brother's killer. He goes undercover at his brother's school, protecting his niece while bringing a carjacking-murder ring to justice. In *The Substitute 3* (1999), Thomasson is back, undercover at a college to investigate the beating of a fellow mercenaries daughter—a professor at the school. The martial arts sequences are top flight, especially Thomasson teaching a lesson in the manly art of self-defense to a football star–bully. In *The Substitute 4* (2000), Thomasson takes a break from his mercenary endeavors to teach at a military academy and finds that, with support from the staff, a neo–Nazi element is growing. This had the weakest of all plots, with the students acting as terrorists, but sported top-of-the-line martial arts sequences choreographed by Simon Rhee.

Gunplay and fisticuffs, important aspects of both crime and martial arts narratives, are weighted differently, however, with the 30s gangsters-cops primarily utilizing the former, while the martial arts protagonists rely mostly on the latter. The

* *Compare Julie's situation with that of Steven Seagal's John Hatcher in* Marked for Death. *If nothing else, both films indicate the war on drugs is failing badly.*

stylized shootouts and fights are not mutually exclusive, though: Edward G. Robinson and James Cagney were as quick and good with their fists as Don Wilson proves to be with a variety of firearms in *Ring of Fire III* (1994), which featured Wilson reprising his role as Dr. Johnny Wu, who takes on a global conspiracy of Mafias that plan to sell nuclear weapons (stolen from the old Soviet Union) to third world countries.

The film features wall-to-wall fights, starting with a breakneck opening sequence that pits Wilson against some Mafia hoods trying to break out their Don from the hospital Wilson works in. In the "Hitchcockian" twist that is so common to Wilson's movies, his medical bag is switched with that of a thief who stole a computer disk outlining all the "global Mafia's" plans, and soon they are hot on his trail. It leads to a mountain cabin—and one very sexy female, karate-kicking park ranger.

Arguably the best of the series (Rick Jacobson directed), *Ring of Fire III* elicits subtle humor from the contrast between the foul and deadly Italian Mafiosos and the cool and deadlier Russian thugs. Style-wise the film's a gem, with the city scenes being shot at night or in dim light, accenting the claustrophobia of the urban area. When Wilson gets to the mountain, however, the lighting is bright and cheery, highlighting the openness of the countryside. The film's end is ambiguous. The ranger, Wilson, and his son are at the lake fishing. But as the ranger pointed out earlier in the film, Wilson is a creature of the city, and she likes the desolation of the wide outdoors. Only a fourth film will tell if the two can reconcile their differences.

Repetition within these films is often the rule rather than an exception, and date back to the action "B" movies of the 30s. In *The Leathernecks Have Landed* (1936), three marines are stationed in China: the rash one (Lew Ayres); the sincere one (James Ellison); and the chubby one (Maynard Holmes). Rash starts a fight in a nightclub and chubby is killed. Disgraced, rash discovers that chubby was really killed by a gang, then goes undercover to smash the criminal ring and restore his reputation. Three years later, *Forged Passport* features the same story, albeit with a change in locale to the U.S.–Mexico border, and the marines are now Border Patrol officers.[17] Three other films follow, all using the same general storyline.

Some 50 years later, the echo reverberates at New Horizon. In *Bloodfist*, a kickboxing champion's brother is mysteriously murdered after winning an illegal tournament fight in Manila. The champion comes looking for answers and is trained by his dead brother's coach for the next tournament to fight the man who it appears killed his brother. The champion is befriended by another fighter and his beautiful sister. The champion and the sister fall in love, the brother is killed during the tournament, the champion kills the fighter he thinks killed his brother only to find his trainer-coach is the real killer. Fast forward four years. *Full Contact* features Jerry Trimble as a hick arriving in the big city to find out who killed his tournament-fighting brother. The locale is now Los Angeles but the story remains the same. *Dragon Fire* takes us centuries into the future, and the action takes place in a dystopic Los Angeles, but the usual suspects are all present.

Angelfist turns the entire model on its head, featuring women in the men's roles. Cat Sassoon plays Kat, a tough LA cop who goes to the Philippines to find out who killed her sister. Against the backdrop of rising anti–American feelings,

Kat maneuvers the back alleys of Manila looking for information about the murder. She enters the karate tournament in which her sister was fighting and is trained by her sister's mentor, only to find that he is her killer and the notorious head of a terrorist group determined to rid the PI of Americans. In usual Roger Corman fashion, the film boasts full nudity, including a couple of battles where the women fight their assailants topless, but also adds a political dimension not always present in these films. Is the American presence in the Philippines beneficial? Is it desired by the people? The film provides no hard answers, but the questions force one to think about the situation nonetheless.

While the action thriller narrative pattern has proven quite popular, world instability still allows for the stalwart plots of ex-cops, military or government agents saving the world. *Maximum Security* (1997) features Paul Michael Robinson, heretofore famous for the softcore porn *Emmanuelle* cable series, as a cop sentenced to time in prison, only the prison is new and he is transferred there with a few other prisoners. The rest of the story finds him fighting felons, and terrorists, finding time for a little sex, and defusing bombs. Not necessarily in that order.

The Tournament

Of course, if saving the world has already been done by someone else, there is always the basic out-for-revenge story. One of the most common plots is that of the "big tournament," wherein the hero must fight in a no-holds-barred match (*a la Enter the Dragon* and *Bloodsport*) to redeem his sensei, or master's honor. These types come close to the pure martial arts story, and prove to be the most inexpensive, since guns and other special effects are generally not needed.

One of the best is *Fists of Iron* (1995), which finds Michael Worth on the revenge kick when his best friend is killed in a tournament run by a sadistic millionaire. Worth has a hard punch and good jaw, but is no match for the brute who killed his buddy—that is, until he convinces two fighters to train him for the big match, *Rocky*-style. *Bloodsport 2* (1996) featured Daniel Bernhardt fighting in a major kumite while helping the authorities bust his ex-partner, a white collar thief and the man who double-crossed him. *Bloodsport 3* (1996) finds Bernhardt back at the kumite, fighting the mobster who killed his mentor, while the final installment of the series, *Bloodsport 4* (1998), was a stranger version of the first three, finding Bernhardt fighting in death matches in some weird, almost gothic-looking place.

Champions (1997) was interesting for its co-star Ken Shamrock, a professional wrestler, ultimate fight champion and one of the best combatants in the world. Shamrock played King, an undefeated no-holds-barred champion who is forced to fight for a greedy, bloodthirsty promoter who holds his wife hostage. When King unknowingly kills an ex-champion's brother in a fight, the stage is set for the two champs to meet in an underground televised bout, with hundreds of millions to be made on wagers. Eventually all the fighters in the tournament band together and shut down the operation, but not before most of them are killed in the cage matches.

Death Ring (1993) featured a slam-bang threesome in a story about a psychotic hunter who finances live human hunts on his island off the Mexican coast. Mike Norris (son of Chuck), Chad McQueen (son of Steve) and Don Swayze (brother of Patrick) play the trio impacted by the hunter. Norris and his girlfriend are kidnapped by the hunter and spirited away to the island, where a group of millionaires prepare to hunt him. A former Special Forces soldier and expert survivalist, Norris' character uses his martial arts skills to good effect, fighting off a pack of killers tracking him and Swayze. McQueen, a fair martial artist himself, leaves the kicking to Norris and settles for playing his helicopter-flying best friend.

Shoot Fighter showcases the talents of Bolo Yeung as Shingo, the king of all shoot fighters. He is the target of Lee, a ruthless shoot fighter who believes in killing his opponents in the ring. Lee is everything Shingo is not: vengeful, evil, bloodthirsty. Shingo is a man of honor attempting to build a new life in America. Reversing the student-fighting-for-master paradigm, Shingo must fight Lee in a death match to save his students, who have been lured into the shoot fighting circuit for just that purpose.

Shoot Fighter accentuates character more than most films in the genre, as Shingo's students struggle with the implications of fighting not for sport or honor, but for blood and money. Nick is a streetwise loner whose best friend Ruben is a straight-arrow karate instructor being trained by Shingo to compete in the national championships. Driven by debt and the need to save his studio, Ruben agrees to enter a shoot fight contest run by Lee, and is eventually seduced by the violence. Nick, however, is repelled by it, and the two men take divergent paths and reverse roles, as Nick trains with Shingo and Ruben trains alone. When Nick attempts to save Ruben from the death match, Lee catches him, and Ruben and Nick are forced to fight, until Shingo appears to destroy Lee and his tournaments once and for all— or at least until the sequel.

Illegal no-holds-barred fighting is a prevalent variant of the tournament revenge story. Stock iconography in these tales are abandoned warehouses (where the fighting takes place), well-dressed patrons (who flash loads of money as the combatants battle it out), reluctant heroes (or those forced to fight), reporters or lone undercover police out to bust the operation, sadistic, wealthy men who finance the events, and the seeming lack of any organized law enforcement to stop the fights.

In *The Cage* (1990), Reb Brown and former Mr. Universe Lou Ferrigno play best pals and Vietnam vets who own a bar together. Ferrigno, wounded in the head, is almost like a child, but has incredible fighting abilities which are exploited by two gamblers who trick him into fighting in an underground tournament run by an Asian Mafia. *The Cage II* (1995) returns the leads to illegal tournament fighting, only this time it is the Mafia who has tricked Ferrigno into fighting.

Triple Impact (1993) can easily be called the "Kickboxing *Raiders of the Lost Ark*." Martial arts champ Dale Cook teams with Ron Hall and female fighter Bridgett "Baby Doll" Riley in a rollicking, non-stop, action-packed tale about adventurers trying to recover an ancient golden statue in Cambodia. The story revolves around a number of pit fights which set the heroes into various phases of action, whether it be conning bettors out of money when they fight one another, fighting *the* kickboxing champion to earn expense money, or battling drug smugglers in the "ring of death." The personal chemistry between the leads is phenomenal, and Riley exhibits a tender underside to a rather tough exterior.

The year 1997 saw the release of two more pit fighting movies, *Blade Boxer* and *Kick of Death*. In the former, a loner detective goes deep undercover to bust a murderous no-holds-barred tournament that features combatants killing one another with steel talon claws. While the fight sequences are so-so, the film does utilize a unique flashback style, with the cop telling his side of the story to Internal Affairs investigators who are never seen. The film co-starred Dana Plato, and was one of her last screen appearances before her untimely death.

Kick of Death followed McQuade, a Hong Kong kickboxer who runs afoul of both the Italian Mafia and the Hong Kong syndicate for refusing to take a dive in an underground tournament fight. He flees to Vegas, where he takes the identity of a hit man as well as a job as a bouncer—until the mob finds him and forces him to fight in a closed circuit broadcast pit fight. The martial arts sequences are good, and realistic in the sense that McQuade is not invincible. The body count is high by the film's end, most of the deaths by gunfire, and it is clear that while McQuade might have a kick of death, he is surely the *kiss* of death, as every character that comes in contact with him is killed, save one. The film was shot on video, a precursor of things to come.

The Ultimate Game (2000) reworks *Enter the Dragon*, with TJ Rifkin assembling a team to fight in a tournament on a rich man's island. The fights were choreographed by TJ Storm, who did an amazing job, and the script featured a slight twist with one of the contestants having to fight his way across the island through ninja warriors. *The Strike* (2002) featured a mostly black cast in the tale of two brothers, the older one a successful ex-cop going to law school who also owns a martial arts studio, the younger one always in trouble. When younger brother gets mixed up in no-holds-barred fights run by the local mobs, older brother has to kick some serious ass to get him out of the game.

In *Kickboxer 2* (1991), Sasha Mitchell takes over for Jean-Claude Van Damme as David Sloan, who must fight the nasty Tong Po to get revenge for Tong Po's murder of his brother. His brother's teacher travels to Los Angeles, as much to help David get in touch with himself as to train him for his match with Tong Po. A great supporting cast, including Peter Boyle, round out the film's rough edges. *Kickboxer 3* (1992) takes David Sloan to Rio, where he defends his title, but is then captured and forced to compete against a rich man's fighter. *Kickboxer 4* (1994) finds Sloan in prison, framed for murder by Tong Po. He is released by the authorities and sent on a mission to break up Tong Po's fortress of killers by fighting in a death match. Good action and fight scenes punctuate a ridiculous story, and one wonders why the Sloan family's perpetual nemesis can't recognized his sworn enemy.

Live Entertainment's *Without Mercy* (1995) stars Frank Zagarino as an ex–Marine forgotten by his country when he is captured and tortured by Somalian warlords during a UN Peacekeeping mission. He eventually winds up in a country that looks a lot like Indonesia, fighting in kumites whenever he needs some scratch. While the fights, coordinated by Zagarino, were fine, including a bare-knuckles anything-goes match between Zagarino and an opponent, and a battle between him and a sword-wielding drug lord, of more interest were the political implications at the beginning of the story.

The warlords running Somalia are venal and merciless, co-opting the humanitarian relief efforts to line their own pockets, while it is apparent that the local population did not value the world or America's assistance. As a UN convoy of Peacekeepers roll down the street to secure a food distribution point, they are pelted with rocks by the locals. Shortly thereafter, the warlord's thugs open up and wipe out the convoy. *Without Mercy* doesn't specifically say that American relief efforts in the third world are foolish, but it does give credence to the old maxim, "If the shoe fits...."

American Samurai (1993) is a cross between *The Octagon* and *Bloodsport*, featuring Anglo David Bradley once again as an orphaned child raised by a Japanese martial artist, this time a samurai. Mark Dacascos plays his stepbrother, a young man filled with hate because of his father's adoption of Bradley. Dacascos joins the Yakuza, is disowned by his father and becomes the champion of a death match swordplay tournament being held in Istanbul. Bradley goes to find him and is forced to enter the death match, where after a lot of soul searching and hand wringing, he defeats all comers and Dacascos. The swordplay and martial arts are evenly balanced, and the huge Texan that Bradley befriends lends a sad touch of comic relief.

Kickboxing Academy was a children's movie that used the martial arts as a backdrop to teach valuable lessons that all kids need to know. The local kickboxing academy is faced with losing its lease and the only way to save the school is for them to take on a rival dojo in a special match. But the rival academy is not concerned with fair play, only winning, and the millionaire holding the lease on the "good" kickboxing academy has a grudge against them because his son died there years before. Up until the big fight the bad martial artists harass the good ones, trashing their dojo, and they even sabotage one kickboxer's car.

When the day of the final match arrives, the kids from the good academy have persevered and overcome great obstacles (lesson one); have conquered their fear (lesson two); learned that respect and fair play are more important than just winning (lesson three); understand that sex is not something to be taken lightly (lesson four); and that drunk driving is not a good thing (lesson five). In the final showdown, the good kickboxing academy defeats the bad one and the millionaire sees the error of his ways, learning to forgive (lesson six). Because *Kickboxing Academy* is a kid's movie, the fight scenes are not as well-executed as in other films, but they are plentiful, and most parents are probably more concerned with the content than with the martial arts.

Horror

Horror and science fiction, among the most popular film genres, are similarly popular with martial arts filmmakers, and they provide an especially fertile ground for cultural analysis. The year 2000 saw Lorenzo Lamas in *The Immortal*, a horror-based martial arts film-turned-TV series in which Lamas plays Rafael Cain, a being who stalks demons, killing them with a special sword. The film mirrors the strong economic growth taking place in the country at the time, with Lamas a raconteur-like character who travels in a large, spacious motorcoach, apparently wealthy, while the characters on the show were well-dressed and urbane. Topical social and economic problems took a back seat to the more fanciful realm of the occult. The resemblance to *Highlander* is probably not coincidental. The show, which only lasted a year, boasted some good martial arts sequences and some really bad demons.

Tiger Claws 3 invoked shades of the *Superman II* plot, this time featuring three deadly kung fu ghosts who terrorize New York City and can't be stopped. This film strays from the first two, concentrating on Hong Kong–style martial arts moves. Rothrock's character, Linda Masterson, is killed early on. Or is she...? Once again the task falls upon Jalal Merhi to learn the requisite martial arts skills from an elder master in order to defeat the ghosts before they destroy the city. Like in *Rocky IV*, Merhi's character must retreat to nature to find the strength necessary to complete his task. A surprise ending saves the story—and opens up the possibility of another sequel.

Instinct to Kill (2001) was a horror thriller starring Mark Dacascos as a martial arts–trained ex-cop, now a bodyguard who agrees to teach a young woman to defend herself. The opponent happens to be her ex-husband, a former cop who was a serial killer, a brutal rapist who murdered a score of women. He escapes from an institute for the criminally insane and goes on the hunt for her, murdering everyone in his path, starting with the guards in the institute, his father, some cops and his mother-in-law.

Tim Abell, as the serial killer, steals the show, appearing throughout in a number of disguises, from a withered old lady to a Mexican cop, from an ER patient to a doctor, often mixing dark humor into his gruesome killing, such as when he disguises himself as a rock star to get at his wife's friend. Dacascos, as the bodyguard, spends most of his time either fighting or shooting at Abell, neither very successfully, at least until the final showdown, where the two engage in a knock-down, drag-out donnybrook.

Instinct to Kill was based on a best-selling novel by Lisa Gardner, a rare occurrence of adaptation at this production level and genre. The celluloid version will probably best be remembered by feminists as a misogynistic nightmare. From the opening sequence, where women are viewed in the serial killer's camcorder, to pieces of their fingers, and lingering shots of both their naked bodies and plastic bags tied around their heads, women's body parts are fetishized, perhaps, as the Lacanians would hold, to ease man's fear of castration.

After they are married, the husband, obviously reading from the Ike Turner guide to marriage, beats his wife unmercifully just for failing to make the bed properly. The wife, who is the victim, nonetheless becomes the locus for killing as everywhere she goes, her ex-husband leaves bodies behind following her. Eventually the ex-husband gets his at the hands (and gun) of the wife, echoing (or perhaps advocating) the *Burning Bed* solution to a very bloody and violent marriage.

Soul of the Avenger (1998) is an interesting film whose tension comes not so much from the supernatural elements doing battle over a warrior's spirit but rather from watching the mental and physical torment that individuals can subject themselves to. James Lew plays Kaan, a martial arts master of the Black Dragon sect who has defected from the group because they have evolved into an evil organization. The sect tracks Kaan to America, where they try to persuade him to come back. When that fails, they attempt to kill him, first at the beach, where scores of cultists somersault and flail at him with fists and various weapons, and then later at his house, where another large number attacks him with swords. When Kaan's attackers murder Earl, a drunken vagrant whom Kaan had earlier helped, the latter sees a way of escape by miraculously merging his spirit into the body of the dead man.

Kaan makes mention that between life and death there is a shadow world, and for much of his time, that's where he finds himself, caught between two forces, one evil beyond description, the other destructive beyond imagination. The Black Dragons place no value on life, neither their own or others; in fact, at times they partake in human sacrifice. At the other end of the spectrum is Earl, one of the dregs of society. Earl's life is a broken reflection of Kaan's. He is destitute, in the grip of alcohol, and sleeps in alleyways and trashcans. His girlfriend is a hooker who services johns on a dirty couch near a freeway overpass. Kaan walks the middle ground, hunted, but at the same time successful and prosperous. His wife owns an *avant garde* gallery and is an accomplished artist. However, once inside Earl's body, Kaan must live through the same experiences of his sotted host, which is no picnic.

When Earl awakens, he finds himself in a daze and unable to remember clearly much of what he experienced. He also knows that something is not right with him. But, then again, *what* would be difficult to pinpoint because there are *so* many things wrong with Earl. He is literally drinking himself to death and his girlfriend is addicted to drugs, if not sex. As Earl stumbles through the haze of his life, he finds himself torn much the same way Kaan was, between the depraved spirits of the Black Dragon, which are trying to get Kaan back, and good spirits trying to keep him on the straight and narrow.

Earl's plight is a sorry one and seems to be leading straight to hell. He cannot stop drinking, and flounders about, dirty and unkempt, barely able to speak at times, and rarely making sense. Eventually he checks into a cheap motel and, with Kaan's spiritual guidance, intends to dry out. The hours pass into days, and he sweats and groans, hallucinates and talks to himself, huddling down over the toilet when the pain and nausea becomes unbearable. As Earl descends to his nadir, conversely his hooker girlfriend ascends as high as she can, fueled by copious quantities of coke.

But such a variance is short-lived. When Earl emerges from the hotel, he is hardly recognizable as the man he was—and he is off the booze. His girlfriend, however, is still addicted. Now their respective positions have switched. Earl is on the rise, having changed from what he once was, while his girlfriend can't see beyond her nose and continues to spiral down into a vicious circle of drugs and sex. When Earl gives her money to get another motel room, making her swear not to buy drugs, it is sickening apparent she will choose cocaine and not shelter.

Now sober, Earl feels he must retrace his steps on the night that Kaan was attacked, and starts at Kaan's apartment, where Kaan's wife tells Earl that her husband's spirit is inside of him. Earl takes Kaan's wife to where Kaan and the Black Dragons fought, and there Kaan emerges from within Earl to fight with the evil sect once again, this time assisted by not only Earl, but the Master Spirit, who represents the forces of good. Kaan is victorious this time, but at a price: Kaan or Earl must die. Both cannot live. Kaan prepares to make the sacrifice but Earl stops him and takes his place. As Earl disappears in a mist, Kaan is reunited with his wife and a sense of balance is restored to the universe with the Black Dragons vanquished.

Soul of the Avenger reworks the *Angel Heart* theme but loses some of its dread just by virtue of its martial arts angle. While the Black Dragons are vile killers, and surely something to be frightened of, the real horror is watching Earl slowly realize that not only is something inside of him, but that he is really dead. The martial arts are a nice sideshow, albeit the ultimate irony comes when, after beating back his alcoholism, Earl finds it was all for naught, as he has to die anyway.

In the horror-infested *Night Hunter* (1995), Don Wilson takes his turn as a martial arts–trained vampire hunter working the streets of Los Angeles. The story is eerie and at the same time compelling, from the opening scenes of Wilson's character as a child watching his parents murdered by vampires to his later inability to trust anyone, including the reporter trying to help him. The story takes the *Blade Runner* route in the sense that Wilson must fight beings much stronger than himself, and gets kicked around much more than he kicks, though in the end he prevails.

Night Hunter adopts the opposite approach of Lamas' *The Immortal,* and can be read as a populist attack on wealth and privilege. The vampires are morbid symbols of capitalism gone wild, with its greed and corruption. They are rich and cultured, used to fine wine and foods. Some appear to be fashion plates, with the latest styles of clothes, makeup and accessories. The head vampire is mannered and refined, but completely without scruples. Contrast this with the poor, who are the faceless oppressed. A whole score of homeless people, cold, hungry, shabbily dressed and dirty, encamped beneath a freeway, are beset upon by the vampires in a ravishing bloodlust, figuratively speaking, the rich eating the poor. Wilson, as a protector of the people, represents the direct action needed to stop the inequality, while the reporter and cop who help him embody the characteristics of truth and justice.

Science Fiction

Wilson also got around to the sci-fi *Future Kick,* which also reworked the *Blade Runner* scenario, playing a sole surviving cyborg that is hunted by corporate police and bounty hunters who remain hot on his trail. Earth has turned into a living hell, where human life has utterly no value, except in death, when faceless corporations can then harvest the organs of the destitute to keep the wealthy alive indefinitely. The ultra-rich have retreated to the Moon, while essential corporate personnel who remain on Earth live in luxurious buildings insulated from the outside horrors they have created.

The irony here is palpable. In the future, "New Los Angeles" and the rest of the advanced industrial countries have become nothing more than an exploitable resource for the various multi-national corporations, just as the third world currently is. In fact, exploitation becomes the only sure thing besides death in a place where governments are routinely overturned by terrorists and the police stations are so crowded it takes days to talk to an officer. The rich prey on the poor; the poor prey on each other. Endless miles of strip clubs feature women who have only their bodies to sell to keep alive. Violence is the exception, not the rule, and when a corpse hits the street it is plucked clean before it can bounce.

Struggling to endure not only the savagery of the city but the corporate police pursuing him is Wilson, the soul survivor of a martial arts–trained group of cyborgs created by the corporations to fight crime, only to rebel once they found that the corporations were the real criminals. Helping a widow whose husband was murdered, Wilson tracks down the killers, playing up the irony that in such a dystopia, where there is little difference between the police, the killers or the general public for that matter, only a non-living thing can form a sense of compassion

Wilson followed up with *Cyber Tracker* (1994). This time, instead of playing a cyborg being hunted by humans, he was a human hunted by cyborgs, in this case playing a Secret Service agent framed for murder by a corrupt politician. The America of the not-too-distant future is a libertarian horror, where all manner of drugs and weapons are legal, and where Cybercore, the world's most advanced computer company, is increasing its influence over most spheres of life. Paralleling Cybercore's push for power is an exponentially expanding human reliance on computers, to the point where they begin to not only sap the masses of their ability to make decisions, but condition them to become obedient and, eventually, subservient.

As the police and cyborg trackers close in on him, Wilson is aided by the very terrorist organization he had been fighting. More or less hi-tech geeks, the group is opposed to Cybercore's establishment of a computerized justice system that deploys unstoppable cyborgs to hunt and summarily execute criminals, viewing it as the first step in the erosion of the Constitution. Much like the cop in *Nemesis*, Wilson finds that he has been on the wrong side of the war, and throws in with the group, eventually destroying the cyborg trackers and exposing Cyborcore for what it really is: a corporate attempt to enslave the populace by undermining and controlling the government. Wilson followed up with *Cyber Tracker 2* (1995), again battling the cyborgs, only this time with help from the media.

This theme, then, of a twisted, nightmarish future where technology has worked to imprison rather than liberate is a common thread within many of these films. In *T C 2000*, the year is 2020 and civilization has been destroyed by pollution. Survival of the fittest has been replaced by survival of the wealthiest. The dichotomy between the haves and have-nots, touched upon in other such films, has become a Darwinian fact of existence here. The rich have retreated below the surface, where they have managed to continue a prosperous, technology-driven society at the expense of the poor, who were methodically excluded and left to die above ground. Both in the "underworld," where the wealthy live, and the "surface world," where the surviving dregs remain, brute strength is the sole determinant of political power and social position.

The underworld, which has degenerated into a semi-fascist state, is ruled by an "Overlord" and regulated by the "Controller," who not only directs the internal security forces but the "Tracker-Communicators" as well—the "T-Cs" of the story's title, an army of scouts specially trained to prevent the dregs from getting through the laser grids that protect the lower dominion. Topside, the weak are routine quarry for the gangs that roam the streets, and death matches provide the only organized form of entertainment. As in the underworld, the fighters in the surface world live a privileged life free of want in abandoned mansions—so long as they have the power to defend it.

Into this desolate milieu strides Billy Blanks, a renegade TC being hunted in the surface world by the Controller for uncovering his plot to destroy the Earth's ozone layer, which has recently replenished itself, thereby making it theoretically possible to one day return to a normal life above ground. Blanks helps organize the death match fighters and, after a pitched battle, kills the Controller. The fight sequences are well-choreographed and feature a variety of styles, from kung fu to karate, kickboxing and wrestling. And while there is rarely, if ever, a break in the action, it is the story's bleak political ambiguity that is most striking. Blanks and the others have saved the world, but for how long? There is no organized government above ground while those in power below ground, the fascists, are more than willing to re-destroy the hope of ever returning to the surface rather than give up their domination of the underworld they rule.

Virtual Combat (1996) also posits a semi-fascist future, where freedom has been replaced in large part by virtual decadence. The masses spend their time living out their dreams and hopes courtesy of virtual reality programs which make even the most ridiculous fantasy seem real, at least long enough to prevent the population from rising up against their corporate oppressors. Those *not* buying into virtual happiness and, who attempt to escape, are hunted by trackers, a highly mobile border police force that employs more force than reason when catching violators.

Heatseeker (1995) is a futuristic tale that finds Keith Cooke playing a champion kick boxer who declines an invitation to fight in a corporate-sponsored martial arts tournament. When big business kidnaps his fiancée, he is forced to fight with Gary Daniels, a cyborg ultimate warrior manufactured by the corporation. This is another in a series of films where multi-national business has either taken over the world or is close to doing so. And while humanity, in the form and representation of Cooke, prevails in the end, can there really be a conclusion? The corporation can merely continue to remake the cyborg warriors until they can't be beaten, thereby raising the dark specter that one day people will be stripped of all that makes them human.

Director Albert Pyun's *Knights* (1993) went the post-apocalypse route, with the world destroyed and civilization at its ebb. Cyborgs, created by the government as assassins, now roam the planet, preying on humans. Built with a finite life span, the cyborgs have engineered a way to remain alive forever—by consuming human blood, like vampires—and set up a number of thematic opposites and similarities with their human enemies. Humans are creatures with feelings; cyborgs have none. Humans are sentient; cyborgs are mechanical. Humans have a sense of spirituality, of nature and of God; so do the cyborgs, who worship the Master Builder, the one who created them. Both share what is left of the Earth, but only one can eventually survive.

Into this nightmare rides Gabriel, played by Kris Kristofferson, a "good" cyborg created to destroy other "bad" cyborgs. Gabriel rescues Nea, a young woman whose parents were massacred by the cyborgs, and in return for her showing him a shortcut to the cyborgs' location, he agrees to train her in cyborg fighting skills. Nea, played by multiple martial arts champion Kathy Long, is a good student who learns quickly. When they finally meet the cyborg army, Gabriel is blown in half, leaving Nea to fight the battle. In a number of encounters, both against cyborgs (including Gary Daniels) and their human army of mercenaries, Nea proves more than a match, kicking, punching and slashing her way through scores of opponents. After Gabriel repairs himself, they team up and destroy the cyborg army, only to have to set out to find the Master Builder before he creates more.

The film's title is clearly a reference to the chivalric period of a bygone era. However, in that past as well as this future, there was nothing very heroic about the knights, who in both times tended to oppress and exploit rather than protect the peasants. These futuristic peasants in Pyun's film, garbed in loin skins or leather breeches, are massacred by the technologically advanced skin-covered robots with the strength of 50 men. Even the cyborgs dress in long flowing garb, leaving the impression the film was suspended in a time warp. However, only with the arrival of Kristofferson does *Knights* acquire a more typical Arthurian narrative, with Kristofferson taking on the persona of the errant knight and Kathy Long his retainer.

Knights rests upon an evident paradox set up in the film's thematic structure: When Nea finds herself attracted to Gabriel, either as the father she lost or a romantic figure, she learns from him that he has only a one-year life span. Nea protests that there must be some way to keep him alive, to prolong his existence. When Gabriel asserts that he is not sentient, Nea continues to apply human characteristics to him, which brings us back to the ultimate point: If the cyborgs are merely machines, then their killing of humans is not justified, for it accomplishes nothing and terminates a life. However, if the cyborgs can be like humans, as Nea seems to feel about Gabriel, then they have every right to feed upon species which keep them alive, much the way humans do. The film doesn't give an answer, and no sequel was forthcoming, though the door was climactically left open for one.

Spoiler (1998) took us into a number of hellish futures, all courtesy of Gary Daniels, who plays Roger Mason, a man wrongly convicted of a crime and sentenced to a year in prison. But as punishment for his escape attempts, he must be put through a process similar to cryogenic freezing that lasts decades. Each time Mason escapes he is recaptured and beaten, frozen again for ever-increasing periods, and then thawed to resume his living incarceration. With each escape Mason's reputation grows until he is a living legend—and that is something the police and corrections people will not tolerate.

In essence Roger Mason is a twenty-first century Cool Hand Luke, a man imprisoned for but a short time, but whose love of freedom and family drive his ever-futile escape attempts. It is never made clear what Mason's job was, or whether he was a loser in life, but what is painfully apparent—and what a guard tauntingly points out to him—is that no one even thinks about escaping from a one-year sentence, for any reason. Yet Roger did. So like Luke, his sentence continues to grow. The first time he is reanimated, he finds both his parents had died. The second time he is reanimated, his wife had just passed. The third time, his daughter is now 72, yet Roger remains 35, and the little girl he left behind is now on her death bed.

The society Roger lives in is a crowded, claustrophobic nightmare, filled with bounty hunters and jackbooted, trenchant-wielding police in black jumpsuits. Like a futuristic Nazi Germany, people must carry papers, and the government has banned all pernicious objects, from tobacco to violent DVDs. One not-so-subtle implication of the driving force behind the repression is the religious iconography visible everywhere, from crucifixes to statues and churches. But despite the repression, or as some would argue because of it, the society is still violent nonetheless, as evidenced by the metal detectors placed in establishments to keep out weapons.

Corruption is also widespread in all sectors of the community. The police are brutal thugs, worse than those incarcerated, and have access to banned or outlawed substances. Government officials are mere toadies going through the motions of their job, not really caring about the people their work affects. Priests, nuns, even judges support the new order. It was a nun who spotted Roger and turned him in to the police when she saw him in a priest's garb. In Roger's last go-round it was the Godly family he stayed with who called the authorities.

Roger is eventually reunited with his daughter, who lies dying in the same hospital as he. But the reunion is quick and brings little comfort to him. He stumbles out of the room, dazed from their meeting and the savage beating the police had given him. When the police order him to halt, Roger keeps going, they fire … and the frame freezes. Why he failed to stop is left ambiguous, but there is a clue. Midway through the film, just after being thawed out, Roger tells the other inmates, who all look at him like a hero, that he didn't escape for them, that he did it for himself. But those words belie his thoughts and actions. By the film's end it becomes apparent that Roger really did do it for all those who value freedom even more than life itself.

In Pepin-Merhi's production *Hologram Man* (1995), multi-national corporations of the future are once again calling the shots, having taken control of the cities, literally, by placing "bio-domes" over them, as much to keep pollution out as to keep the populace in. Government is largely a corrupt figurehead that rubber stamps the activities of the corporate board. Gallagher, a martial arts–trained killer and madman, escapes from the hologramic stasis where he has been imprisoned, yet by remaining a bio-electric energy field of immense power, he is virtually unstoppable.

He violently attacks the corporate structure, robbing banks and pirating the television waves in an attempt to rally the people behind him. The corporation fights back by declaring martial law. Paramilitary police are ordered to kill Gallagher no matter how many civilian casualties are incurred. Into the fray comes Decoda, the tough police detective who originally brought Gallagher to justice. Distrustful of the corporation but hating Gallagher even more, he not only fails to kill the terrorist but cannot stop the corporation's slaughter of innocent bystanders—that is, until he becomes a hologram man himself.

The film raises as many philosophical questions as there are fights and explosions. Are some freedoms more important than others? When both sides are equally bad, what can a man of conscience do? The battle clearly pits totalitarianism against anarchy, with Decoda staking a dubious claim to the middle ground. In return for alleviating poverty and deprivation, the corporation has usurped power and denies all political freedom. Those questioning its board can be summarily executed. Gallagher and his "World Liberation Movement" advocate the destruction of the corporate oligarchy, but have no plan for a future system of government to replace the one he proposes to topple. In fact, he goes so far as executing one of his allies who was bold enough to submit a social action plan to him.

Both the corporation and Gallagher become opposite sides of the same corrupt coin, where the ends justify the means and civilian casualties are merely a natural byproduct of the struggle for power. Decoda, with all his flaws, represents the democratic view, that all freedoms should be respected. However, his rhetoric doesn't always match his actions. In becoming a bio-electrical hologram himself, and harnessing the unlimited power it represents, he sides with the corporation and wipes out Gallagher and his followers. When the battle is over, the corporate leader offers him a position as his company enforcer, but Decoda refuses, instead killing him there on the spot. His reply to his girlfriend's question of what will happen next rings hollow: "We vote." Like the Norris character in *Good Guys Wear Black*, Decoda finds that when one finally gets some power, the perspective regarding ends and means changes drastically.

Olivier Gruner's *Automatic* covers much the same ground: a future dominated by massive corporations and endless duplicity that blurs the lines between reality and obscures the truth beyond recognition. As Gruner fights to uncover the facts behind his existence, his discovery marks him as the very personification of the corporation he battles: He is a machine. In *Interceptor Force* (1999), Gruner stars as a military alien hunter who tracks a Predator-like being to a small Mexican town, where he fights it tooth and nail. In *Velocity Trap* (1998), Gruner shifts gears, returning to the future but this time as the all-too-human police officer on a space transit ship overrun with villains trying to hijack a cargo of money. Not only must he fight off the bad guys, but he has to find a way to save the ship from a fast-approaching meteor.

War

Counting the Persian Gulf War, and the subsequent Iraqi Freedom campaign, America has had a number of problems abroad, including bombing engagements against the Yugoslavian government and peace-keeping duties in Kosovo. However, war films have been few and mostly confined to big-budget bonanzas which look back and not at the present. Spielberg's World War II epic *Saving Private Ryan* (1998) was a box office smash that garnered him a Best Director Academy Award; a more existential look at the war in the Pacific, *The Thin Blue Line*, Terence Malik's first film in over 20 years, was a dud that garnered heaps of critical praise, a slew of Oscar nominations, but no wins and no money.

A few martial arts DTVs have used the military or war as a backdrop. In *The Base* (1999), Mark Dacascos plays an officer who goes undercover to break up illegal activities on a military base, while in *Crash Dive* (1996) Michael Dudikoff plays a Naval officer and troubleshooter called upon to stop terrorists who have captured an American nuclear submarine. If getting on the sub—no small accomplishment—was tricky, Dudikoff has his work cut out for him as he battles the villains tooth and nail.

Another interesting Dudikoff film was *The Human Shield* (1992), a Cannon release that focused on the horror that was (and is) Iraq. Dudikoff plays Mathews, an American military advisor to the Iraqi army during the 1980s. He runs afoul of a colonel over the massacre of a village and barely escapes with his life. Later, as Americans are fleeing Iraq prior to the Persian Gulf War, the colonel seizes Mathews' brother to use as bait to lure Mathews back to the country so the colonel can kill him.

The martial arts scenes (few and obligatory) include a knife fight between

Dudikoff and the colonel to open the film, a gun takeaway and Dudikoff fighting off a couple of Iraqi soldiers to escape from prison. However, beyond the fights, the film's implications about American foreign policy are worthy of note. Mathews is assigned to help the Iraqis fight the Iranians, in a war started by the Iraqis, in which the Iraqis used chemical weapons. Mathews' objection over the colonel slaughtering a village of Iranians was clearly meant as a symbolic gesture which indicated America's disapproval of such tactics and to wash our hands clean. However, symbol or no symbol, America's backing of Saddam Hussein and possible tacit approval of his invasion of Iran clearly led to the problems of Desert Storm and Operation Iraqi Freedom, in which American forces had to personally deal with the monster its own government helped create.

Nu Image Productions has released a whole slate of war films, from *The Operation Delta Force* series to the *U.S. Seals* group, in which martial arts–trained military men take on all manner of threats facing our nation. In *U.S. Seals II* (2001), Michael Worth leads a commando team to an island where terrorists are threatening to launch a ballistic missile at the United States. The plot itself is weak, but the action sequences are on the ball, and for once the hero isn't the best martial artist, just the one who survives the mission.

American Tigers revisits *The Dirty Dozen*, featuring "B" action favorite Sam J. Jones as an Army sergeant who recruits and drills a group of military prisoners for a special mission against narco-terrorists. In a testament to her personal popularity within the genre, Cynthia Rothrock makes a guest appearance as none other than herself, training the men in the hand-to-hand combat they will need to master if they are to survive their suicide attack.

In *Perfect Target,* mercenary Daniel Bernhardt is set up to take the fall when a popular Latin American president is assassinated; while the plot is standard, its implications are not. The forces behind the scenes running the country are American military personnel, a not-so-subtle reminder of this country's duplicitous involvement in the affairs of its south-of-the-border neighbors. Olivier Gruner's *Mercenary* (1997) and *Mercenary 2* (1998) find the Frenchmen knee-deep in military action. In the former film he sets out to rescue the kidnapped wife of a meek accountant. In the latter he trudges through the jungle to bring home a flamboyant accountant kidnapped by drug dealers. In both films, nothing is what it seems. The women can't be trusted, and martial arts takes a back seat to broad humor and gunplay.

In *Delta Force: The Lost Patrol* (1999), Gary Daniels leads some UN peacekeepers on an observation mission in an unnamed desert of the Middle East. The story's premise is unintentionally controversial: Throughout the world, UN peacekeepers are deployed, often without guidance or clear protocols on when to use force or defend themselves. Which begs the question: Why deploy them in the first place? No explicit answers are provided, but the sorry nature of the situation definitely provokes thought.

During their patrol, the squad is ambushed and left for dead. Daniels has to somehow rally the few remaining men he has to keep going, and then break orders to take out an illegal missile site. The end allows for two contradictory but valid readings: first, that peacekeepers are just as willing to break rules as the nations in which they are deployed; or second, that peacekeepers must use whatever means are necessary to preserve the peace, including using force. Like the *Mercenary* series, martial arts in *Delta Force: The Lost Patrol* plays second fiddle to firepower, though Daniels does take the time to put Mike Norris in his place.

Black Sea Raid (1997) casts Daniel Bernhardt as Rick, a CIA agent who leads a covert operation to rescue an old friend's ex-wife from a Russian mental institution. Complicating matters for Bernhardt is a nuclear missile which rogue elements of the army are trying to sell, and a member of the commando team, who is a schemer to say the least. In any event, the boys come through in the end. Location filming in the Ukraine along with Russian-style helicopters added to the film's flavor. Bernhardt choreographed the exceptional fight scenes, and the action held the film together even when the story didn't. Of particular interest, however, is the opening scene, in which Chechen rebels hold a hostage in Moscow. Five years later, the same scene would be repeated for real, with close to 500 hostages.

Sequels

Sequels are common in cinema, and successful martial arts films are no different, spawning any number of follow-ups so long as they are profitable. However, of note are the series that take on a life of their own and go down a different path than originally foreseen. Imperial Entertainment's *Nemesis*, a cross between action thriller and sci-fi, was one such example. The first story concerns a martial arts–trained cop fighting gangster-cyborgs; where the plot broke with other films of its ilk was its unusual accent on character. In a futuristic America, detective Alex Rain becomes the noirish filter through which we not only view this world-gone-wild dystopia but its devastating effects on his own humanity. Like a Philip K. Dick novel, what is real becomes increasingly difficult to identify, and the protagonist's trepidation over his diminishing human nature is well-founded: Like the cyborgs he hunts, beneath whose imitation skin is visible a sinister metal skull, Rain also contains non-organic parts. In fact, with almost each confrontation, he must be patched together with new eyes, limbs and bones to the point where the man resembles a machine and the detective needs to wonder whether he must one day hunt himself.

Two years later, Imperial returned with *Nemesis II*, keeping the same director, Albert Pyun, but jettisoning the original cast. One familiar aspect, however, was the postmodern strains that were so visible and confounding in the first installment. Alex returned, only this time as a woman, albeit rather buffed and manly. Biblical allusions abound, with the new Alex positioned as a savior figure. Where the initial Alex was a decent man confused by a world where reality changed in the fraction of a second it takes to blink, this Alex was a stock character pulled from a hundred other films, a killing machine who just happened to be a woman. The series' third and fourth installments were just as unseemly, though they boasted "B" favorite Tim Thomerson in a supporting role.

In *Blackbelt*, a New Horizons release, Don Wilson plays an ex-cop now putting his martial arts skills to good use as a private investigator–bodyguard. Hired to protect a singer, he finds himself up against a psychotic hit man. The film presented terrific fight scenes, as do almost all Wilson movies, and featured some gruesome moments as well as some twisted ones, such as when the hit man flashes back to his mother's abuse of him as a boy. In *Blackbelt II* (1993), Wilson's character—and Wilson—has disappeared, and what appears to be the outtakes from a war movie are patched into an action film. The result is an incongruous tale of a martial arts–trained cop taking on some mercenaries in a place that looks suspiciously like the Philippines but is supposed to be Hawaii.

The *American Kickboxer* and *American Streetfighter* series go the same way. In the former film, John Barrett stars as the drunken ex-champ who, following a prison stretch, has to work his way back into shape to fight his nemesis. He wins the battle and his girl, so the stage is set in *American Kickboxer II* for Barrett's return, right? Wrong! Dale Cook takes over as star, along with Evan Lurie, and all the characters have changed. However, in this series there is no marked drop-off between the original and the sequel, with both standing on their own merit. No such accolades apply to *American Streetfighter*, a muddled film in which Gary Daniels tries to save his brother's life. The sequel, *American Streetfighter 2*, kept Daniels, but appeared to feature outtakes of the first film, plus some new footage thrown in, to make for unintelligible muddle about the search for a serial killer of prostitutes. Tons of nudity and some requisite fights (choreographed by Daniels) round out the mess.

Decade's End

As the 90s came to a close, production of low-budget martial arts films declined. With a recession hitting Germany and continuing in Japan, and then plaguing the United States at the turn of the millennium, the money previously available for film production was gone. What started out as a promising decade ended in ambiguity as no new martial arts stars appeared, and many of the older ones were looking to break out of low-budget action films. So, while budgets climbed slightly, in many cases story values did not, and higher-priced schlock became the rule and not the exception. As America moved into the twenty-first century, uncertainty and caution wracked the film industry at all levels, and martial arts films, which make up the lower realms, found themselves operating much like "A" films, with productions green-lighted for only its biggest stars.

VIII

2000 and Beyond

As the world moved into the twenty-first century, much of the paranoia and discordance present in the narratives of martial arts films like *Bloodfist IV* or *Automatic* subsided. However, a war in Iraq, a crisis on the Korean peninsula and economic pressures from a lingering recession forced a cutback in the production of martial arts films. Old favorites turned out fewer movies, and new martial arts stars have yet to be discovered. Cynthia Rothrock and Don Wilson have just finished shooting *Sci-Fighters*, but it has yet to be released. Steven Seagal completed *Out for a Kill* (2003) and *Belly of the Beast* (2003) for Nu Image. Jean-Claude Van Damme is also filming for Nu Image. In *The Savage*, he plays a white collar worker who is sentenced to a brutal prison for taking the law into his own hands and killing his wife's rapist-murderer. The prison guards stage vicious battles for the warden's entertainment—and Van Damme has to fight to survive.[1]

Chuck Norris has stayed in television for the most part; other martial arts stars such as Ron Marchini, James Ryan, and Jim Kelly haven't made a movie in years. Mark Dacascos continues to remain busy, but TJ Storm, Loren Avedon, Ron Hall and Phillip Rhee have not been. Even those who have kept filming, like Olivier Gruner, find their movies are not released in the States, not on television, cable, or video, at least to this point anyway. Jalal Merhi has continued to direct, just finishing *The Circuit 2*, which (at least according to a review on the IMDb) makes it sound just like Van Damme's new film, something about fighting for a prison warden's enjoyment.

Lorenzo Lamas has kept quite active, shooting two films in 2002 and three in 2003. However, the shift he began making in the late 90s from martial arts to thrillers appears to be accomplished. In *Rapid Exchange* (2003), Lamas has completed a genuine 180, playing Ketchum, an international thief who teams up with some experts to rip off a quarter of a billion dollars held in a vault on a Boeing 747. Lamas and the others manage to sneak their plane behind the 747 and gain entry to it, but lose a man in the process. Once aboard, the team gets most of the money out of the vault and loads it into their waiting aircraft, but Lamas and his partner are double-crossed and appear to be killed. When the rest of the team tries to launder their money through a bank in Yugoslavia, they are conned by Lamas and he makes off with the cash.

Rapid Exchange has its moments, but for the most part does not showcase the physicality that viewers have come to expect from a Lamas film. The plot is difficult to follow at times, especially when the characters are talking computer lingo, yet the special effects are good, particularly the scenes of the crooks going from one aircraft to the other. The fact that Lamas and his partner are still alive after falling 10,000 feet from a plane is never explained. As for action, there is none, though Lamas has a number of occasions where he *could* fight. In fact, in his one altercation in the hold of the 747, Lamas is beaten by a weasly punk he wouldn't have thought twice about in past films. However, here his character seems to be a lover and a con man, not a fighter. In comparison with Jonathan Damone, the karate-kicking head hunter in *Bounty Tracker* (filmed ten years before), Ketchum is a kindler, gentler character—the same sharp tongue and breezy nature, only nothing to back it up.

Aussie Richard Norton co-starred in *Amazons and Gladiators* (2000), a sword-play story set in the days of the Roman Empire. He plays Lucious, captain of the Amazon Queen Zenobia's guard. The Amazons are a tribe of escaped women slaves who roam the European countryside, training in martial arts and all manner of edged weapons. Caesar wants the Amazons eliminated, so he orders the sadistic Crassius, the same general who defeated Spartacus, to find the women and destroy them. Crassius does but, unknown to him, one of the women whom he has taken captive has sworn revenge. In a duel to the death in the gladiator ring, she kills the general.

Amazons and Gladiators continues in the lengthy tradition of Roman Empire films which attempt to posit current sensibilities, ethical standards and morals to a long-ago time when slavery was an accepted practice all over the world and women were either third tier citizens or, worse yet, not recognized at all. Zenobia and her forces preach tolerance and respect and do not recognize the right of one person to own another. Their villages are egalitarian structures where men and women are equal and everyone goes about happily. In outlying villages, when a woman is somehow wronged, the Amazons will administer justice for her. In one speech taken from Clint Eastwood's *Unforgiven*, the heroine of the film advises the Roman citizens that if they harm any women or slaves, she will be back to kill them all.

Norton's role as captain of the guard allows him to demonstrate his talent with the sword, which he does in a number of fights, not to mention throwing in a few kicks and punches. In a montage scene of the battle of Greyhaven, Norton can be seen slashing and stabbing through scores of Romans, his sword a blur. The women fighters, clearly not as skilled or fluid as Norton, distract attention from their lack of ability through their revealing forms of dress, which highlight their attractiveness if not their talent. This scheme of distraction works throughout the film to disguise the relatively low budget of the shoot. The gladiator ring is hardly of epic proportion, so the fights in them are particularly bloody and gruesome, diverting attention. Similarly, the battles between the Roman troops and the Amazons are relatively small, but they are counterbalanced by scenes of enormous luxury and decadence, such as Crassius' bath, which is prepared by naked slave women.

In another scene, this one seemingly lifted from *Spartacus*, Norton and his lover, the Amazon heroine, battle a whole group of gladiators. However, once they destroy them, Crassius orders them to fight one another—to the death. Norton throws down his sword, refusing to fight, and he is killed by a volley of arrows. In the end, the Amazons prevail and flee into the forest, where the disembodied voice of a soothsayer tells us that, along with the Visigoths and other barbarian tribes, the Amazons help bring down the Roman Empire. However, considering what followed in Europe for the next 800 years or so, this was an accomplishment of questionable merit.

Gary Daniels maintained a busy schedule, shooting five films in 2000. *City of Fear* (2000) plumbed the depths of the Sophian underworld in a post–Communist Bulgaria that doesn't look much different than its Stalinist days. Daniels plays Steve, an adventuresome reporter coasting through life. His sensei beats him in a full contact match, then tells him he has to focus on the spiritual side of himself so that he can follow through on the important things in life. Steve isn't worried so much about following through as he is getting ahead.

Steve is hired to write a story about his best friend Charlie, a brilliant research scientist in Sophia working on a cure for AIDS. Steve arrives in Bulgaria just as Charlie is being buried, the victim of a freak fishing accident. Just as Steve prepares to fly home, his interest is piqued by a woman, Alexa, whom he saw at Charlie's funeral. He talks to her at a strip bar where she works and becomes convinced that Charlie was murdered. He decides that this time he is going to follow things through, for Charlie's sake, if for nothing else. As Steve works his way through the dangerous streets of Sophia, he learns more about Charlie than he ever wanted to, not to mention a lot about himself.

City of Fear is one of those interesting stories that follow a parallel track: As Steve grows from an immature adult to a man committed to justice, the sunny side of Bulgaria is exposed as a treacherous mask which hides much socio-economic uncertainty. While trying to fathom the reasons behind Charlie's demise, Steve is warned several times to leave the case alone and go home. For Steve, that would be the easiest thing to do, but the longer he is pushed and prodded, the more intent he is on finding out the truth behind his friend's death. He is shadowed, shot at and attacked, sometimes by the police and sometimes by the Russian Mafia which Steve learns the hard way that Charlie had been working for. But with each fight, he becomes more committed to what he is doing, and his skills as a martial artist improve from the confidence that he is doing the right thing.

Eventually, with the help of Alexa, Steve learns the reason that everyone is so interested in Charlie: He was developing a highly addictive narcotic called Blue Myst which is so potent that it actually destroys DNA material in the user. But by this time, Steve is convinced that Charlie is actually alive—and a criminal—so he and Alexa go to the police with their suspicions. Steve eventually unmasks Charlie, only to find him a shell of the person he once was, addicted to Blue Myst, and preparing to double-cross his Russian Mafia sponsors by heading to Turkey to work for their underworld.

Steve has finally followed something through to its conclusion, and while his was a journey of personal enlightenment and courage, a more public trek through the wasteland of Bulgaria reveals trouble in paradise. Crime is rampant, and anyone with money must have a bodyguard. Shootings seem as common on the streets of Sophia as on those of Central Los Angeles. In one instance, a fishing boat captain is gunned down for talking to Steve, while another character is machine gunned while eating his breakfast at a swank outdoor cafe. Bulgaria may have embraced democracy and freedom, but there is no freedom from poverty, which still affects significant portions of the population.

While a Communist nation, Bulgaria and other Eastern bloc countries were relatively free from the vices that plagued Western Europe and the United States. With the end of Soviet influence and totalitarian control, drugs and prostitution flourished. While fleeing their pursuers, Steve and Alexa wander into an encampment of homeless, dying and sometimes violent drug addicts, strung out from Charlie's Blue Myst, begging for food, money, anything they can get their hands on.

AIDS, the disease Charlie was supposed to be attempting to cure, has spread across the country and is a virtual death sentence for those afflicted. The government restricts employment, movement, even exit from the country to anyone found with the disease, and the police, who have not completely freed themselves of Stalinist tendencies, use forged positive blood tests to control anyone considered undesirable. As the story's title suggests, Sophia can at times be a city of fear.

The martial arts sequences in the film were plentiful, fast and furious, and begin right away. Daniels takes on his sensei in a full contact match to open the story; once in Bulgaria he fights off a number of mobsters in a garage, and a whole slew of police officers chasing him through an outdoor market. He battles a few hospital security guards and, in the film's finale, clashes with two martial arts–trained members of the Turkish Mafia there to pick up Charlie. Daniels even has time for a rather humorous encounter with the hulking bodyguard protecting Alexa.

In many ways, *City of Fear* is an homage to *Citizen Kane* and *The Third Man*. Steve is a reporter and writer, like the characters in those two classics who investigate what happened to Charles Foster Kane and Harry Lime, respectively. Steve breaks Charlie's computer code using a password taken from *Citizen Kane*, Charlie's favorite movie, and when Charlie is facing his demise, he bravely announces that it's not his "Rosebud" yet. Even the story line follows *The Third Man*. Both Harry Lime and Charlie are involved with drugs, both men fake their own death to avoid capture, both are being investigated by their friends, and both tales take place in Central Europe.

However, unlike most films of this nature, *City of Fear* ends with mixed emotions. Charlie has gotten what he deserved, the spread of Blue Myst has been stopped, but Alexa has been revealed as Charlie's accomplice, which is a betrayal of Steve, who had fallen in love with her. Steve leaves Bulgaria, hurt and disgusted by Alexa, but at the same time proud of the way he conducted himself. For once, Steve has followed through on something. Alexa remains behind, with no way to leave and no one to look out for her.

Black Friday (2000) found Daniels as a one-time government assassin turned successful lawyer who drives home one day to find his residence surrounded by a secret government strike team that tracks and safeguards chemical weapons. Purportedly terrorists have taken up positions inside and are holding his wife and child hostage. Why they specifically targeted Daniels' home (a luxury mansion in a secluded area) and why they subsequently try to kill him is a mystery that Daniels has to unravel—or does he? As the story unfolds, we find that Daniels is in with the so-called terrorists and that they are the good guys.

The plot of *Black Friday* is muddled to say the least, and it's cinematographically bizarre. In the first martial art sequence, Daniels takes on his nemesis in a parking garage that is bathed in green light, making the entire area look like the water in a dirty pool. Prior to that, Daniels enters a room that is completely white, including the uniforms of the employees. Why is not exactly clear, except perhaps to highlight the red of blood when Daniels shoots up the entire place and kills everyone.

Editing is choppy in places, as with most films of this nature, with flashbacks marring the middle of the film and breaking the story's rhythm. Fight scenes are also rocky, particularly during the final conflict, which has Daniels taking on an old foe from his assassin days. However, the fight in the garage is filmed mostly in master shot, with few closeups, slowing down the action but also heightening its sense of realism.

While *Black Friday* adds nothing new to the genre, and is in fact much slower than most Gary Daniels films, it does point up an old phenomenon: distrust of government and authority. While the conservative nature of most martial arts films of the 80s often gave the government a pass, many subsequent films of the 90s and new millennium do not. Whether this cynicism is due to the moral disgrace of the Clinton Administration or the continual big business ethical debacles is unclear. It could quite possibly be a combination of both. In any event, Daniels' character is sickened by the killing he had done and has started a new life, only to find that the government is out to test chemical weapons on American civilians. As the grunge rock soundtrack rolls on, time and again Daniels and others refer to the people they work for as "faceless entities," or blast through tirades of how "they" (meaning the government) are in control of everything. Whether this trend will continue or not remains open. With tensions high in the Middle East, most Americans seem to be back in a conservative mode, so we will see, indeed, if art reflects life.

Daniels took a sharp right turn away from the martial arts in *Epicenter* (2000), an adventure drama featuring him as a spy in the custody of FBI agent Tracy Lords. Daniels only had one fight in the film, and that was while handcuffed, but this is not to say the film was lacking excitement. Replacing the hand-to-hand combat were tremendous special effects which produced the illusion of a massive earthquake rocking the Los Angeles area.

Daniels plays Nick, a computer programmer with a chip on his shoulder regarding his employer. He steals some top secret data involving stealth bomber technology from his company, then arranges to sell it to the Russian Mafia. But he is caught by Amanda (Lords), an FBI agent infiltrating the mob. As Nick is being transported to a safe house in L.A., the Russians find him and Amanda, but so does the earthquake, and the entire city is destroyed. Amanda and Nick make their way through the rubble that was once Los Angeles, all the while being chased by the Russians, who want the microchip with the top secret information.

Epicenter boasted some exciting car chases and shootouts, and a refreshing emphasis on characters, most of whom are troubled in one way or another. Nick has lost his wife to leukemia, in part because his company wouldn't help to pay for an experimental procedure to save her. His bitterness toward the firm motivates him to steal the top secret data, hoping to destroy their business when the Russians put the information for sale on the open market. Amanda is an agent obsessed with her job: She smokes too much, her husband has left her and she dedicates all of her time to bringing down the Russians. She has little or no time to spend with her young daughter, who is becoming rebellious and distraught because of her mother's inattention. Even Tanya, the Russian in charge of getting the microchip from Nick, is coping with the death of her brother, who was killed by the police in a shootout. Her sex life suffers (to say the least), and she becomes a mirror image of Nick, seeking revenge against the person she believes to be the cause of her family loss: Nick.

The film is divided into distinct sections. The first segment is part thriller, part drama, where we learn what is eating at and motivating the characters. The second is all action as Amanda and Nick struggle to get to Amanda's daughter, who is waiting for her at a large mall. Amanda and Nick eventually prevail, but more importantly they profit from their experience and change their ways. Tanya, blinded by hate, does not, and faces the consequences. Early in the story, a character describes an earthquake as two geological plates pushing against one another, creating tremendous pressure. In many ways, that represents these characters and their fractious relationship with others and the world around them.

The Road Ahead

As the new millennium rolls in, the future of low-budget martial arts films is uncertain. On the up side, television is one avenue where martial arts continue to make its presence known. *Black Sash* (2003) is a new show from the WB Network that stars Russell Wong as Tom Chang, a former San Francisco cop who was framed and imprisoned in Hong Kong for pedaling narcotics. Chang returns to San Francisco and takes over his old master's studio, attracting a clientele of mostly troubled kids. To make ends meet in one episode, he takes on work as a skip tracer, hunting down criminals with a price on their head.

The first episode introduced the characters, including one played by the venerable Mako, a veteran of many martial arts films. He plays Chang's sifu, or master, and follows Chang as he tracks down the killer of one student's father. The fighting sequences follow a dual track: Those in the studio are almost spiritual, as Chang teaches his students the art and philosophy behind the martial arts, imparting wisdom that will help them in their daily lives. The street scenes are florid but violent, excellently choreographed and executed, and feature Hong Kong–style action, including a sequence on a bus where Chang kicks in the front windshield and fights with the man who framed him.

Besides presenting martial arts combat, the show also concentrates on character. Chang is not a "brutal" instructor but rather a committed teacher interested in both the kids' wellbeing and their training progress. Each show usually imparts a lesson or two about life—balanced out by a fight or two to keep things moving. In one episode, a student plans to settle a dispute with his father's jailhouse enemies with a gun. Another student protests, and accompanies the boy when he faces the men. Chang eventually saves the day by dispatching the felons, but the message was clear: Guns do not solve problems—they create them. The show was eventually placed on hiatus after a few episodes, but there is talk of bringing it back in a series of movie specials.

On the down side, two issues continue to plague the financial viability of American martial arts films. First, as already noted, the budgets of theatrically released feature films persist in climbing, putting the squeeze on lower-budgeted DTVs which have to compete for shelf space with the "A" list films at the video store. *Titanic, Lord of the Rings* and the *Star War* trilogies all cost in the hundreds of millions of dollars and were big hits that made it to the video store a few months after they closed in the theaters. Box office bombs with big budgets make it to the video stores even faster.

And just as important, higher-budgeted films that have nothing to do with the martial arts have appropriated martial arts moves and fights for cool effect. While this type of appropriation has always been done in Hollywood, the use of wires and computer generated effects to present outlandish fight sequences have upped the ante, so to speak, making "normal" martial arts films seem tame. *The Matrix* and *Charlie's Angels* are two films that feature impossibly expensive choreographed stunts which viewers then come to expect regularly in their films, and which most true DTV martial arts films cannot duplicate. Watching three beautiful women leaping high into the air, long jumping 30 or more feet while spinning in preposterous fashion, lets viewers know the fact that they are well-trained fighting machines.

Even a foreign martial arts film like *Crouching Tiger, Hidden Dragon,* which was certainly a blockbuster, had negligible effects on domestically produced martial arts DTVs, mostly for the same reason: Its special effects and large budget resulted in visuals which cannot be replicated in its lower-budgeted American counterparts. As the characters walked on tree limbs, flipped across buildings and whirled violently in front of a blue screen that was filled in by background later, audience expectations increased dramatically for films of this type. And the martial arts films it has inspired, like *Bullet Proof Monk* (2003), which was based on an underground comic book, are similarly budgeted. With the bar so raised, an introspective martial arts film like *Redemption,* or a plucky, oddball partner film like *Irresistible Force,* will not attract the fans that the "A" movie releases will.

The result has been a steady decrease in martial arts DTVs.

One path to keep the martial arts films flowing is to drop the budgets even further, to rock bottom, and concentrate on distribution of DVDs to smaller chain and mom and pop video stores. With digital video about to become a cinema reality, the opportunity to shoot ultra low-budget films is a distinct possibility. Distributors like Spectrum/DAP market films shot on DV, with budgets anywhere from a few thousand dollars up. In such an environment, stripped-down martial arts films are definitely an option. As it stands, Landmark Theatres will outfit all its U.S. locations with digital playback systems to facilitate the showing of movies shot digitally, a cinema trend which is increasing every year.[2]

A second alternative is cable television. As the number of stations grow, eventually specialty stations will arise addressing action and/or martial arts films. Blackbelt television, a network devoted to martial arts films and their devotees, is scheduled to start running in 2004. Martial arts film funding for new

Crouching Tiger, Hidden Dragon's Michelle Yeoh defies gravity. Such activity, facilitated by wires and hidden with computer generated effects, raises expectations for lower budgeted martial arts films—expectations that they cannot meet.

programming is almost a certainty. As always, video will remain a secondary out-let to recoup revenue.

The third (and probably most controversial) option is for independent stu-dios to raise their budgets and fight for their share of the market. A well-crafted film does not have to cost $100,000,000, but these days it is good to look that way. However, in doing this, independents run the risk of spending more money and still losing the battle to the major studio releases. That said, a number of inde-pendent production companies have been increasing their budgets and the quality of their films.

Promark Entertainment Group, Nu Image, New Cannon, Concorde–New Horizons and American World Pictures are among the leading independent production companies making DTV films today. Like their counterparts in Holly-wood's golden age, many are linked to a particular genre of film. Promark, clearly the pre-eminent of the group,* focuses on well-made thrillers, while Roger Cor-man's outfit, Concorde–New Horizons, is the jack of all trades, often mixing genres like martial arts and sci-fi, or erotica and horror—in short, whatever he thinks will sell. Nu Image has kept on churning out the action films, while Simon Tse Productions does the same, producing top-notch martial arts films, often star-ring British sensation Gary Daniels. American World Pictures has on occasion, made some good films with Mark Dacascos while New Cannon has teamed with Olivier Gruner and is attempting to reestablish the old company and its audience base.

As hi-definition television and DVD technology become more popular and accessible, the demand for quality film entertainment will remain steady, if not increase. Promark has already opened a children's division of film, while Nu Image has formed Millennium, a subsidiary which will handle higher-budgeted films like *Shadrach* (1998), a critically acclaimed film based on a William Styron short story. The film, starring Harvey Keitel, cost 5,000,000, and was not expected to make a profit. The company would settle for a little prestige in this instance.[3]

The Internet has also begun playing an important role in the film world, both as an advertising tool and as a means of exhibition. In the late 90s, websites, both official and unofficial, began springing up, dedicated to films, directors and actors. Official studio websites promoted films; the *Boogie Nights* site provides background information on the filming and movie's stars, while also offering for sale the 70s and 80s hits which make up its soundtrack. Independent Concorde-New Hori-zons' website lists its current films and other pertinent information about the com-pany and its product. Unofficial websites abound, mostly run by fans, celebrating low-budget icons like Don Wilson, Cynthia Rothrock or, in some cases, entire film genres like the *martial arts*. A number of websites are dedicated solely to the "B" movie and its fans!

As both cable Internet and digital subscriber lines (DSL) increase in popu-larity for both work and home use, the potential for "web-cast" films increase. Already a number of companies have sprung up to provide short films for Internet

* *Promark's budgets are higher than most if not all of the independents mentioned, and their films have con-sistently starred major A feature talent like Ray Liotta, Kiefer Sutherland and Academy Award William Hurt.*

Another computer generated effect makes Zhang Ziyi "float" in the air in *Crouching Tiger, Hidden Dragon.*

consumption (shorts being up to five minutes). They address topics germane to the particular website, be it cooking, gardening or home improvement.

Even feature-length films, mostly undistributed independents, have the potential to be broadcast in their entirety in low resolution.[4] Along those lines, major studios like Sony, Disney and Twentieth Century–Fox are looking into ways to eventually provide pay movie services to PCs, thereby circumventing the web pirates who currently download thousands of movies a day by relying on various file-swapping schemes.[5] One plan calls for new films to be released on the Internet *after* they are available in video stores, thereby preventing any losses from their biggest revenue draw. In fact, Twentieth Century–Fox has teamed up with CinemaNow, Inc., to offer newly released Fox movies for Internet download on the same day that the films become available to pay-per-view outlets. Previously released Fox films will also be available.[6]

And finally, with satellite transmissions of digitized film[7] (which could eventually replace actual celluloid reels) fast becoming an inexpensive reality, the prospect of once again displaying low-budget films in theatrical release is a possibility. The martial arts film may yet be back on the big screen. Where it belongs.

Selected Martial Arts Filmography

All films listed are in color unless otherwise noted.

Above the Law (1988): Martial arts. Directed by Andrew Davis. Screenplay by Steven Pressfield, Ronald Shusett and Andrew Davis, story by Davis and Seagal. Starring Steven Seagal and Pam Grier. (Cop with past CIA ties fights government corruption.) Warner Bros. 99 minutes.

Amazons and Gladiators (2000): Action. Directed by Zachary Weintraub. Screenplay by Zachary Weintraub. Starring Richard Norton and Patrick Bergin. (Amazonian gladiators fight for freedom against the decadent Roman Empire.) Weintraub/Kuhn Productions. 94 minutes.

American Chinatown (1996): Martial arts. Directed by Woo-Sang Park. Screenplay by Woo-Sang Park. Starring Robert Z'Dar. (Martial artist attempts to escape from the United States with his girlfriend and head back to Korea.) Woo-Sang Park Productions.

American Kickboxer 1 (1991): Martial arts. Directed by Frans Nel. Screenplay by Emil Kolbe. Starring John Barrett and Keith Vitali. (Kickboxing champion overcomes prison, then trains for big match against arch rival.) Cannon Films. 92 minutes.

American Kickboxer 2 (1993): Martial arts. Directed by Jeno Hodi. Screenplay by Jeno Hodi and Greg Lewis. Starring Dale Cook and Evan Lurie. (Two rivals join forces to rescue their ex-lover's child.) Vidmark Entertainment.

American Ninja (1985): Martial arts. Directed by Sam Firstenberg. Screenplay by Paul de Mielche. Starring Michael Dudikoff and Steve James. (Soldier trained in ninjitsu fights terrorists in the Philippines.) Cannon Films. 95 minutes.

American Ninja 2 (1987): Martial arts. Directed by Sam Firstenberg. Screenplay by Gary Conway and James Booth. Starring Michael Dudikoff and Steve James. (Soldier trained in ninjitsu fights drug dealers on a Caribbean island.) Cannon Films. 89 minutes.

American Ninja 3 (1989): Martial arts. Directed by Cedric Sundstrom. Screenplay by Gary Conway. Starring David Bradley and Steve James. (Two ninjitsu-trained warriors battle a maniac during a martial arts tournament.) Cannon Films. 90 minutes.

American Ninja 4 (1991): Martial arts. Directed by Cedric Sundstrom. Screenplay by David Geeves. Starring Michael Dudikoff and David Bradley. (Two ninjitsu warriors team up to battle an evil ninja terrorist army to rescue American POWs.) Cannon Films. 95 minutes.

American Ninja 5 (1993): Martial arts. Directed by Bobby Jean Leonard. Screenplay by John Bryant Hedberg, Greg Latter and George Saunders. Starring David Bradley and Pat Morita. (A martial artist helps a young boy discover his destiny to be a ninja.) Cannon Films. 102 minutes.

American Samurai (1993): Martial arts. Directed by Sam Firstenberg. Screenplay by Greg Corcoran. Starring David Bradley and Mark Dacascos. (Two men raised as brothers fight one another in an underground cage match in Istanbul.) Cannon Films. 82 minutes.

American Streetfighter 1 (1992): Martial arts. Directed by Steve Austin. Screenplay by Steve Austin, David Huey and Dom Magwili. Starring Gary Daniels and Ian Jacklin. (Martial artist fights to keep his brother alive.) Cine Excel Entertainment.

American Streetfighter 2 (1997): Martial arts. Directed by David Huey. Screenplay by David Huey and Marc Messenger. Starring Gary Daniels. (Martial arts cop tracks murderer.) Cine Excel Entertainment. 72 minutes.

American Tigers (1996): Martial arts. Directed by David Worth. Screenplay by Jim Fryman, story by Bob Kronovet. Starring Sam J. Jones and Cynthia Rothrock. (Military prisoners and their tough sergeant train for a suicide mission.) Gun for Hire Films. 95 minutes.

American Yakuza (1994): Crime. Directed by Frank A. Cappello. Screenplay by John Allen Nelson and Max Strom, story by Taka Ichise. Starring Viggo Mortensen. (Undercover FBI agent infiltrates Japanese crime gang.) Twister Digital Video. 96 minutes.

Angel Town (1990): Martial arts. Directed by Eric Karson. Screenplay by S. Warren. Starring Olivier Gruner and Theresa Saldana. (Graduate student skilled in martial arts battles street gangs while going to school.) Imperial Entertainment Corporation. 102 minutes.

Angelfist (1993): Martial arts. Directed by Cirio H. Santiago. Screenplay by Anthony L. Greene. Starring Catya Sassoon. (Female detective travels to Manila to find the killer of her sister.) Concorde–New Horizons. 80 minutes.

Armed Response (1986): Action. Directed by Fred Olen Ray. Story by Paul Hertzberg, TL Lankford and Fred Olen Ray. Starring

David Carradine and Lee Van Cleef. (Bar owner and ex-vet protects his family from mobsters.) Cinetel Films. 85 minutes.

Automatic (1994): Sci-fi/Martial arts. Directed by John Murlowski. Screenplay by Patrick Highsmith and Susan Lambert, story by Highsmith. Starring Olivier Gruner. (Man resists corporate corruption trying to save an android, only to learn a secret about himself in the process.) Republic Pictures Home Video. 90 minutes.

Bad Day at Black Rock (1955): Drama. Directed by John Sturges. Screenplay by Millard Kaufman. Starring Spencer Tracy and Robert Ryan. (Veteran stops in a small town to look up an Army buddy's family but finds nothing but trouble.) MGM. 81 minutes.

The Barbarian and the Geisha (1958): Drama. Directed by John Huston. Screenplay by Charles Grayson, story by Ellis St. Joseph. Starring John Wayne and Sam Jaffe. (First American ambassador to Japan encounters many problems.) 20th Century–Fox. 105 minutes.

The Base (1999): Action. Directed by Mark L. Lester. Screenplay by Jeff Albert and Hesh Rephun, story by Craig J. Nevius. Starring Mark Dacascos and Tim Abell. (Military officer goes undercover to break up corruption at a military base.) American World Pictures. 93 minutes.

Best of the Best (1989): Martial arts. Directed by Robert Radler. Screenplay by Paul Levine, story by Philip Rhee. Starring Eric Roberts and Phillip Rhee. (Five men picked to represent the USA in a martial arts tournament overcome their differences.) 20th Century–Fox. 97 minutes.

Best of the Best 2 (1993): Martial arts. Directed by Robert Radler. Screenplay by Max Strom and John Allen Nelson. Starring Eric Roberts and Phillip Rhee. (After their friend is murdered in an illegal fighting tournament, two martial artists prepare to take on its brutal champion.) 20th Century–Fox. 101 minutes.

Best of the Best 3 (1995): Martial arts. Directed by Phillip Rhee. Screenplay by Barry Gray and Deborah Scott. Starring Phillip Rhee. (Martial artist takes on some militia men who cross him.) Dimension Film. 90 minutes.

Best of the Best 4 (1998): Martial arts. Directed by Phillip Rhee. Screenplay by Phillip Rhee and Fred Vicarel. Starring Phillip Rhee. (Martial arts instructor on the run from mobsters who want something he possesses.) Dimension Film. 90 minutes.

Billy Jack (1971): Drama. Directed by TC Frank. Screenplay by Frank and Teresa Christina. Starring Tom Laughlin and Delores Taylor. (Half-breed Indian protects Freedom School from bigoted townspeople.) Warner Bros. 114 minutes.

Bionic Ninja (1986): Martial arts. Directed by Tim Ashby and Godfrey Ho. Screenplay by Alan Jackson. Starring Alan Hemmings and Rick Wilson. (Two ninja organizations fight over some top secret film.) Force 10. 89 minutes.

Black Belt Jones (1974): Martial arts. Directed by Robert Clouse. Screenplay by Alex Ross, Fred Weintraub, and Oscar Williams. Starring Jim Kelly. (Martial artist-community activist fights mobsters threatening a karate school.) Warner Bros. 87 minutes.

Black Eagle (1988): Martial arts. Directed by Eric Karson. Screenplay by Shimon Arama. Starring Sho Kosugi and Jean-Claude Van Damme. (U.S. agent battles Russian agent to recover weapons system from sunken aircraft.) Taurus Entertainment. 93 minutes.

Black Samurai (1976): Martial arts. Directed by Al Adamson. Screenplay by B. Radnick. Starring Jim Kelly. (Secret agent fights occultists who have kidnapped his girlfriend.) Magnum Video. 88 minutes.

Black Sea Raid (1997): Martial arts. Directed by Jeno Hodi. Screenplay by Jeno Hodi. Starring Daniel Bernhardt. (Man risks suicide mission for former lover.) Beam Entertainment. 82 minutes.

Blackbelt (1992): Martial arts. Directed by Charles Philip Moore. Screenplay by Robert Easter, Neva Friedenn, Paul Maslak and Charles Philip Moore. Starring Don Wilson and Mathias Hues. (Martial arts–trained detective protects a celebrity from a mad stalker.) New Horizons Picture Corporation.

Blackbelt 2 (1993): Martial arts. Directed by Joe Mari Avellana and Kevin Trent. No writer listed. Starring Blake Bahner and Gary Rooney. (Man tracks down partner's killer in Hawaii.) Concorde-New Horizons.

Blade Boxer (1997): Martial arts. Directed by Bruce Reisman. No writer listed. Starring Kevin King and Cass Magda. (Police detective goes undercover in the world of leather bars to find the killers of his partner.) 109 minutes.

Blood for Blood (1994): Martial arts. Directed by John Weidner. Screenplay by J.B. Lawrence, story by Moshe Diamant. Starring Lorenzo Lamas and James Lew. (Police officer tangles with Cambodian Mafia and discovers his own heritage.) MDP Worldwide. 93 minutes.

Blood on the Sun (1945): Action. Directed by Frank Lloyd. Screenplay by Lester Cole, story by Garrett Fort. Starring James Cagney and Sylvia Sydney. (Tough American newspaperman investigates the Japanese in pre–WWII Tokyo.) Cagney Productions. BW. 98 minutes.

Blood Warriors (1993): Martial arts. Directed by Sam Firstenberg. Screenplay by Jon Stevens and David Bradley. Starring David Bradley and Frank Zagarino. (Ex-Marine tangles with best buddy after refusing to join in drug trade with him.) Imperial Entertainment Corporation. 90 minutes.

Bloodfist (1989): Martial arts. Directed by Terence H. Winkless. Screenplay by Robert King. Starring Don Wilson. (Martial artist travels to the Philippines to track down killer of his brother.) Concorde–New Horizons. 85 minutes.

Bloodfist II (1990): Martial arts. Directed by Andy Blumenthal. Screenplay by Catherine Cyran. Starring Don Wilson. (Martial artist and some of his buddies fight drug kingpin.) Concorde–New Horizons. 85 minutes.

Bloodfist III (1992): Martial arts. Directed by Oley Sassone. Screenplay by Allison Burnett. Starring Don Wilson and Richard Roundtree. (Prisoner is forced to fight both the Aryan Brotherhood and the Black Guerrilla Family to stay alive.) Concorde–New Horizons. 88 minutes.

Bloodfist IV (1992): Martial arts. Directed by Paul Ziller. Screenplay by Paul Ziller, story by Rob Kerchner. Starring Don Wilson. (Car repo man is on the run from terrorists after repossessing their car.) Concorde–New Horizons. 86 minutes.

Bloodfist V (1993): Martial arts. Directed by Jeff Yonis. Screenplay by Jeff Yonis, story by Rob Kerchner. Starring Don Wilson. (Martial artist loses his memory and is on the run.) Concorde–New Horizons.

Bloodfist VI (1994): Martial arts. Directed by Rick Jacobson. Screenplay by Brendan Broderick and Rob Kerchner. Starring Don Wilson. (Airmen defend missile silo against entrenched terrorists trying to launch a nuclear missile.) Concorde-New Horizons. 86 minutes.

Bloodfist VII (aka *Manhunt*) (1995): Martial arts. Directed by Jonathan Winfrey. Screenplay by Brendan Broderick and Rob Kerchner. Starring Don Wilson. (Man is chased around city by the police after being set up as a cop killer.) Concorde–New Horizons. 95 minutes.

Bloodfist VIII (1996): Martial arts. Directed by Rick Jacobson. Screenplay by Alex Simon, story by Rob Kerchner. (Former CIA agent goes after partners who kidnap his son.) Concorde–New Horizons. 85 minutes.

Bloodmatch (1991): Martial arts. Directed by Albert Pyun. Screenplay by K. Hannah. Starring Thom Mathews and Michel Quisi. (Obsessed martial artist kills those he feels responsible for his brother's death.) 21st Century Film Corporation. 86 minutes.

Bloodmoon (1997): Martial arts. Directed by Tony Leung Siu Hung. Screenplay by Keith W. Strandberg. Starring Gary Daniels and Frank Gorshin. (Serial profiler tracks down a psychopath who murders famous martial artists.) Seasonal Film Corporation. 102 minutes.

Bloodsport (1988): Martial arts. Directed by Newt Arnold. Screenplay by Christopher Cosby, Mel Friedman and Sheldon Lettich, story by Lettich. Starring Jean-Claude Van Damme and Forest Whitaker. (Airman goes AWOL to fight in big underground tournament in Hong Kong.) Cannon Films. 92 minutes.

Bloodsport 2 (1996): Martial arts. Directed by Alan Mehrez. Screenplay by Jeff Schechter. Starring Daniel Bernhardt and Ron Hall. (Thief trains with martial artist in prison to get back at his double-crossing partner, then fights in the kumite.) F.M. Entertainment International. 90 minutes.

Bloodsport 3 (1996): Martial arts. Directed by Alan Mehrez. Screenplay by Steve Tymon and James Williams. Starring Daniel Bernhardt and Pat Morita. (Martial artist gets revenge on the man who killed his trainer.) F.M. Entertainment International. 91 minutes.

Bloodsport 4 (1998): Martial arts. Directed by Elvis Restaino. Screenplay by George Saunders. Starring Daniel Bernhardt. (Prisoners must fight in warden's underground matches.) Prisvideo. 100 minutes.

Cage (1989): Action. Directed by Lang Elliot. Screenplay by Hugh Kelley. Starring Lou Ferrigno and Reb Brown. (Two Army vets are forced to fight cage matches for Asian mobsters.) Orion Home Video. 101 minutes.

Cage II (1994): Action. Directed by Lang Elliott. Screenplay by Hugh Kelley. Starring Reb Brown and Lou Ferrigno. (Two Army vets are again forced to fight in the cage for Asian mobsters.) Image Entertainment. 106 minutes.

Call Him Mr. Shatter (1974): Martial arts. Directed by Michael Carreras. Screenplay by Don Houghton. Starring Stuart Whitman and Peter Cushing. (Double-crossed hitman teams with martial artist to get the money he is owed.) Hammer Films. 90 minutes.

Capital Punishment (1991): Martial arts. Directed by David Huey. Screenplay by David Huey. Starring Gary Daniels. (Martial artist goes up against his former sensei, who is now a drug kingpin.) Cine Excel Entertainment. 89 minutes.

Carnosaur (1993): Sci-fi. Directed by Adam Simon. Screenplay by Adam Simon, novel by John Brosnan. Starring Diane Ladd. (Prehistoric monster on the loose.) Concorde–New Horizons. 83 minutes.

Carnosaur 3 (1996): Sci-fi. Directed by Jonathan Winfrey. Story by Rob Kerchener. Starring Scot Valentine and Rick Dean. (Elite Army unit traps a prehistoric monster in a warehouse.) Concorde–New Horizons. 85 minutes.

The Challenge (1982): Martial arts. Directed by John Frankenheimer. Screenplay by John Sayles and Richard Maxwell. Starring Scott Glenn and Toshiro Mifune. (American boxer gets caught up in deadly struggle between two brothers over family sword.) Embassy Pictures Corporation. 112 minutes.

Champions (1998): Martial arts. Directed by Peter Gathings Bunche. Screenplay by Peter McAlevey and Thomas S. McNamara. Starring Louis Mandylor and Ken Shamrock. (Two undisputed cage-fighting champions are forced to fight by an unscrupulous promoter.) A-Pix Entertainment Corporation. 99 minutes.

China O'Brien (1990): Martial arts. Directed by Robert Clouse. Story by Sandra Weintraub. Starring Cynthia Rothrock and Richard Norton. (Female martial artist cleans up town after her sheriff father is murdered.) Golden Harvest Company. 86 minutes.

China O'Brien II (1991): Martial arts. Directed by Robert Clouse. Screenplay by Craig Clyde and James Hennessey, novel by Sandra Weintraub. Starring Cynthia Rothrock and Richard Norton. (Female martial artist continues her campaign against crime.) Golden Harvest Company. 92 minutes.

Circle of Iron (1979): Martial arts. Directed by Richard Moore. Screenplay by Stirling Silliphant and Stanley Mann, story by Bruce Lee and James Coburn. Starring David Carradine and Jeff Cooper. (Young martial artist goes on a mythic journey to discover knowledge and enlightenment.) AVCO Embassy Pictures. 102 minutes.

City of Fear (2000): Martial arts. Directed by Mark Roper. Screenplay by Harry Alan Towers and Les Weldon. Starring Gary Daniels. (Newspaperman investigates the death of a friend in Budapest, only to find out more than he bargained for.) Nu Image. 90 minutes.

Code Name Vengeance (1989): Action. Directed by David Winters. Screenplay by Tony Palmer. Starring James Ryan and Robert Ginty. (Ex-CIA operative tracks terrorist in Africa.) Action International Pictures. 96 minutes.

Cold Harvest (1998): Martial arts. Directed by Isaac Florentine. Screenplay by Frank Dietz. Starring Gary Daniels. (Adventurer protects his sister-in-law, who is carrying his late brother's baby.) Nu Image. 89 minutes.

Crash Dive (1996): Action/War. Directed by Andrew Stevens. Screenplay by William

C. Martell. Starring Michael Dudikoff and Frederick Forrest. (Agent battles terrorists on a nuclear submarine.) Royal Oaks Entertainment. 90 minutes.

Cyber Tracker (1994): Sci-fi/Martial arts. Directed by Richard Pepin. Screenplay by Jacobsen Hart. Starring Don Wilson. (Martial artist battles cyborgs and big business corruption.) PM Entertainment Group. 91 minutes.

Cyber Tracker 2 (1995): Sci-fi/Martial arts. Directed by Richard Pepin. Screenplay by Richard Preston, Jr. Starring Don Wilson. (Media helps martial artist in his battle with cyborgs and corruption.) PM Entertainment Group. 97 minutes.

Cyborg (1989): Sci-fi/Martial arts. Directed by Albert Pyun. Screenplay by Kitty Chalmers. Starring Jean-Claude Van Damme. (Post-apocalypse adventurer escorts a cyborg across dangerous territory.) Cannon Films. 86 minutes.

Cyborg 2 (1993): Sci-fi/Action. Directed by Michael Schroeder. Screenplay by Michael Schroeder, Mark Geldman and Ron Yanover, story by Geldman and Yanover. Starring Angelina Jolie and Billy Drago. (Security expert and his cyborg lover escape from the Corporation and are pursued across a ravaged city.) Trimark Pictures. 99 minutes.

Day of the Panther (1988): Martial arts. Directed by Brian Trenchard-Smith. Story by David Groom and Peter West. Starring Edward John Stazak and John Stanton. (Hong Kong police detective stalks the Australian drug kingpin who murdered his partner.) TVM Studios. No minutes given.

Deadly Bet (1992): Martial arts. Directed by Richard W. Munchkin. Screenplay by Joseph Merhi and Robert Tiffi. Starring Jeff Wincott and Charlene Tilton. (Martial artist trains to defeat rival and regain girlfriend, whom he lost in a bet.) PM Entertainment Group. 92 minutes.

Deadly Ransom (1997): Martial arts. Directed by Robert Hyatt. Screenplay by Loren Avedon and Robert Hyatt. Starring Loren Avedon and Brion James. (Navy SEAL tracks men who have kidnapped his girlfriend in South America.) York Entertainment. 92 minutes.

Deadly Target (1994): Martial arts. Directed by Charla Driver. Screenplay by James

Adelstein and Michael January. Starring Gary Daniels and Ken McLeod. (Hong Kong cop works with LAPD to bring in a vicious Asian gangster.) PM Entertainment. 92 minutes.

Death Machines (1976): Martial arts. Directed by Paul Kyriazi. Screenplay by Paul Kyriazi and Joe Walders. Starring Ron Marchini. (Multi-racial martial arts killing machines wreak havoc on a city.) Crown International Pictures. 90 minutes.

Death Race 2000 (1975): Sci-fi/Action. Directed by Paul Bartel. Screenplay by Robert Thom and Charles B. Griffith, story by Ib Melchior. Starring Sylvester Stallone and David Carradine. (Drivers race across country running over pedestrians to obtain points.) Concorde–New Horizons. 78 minutes.

Death Ring (1993): Martial arts. Directed by R.J. Kizer. Screenplay by George T. Le-Brun, story by Mike Norris and LeBrun. Starring Billy Drago and Mike Norris. (Psychotic occultist runs death hunts on his island estate.) Trans Atlantic Entertainment. 92 minutes.

Delta Force (1986): Action. Directed by Menahem Golan. Screenplay by James Bruner and Menahem Golan. Starring Chuck Norris and Lee Marvin. (Delta Force team moves in to rescue hostages from Arab terrorists.) Cannon Films. 129 minutes.

Delta Force I: The Lost Patrol (1999): Action/War. Directed by Joseph Zito. Screenplay by Clay McBride. Starring Gary Daniels and Mike Norris. (UN peacekeepers are forced into battle with Arab terrorists despite orders not to engage the enemy.) Frontline Entertainment Group. 93 minutes.

Delta Force 2 (1990): Action. Directed by Aaron Norris. Screenplay by Lee Reynolds. Starring Chuck Norris and Richard Jaeckel. (Delta Force is called into action against drug cartel using chemical weapons.) Cannon Films. 110 minutes.

Derailed (2002): Martial arts. Directed by Bob Misiorowski. Screenplay by Jace Anderson and Adam Gieracsh. Starring Jean-Claude Van Damme and Thomas Arana. (Government agent tries to stop terrorist from gaining possession of small pox virus.) Millennium Films. 89 minutes.

DNA (1997): Action. Directed by William Mesa. Screenplay by Nick Davis. Starring Mark Dacascos and Jurgen Prochnow. (Researchers run across troubling goings-on in the jungle.) Interlight. 105 minutes.

Double Blast (1993): Martial arts. Directed by Tim Spring. Screenplay by Joseph Paul Gulino, story by Gulino, Tim Spring and Paul Wolansky. Starring Dale Cook and Linda Blair. (A martial artist and his kids rescue a professor being pursued by mobsters.) Home Box Office. 89 minutes.

Double Dragon (1993): Martial arts. Directed by James Yukich. Screenplay by Michael Davis and Peter Gould, story by Paul Dini and Neal Schusterman. Starring Mark Dacascos and Robert Patrick. (Two martial artist brothers battle an evil billionaire in the future.) Imperial Entertainment Corporation. 89 minutes.

Double Impact (1991): Martial arts. Directed by Sheldon Lettich. Screenplay by Sheldon Lettich and Jean-Claude Van Damme, story by Lettich, Van Damme, Steve Meerson and Peter Krikes. Starring Jean-Claude Van Damme and Geoffrey Lewis. (Two twins, separated at birth, reunite to find parent's killers.) Columbia Pictures. 118 minutes.

Double Team (1997): Martial arts. Directed by Hark Tsui. Screenplay by Don Jakoby and Paul Mones, story by Jakoby. Starring Jean-Claude Van Damme and Dennis Rodman. (Agent escapes his prison and seeks out his nemesis, who is holding the agent's wife captive.) Columbia Pictures. 93 minutes.

Enter the Dragon (1973): Martial arts. Directed by Robert Clouse. Screenplay by Michael Allin. Starring Bruce Lee and John Saxon. (A martial artist working for the government competes in a secret fighting tournament.) Warner Bros. 97 minutes.

Enter the Ninja (1981): Martial arts. Directed by Menahem Golan. Screenplay by Dick Desmond and Mike Stone. Starring Franco Nero and Sho Kosugi. (White ninja protects his friend's plantation from greedy developers.) Cannon Films. 94 minutes.

Epicenter (2000): Action. Directed by Richard Pepin. Screenplay by Greg McBride. Starring Gary Daniels and Tracy Elizabeth Lords. (Harried female FBI agent escorts a prisoner to Los Angeles when a massive earthquake destroys the city.) PM Entertainment Group. 98 minutes.

Escape from Atlantis (1997): Fantasy. Directed by Strathford Hamilton. Screenplay by Arne Olson. Starring Jeff Speakman. (A lawyer and his kids sail into the Bermuda Triangle and find Atlantis.) Universal Home Entertainment. 97 minutes.

Excessive Force (1993): Martial arts. Directed by Jon Hess. Screenplay by Thomas Ian Griffith. Starring Thomas Ian Griffith and James Earl Jones. (Martial arts–trained cop is framed for murder and has to set things right.) New Line Cinema. 90 minutes.

Exit Wounds (2000): Martial arts. Directed by Andrzej Bartkowiak. Screenplay by Ed Horowitz and Richard D'Ovidio, novel by James Westermann. Starring Steven Seagal and DMX. (Beat cop investigates corruption in his precinct and uses his martial arts skills to break it up.) Village Roadshow Entertainment. 101 minutes.

Expect No Mercy (1995): Sci-fi/Martial arts. Directed by Zale Dalen. Screenplay by J. Stephen Maunder. Starring Billy Blanks and Jalal Merhi. (A government agent enters a dangerous virtual reality training ground to rescue another agent.) Film One Productions. 91 minutes.

The Expert (1994): Martial arts. Directed by Rick Avery and William Lustig. Screenplay by Larry Cohen and Max Allen Collins, story by Jill Gatsby. Starring Jeff Speakman and James Brolin. (Police SWAT advisor takes matters into his own hands after the man who murdered his sister gets a light sentence.) Axis Films. 92 minutes.

Extreme Force (2000): Martial arts. Directed by Michel Qissi. Screenplay by Johnathan Davenport. Starring Hector Echavarria. (Thief helps government get back artifact stolen by his partners, but finds trouble along the way.) Creative Light Entertainment. 90 minutes.

Final Impact (1992): Martial arts. Directed by Joseph Merhi and Stephen Smoke. Screenplay by Stephen Smoke. Starring Lorenzo Lamas and Michael Worth. (Ex-champion trains new kid for fight with his arch rival.) PM Entertainment Group. 99 minutes.

Final Round (1993): Martial arts. Directed by George Erschamer. Screenplay by Arne Olson. Starring Lorenzo Lamas and Kathleen Kinmont. (Martial artist is tracked down by mercenaries in a televised hunt.) Mike Erwin (Ex. Producer).

Fire Down Below (1997): Martial arts. Directed by Felix Enriquez Alcala. Screenplay by Jeb Stuart and Philip Morton, story by Stuart. Starring Steven Seagal and Marg Helgenberger. (EPA agent takes on corporate polluters in a rural mountain community.) Warner Bros. 105 minutes.

Firewalker (1986): Action/Comedy. Directed by J. Lee Thompson. Screenplay by Norman Aladjem, Robert Gosnell and Jeffrey M. Rosenbaum. Starring Chuck Norris and Louis Gossett, Jr. (Two adventurers and a tag-along woman hunt treasure in Central America.) Cannon Films. 104 minutes.

Fist of Fury (1972): Martial arts. Directed by Wei Lo. Screenplay by Wei Lo. Starring Bruce Lee. (Martial arts student avenges teacher's death.) Golden Harvest. 110 minutes.

Fist of Glory (1990): Martial arts/War. Directed by Joe Mari Avellana. Screenplay by Joe Mari Avellana. Starring Dale Cook. (Veterans return to Vietnam to help a friend.) Trimark. 93 minutes.

Fist of Iron (1995): Martial arts. Directed by Richard W. Munchkin. Screenplay by Sean Dash, story by Aron Schifman. Starring Michael Worth and Sam J. Jones. (Young fighter trains to avenge his best friend's death at the hands of a brutal martial artist.) Century Film Partners. 95 minutes.

Fist of the North Star (1995): Martial arts. Directed by Tony Randel. Screenplay by Buronson, graphic novel by Tetsuo Hara. Starring Gary Daniels and Malcolm McDowell. (Warrior fights various battles and rescues princess.) Overseas Film Group. 103 minutes.

Force: Five (1981): Martial arts. Directed by Robert Clouse. Screenplay by Robert Clouse. Starring Joe Lewis and Richard Norton. (Action team penetrates a cult fortress to rescue some girls.) Astral Films. 95 minutes.

A Force of One (1979): Martial arts. Directed by Paul Aaron. Screenplay by Ernest Tidyman, story by Pat Johnson and Tidyman. Starring Chuck Norris and Jennifer O'Neill. (Martial arts champion helps police find a brutal killer.) American Cinema Productions. 90 minutes.

Forced Vengeance (1982): Martial arts. Directed by James Fargo. Screenplay by Franklin Thompson. Starring Chuck Norris. (Casino security chief protects his boss' daughter from mobsters who want them both dead.) MGM. 90 minutes.

The Foreigner (2002): Action/Thriller. Directed by Michael Oblowitz. Screenplay by Darren O. Campbell. Starring Steven Seagal. (CIA operative walks a tightrope between various factions as he tries to unravel a mystery.) Franchise Pictures. 96 minutes.

The Forgotten Warrior (1986): Martial arts. Directed by Nick Cacas and Charlie Ordonez. Screenplay by Tom McKenzie. Starring Ron Marchini. (Army vet living in jungle protects a village from the Communists.) Interwood Films. 76 minutes.

Fugitive X (1996): Action. Directed by David Heavener. Written by David Heavener. Starring David Heavener and Richard Norton. (Ex-cop suffering from post traumatic stress is hunted for sport through the city.) Silverlake International Pictures. 97 minutes.

Future Fear (1997): Sci-fi. Directed by Lewis Baumander. Written by Lewis Baumander, Glen Cullen, Jules Delorme and Philip Jackson. Starring Jeff Wincott and Maria Ford. (Scientist goes up against fascists trying to take over the world using a deadly virus.) Aliceco. 77 minutes.

Future Kick (1991): Sci-fi/Martial arts. Directed by Damian Klaus. Screenplay by Catherine Cryan and Damian Klaus. Starring Don Wilson and Meg Foster. (A cyborg helps a widow find the killers of her husband.) Concorde–New Horizons. 76 minutes.

Future War (1994): Sci-fi/Martial arts. Directed by Anthony Doublin. Screenplay by Dom Magwili, story by David Huey. Starring Daniel Bernhardt. (Alien slave is pursued by cyborgs who use dinosaurs as trackers.) Cine Excel Entertainment. 90 minutes.

Girl's Town (1959): Drama. Directed by Charles Haas. Screenplay by Robert Smith, story by Robert Hardy Andrews. Starring Mamie Van Doren. (Wisecracking girl is sent to a home run by nuns and discovers

there is a lot to learn about life.) MGM. BW. 90 minutes.

Gladiator Cop (1994): Martial arts. Directed by Nick Rotundo. Screenplay by Nick Rotundo, Paco Alvarez and Nicolas Stiliadis. Starring Lorenzo Lamas. (Psychic cop hunts down killers running an illegal fighting tournament.) SC Entertainment. 92 minutes.

The Glimmer Man (1996): Martial arts. Directed by John Gray. Screenplay by Kevin Brodbin. Starring Steven Seagal and Keenan Ivory Wayans. (Detective with secret past hunts a serial killer while coming under suspicion for the murders.) Warner Bros. 88 minutes.

The Glove (1978): Action. Directed by Ross Hagen. Screenplay by Julian Roffman and Hubert Smith. Starring John Saxon and Roosevelt Grier. (Down-on-his-luck bounty hunter goes after a killer who uses a special glove to do his dirty work.) Tommy J. Productions. 91 minutes.

G.O.D. (2000): Action. Directed by Dean Rusu. Screenplay by Dean Rusu. Starring Jalal Merhi and Olivier Gruner. (Delivery man finds he has human female cargo and battles white slavers trying to get the girl back.) Amsell Entertainment.

Golden Needles (1974): Action. Directed by Robert Clouse. Screenplay by S. Lee Pogostin and Sylvia Schneble. Starring Joe Don Baker and Jim Kelly. (A millionaire seeks some golden acupuncture needles which will restore a man's vitality.) American International Pictures. 92 minutes.

Good Cop Bad Cop (1998): Action. Directed by John DeBello. Screenplay by John DeBello. Starring Lorenzo Lamas and Catherine Lazo. (Cop crosses into Mexico to catch a drug dealer.) Four Square Productions. 102 minutes.

Good Guys Wear Black (1978): Martial arts. Directed by Ted Post. Screenplay by Bruce Cohn and Mark Medoff, story by Joseph Fraley. Starring Chuck Norris and Dana Andrews. (Army vet-turned-college professor investigates the killings of members of his old unit.) Mar Vista Productions. 96 minutes.

The Green Berets (1968): War. Directed by John Wayne, Ray Kellogg and Mervyn

LeRoy. Screenplay by James Lee Barrett, Col. Kenneth B. Facey, novel by Robin Moore. Starring John Wayne and Jim Hutton. (Special Forces unit fights the Communists in Vietnam.) Warner Bros. 141 minutes.

Guardian Angel (1994): Martial arts. Directed by Richard W. Munchkin. Screenplay by Jacobsen Hart. Starring Cynthia Rothrock. (Ex–police officer hires herself out as a bodyguard.) PM Entertainment Group. 97 minutes.

Gymkata (1985): Martial arts. Directed by Robert Clouse. Screenplay by Charles Robert Carner, based on the novel by Dan Tyler Moore. Starring Kurt Thomas and Richard Norton. (Gymnast trains in karate to compete in special tournament in a third world country.) MGM. 90 minutes.

Half Past Dead (2002): Action. Directed by Don Michael Paul. Screenplay by Don Michael Paul. Starring Steven Seagal and Morris Chestnut. (FBI agent goes deep undercover in prison to break up a car theft ring.) Franchise Pictures. 98 minutes.

Hard as Nails (2001): Martial arts. Directed by Brian Katkin. Screenplay by Brian Katkin, story by Katkin. Starring Allen Scotti and Kim Yates. (Undercover cop infiltrates Russian Mafia to break up arms trafficking.) Concorde–New Horizons.

Hard to Kill (1990): Martial arts. Directed by Bruce Malmuth. Screenplay by Steven Kaye. Starring Steven Seagal and Kelly LeBrock. (Cop awakens from coma, learns his family has been killed and goes after the murderers.) Warner Bros. 95 minutes.

Hawk's Revenge (1996): Martial arts. Directed by Mark Voizard. No writer listed. Starring Gary Daniels and Cass Magda. (British SAS officer hunts down his brother's killers in NYC.) Buena Vista. 92 minutes.

Heatseeker (1995): Martial arts. Directed by Albert Pyun. Screenplay by Albert Pyun and Christopher Borkgren. Starring Gary Daniels and Keith Cooke. (Martial artist must fight a corporation's cyborg in major tournament.) Trimark Pictures. 91 minutes.

Hell to Eternity (1960): War. Directed by Phil Karlson. Screenplay by Walter Roeber Shmidt and Ted Sherdeman, story by Gil Doud. Starring Jeffrey Hunter and David Janssen. (Man raised by Japanese family is drafted to fight in WWII.) Allied Artists. 132 minutes.

Hellbound (1993): Martial arts. Directed by Aaron Norris. Screenplay by Brent V. Friedman and Galen Thompson, story by Ian Rabin and Anthony Ridio. Starring Chuck Norris and Calvin Levels. (Tough cop takes on Satan's minions.) Cannon Films. 95 minutes.

The Hero and the Terror (1988): Martial arts/Horror. Directed by William Tannen. Screenplay by Dennis Shyrack and Michael Blodgett. Starring Chuck Norris and Steve James. (Cop battles an escaped mass murderer who is terrorizing a city.) Cannon Films. 96 minutes.

The Hitman (1991): Martial arts: Directed by Aaron Norris. Screenplay by Robert Geoffrian and Galen Thompson, story by Thompson. Starring Chuck Norris. (Undercover FBI agent works against feuding Mafias in Seattle.) Cannon Films. 95 minutes.

Hologram Man (1995): Sci-fi/Action. Directed by Richard Pepin. Screenplay by Evan Lurie and Richard Preston, Jr., story by Lurie. Starring Joe Lara and Evan Lurie. (Cop becomes an electric energy field to destroy a madman bent on taking over the city.) PM Entertainment Group, Inc. 101 minutes.

Hot Potato (1976): Martial arts. Directed by Oscar Williams. Screenplay by Oscar Williams. Starring Jim Kelly and Irene Tsu. (A government agent and his team head into the jungle to rescue a Senator's daughter from the clutches of a warlord.) Warner Bros. 87 minutes.

The Human Shield (1992): Action. Directed by Ted Post. Screenplay by Mann Rubin, story by Mike Werb and Rubin. Starring Michael Dudikoff. (Former military man returns to Iraq to rescue his brother.) Cannon Films.

The Immortal (2000): Horror/Martial arts. Directed by Harley Cokeliss. Screenplay by Rick Drew. Starring Lorenzo Lamas. (A man with a very long life span hunts demons and other manifestations of evil.) Immortal Productions, Inc. 95 minutes.

Immortal Combat (1994): Martial arts. Directed by Dan Neira. Screenplay by

Robert Crabtree and Dan Neira. Starring Roddy Piper and Sonny Chiba. (A tough cop and his Japanese partner take on bloodthirsty ninjas.) A-Pix. 109 minutes.

Instinct to Kill (2001): Martial arts/Horror. Directed by Gustavo Graef-Marino. Screenplay by Randall Frakes and Josh Olson, novel by Lisa Gardner. Starring Mark Dacascos and Tim Abell. (An ex-cop protects a woman from her psychotic spouse.) American World Pictures. 90 minutes.

Interceptor Force (1999): Sci-fi/Martial arts. Directed by Philip J. Roth. No Writer Listed. Starring Olivier Gruner and Ernie Hudson. (A team of specialists tracks some aliens who crash land in Mexico.) UFO Productions. 97 minutes.

Invasion USA (1985): Martial arts. Directed by Joseph Zito. Screenplay by James Bruner and Chuck Norris. Starring Chuck Norris and Richard Lynch. (A CIA agent comes out of retirement to take on terrorists.) Cannon Films. 107 minutes.

Ironheart (1992): Martial arts. Directed by Robert Clouse. Screenplay by Larry Riggins. Starring Britton K. Lee and Richard Norton. (A detective seeks to solve his ex-partner's murder.) Morning Calm Entertainment Group. 92 minutes.

Irresistible Force (1993): Martial arts. Directed by Kevin Hooks. Screenplay by Carleton Eastlake. Starring Stacy Keach and Cynthia Rothrock. (A veteran detective gets a rookie partner straight out of the Academy and they fight terrorists who have taken over a shopping mall.) CBS Entertainment Productions. 80 minutes.

Journey of Honor (1992): Martial arts/Historical. Directed by Gordon Hessler. Screenplay by Nelson Gidding, story by Gidding and Sho Kosugi. Starring Sho Kosugi and David Essex. (A noble sends his most valued samurai to accompany his son to Spain to purchase guns.) Universal Pictures. 90 minutes.

Karate Cop (1991): Martial arts. Directed by Alan Roberts. Screenplay by Dennis Grayson, Ron Marchini and Bill Zide. Starring Ron Marchini and David Carradine. (The last cop in America protects a woman and a large group of children from scavengers.) Imperial Entertainment Corporation. 90 minutes.

Karate—the Hand of Death (1964): Martial arts. Directed by Joel Holt. Screenplay by Joel Holt. Starring Joel Holt. (A tough American karateka unravels the mystery of a woman who looks like his late wife while tracking down a treasure.) Joel Brenner Productions. BW. 80 minutes.

Karate Warrior (1987): Martial arts. Directed by Fabrizzio De Angelis. Screenplay by Fabrizzio De Angelis and Dardano Sacchetti. Starring Kim Rossi Stuart and Jared Martin. (A boy learns martial arts from an ancient master, then takes on the village bully.) Fulvia Film. 94 minutes.

Kick of Death (1997): Martial arts. Directed by David Avellone. Screenplay by David Avellone. Starring Michael Guerin and Vernon Wells. (A Hong Kong kickboxer, on the run from triads, heads to Las Vegas, where he finds more trouble.)

Kickboxer (1989): Martial arts. Directed by Mark DiSalle and David Worth. Screenplay by Glenn Bruce, story by Mark DiSalle and David Worth. Starring Jean-Claude Van Damme and Dennis Chan. (A martial artist trains to avenge the crippling of his brother.) Cannon Films. 105 minutes.

Kickboxer 2 (1991): Martial arts. Directed by Albert Pyun. Screenplay by David Goyer. Starring Sasha Mitchell and Peter Boyle. (Kickboxer must take on the brute who killed his brother.) Kings Road Entertainment. 89 minutes.

Kickboxer 3 (1992): Martial arts. Directed by Rick King. Screenplay by Dennis A. Pratt. Starring Sasha Mitchell and Dennis Chan. (Kickboxing champion is taken hostage and must face a rich man's fighter.) Kings Road Entertainment. 92 minutes.

Kickboxer 4 (1994): Martial arts. Directed by Albert Pyun. Screenplay by Albert Pyun and David Yorkin, story by Albert Pyun. Starring Sasha Mitchell and Nicholas Guest. (Framed kickboxer is recruited from prison by the DEA to fight in a drug dealer's tournament. Kings Road Entertainment. 90 minutes.

Kickboxer 5 (1995): Martial arts. Directed by Kristine Peterson. Screenplay by Rick Filon. Starring Mark Dacascos and James Ryan. (Champion martial artist goes after the psychotic millionaire who tried to have him killed.) Kings Road Entertainment. 87 minutes.

Kickboxing Academy (1997): Martial arts/ Family. Directed by Richard Gabai. Screenplay by Richard Gabai and L.A. Maddox. Starring Michael Nouri and Chyler Leigh. (A martial arts studio must take on its rival to remain in business.) Pan Am Pictures. 84 minutes.

Kill and Kill Again (1981): Martial arts. Directed by Ivan Hall. Screenplay by John Crowther. Starring James Ryan and Ken Gampu. (A martial artist is hired to rescue a scientist from the clutches of an evil millionaire.) Kavalier Films. 100 minutes.

Kill or Be Killed (1980): Martial arts. Directed by Ivan Hall. Screenplay by CF Beyers-Boshoff. Starring James Ryan and Charlotte Mitchell. (A martial artist fights in a madman's tournament.) Kavalier Films. 90 minutes.

King of the Kickboxers (1991): Martial arts. Directed by Lucas Lowe. Screenplay by Keith W. Strandberg and John Kay. Starring Loren Avedon and Billy Blanks. (Cop goes after the man who killed his brother and filmed it on video.) Imperial Entertainment Corporation. 99 minutes.

Kiss of the Dragon (2001): Martial arts. Directed by Chris Nahon. Screenplay by Luc Besson and Mark Robert Kamen, story by Jet Li. Starring Jet Li and Bridget Fonda. (Chinese agent is double-crossed in France and fights overwhelming odds to survive.) 20th Century–Fox. 98 minutes.

Knights (1993): Sci-fi/Martial arts. Directed by Albert Pyun. Screenplay by Albert Pyun. Starring Kathy Long and Kris Kristofferson. (Female warrior teams with good cyborg to take on bad cyborgs out to destroy what's left of the post-apocalyptic world.) Kings Road Entertainment.

Knock Off (1998): Martial arts. Directed by Hark Tsui. Screenplay by Steven E. de Souza. Starring Jean-Claude Van Damme and Rob Schneider. (Merchandise copier battles mobsters in league with renegade CIA agents.) Tri Star Pictures. 91 minutes.

Kung Fu: The Movie (1986): Martial arts. Directed by Richard Lang. Screenplay by Durrell Royce Crays. Starring David Carradine and Brandon Lee. (A wealthy Chinese noble uses a monk's son to obtain vengeance on him.) Warner Bros. 100 minutes.

L.A. Wars (1994): Martial arts. Directed by Tony Kandah and Martin Morris. Screenplay by Tony Kandah and Addison Randall. Starring Vince Murdocco and Kerri Kasem. (Disgraced cop becomes a bodyguard for mafiosa.) Starlight.

Lady Dragon (1992): Martial arts. Directed by David Worth. Screenplay by Clifford Mohr. Starring Cynthia Rothrock and Richard Norton. (Ex-government agent tracks the man who killed her husband.) Rapi Films. 97 minutes.

Lady Dragon II (1993): Martial arts. Directed by David Worth. Screenplay by Clifford Mohr. Starring Cynthia Rothrock and Billy Drago. (Woman hunts men who raped her and killed her husband.) Rapi Films. 92 minutes.

Land of the Free (1997): Martial arts/ Thriller. Directed by Jerry Jameson. Screenplay by Maria James, story by Ronald Jacobs and Jerry Jameson. Starring Jeff Speakman and William Shatner. (Political consultant battles evil Senatorial candidate tied up with militia groups.) PM Entertainment Group. 100 minutes.

Laser Mission (1990): Martial arts. Directed by Beau Davis. Screenplay by Phillip Gutteridge, story by David Frank. Starring Brandon Lee and Ernest Borgnine. (Freelance agent tries to rescue scientist from Russians.) Azimuth. 83 minutes.

Last Man Standing (1996): Martial arts. Directed by Joseph Merhi. Screenplay by Joseph Merhi. Starring Jeff Wincott and Jonathan Fuller. (Martial arts cop unravels who killed his partner.) PM Entertainment Group. 96 minutes.

The Last Samurai (1990): Martial arts. Directed by Paul Mayersberg. Screenplay by Paul Mayersberg. Starring Lance Henriksen and James Ryan. (Ex–Vietnam vet flies Japanese businessman into the African bush for a fateful adventure.) Arrow Video.

Legionnaire (1998): Adventure. Directed by Peter MacDonald. Screenplay by Sheldon Lettich and Rebecca Morrison, story by Lettich and Jean-Claude Van Damme. Starring Jean-Claude Van Damme and Steven Berkoff. (French boxer on the run to America joins Foreign Legion and fights Arabs.) Edward R. Pressman Film Corporation. 98 minutes.

Lionheart (1990): Martial arts. Directed by Sheldon Lettich. Screenplay by Sheldon Lettich, Jean-Claude Van Damme and S.N. Warren, story by Van Damme. Starring Jean-Claude Van Damme and Harrison Page. (Foreign Legionnaire goes AWOL to find out who murdered his brother, and becomes a streetfighter to survive.) Imperial Entertainment Corporation. 105 minutes.

Lone Wolf McQuade (1983): Martial arts. Directed by Steve Carver. Screenplay by B.J. Nelson, story by H. Kaye Dial and Nelson. Starring Chuck Norris and David Carradine. (Texas Ranger teams with FBI agent and local sheriff to bust master criminal.) Lone Wolf McQuade Associates. 107 minutes.

Martial Law (1990): Martial arts. Directed by Steve Cohen. Screenplay by Richard Brandes. Starring Cynthia Rothrock and Chad McQueen. (Two cops go after a smuggler and his gang.). Media Home Entertainment. 89 minutes.

Martial Law 2 (1992): Martial arts. Directed by Kurt Anderson. Screenplay by Richard Brandes and Jiles Fitzgerald, story by Pierre David. Starring Cynthia Rothrock and Jeff Wincott. (Detectives investigate shady goings-on in a nightclub run by gangsters.) 87 minutes.

Martial Outlaw (1993): Martial arts. Directed by Kurt Anderson. Screenplay by John Bryant, Pierre David and Thomas Ritz, story by George Saunders. Starring Jeff Wincott and Gary Hudson. (Two brothers, one a Fed, the other a local cop, battle the Russian Mafia.) The Image Organization. 86 minutes.

Mask of Death (1996): Action. Directed by David Mitchell. Screenplay by R.C. Rossenfier. Starring Lorenzo Lamas and Rae Dawn Chong. (Cop takes on the identity of a hit man to capture the mobster responsible for his family's death.) Lions Gate Film, Inc. 89 minutes.

Maximum Risk (1996): Martial arts. Directed by Ringo Lam. Screenplay by Larry Ferguson. Starring Jean-Claude Van Damme and Natasha Henstridge. (French police officer assumes the identity of his own twin brother to solve his murder.) Columbia Pictures Corporation. 100 minutes.

Memorial Day (1998): Action/Thriller. Directed by Worth Keeter. Screenplay by Steve Latshaw. Starring Jeff Speakman and Bruce Weitz. (Marine kept in a psycho ward escapes and is manipulated into killing a candidate.) Artisan Entertainment. 95 minutes.

Mercenary 1 (1997): War. Directed by Avi Nesher. Screenplay by Steven Hartog. Starring Olivier Gruner and John Ritter. (Mercenary is hired to rescue a man's wife.) Home Box Office. 102 minutes.

Mercenary 2 (1998): War. Directed by Phillip De Mora. No Writer Listed. Starring Olivier Gruner and Robert Townsend. (Mercenary travels through the jungle to find a businessman on the run.) Buena Vista. 96 minutes.

Missing in Action (1984): Martial arts/ War. Directed by Joseph Zito. Screenplay by James Bruner and Lance Hool. Starring Chuck Norris and James Hong. (An ex-prisoner of war returns to Vietnam to rescue some POWs still being held by Communists.) Cannon Films. 101 minutes.

Missing in Action II (1985): Martial arts/ War. Directed by Lance Hool. Screenplay by Steve Bing, Larry Levinson and Arthur Silver. Starring Chuck Norris and Soon-Tek Oh. (A POW colonel and his men suffer under the cruel Vietnamese during the war.) Cannon Films. 96 minutes.

Missing in Action III (1988): Martial arts/ War. Directed by Aaron Norris. Screenplay by James Bruner and Chuck Norris. Starring Chuck Norris and Aki Aleong. (Ex-POW returns to Vietnam to rescue his wife and son.) Cannon Films. 101 minutes.

Mission of Justice (1992): Martial arts. Directed by Steve Barnett. Screenplay by John Bryant Hedberg. Starring Jeff Wincott and Bridgette Nielson. (Man goes after mayoral candidate using Guardian Angel–like posses that keep the streets under control.) The Image Organization. 84 minutes.

Moving Target (2000): Martial arts. Directed by Paul Ziller. No Writer Listed. Starring Don Wilson and Bill Murphy. (Man on the run must take on all comers.) New Concorde.

Murder in the Orient (1974): Martial arts. Directed by Manuel G. Songo. Screenplay by Manuel Songo. Starring Ron Marchini and Leo Fong. (Two martial artists team up to catch the gang responsible for the murder of one of the men's sister.) Ilochondria Films. 73 minutes.

My Samurai (1992): Martial arts. Directed by Fred H. Dresch. Screenplay by Richard Strahle. Starring Julian Lee and Mako. (A martial arts instructor protects one of his students who witnessed a murder.) Starmax. 87 minutes.

Nemesis (1993): Sci-fi/Martial arts. Directed by Albert Pyun. Screenplay by Rebecca Charles. Starring Olivier Gruner and Tim Thomerson. (A cop who hunts down cyborgs finds out he is on the wrong side and must get a computer chip to the resistance forces before it is too late.) Imperial Entertainment Corporation. 94 minutes.

Nemesis II (1995): Sci-fi/Martial arts. Directed by Albert Pyun. Screenplay by Albert Pyun. Starring Sue Price and Chad Stahelski. (A female warrior rises to fight the cyborgs.) Imperial Entertainment Corporation. 83 minutes.

Nemesis III (1995): Sci-fi/Martial arts. Directed by Albert Pyun. Screenplay by Albert Pyun. Starring Sue Price and Tim Thomerson. (A female warrior continues to fight the cyborgs in Africa.) Imperial Entertainment Corporation. 85 minutes.

Nemesis IV (1995): Sci-fi/Martial arts. Directed by Albert Pyun. Screenplay by Albert Pyun. Starring Sue Price and Andrew Divoff. (Hitmen chase a giant hitwoman.) Imperial Entertainment Corporation. 65 minutes.

Never Say Die (2001): Martial arts. Directed by Jorge Montesi. Screenplay by Rob Gilmer. Starring Cynthia Rothrock and Jeff Wincott. (A DEA agent on the run stops in a town run by a drug dealer and brings him down.) Alexander/Enright and Associates. 90 minutes.

New York Cop (1996): Martial arts. Directed by Toru Murakawa. Screenplay by Hiroshi Kashiwabara, story by Jiro Ueno. Starring Toru Nakamura and Chad McQueen. (Japanese immigrant works for the NYPD and goes undercover to bust a gang.) STP International. 88 minutes.

Night Hunter (1995): Horror/Martial arts. Directed by Rick Jacobson. Screenplay by William C. Martell. Starring Don Wilson and Maria Ford. (Martial arts–trained vampire hunter takes on a group infiltrating Los Angeles.) Amritraj Premiere Entertainment. 86 minutes.

Night of the Warrior (1991): Martial arts. Directed by Rafal Zielinski. Screenplay by Thomas Ian Griffith. Starring Lorenzo Lamas and Kathleen Kinmont. (Bar owner fights in illegal street matches to pay off debt to Mafia.) Trimark Pictures. 99 minutes.

Night Vision (1997): Martial arts. Directed by Gil Bettman. Screenplay by Michael Thomas Montgomery. Starring Cynthia Rothrock and Fred Williamson. (Cops go after a video-obsessed serial killer.) Fred Williamson. 93 minutes.

9 Deaths of the Ninja (1986): Martial arts. Directed by Emmett Alston. Screenplay by Emmett Alston. Starring Sho Kosugi and Brent Huff. (Government agents take on misfit terrorist holding a bus load of hostages.) Crown International Pictures. 94 minutes.

Ninja Warriors (1985): Martial arts. Directed by John Lloyd. No Writer Listed. Starring Ron Marchini and Paul Vance. (American ninja helps the police track down ninja killers.) 90 minutes.

No Exit (1995): Martial arts. Directed by Damian Lee. Screenplay by John Lawson and Damian Lee. Starring Jeff Wincott and Sven-Ole Thorsen. (Professor trained in martial arts is forced to fight in death matches televised all over the world.) New City Releasing. 93 minutes.

No Retreat, No Surrender (1985): Martial arts. Directed by Cory Yuen. Screenplay by See-Yuen Ng. Keith W. Strandberg and Cory Yuen. Starring Kurt McKinney and Jean-Claude Van Damme. (Young martial artist trains to fight Russian to save local martial arts studio.) Seasonal Film Corporation. 85minutes.

No Retreat, No Surrender II (1989): Martial arts. Directed by Cory Yuen. Screenplay by Maria Elleno Cellino, Roy Horan and Keith W. Strandberg. Starring Loren Avedon and Cynthia Rothrock. (Grizzled veteran leads young martial artist into the jungle to rescue his girlfriend from the Communists.) Seasonal Film Corporation.

No Retreat, No Surrender III (1990): Martial arts. Directed by Lucas Lowe.

Screenplay by Keith W. Strandberg. Starring Loren Avedon and Keith Vitali. (Feuding brothers team up to get father's killers.) Seasonal Film Corporation. 101 minutes.

The Octagon (1980): Martial arts. Directed by Eric Karson. Screenplay by Paul Aaron and Leigh Chapman. Starring Chuck Norris and Lee Van Cleef. (American ninja hunts his brother, who is training terrorists in Central America.) American Cinema Productions. 103 minutes.

Omega Cop (1990): Martial arts. Directed by Paul Kyriazi. Screenplay by Denny Grayson, Salli McQuade and Joe Meyer. Starring Ron Marchini and Stuart Whitman. (During the breakdown of civilization, a lone cop protects three women from slave traders.) Hemdale Home Video. 89 minutes.

On Deadly Ground (1994): Martial arts. Directed by Steven Seagal. Screenplay by Ed Horowitz and Robin U. Russin. Starring Steven Seagal and Joan Chen. (Oil rigger goes after his boss, who is polluting the Alaskan environment.) Warner Bros. 101 minutes.

One Down, Two to Go (1982): Action. Directed by Fred Williamson. Screenplay by Jeff Williamson. Starring Jim Brown and Jim Kelly. (After being cheated out of the money they won on a bet, three men go after the welcher, taking on all his men in the process.) Po' Boy Productions. 84 minutes.

Only the Strong (1993): Martial arts. Directed by Sheldon Lettich. Screenplay by Luis Estaban and Sheldon Lettich. Starring Mark Dacascos and Geoffrey Lewis. (Young Army vet returns to his old school and tries to clean things up.) Davis Entertainment. 96 minutes.

Open Fire (1994): Martial arts. Directed by Kurt Anderson. Screenplay by Thomas Ritz. Starring Jeff Wincott and Patrick Kilpatrick. (On a rescue mission, a disgraced cop works his way into a chemical plant where terrorists are holding his dad and others hostage.) Marketing-Film.

Operation Cobra (1997): Martial arts. Directed by Fred Olen Ray. Screenplay by Sean O'Bannon. Starring Don Wilson and Evan Lurie. (Cop tracks the killer of his partner to India.) Royal Oaks Entertainment. 82 minutes.

Operation Golden Phoenix (1993): Martial arts. Directed by Jalal Merhi. Screenplay by J. Stephen Maunder. Starring Jalal Merhi and Loren Avedon. (High-risk security specialist, framed by his partner for a heist, goes on the run.) Le Monde Entertainment. 95 minutes.

The Order (2001): Martial arts. Directed by Sheldon Lettich. Screenplay by Sheldon Lettich and Jean-Claude Van Damme. Starring Jean-Claude Van Damme and Charlton Heston. (An art thief goes to Israel to find his missing father.) Millennium Films. 89 minutes.

Out for Justice (1991): Martial arts. Directed by John Flynn. Screenplay by David Lee Henry. Starring Steven Seagal and William Forsythe. (Cop spends a long night tracking the mass-murdering psychopath who killed his partner.) Warner Bros. 91 minutes.

The Patriot (1998): Action. Directed by Dean Semler. Screenplay by M. Sussman and John Kingswell, story by Sussman, novel by William Heine. Starring Steven Seagal. ("New Age" doctor takes on militia men who release a deadly biological weapon.) Baldwin/Cohen Productions. 90 minutes.

The Perfect Weapon (1991): Martial arts. Directed by Mark DiSalle. Screenplay by David C. Wilson. Starring Jeff Speakman and Mako. (Martial arts master takes on the Korean mobsters who killed his mentor.) Paramount. 112 minutes.

The President's Man (2000): Action. Directed by Eric Norris and Michael Preece. Screenplay by Bob Gookin. Starring Chuck Norris and Dylan Neal. (The president's personal troubleshooter trains a replacement.) Norris Brothers Entertainment. 90 minutes.

Prince of the Sun (1990): Martial arts. Directed by Wellson Chin and I-Jung Hua. No Writer Listed. Starring Cynthia Rothrock and Conan Lee. (Female martial artist helps protect a special child.) Golden Sun Films. 84 minutes.

Pursuit (1991): Action. Directed by John H. Parr. Screenplay by Paul S. Rowlston, story by Ronnie Isaacs. Starring James Ryan and Andre Jacobs. (Mercenary is hired to recover stolen gold and is double-crossed by his partners.) Kevron Entertainment. 95 minutes.

The Rage (1997): Action. Directed by Sidney J. Furie. Screenplay by Greg Mellot and Furie. Starring Lorenzo Lamas and Roy Scheider. (FBI agents track a group of militia men who are leaving a trail of bodies across the country.) Miramax Film Group. 93 minutes.

Rage and Honor (1992): Martial arts. Directed by Terence H. Winkless. Screenplay by Terence H. Winkless. Starring Cynthia Rothrock and Richard Norton. (Karate teacher and Australian cop battle to keep streets clean of gangsters.) IRS Media. 89 minutes.

Rage and Honor II (1993): Martial arts. Directed by Guy Norris. Screenplay by Steven Reich and Louis Sun. Starring Cynthia Rothrock and Richard Norton. (Government agent teams with wanted cop to bring down crime lord.) IRS Media. 98 minutes.

Rage of Honor (1987): Martial arts. Directed by Gordon Hessler. Screenplay by Walter Bennet and Robert Short. Starring Sho Kosugi and Kane Kosugi. (A government agent avenges the death of his partner.) Transworld Entertainment. 98 minutes.

Rage to Kill (1987): Action. Directed by David Winters. Screenplay by Ian Yule and David Winters. Starring James Ryan and Cameron Mitchell. (Race car driver attempts to rescue his brother, a hostage on an island taken over by the Communists.) Hope Holiday Productions.

Rapid Exchange (2003): Thriller. Directed by Tripp Weed. Screenplay by Tripp Weed and Sam Wells. Starring Lorenzo Lamas and Lance Henriksen. (Thieves plan a bold heist aboard an aircraft carrying millions of dollars in U.S. currency.) First Look Home Entertainment. 97 minutes.

Rapid Fire (1992): Martial arts. Directed by Dwight H. Little. Screenplay by Alan McElroy, Cindy Cirile and Paul Attanasio, story by Cirile and Bob McElroy. Starring Brandon Lee and Powers Boothe. (An art student is on the run after witnessing an execution committed by mobsters.) 20th Century–Fox. 95 minutes.

Red Sun Rising (1993): Martial arts. Directed by Francis Megahy. Screenplay by

Robert Easter, Neva Friedenn and Paul Maslak. Starring Don Wilson and Mako. (Japanese cop in Los Angeles hunting Yakuza.) Amritraj Entertainment. 99 minutes.

Redemption (2002): Action. Directed by Art Camacho. Screenplay by Jack Capece. Starring Don Wilson and Cynthia Rothrock. (A disgraced cop becomes partners with a drug dealer to make ends meet.) Danny De Falco, producer. 90 minutes.

Replicant (2000): Martial arts. Directed by Ringo Lam. Screenplay by Larry Riggins and Les Weldon. Starring Jean-Claude Van Damme and Michael Rooker. (A detective tracks a serial killer using the killer's clone.) Millennium Pictures. 101 minutes.

Return Fire (1991): Martial arts. Directed by Neal Callaghan. Screenplay by Neal Callaghan and Denny Grayson. Starring Ron Marchini and Adam West. (Honest CIA agent is targeted for elimination by his boss, who wants to deal drugs.) Romarc. 97 minutes.

Return of the Dragon (1972): Martial arts. Directed by Bruce Lee. Screenplay by Bruce Lee. Starring Bruce Lee and Chuck Norris. (Waiter helps his family fight off thugs determined to take over their restaurant.) Golden Harvest. 91 minutes.

Revenge of the Ninja (1983): Martial arts. Directed by Sam Firstenberg. Screenplay by James R. Silke. Starring Sho Kosugi and Keith Vitali. (Ninja comes to America but is forced to take on his boss, who is also a ninja.) Cannon Films. 90 minutes.

Ring of Fire (1991): Martial arts. Directed by Richard W. Munchkin. Screenplay by Jake Jacobs, Richard W. Munchkin and Steve Tymon. Starring Don Wilson and Maria Ford. (Martial arts trained doctor advises Asian gang while falling in love with the sister of the rival gang's leader.) PM Entertainment Group.

Ring of Fire II (1993): Martial arts. Directed by Richard W. Munchkin. Screenplay by Paul Maslak, Richard W. Munchkind and Steve Tymon. Starring Don Wilson and Maria Ford. (Martial arts–trained doctor fights his way through a bizarre underworld to rescue his girlfriend.) PM Entertainment Group.

Ring of Fire III (1994): Martial arts. Directed by Rick Jacobson. Screenplay by

Joseph John Barmettler, Art Camacho and Don Wilson. Starring Don Wilson and Art Camacho. (Martial arts–trained doctor is hunted by Russian and Italian mobsters who want a disk he unknowingly picked up.) PM Entertainment Group. 90 minutes.

Riot (1996): Martial arts. Directed by Joseph Merhi. Screenplay by William Applegate, Jr., and Joseph John Barmettler. Starring Gary Daniels and Sugar Ray Leonard. (A British soldier has to navigate a riot zone to rescue an ambassador's daughter.) PM Entertainment Group. 94 minutes.

Road House (1989): Action. Directed by Rowdy Herrington. Screenplay by David Lee Henry and Hilary Henkin. Starring Patrick Swayze and Ben Gazarra. (A famous bouncer is hired to clean up a gin joint, but has to go against the town big shot to do it.) MGM. 114 minutes.

Shootfighter I (1992): Martial arts. Directed by Patrick Allen. Screenplay by Judd Lynn and Pete Shaner. Starring Bolo Yeung and William Zabka. (Two martial artists get mixed up in no-holds-barred matches across the border.) ANA Productions. 100 minutes.

Shootfighter II (1995): Martial arts. Directed by Paul Ziller. Screenplay by Greg Mellot and Pete Shaner. Starring Bolo Yeung and William Zabka. (Two martial artists and their sifu help the police shutdown an illegal cage match.) ANA Productions. 104 minutes.

Showdown (1993): Martial arts. Directed by Robert Radler. Screenplay by Stuart Gibbs. Starring Billy Blanks and Kenn Scott. (A school janitor teaches a young man how to defend himself while breaking up a fight club.) Imperial Entertainment Corporation. 100 minutes.

Showdown in Little Tokyo (1991): Martial arts. Directed by Mark Lester. Screenplay by Stephen Glantz and Calliope Brattlestreet. Starring Dolph Lundgren and Brandon Lee. (Two American cops go after the Yakuza.) Warner Bros. 76 minutes.

Sidekicks (1992): Martial arts/Family. Directed by Aaron Norris. Screenplay by Donald G. Thompson and Lou Illar. Starring Chuck Norris and Julia Nickson. (A boy's daydreams of meeting Chuck Norris come true as he and Norris compete together in a karate tournament.) Gallery Films. 102 minutes.

Silent Rage (1982): Martial arts/Horror. Directed by Michael Miller. Screenplay by Joseph Fraley and Edward Di Lorenzo. Starring Chuck Norris and Brian Libby. (A small town sheriff must take on an unstoppable human psychopath who has been injected with a potion that makes him quite difficult to kill.) Columbia Pictures. 105 minutes.

SnakeEater (1989): Action. Directed by George Erschbamer. Screenplay by John Dunning and Michael Paseornek. Starring Lorenzo Lamas and Josie Bell. (Ex-Marine hunts the hillbilly killers of his family.) Cinepix.

SnakeEater II (1991): Action. Directed by George Erschbamer. Screenplay by John Dunning, Michael Paseornek, and Don Carmody. Starring Lorenzo Lamas and Larry B. Scott. (Cop takes law into his own hands to break up a drug ring.) Starlight.

SnakeEater III (1992): Action. Directed by George Erschbamer. Screenplay by John Dunning, novel by W. Glenn Duncan. Starring Lorenzo Lamas and Minor Mustain. (Suspended cop and his private eye partner take on a motorcycle gang.) Cinepix.

Soul of the Avenger (1998): Martial arts/Horror. Directed by Steve Kaman. Screenplay by Steve Kaman. Starring James Lew and Richard Norton. (A cult goes after a former member, who transplants his spirit into a homeless man.) Royal Oaks Entertainment. 90 minutes.

Space Mutiny (1988): Sci-fi. Directed by Neal Sundstrom and David Winters. Screenplay by Maria Dante. Starring James Ryan and Reb Brown. (Evil mutineers threaten the survival of a giant spaceship.) Action International Productions. 93 minutes.

Spoiler (1998): Sci-fi. Directed by Jeff Burr. Screenplay by Michael Kalesniko. Starring Gary Daniels and Arye Gross. (Prisoner continues to escape from prison, only to be caught again and again and placed in cryogenic freeze.) Ed Ancoates Inc. 90 minutes.

Steel Dawn (1987): Sci-fi/Action. Directed by Lance Hool. Screenplay by Doug Lefler. Starring Patrick Swayze and Lisa Niemi. (A wanderer helps protect a widow and her family from scavengers.) Yellowpine Ltd. 100 minutes.

The Stranger and the Gunfighter (1976): Western/Martial arts. Directed by Antonio Margheriti. Screenplay by Barth Jules Sussman. Starring Lee Van Cleef and Lo Leih. (A gunfighter teams with a martial artist to track down a treasure.) Shaw Brothers. 107 minutes.

Street Fighter (1994): Martial arts. Directed by Steven E. de Souza. Screenplay by Steven E. de Souza. Starring Jean-Claude Van Damme and Raul Julia. (Rugged colonel and his troops fight a madman holding a country hostage.) Capcom Entertainment Inc. 97 minutes.

Street Knight (1993): Martial arts. Directed by Albert Magnoli. Screenplay by Richard Friedman. Starring Jeff Speakman and Christopher Neame. (Ex-cop helps stop gang bloodbath being plotted by criminals out to score a big heist.) Cannon Films. 91 minutes.

The Strike (2002): Martial arts. Directed by Donald Farmer. Screenplay by Andre Buckner and Donald Farmer. Starring Andre Buckner and Stephanie Sinclair. (Older brother fights to keep younger, irresponsible brother out of cage fighting.) Canis Lupus Entertainment. 90 minutes.

The Substitute (1996): Action. Directed by Robert Mandel. Screenplay by Roy Frumkes, Rocco Simonellis and Alan Ormsby. Starring Tom Berenger and William Forsyth. (A mercenary poses as a substitute teacher at an inner city high school to break up a drug ring.) Live Entertainment. 114 minutes.

The Substitute 2 (1998): Action. Directed by Steven Pearl. Screenplay by Roy Frumkes and Rocco Simonelli. Starring Treat Williams and B.D. Wong. (A mercenary poses as a substitute teacher to find the killer of his brother.) Dinamo Entertainment. 89 minutes.

The Substitute 3 (1999): Action. Directed by Robert Radler. Screenplay by Roy Frumkes and Rocco Simonelli. Starring Treat Williams and Rebecca Staab. (Mercenary poses as college professor to root out steroid dealing among football players.) Artisan Entertainment. 89 minutes.

The Substitute 4 (2000): Action. Directed by Robert Radler. Screenplay by Dan Gurskis. Starring Treat Williams and Patrick Kilpatrick. (Mercenary poses as instructor in a military academy to get at a neo–Nazi organization operating there.) Artisan Entertainment. 91 minutes.

Sudden Impact (1983): Action. Directed by Clint Eastwood. Screenplay by Joseph C. Stinson, story by Earl E. Smith and Charles B. Pierce. Starring Clint Eastwood and Sandra Locke. (Touch homicide detective investigates the murder of men by a woman close to them.) Warner Bros. 117 minutes.

Sword of Honor (1994): Martial arts. Directed by Robert Tiffi. Screenplay by Robert Tiffi and Clay Ayers. Starring Steven Vincent Leigh and Jeff Pruitt. (Cop hunts for the killer of his partner and the thief who stole a sacred sword.) PM Entertainment Group. 97 minutes.

Talons of the Eagle (1992): Martial arts. Directed by Michael Kennedy. Screenplay by J. Stephen Maunder. Starring Billy Blanks and Jalal Merhi. (Two agents go undercover to find out if another agent has been corrupted.) Film One Productions. 90 minutes.

TC—2000 (1993): Sci-fi/Martial arts. Directed by TJ Scott. Screenplay by TJ Scott, story by J. Stephen Maunder and Richard M. Samuels. Starring Billy Blanks and Bolo Yeung. (An outcast from a subterranean compound discovers that world is habitable again and must fight to survive the overlord, who does not want it to be known.) MCA Home Video. 97 minutes.

Terminal Rush (1995): Martial arts. Directed by Damian Lee. Screenplay by Mark Sevi. Starring Don Wilson and Roddy Piper. (A Native American deputy fights terrorists holding his father and others in a dam complex.) Triboro Entertainment Group. 94 minutes.

Terminator Woman (1993): Martial arts. Directed by Michel Qissi. Screenplay by Jeanette Francesca Qissi. Starring Jerry Trimble and Karen Sheperd. (Two American cops track down a drug lord in Africa.) Nu Image. 105 minutes.

Three the Hard Way (1974): Action. Directed by Gordon Parks, Jr. Screenplay by Eric Bercovichi and Jerry Ludwig. Starring Jim Brown and Jim Kelly. (Three men face off against white supremacists tainting the water supply to kill blacks.) Allied Artists. 93 minutes.

Thunder Road (1958): Action. Directed by Arthur Ripley. Screenplay by James Atlee Phillips and Walter Wise, story by Robert Mitchum. Starring Robert Mitchum and Gene Barry. (Moonshiner goes up against mobsters and Feds trying to put him out of business.) DRM Productions. 92 minutes.

Ticker (2002): Action. Directed by Albert Pyun. Screenplay by Paul B. Margolis. Starring Steven Seagal and Dennis Hopper. (Detective and demolition cop track mad bomber.) Nu Image. 92 minutes.

Tiger Claws (1992): Martial arts. Directed by Kelly Makin. Screenplay by J. Stephen Maunder. Starring Jalal Merhi and Cynthia Rothrock. (Two detectives track a killer targeting celebrity martial artists.) Film One Productions. 92 minutes.

Tiger Claws 2 (1997): Martial arts. Directed by J. Stephen Maunder. Screenplay by J. Stephen Maunder and Andreas Kyprianou. Starring Jalal Merhi and Cynthia Rothrock. (Two detectives follow the cross-country trail of an escaped killer.) Film One Productions. 90 minutes.

Tiger Claws 3 (1999): Martial arts/Horror. Directed by J. Stephen Maunder. Screenplay by J. Stephen Maunder. Starring Jalal Merhi and Cynthia Rothrock. (A detective fights the supernatural creatures who killed his partner.) Film One Productions. 95 minutes.

Time Cop (1994): Sci-fi/Martial arts. Directed by Peter Hyams. Screenplay by Mark Verheiden, story by Verheiden and Mark Richardson. Starring Jean-Claude Van Damme and Mia Sara. (A policeman travels through time preventing criminals from manipulating past events.) Universal Pictures. 99 minutes.

Timelock (1996): Sci-fi/Martial arts. Directed by Robert Munic. Screenplay by Joseph John Barmettler and J. Reifel. Starring Jeff Speakman and Arye Gross. (Convict tries to escape from frozen prison and only a pilot and a prisoner can stop him.) 90 minutes.

To the Death (1993): Martial arts. Directed by Darrel Roodt. Screenplay by Darrel Roodt, story by Greg Latter. Starring John Barrett and Michael Qissi. (Ex–martial arts champion is forced back into the ring to avenge his girlfriend's death.) Tangent Films Pty Ltd.

Tough and Deadly (1995): Action. Directed by Steve Cohen. Screenplay by Steve Cohen and Otto C. Pozzo, story by Pozzo. Starring Roddy Piper and Billy Blanks. (A tough private eye and a CIA agent team tackle corruption within the government.) Shapiro-Glickenhaus Entertainment. 92 minutes.

Triple Impact (1992): Martial arts. Directed by David Hunt. Screenplay by Steve Rogers. Starring Dale Cook and Ron Hall. (Three martial artists travel the jungle in search of hidden treasure.) Davian International Ltd. 97 minutes.

Under Siege (1992): Martial arts. Directed by Andrew Davis. Screenplay by J.F. Lawton, John Mason and Michael Rae. Starring Steven Seagal and Tommy Lee Jones. (Navy cook fights off terrorist hijacking the USS *Missouri*.) Warner Bros. 102 minutes.

Under Siege 2 (1995): Martial arts. Directed by Geoff Murphy. Screenplay by Richard Hatem and Matt Reeves. Starring Steven Seagal and Nick Mancuso. (Chef on vacation with niece battles terrorist taking over the train they are on.) Warner Bros. 99 minutes.

Universal Soldier (1992): Martial arts. Directed by Roland Emmerich. Screenplay by Richard Rothstein, Christopher Leitch and Dean Devlin. Starring Jean-Claude Van Damme and Dolph Lundgren. (Two dead soldiers, revived and kept as anti-terrorist specialists, square off against one another.) Carolco Pictures. 104 minutes.

Universal Soldier: The Return (1999): Action. Directed by Mic Rodgers. Screenplay by William Malone and John Fasano. Starring Jean-Claude Van Damme and Bill Goldberg. (A military man who was resurrected from the dead by the government fights rampaging dead soldiers also resurrected by the government.) Baumgarten-Prophet Entertainment. 82 minutes.

U.S. Seals II (2001): War. Directed by Isaac Florentine. Screenplay by Michael D. Weiss, story by Boaz Davidson. Starring Michael Worth and Karen Kim. (Navy SEAL leads a crack martial arts team to an island where they intend to neutralize terrorists who are planning to launch a nuclear missile.) Nu Image. 95 minutes.

Virtual Combat (1996): Directed by Andrew Stevens. Screenplay by William C.

Martell. Starring Don Wilson and Loren Avedon. (Man fights against a virtual warrior created by science.) Amritraj/Stevens Productions. 97 minutes.

When the Bullet Hits the Bone (1995): Action. Directed by Damian Lee. Screenplay by Damian Lee. Starring Jeff Wincott and Michelle Johnson. (A doctor is affected by all the violence he witnesses.) Terror Zone Productions. 82 minutes.

White Tiger (1995): Martial arts. Directed by Richard Martin. Screenplay by Gordon Melbourne, Roy Sallows and Don Woodman, story by Bey Logan. Starring Gary Daniels and Julia Nickson. (DEA agent tracks the killers of his partner to Chinatown, where he makes them pay.) Evergreen Entertainment. 93 minutes.

Without Mercy (1995): Action. Directed by Robert Anthony. Screenplay by Robert Anthony. Starring Frank Zagarino and Martin Kove. (A Marine left behind in Somalia makes it to Indonesia, where he becomes an underground fighter.) Rapi Films. 90 minutes.

The Yakuza (1975): Martial arts. Directed by Sydney Pollack. Screenplay by Paul Schrader and Robert Towne, story by Leonard Schrader. Starring Robert Mitchum and Ken Tanaka. (A retired cop returns to Japan to help an old Army buddy retrieve his kidnapped daughter.) Warner Bros. 112 minutes.

Notes

Chapter I

1. *The Hollywood Reporter*: Cannes Special Issue, (May 1997) p. 59; *The Hollywood Reporter*: Cannes Special Issue, (May 1999) p. 41. Only drama had a greater number of produced films during this same time period. Yet, the action numbers may be lower than the actual numbers produced. Some small production companies that do ultra low-budget martial arts/action films do not attend Cannes, or even AFM, and have direct deals with distributors in various countries.

2. Marilyn D. Mintz, *The Martial Arts Films* (Cranbury, N.J.: A.S. Barnes, 1978), p. 11.

3. Mintz, pp. 57–73. All of these definitions are taken from Mintz, a UCLA film and television graduate who is an actress and a filmmaker. She also taught both martial arts as well as the humanities.

4. *Martial Arts Worldwide Network*, "History of Martial Arts" (Internet). MAWN provides a concise history of the development of martial arts throughout the world and is an excellent reference source.

5. Martial Arts World Network.

6. MAWN.

7. Kristin Thompson and David Bordwell, *Film History* (New York: McGraw-Hill, Inc., 1994), p. 284.

8. Sek Kai, Roland Chu and Grant Foerster, *Bright Lights Film Journal*, "The Hong Kong Martial Arts Film" (January 2001), Internet.

9. David Chute, *Premiere*, Year of the Dragon (December 2000), p. 77.

10. Kei.

Chapter II

1. Steve Jacques, "Enter the Dragon," *The Legendary Bruce Lee* (Burbank, Calif.: Ohara Publications, 1986), p. 103.

2. Mintz, p. 180.

3. Randall Clark, *At a Theater or Drive-In Near You* (New York: Garland, 1995), p. 132.

4. Robert Clouse, *The Making of Enter the Dragon* (Burbank, Calif.: Unique Publications, 1988), p. 194.

5. *The Yakuza*, directed by Sydney Pollack, starring Robert Mitchum. Warner Bros., 1975.

6. Pauline Kael, *5001 Nights at the Movies* (CD Rom; 1996).

7. Peter Biskind, *Easy Riders, Raging Bulls* (New York: Touchstone, 1998), p. 291.

Chapter III

1. Savate, a form of "footfighting" developed in France combined boxing and kicking and is one of the few martial arts forms developed in the west.

2. Mintz, p. 205.

3. Carlos Clarens, *Crime Movies* (New York: Da Capo Press, 1997), pp. 54–57.

4. Nicholas Christopher, *Somewhere in the Night* (New York: Henry Holt, 1997), p. 23.

Chapter IV

1. Mark Thomas McGee, *Fast and Furious: The Story of American International Pictures* (Jefferson, N.C.: McFarland, 1984), p. 172. McGee reports that after Laughlin reprised his character in *Billy Jack*, AIP re-released *Born Losers* as "the original Billy Jack." Laughlin demanded but did not receive $5,000,000 in damages.

2. Bey Logan, *Hong Kong Action Cinema* (New York: Overlook Press, 1995), p. 15.

Chapter V

1. Biskind, p. 85.

2. "Billy Jack" pressbook, Warner Bros., 1973, p. 3.

3. Charles Musser, *The Emergence of Cinema: The American Screen to 1907* (Berkeley: University of California Press, 1990), p. 454.

4. Winthrop D. Jordan, Leon F. Litwack , Richard Hofstadter, William Miller, Daniel Aaron, *The United States* (Englewood Cliffs, N.J.: Prentice-Hall, 1985), p. 451.

5. There is some confusion about the actual dates of these movies. IMDb lists them as 1980 and 1981 respectively, while the film release date says 1977. I am using the IMDB dates.

6. The Report of Study Commission on U.S. Policy Toward South Africa, *South Africa: Time Running Out* (Berkeley: University of California Press, 1981), p. 48.

7. IDAF, *Apartheid: The Facts* (London: A.G. Bishop and Sons, 1983), p. 82.

8. The Library of Congress Country Studies, "South Africa: The Impact of World War II (Internet). While the South Africans sided with the Allies during the War, a significant number of Afrikaners favored supporting Germany.

9. Clark calls him a "living justification of the capitalist system." Clark, p. 137.

10. Internet Movie Database.

11. Paul Turse, "Bruce Lee and the Martial Arts Films of the 70s" (Internet, 1980).

12. Clark, p. 137.

Chapter VI

1. Kenneth A. Oye, Robert J. Lieber, Donald Rothchild, *Eagle Defiant* (Boston: Little, Brown, 1983), p. 67.

2. Congressional Quarterly, Inc., *U.S. Defense Policy, Third Edition* (Washington, D.C.: Congressional Quarterly, 1983), p. 64.

3. Glenn P. Hastedt, *American Foreign Policy* (Englewood Cliffs, N.J.: Prentice-Hall, 1988), p. 316.

4. John Belton, *American Cinema/American Culture* (New York: McGraw-Hill, 1994), p. 316. Oliver Stone was one of the writer-directors bucking the trend, his anti-heroic *Platoon* (1986) earning $70,000,000.

5. Roger Ebert, *Video Companion* (The Ebert Company, Ltd. CD rom version, 1996).

6. *Sudden Impact*, directed by Clint Eastwood, Warner Bros., 1983.

7. Patrick Runkle, *cannonfilms.com*, "Cannon Films: The Life, Death, and Resurrection" (Internet).

8. Clark, p. 138.

9. Press Kit, *American Ninja*, Cannon Films, 1985.

10. Ben Morris, "The Equals," *Fighting Stars* (February, 1982), p. 20. *The Challenge* was entitled *The Equals* before release.

11. The same reactions are occurring now, almost 20 years later. With the American occupation of Iraq, the brutal tyrant Saddam Hussein's secular government may very well be replaced by a Fundamentalist one along Iranian lines, while anti–American sentiment is at an all-time high.

12. Chris Betros, *Metropolis—In Person: JapanToday.com*, "Speak Softly and Carry a Big Stick" (Internet).

13. *Baseline Encyclopedia of Film*, "Steven Seagal" (CD rom version, 1996).

14. *E! True Hollywood Story*, "Steven Seagal" (12-22-02).

15. Aaron Anderson, *Jump Cut*, "Violent Dances in Martial Arts Films," (Internet).

16. *Under Siege*, presskit, Warner Bros., 1992.

17. Robert Carl Schehr, *Journal of Criminal Justice and Pop Culture*, "Martial Arts and the Action-Cop Genre: Ideology, Violence, Spectatorship" (University of Illinois at Springfield, 2000), p. 112.

18. *The Fire Down Below*, presskit, Warner Bros., 1997.

19. *Jam Showbiz: Actor Database*, "HBO Salvages Steven Seagal Film" (8-20-98: Internet). The article states that the film cost between $25 and 30 million, meaning its investors would no doubt take a loss.

20. *Exit Wounds*, presskit, Warner Bros., 2001.

21. *Exit Wounds*, presskit.

22. *E! True Hollywood Story*, "Steven Seagal."

23. *Hollywood.com*, "Jean-Claude Van Damme" (Internet).

24. Ben Smith, *TMAN's Martial Arts Network*, "Michel Qissi" (Internet).

25. Logan, p. 176.

26. *Jam Showbiz: Artist Database*, "Jury Finds in Favor of Action Star in Breach of Contract Trial" (Internet).

27. Joseph Campbell, *The Hero with a Thousand Faces* (Princeton, N.J.: Princeton University Press, 1973), p. 51.

28. Harold Schechter and Jonna Gormely Semeiks, *Discoveries: Fifty Stories of the Quest*, 2nd ed. (New York: Oxford University Press, 1992), p. 9. The authors break down Campbell's hero quest into literary form.

29. Natasha Stoynoff, "Flexing New Muscles," *Toronto Sun*, 20 April, 1996. Before going that route, Van Damme should consider what happened with *On Deadly Ground*.

30. *Hollywood.com*, "Lorenzo Lamas" (Internet).

31. *Jam Showbiz: Actor Database*, "Van Damme Plays a Hasidic Jew" (Internet).

32. Jet Li, *Official Jet Li Website*, "Essays on Life" (Internet).

33. *Kiss of the Dragon*, presskit. *Twentieth Century–Fox* 2001, p. 7.

34. Philip Gaines and David J. Rhodes, *Micro-Budget Hollywood* (Los Angeles: Silman-James Press, 1995), p. 121.

35. Douglas Gomery, *Shared Pleasures: A History of Movie Presentation in the United States* (Madison: University of Wisconsin Press, 1992), p. 282.

36. Frederick Jameson, *The Geopolitical Aesthetic* (Bloomington: Indiana University Press, 1995), p. 5.

37. Timothy Corrigan, *A Cinema Without Walls: Movies and Culture After Vietnam* (New Brunswick, N.J.: Rutgers University Press, 1991), p. 23.

38. Benjamin Svetskey, *Entertainment Weekly*, "The Money Pitfall" (12 April 1996), pp. 24–28.

39. Erik Barnouw, *Tube of Plenty: The Evolution of American Television*, 2nd revised edition (New York: Oxford University Press, 1990), p. 502.

40. Sallie Hofmeister, "Lights, Camera, Download? Studios Focus on the Web," *Los Angeles Times*, 30 November 2000: A1 + A24.

Chapter VII

1. Marty Grove, *Hollywood Reporter Online* (KNX Radio 1070), 8-17-00/1355.

2. John McCarty, *The Sleaze Merchants: Adventures in Exploitation Filmmaking* (New York: St. Martin's/Griffin, 1995), p. 143.

3. Gary Cook, Debbie Rochon, Peter Schmideg, *The B Movie Survival Guide* (Minneapolis: Wild Things Publishing, 1998), p. 45.

4. Kris Cox, *Hollywood Connection*, "Virtual Reality Has Just Crossed the Line" (Internet).

5. *Don The Dragon Wilson.com*, "Biography" (Internet).

6. *Don The Dragon Wilson.com*, "Biography" (Internet).

7. Ben Smith, *The Martial Arts Network*, *Cynthia Rothrock* (Internet).

8. Logan, p. 160.

9. Jill Morley, *Jill Morley.com*, "Cynthia Rothrock: The Queen of Martial Arts Films" (Internet).

10. L. Kimball, "Jeff Wincott," *TV Tome* (Internet).

11. Bob Sykes, *Martial Arts Illustrated*, "Interview with Gary Daniels" (Internet).

12. *Kung Fu Cinema*, "Jeff Speakman" (Internet).

13. *Only the Strong* presskit. Twentieth Century–Fox.

14. Todd Hester, *Big City—Bright Lights*, Bio of Richard Norton (Internet).

15. Biography, Karen Sheperd (Internet).

16. City on Fire, Loren Avedon Interview (Internet).

17. *The Substitute* presskit. Live International 1996.

18. Don Miller, *B Movies* (New York: Curtis Books, 1973), pp. 116–117.

Chapter VIII

1. The film's synopsis is listed on the IMDb, written by Nu Image Productions.

2. Greg Hernandez, "Movie Chain Going Digital," *Daily News*, 4 April 2003, B1-2.

3. Mark Singer, *The New Yorker*. "The Flick Factory" (March 16, 1998), p. 51.

4. Greg Merritt, *Celluloid Mavericks: A*

History of Independent Film (New York: Thunder's Mouth Press, 2000), p. 409.

5. Hoffmeister. P A24. Napster, which operated a service to facilitate such sharing, is now defunct, but other downloading services, like Kazaa, still exist.

6. Greg Hernandez, "Movies Only a Click Away," *Daily News* 4 April 2003, B3.

7. *The Hollywood Reporter,* Show East Special Edition (November 2001), P. W17–19. Boeing has already begun advertising its digital transmission system using satellite and fiber optics.

Bibliography

American Ninja 2: The Confrontation. Cannon Films. Presskit. 1987.

Anderson, Aaron. "Violent Dances in Martial Arts Films." *Jump Cut.* Internet.

Barnouw, Erik. *Tube of Plenty: The Evolution of American Television,* 2nd revised edition. New York: Oxford University Press, 1990.

Baseline's Encyclopedia of Film. "Steven Seagal." CD ROM version, 1996.

Belton, John. *American Cinema/American Culture.* New York: McGraw-Hill, 1994.

Betros, Kris. "Speak Softly and Carry a Big Kick." *Metropolis—In Person.* japantoday. com. Internet.

Billy Jack. Warner Brothers. Pressbook. 1973.

Biography. "Karen Sheperd." Internet.

Biskind, Peter. *Easy Riders, Raging Bulls: How the Sex, Drugs, and Rock and Roll Generation Saved Hollywood.* New York: Simon and Schuster, 1999.

Campbell, Joseph. *The Hero with a Thousand Faces.* Princeton, N.J.: Princeton University Press, 1973.

Christopher, Nicholas. *Somewhere in the Night.* New York: Henry Holt, 1977.

Chute, David. "Year of the Dragon." *Premiere,* December, 2000.

City on Fire. "Loren Avedon Interview." Internet.

Clarens, Carlos. *Crime Movies: An Illustrated History of the Gangster Genre from D.W. Griffith to Pulp Fiction.* New York: Da Capo Press, 1997.

Clark, Randall. *At a Theater or Drive In Near You.* New York: Garland, 1995.

Clouse, Robert. *The Making of Enter the Dragon.* Burbank, Calif.: Unique Publications, 1988.

Congressional Quarterly. *United States Defense Policy, Third Edition.* Washington, D.C.: Congressional Quarterly, 1983.

Cook, Gary, Debbie Rochon and Peter Schmideg. *The B Movie Survival Guide.* Minneapolis: Wild Things, 1998.

Corrigan, Timothy. *A Cinema Without Walls: Movies and Culture After Vietnam.* New Brunswick, N.J.: Rutgers University Press, 1991.

Cox, Kris. "Virtual Reality Has Just Crossed the Line." *Hollywood Connection.* Internet.

Don the Dragon Wilson.com. "Biography." Internet.

E! True Hollywood Story. "Steven Seagal." Entertainment Television.

Ebert, Roger. *Roger Ebert's Video Companion.* CD ROM version, 1996.

Exit Wounds. Warner Brothers. Presskit. 1997.

Gaines, Philip, and David J. Rhodes. *Micro-Budget Hollywood.* Los Angeles: Silman-James Press, 1995.

Gomery, Douglas. *Shared Pleasures: A History of Movie Presentation in the United States.* Madison: University of Wisconsin Press, 1992.

Grove, Marty. *Hollywood Reporter Online.* KNX Radio 1070.

Hastedt, Glenn P. *American Foreign Policy.* Englewood Cliffs, N.J.: Prentice-Hall, 1988.

Hernandez, Greg. "Movie Chain Going Digital." *Daily News* (Los Angeles). 4 April 2003.

_____. "Movies Only a Click Away." *Daily News* (Los Angeles). 4 April 2003.

Hester, Todd. "Richard Norton." *Big City—Bright Lights.* Internet.

Hofmeister, Sallie. "Lights, Camera, Download: Studios Focus on the Web." *Los Angeles Times.* 30 November 2000.

Hollywood.com. Jean-Claude Van Damme. Internet.

_____. Lorenzo Lamas. Internet.

The Hollywood Reporter. Cannes Special Issue. May 1997.

_____. Cannes Special Issue. May 1999.

_____. Show East Special Issue. November 2001.

IDAF. *Apartheid: The Facts.* London: A.G. Bishop and Sons, 1983.

Jacques, Steve. *The Legendary Bruce Lee.* "Enter the Dragon." Burbank, Calif.: Ohara Publications, 1986.

Jam Showbiz: Actor Database. "HBO Salvages Steven Seagal Film." Internet. 20 August 1998.

_____. "Van Damme Plays a Hasidic Jew." Internet. 26 September 2000.

Jameson, Frederick. *The Geopolitical Aesthetic.* Bloomington: Indiana University Press, 1995.

Jordan, Winthrop D., Leon F. Litwack, Richard Hofstadter, William Miller, Daniel Aaron. *The United States.* 2nd ed. Englewood Cliffs, N.J.: Prentice-Hall, 1985.

Kael, Pauline. *5001 Nights at the Movies.* CD ROM version, 1996.

Kai, Sek, Rolanda Chu, Grant Foerster. "The Hong Kong Martial Arts Film." *Bright Lights Film Journal.* January 2001. Internet.

Katz, Ephraim. *The Film Encyclopedia.* CD ROM version, 1996.

Kimball, L. *TV Tome.* Jeff Wincott. Internet.

Kiss of the Dragon. Twentieth Century–Fox. Presskit. 2001.

Kung Fu Cinema. Jeff Speakman. Internet.

Li, Jet. "Essays on Life." *Official Jet Li Website.* Internet.

Library of Congress Country Studies. *South Africa: The Impact of World War II.* Internet.

Logan, Bey. *Hong Kong Action Cinema.* New York: Overlook Press, 1995.

McCarty, John. *The Sleaze Merchants: Adventures in Exploitation Filmmaking.* New York: St. Martin's/Griffin, 1995.

McGee, Mark Thomas. *Fast and Furious: The Story of American International Pictures.* Jefferson, N.C.: McFarland, 1984.

Martial Arts World Network. "A History of Martial Arts." Internet.

Mast, Gerald, and Bruce Kawin. *A Short History of the Movies.* New York: Macmillan, 1992.

Merritt, Greg. *Celluloid Mavericks: A History of Independent Film.* New York: Thunder's Mouth Press, 2000.

Miller, Don. *B Movies.* New York: Curtis Books, 1973.

Mintz, Marilyn D. *The Martial Arts Films.* Cranbury, N.J.: A.S. Barnes, 1978.

Morley, Jill. "Cynthia Rothrock: The Queen of Martial Arts Films." Jill Morley.com. Internet.

Morris, Bruce. "The Equals." *The Fighting Stars.* February 1982.

Musser, Charles. *The Emergence of Cinema: The American Screen to 1907.* Berkeley: University of California Press, 1990.

The Onion AV Club. Interview with Roger Corman. Internet.

Only the Strong. Twentieth Century–Fox. Presskit. 1993.

Oye, Kenneth, Robert J. Lieber and Donald Rothchild. *Eagle Defiant.* Boston: Little, Brown, 1983.

The Report of the Study Commission on U.S. Policy Toward South Africa. *South Africa: Time Running Out.* Berkeley: University of California Press, 1981.

Runkle, Patrick. "Cannon Films: The Life, Death, and Resurrection." CannonFilms. com. Internet.

Schechter, Harold. *Discoveries: Fifty Stories of the Quest.* 2nd ed. New York: Oxford University Press, 1992.

Schehr, Robert. *Journal of Criminal Justice and Pop Culture.* "Martial Arts Films and the Action—Cop Genre: Ideology, Violence, and Spectatorship." Champaign: University of Illinois, 2000.

Singer, Mark. "The Flick Factory." *The New Yorker.* 16 March 1998.

Smith, Ben. Michel Qissi. *The Martial Arts Network.* Internet.

_____. Cynthia Rothrock. *The Martial Arts Network.* Internet.

Stoynoff, Natasha. "Flexing New Artistic Muscles." *Toronto Sun.* 20 April 1996.

Svetkey, Benjamin. "The Money Pitfall." *Entertainment Weekly.* 12 April 1996.

Sykes, Bob. Interview with Gary Daniels. *Martial Arts Illustrated.* Internet.

Thompson, Kristen, and David Bordwell. *Film History.* New York: McGraw-Hill, 1994.

Turse, Paul. *Bruce Lee and the Martial Arts Films of the 70s.* 1980. Internet.

Under Siege. Warner Brothers. Presskit. 1992.

Index